A FIELD GUIDE TO
ROCKY MOUNTAIN AND
SOUTHWEST FORESTS

THE PETERSON FIELD GUIDE SERIES®

A FIELD GUIDE TO

ROCKY MOUNTAIN AND SOUTHWEST FORESTS

JOHN KRICHER

Illustrated by
GORDON MORRISON

Photographs by
JOHN KRICHER

SPONSORED BY THE NATIONAL AUDUBON SOCIETY,
THE NATIONAL WILDLIFE FEDERATION, AND
THE ROGER TORY PETERSON INSTITUTE

HOUGHTON MIFFLIN COMPANY
BOSTON   NEW YORK   1998

For information about permission to reproduce selections from this
book, write to Permissions, Houghton Mifflin Company,
215 Park Avenue South, New York, NY 10003

PETERSON FIELD GUIDES and PETERSON FIELD GUIDE SERIES
are registered trademarks of Houghton Mifflin Company.

LIBRARY OF CONGRESS CATALOGING-IN-PUBLICATION DATA

Kricher, John C.
A field guide to Rocky Mountain and southwest forests /
John C. Kricher ; illustrated by Gordon Morrison.
p. cm. — (The Peterson field guide series ; 51)
Rev. ed. of: A field guide to the ecology of western forests. 1993.
"Sponsored by the National Audubon Society, the National Wildlife
Federation, and the Roger Tory Peterson Institute."
Includes bibliographical references and index.
ISBN 0-395-92897-4
1. Forest ecology — West (U.S.) I. Kricher, John C. Field guide to
the ecology of western forests. II. Title. III. Series.
QH104.5.W4K735 1998   98-17822
577.3'0978 — dc21   CIP

Book design by Anne Chalmers
Typeface: Linotype-Hell Fairfield; Futura Condensed (Adobe)

PRINTED IN THE UNITED STATES OF AMERICA
RMT 10 9 8 7 6 5 4 3 2 1

EDITOR'S NOTE

During the last two or three decades, interest in the natural world has been increasing exponentially; more people are taking to the woods and fields. Some are birdwatchers, others are botanically oriented, many others hunt or fish. Those who are just introducing themselves to the outdoors—those who may recognize fewer than a dozen kinds of birds, even fewer wildflowers or trees, and *no* butterflies except perhaps the Monarch—find a wealth of information in Field Guides. These useful books make it simple to attach names to things and then go on to learn what animals do, where they live, and how they interact with each other and with their environment.

Many of these people find that spending time outdoors has caused them to embrace the environmental ethic; yet they know very little about the interrelationships of nature. *A Field Guide to Rocky Mountain and Southwest Forests* is designed to help those who want to know what makes the wild world tick. It is one of a new generation of field guides that goes beyond identification to interpretation.

In 1934, my first *Field Guide to the Birds* was published, covering the birds of eastern and central North America. It was designed so that live birds could be readily identified at a distance by their field marks without resorting to the "bird in hand" characters that the early ornithologists relied on. During the last half century, the binocular and the spotting scope have replaced the shotgun. In like manner, the camera has become the modern vehicle for making collections of plants and butterflies. No more picking rare flowers and putting them in the vasculum and then the plant press until they are dry enough to fasten to herbarium sheets; butterflies need not be caught, put into the killing jar, then pinned through the thorax in a specimen tray.

The Peterson System, as it is now called, is based primarily on patternistic drawings with arrows that pinpoint the key field marks. The rather formal schematic illustrations and the direct comparisons between similar species are the core of the system, a practical method that has gained universal acceptance. This system, which is, in a sense, a pictorial key based on readily noticed visual impressions rather than on technical features, has been extended from birds to other branches of natural history—there are now nearly four dozen titles in the Peterson Field Guide Series. In this book, the Peterson System has been extended to forest types; each forest can be identified by its "field marks," a unique combination of plant and animal species.

Most readers of this guide by John Kricher probably have already learned to name many of the trees by using George Petrides's field guides, *Eastern Trees* and *Western Trees*. Likely as not they also own *A Field Guide to the Birds*, as well as other guides in the series, including the companions to this book, *California and Pacific Northwest Forests*, and *Eastern Forests*.

Do not be concerned, however, that you need to know the name of everything that grows or flies or crawls in the woods before you can understand and enjoy this guide. For the visually oriented, the illustrations of Gordon Morrison artfully support the scholarly text so that we can more quickly put things in order. And Professor Kricher skillfully integrates information of many kinds so that the woodswalker arrives at a more sophisticated or holistic understanding of the forest and its inhabitants. He explains the diversity and symbiotic relationships that allow them to live together, even though some are rooted to the earth, while others, like the birds and butterflies, fly free. This book has something to teach everyone who reads it.

ROGER TORY PETERSON

ACKNOWLEDGMENTS

The following people generously gave of their time to read and comment on various sections of this guide as it was in preparation: Robert A. Askins, Edward H. Burtt Jr., James Berry, Brian Cassie, William E. Davis Jr., Ann Dewart, Victor Emanuel, Bruce Hallett, Lisa Floyd-Hanna, Edward Harper, Janet Lee Heywood, Jerome Jackson, Paul Miliotis, David Morimoto, Scott Shumway, Martha Steele, Robert Stymeist, and especially to Martha Vaughan. To each of you I extend my warmest thanks for helping make this a better, more useful book. Any errors that have managed to pass through the various filters employed to stop them are, of course, entirely my responsibility.

Harry Foster and Susan Kunhardt of Houghton Mifflin devoted the full measure of their considerable editorial skills to this guide, for which I am extremely grateful. Deborah Fahey, Donna Kowalczyk, and Stephanie Sherwin were most helpful in preparing the manuscript. Linda Kricher accompanied me on most of my trips to the West, and I am very grateful for her companionship. Some of my field work was supported by grants from Wheaton College during my tenure as Bojan Hamlin Jennings Professor of Natural Sciences, and I extend my thanks to Wheaton for the support I received. This book is dedicated to Ethel, Charles, and Bruce Carrick.

John C. Kricher

Through my work, I have come to know many interesting and exciting people. Many of these people have unselfishly shared their knowledge and expertise or given me access to valuable collections, gardens, or properties. Without their generosity, much of what I do would be less successful.

A few, by their sharing, have deepened my love and understanding of nature, thereby improving my work. David Clapp, Larry Newcomb, John Mitchell, Christopher Leahy, Jack Moore, James Baird, and Raymond Payntor are counted among these people, and for their help I am deeply grateful.

Harry Foster of Houghton Mifflin has been very supportive, especially in dealing with an illustration style that broke away from the typical field guide look in favor of one combining a sense of place with the details.

I would like to extend a special thanks to John Kricher, an individual whose intelligence and wit are closely entwined and whose broad base of knowledge has supported our partnership through this and other projects we've shared.

A sincere thank-you to my wife, Nancy, who has shared all the highs and lows inherent in a work of this sort.

And to my parents, Hugh and Margaret, I dedicate this work with love.

Gordon Morrison

PREFACE

For most people, thoughts of the American West bring to mind the romantic images of staunch pioneers, covered wagons, immense Bison herds, Indian tribes, and vast expanses of uninterrupted scenery. The West beckons, truly a land of "purple mountains' majesty above the fruited plains." From the first accounts of Lewis and Clark returning in 1806 from their historic trek along the Missouri and Columbia rivers to the Pacific shore, to the present day, when people crowd into the many campgrounds of Yellowstone, Yosemite, Rocky Mountain, and other national parks, this nation has had a love affair with the West. In 1990, 258 million people visited national parks, up 27 percent from 10 years earlier. Yellowstone National Park, the nation's oldest national park, hosted nearly 3 million people in the summer of 1991. Lewis and Clark started a trend that has only accelerated through the years!

It is no accident that most national parks and national forests are located in the western states. Here is where one finds the greatest diversity of forests that this country has to offer, from "pygmy forests" of pinyon pines and juniper to majestic redwood giants and sequoias wide enough to drive an automobile through. High atop some western mountains grow the world's oldest things: Bristlecone Pines, some of which approach 6,000 years in age.

Western mountains, unlike their eastern counterparts, are geologically young and active. The eruption of Mount St. Helens on May 18, 1980, as well as the many fires that burned parts of Yellowstone National Park in the summer of 1988, provide ample proof that the West is both geologically and ecologically dynamic. Western mountain peaks are tall and sharply defined, and have yet to experience the slow erosion that will eventually smooth them to resemble the much older Appalachians of the East.

This is a book about western natural history, with a focus on the Rocky Mountains and the Southwest. A companion volume treats California and the Pacific Northwest. It is not designed primarily to be a guide to identification, though it will certainly help you identify most of what you see during your western travels. Instead, this guide will help you to *interpret* what you see, to understand what's going on ecologically. Ecology, the modern science of natural history interpretation, provides the keys that unlock the many mysteries that seem to enshroud the lives of plants and animals. This guide is your set of keys.

I recall watching a group of Yellowbellied Marmots along Trail Ridge Road, the scenic alpine highway that winds through Rocky Mountain National Park. A man and his young son were standing nearby, and I overheard the boy ask his father, "What are those big mouselike animals?" "Beavers," replied dad. "What are they doing?" asked the inquisitive youngster. "Guess they're just hanging out together," was the answer. The dubious lad persisted, suggesting that Beavers ought to have wide, flat tails and be in streams and ponds, not on a dry mountainside. His father changed the subject, suggesting that he and the boy go to the lodge and get hot dogs.

Marmots, of course, are not Beavers, and they lead very different lives. Some marmots defend territories, each keeping exclusive hold on its real estate, while others are highly social, living in cooperative groups. It's fun not only to learn how to differentiate between a Yellowbellied Marmot and a Beaver but also to learn something about how each lives its life. This guide is designed to help all parents of curious children—and to help satisfy the parents' own curiosity as well.

Nature is dynamic, though its changes may not be immediately apparent to the uninitiated human observer. A drive through the grasslands of Wind Cave National Park in South Dakota reveals a landscape of waving grasses and prairie wildflowers, with occasional prairie dog towns and small herds of Bison. Interspersed among the tracts of prairie grasses are forests composed mostly of Ponderosa Pine. These dark-foliaged pines give the area its name, the Black Hills. But you may not be aware that the forests are moving into the prairie. Windblown seeds of Ponderosa Pines are constantly invading the grassland and would eventually replace it, were it not for periodic fires that kill the seedling pines.

The West is diverse, rich in many kinds of habitats. A drive in the Rocky Mountains will take you through an unforgettable panorama of tall forests, alpine meadows rich in wildflowers, and high tundra, where the weather is so severe that only the hardiest plants and animals survive. At lower elevations, forests yield ecological dominance to prairies, plains, and deserts. Although this guide focuses primarily on forests, it will provide an introduction to all of the West's fascinating habitats, as well as to the complex lives of the plants and animals they comprise.

The American West provides a cornucopia for anyone interested in natural history. Lewis and Clark began a journey of discovery that is just as exciting today as it was then, for those who know how to look. Be an explorer and let this little book be your guide. I hope it will earn its place in your car, your camper, or your backpack as you venture throughout the West.

The legacy of America's great naturalist, Roger Tory Peterson, is preserved through the programs and work of the Roger Tory Peterson Institute of Natural History. The RTPI mission is to create passion for and knowledge of the natural world in the hearts and minds of children by inspiring and guiding the study of nature in our schools and communities. You can become a part of this worthy effort by joining RTPI. Just call RTPI's membership department at 1-800-758-6841, fax 716-665-3794, or e-mail (webmaster@rtpi.org) for a free one-year membership with the purchase of this Field Guide.

Contents

A FIELD GUIDE TO
ROCKY MOUNTAIN AND
SOUTHWEST FORESTS

How to Use This Book

A *Field Guide to Rocky Mountain and Southwest Forests,* like our previous field guide, *Eastern Forests,* represents a departure from traditional field guide organization. This guide is not organized taxonomically—you won't find the plants first, the mammals next, followed by birds, reptiles, etc. What you will find, both on the plates and in the text, are *combinations* of species that serve as *indicators* of particular forest types. This organization reflects the purpose of the guide: to interpret natural history rather than merely identify which species are present. Indeed, identification, though important as a first step, is not the primary purpose of this book. Although this book will allow you to identify many, if not most, of the common species you are likely to encounter, *Rocky Mountain and Southwest Forests* is not a comprehensive guide to identifying the myriads of plants and animals that inhabit the American West. Other books in the Peterson Field Guide Series are directed toward identification. Instead, this book is a primer on the *ecology* of one of the most fascinating areas of western North America.

Ecology is the scientific study of natural history. Ecologists ask broad questions about nature, such as: Why are some forests dominated by evergreens while others are composed mostly of broad-leaved deciduous trees? Why does vegetation dramatically change as one travels up a mountain slope? Why do Pinyon Jays travel in large flocks? What is the natural role of fire in structuring forests? Ecologists interpret natural history. One of the most satisfying feelings for an observer of nature is to understand something about what is actually happening in a habitat, in addition to merely knowing, for instance, that those little birds flitting about in the Ponderosa Pines are Pygmy Nuthatches. Though nature, at first glance, may look almost hopelessly complex, there are patterns that are not difficult to see once you know how to look. Fortunately, much of ecology is quite readily understandable by anyone willing to really look at nature. This book is meant to be your guide to nature interpretation.

ORGANIZATION OF THE GUIDE

This chapter will tell you how to use the lists provided in the descriptions of each habitat. It will also help you learn how to identify plants and animals as well as how to observe nature from an ecological perspective.

Chapter 2, "Forest Ecology," and Chapter 3, "Life Zones," will provide some basic information about ecology. They will teach you how to ask ecological questions about nature—and give some of the answers.

Chapter 4 will acquaint you with some widespread western mammals and birds, especially the ones most frequently sighted by the automobile traveler. This chapter will also give you a lesson on how to look at animals in a way that helps you understand their adaptations for survival.

The next chapters deal specifically with great plains riverine forests, southern and central Texas, and the altitudinal variation within the Rocky Mountains and the Southwest.

It is a good idea to familiarize yourself with all the color plates, because many species occur in more than one forest type. For instance, the Violet-green Swallow, shown on the plate illustrating the Aspen forest, is widespread in the West and can be encountered in many different places. The more you study the plates, the more you will develop a holistic sense about western natural history. The many photographs scattered throughout the text are meant to convey a "sense of place" and help you to develop your observational skills, seeing nature as an ecologist sees it.

FOREST DESCRIPTIONS

Each forest type can be recognized by looking for certain species that, by their combined presence and abundance, define that forest. When you survey a forest, first note which tree species are dominant. The dominant species are those you notice first, conspicuous by their size and numbers. It won't be difficult; there may be as few as one or two, and it is rare for a western forest to have more than a half dozen abundant tree species. The numerically dominant species are *indicator species* for that particular type of forest. You may even be able to use the dominant species to name the forest: Engelmann Spruce forest, for example, or pinyon-juniper forest.

In addition, there will usually be associated species, trees that are not dominant but present in fewer numbers. There is often also an understory of smaller trees. Below the understory is often a layer of shrubs, and below that, a layer of herbaceous species such as wildflowers and ferns. Animal species are equally important in defining the habitat; some birds nest only in old-growth forests, for example, and many amphibians are found only in damp environments.

Most indicator species are not found exclusively in one kind of forest. For instance, the Black Hills forest, described in Chapter 5, is a unique combination of species, some of which, such as American Elm and Blue Jay, originate in the East and many of which, such as Ponderosa Pine and Lewis's Woodpecker, are fundamentally western in range. It is the *combination* of indicator species that defines the habitat.

Each forest description begins by listing INDICATOR PLANTS, followed by INDICATOR ANIMALS. The species listed in italics are those that are most indicative of the habitat, including those that occur exclusively there. The other species listed are usually common in the habitat, but they are less important in defining that forest type.

Indicator plants are divided into three categories: canopy trees, understory trees and shrubs, and herbaceous species. Indicator animals are divided into four categories: birds, mammals, reptiles, and amphibians. Of course, by far the most abundant animal species in any habitat are insects, spiders, and other invertebrates, but most visitors are attracted to the larger creatures, especially birds and mammals. As with the selected plants, the animals listed are usually common enough that you ought to be able to find most of them with some diligent searching. Please bear in mind that neither the plant list nor the animal list is meant to be comprehensive for the given forest. You will probably find many species that are not on the list.

Following the list of indicator species is a brief DESCRIPTION of the habitat, a comparison with SIMILAR FOREST COMMUNITIES, and the overall geographic RANGE of the habitat being described. This is followed by REMARKS, which provide brief accounts of the species illustrated on the corresponding plates as well as an interpretation of the natural history of the habitat. Remarks are followed by suggestions for WHERE TO VISIT in order to best see the habitat described.

A Note to the Birder: This guide should be useful to birders who wish to learn more about how birds fit into their habitats. Birds, probably more than any other group of plants or animals, stimulate interest in natural history. Many birders begin by merely

Clark's Nutcracker is an important animal in the ecology of Rocky Mountain forests.

wishing to know what birds are around, listing as many species as possible. Soon, however, this need to list is supplemented by a desire to understand something not only about birds, but about the habitats in which they are found. In other words, what began as a simple curiosity about creatures with feathers becomes a broad curiosity about the natural world. This guide should help birders learn how birds are part of ecology.

IDENTIFYING PLANTS AND ANIMALS

Though species identification is not the main purpose of this guide, you will need to do some basic sorting of the plants and animals in order to make the book more useful. Nature is so bountiful that identification can seem downright intimidating at times. However, with a little practice, the task of accurately putting a name on what you are seeing is both fun and satisfying. You may be unsure what penstemon you are seeing, but you want to know at least that it's a penstemon. You may wish, of course, to use this guide in conjunction with others in the Peterson Field Guide Series that place their entire emphasis on identification.

PLANTS

One convenient thing about plants is that they don't run or fly away. Perhaps for this reason, botanists use the term *stand* to describe a group of plants in a single location. Throughout this guide you will read about stands of Ponderosa Pines, stands of Fireweed, and stands of Gambel Oak, to name a few. Plant identification is usually a more leisurely activity than trying to identify warblers flitting among branches 1 oo feet above you, or attempt-

Mesquite is typical of trees with compound leaves.

ing to put a name on a ground squirrel as it disappears into its burrow. You can look closely at a plant, noting many important characteristics. Look at the leaves. If it is a tree, observe the pattern of the bark. If cones or flowers are present, you have an even easier time identifying the plant.

Trees are usually the first plants to attract our attention. Trees come in two basic kinds, *broad-leaved* and *needle-leaved.* Broad-leaved trees such as oaks, maples, and cottonwoods have wide, flat leaves. Their wood tends to be quite hard, hence broad-leaved trees are often called hardwoods. Most broad-leaved trees in our region are *deciduous,* which means that they drop their leaves in autumn and regrow new leaves in spring. However, some broad-leaved species, particularly those in the Southwest, are *evergreen* and some are partially evergreen, with leaves remaining throughout most of the winter, but with new leaves replacing them in spring.

Broad leaves may be either *simple* or *compound.* A simple leaf, such as those found on oaks, consists of a single blade on its leaf-stalk. A compound leaf consists of several leaflets on a single leaf-stalk. Trees with compound leaves include Ashleaf Maple (Box-elder) and Honey Mesquite.

The way leaves are arranged on the stalk is also helpful in identification. Most plants, including wildflowers and shrubs as well as trees, have *alternate* leaves, but some, especially among the wildflowers, have *opposite* leaves. Leaves may be oval, heart-shaped, pointed, lobed, or long. Some leaves have smooth margins, others are toothed. For example, among the cottonwoods, Fremont Cottonwood has broad, heart-shaped leaves with large teeth along the margins. Black Cottonwood leaves are also heart-

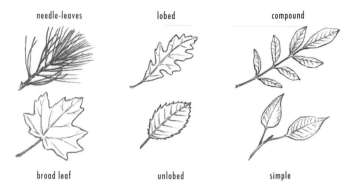

needle-leaves	lobed	compound
broad leaf	unlobed	simple

Figure 1. Leaf types

shaped but have very tiny teeth. Narrowleaf Cottonwood has long leaves with tiny teeth along the margins. The feel of a leaf is also occasionally helpful in identification. Some leaves feel quite waxy and leathery; others are thinner and feel more like paper. Some are covered with fine hairs, usually on their undersurface.

Needle-leaved trees tend to dominate most western forests. Common Douglas-fir, Ponderosa Pine, Pinyon Pine, White Fir, Engelmann Spruce, and Rocky Mountain Juniper are all examples of needle-leaved trees. With very few exceptions (the American Larch, or Tamarack, is one), all are evergreen. Needles may be stiff or soft, long or short. They usually grow in clumps or clus-

Vast conifer forests occur throughout the West, especially in the mountains.

ters called *bundles,* and the number of needles per bundle helps identify the tree. Needle-leaved trees tend to have softer wood than most broad-leaved species.

Needle-leaved trees are conifers, which means that they do not have flowers but produce seeds contained in cones. Cones are initially green but become brown as they age. There are two kinds of cones on most conifers: pollen-producing cones (male) and seed-producing cones (female). Pollen-producing cones are small, usually clustered at the branch tips. Seed-producing cones are larger in size and much more conspicuous. They may feel prickly or smooth. The seed-producing cones of pines, spruces, hemlocks, and Douglas-firs dangle beneath the branch, but cones of true firs stand upright. Yews and junipers, unlike other conifers, have berrylike, pollen-producing and seed-producing cones on separate male and female plants.

Bark color and texture are often useful for identifying trees. Bark may be scaly, smooth, ridged, or furrowed. It may be brown, gray, reddish, or some other color. It may adhere tightly or peel off in strips, scales, or plates. Bark characteristics often change as a tree ages. Young trees tend to have smoother-textured bark than older trees, which usually have furrowed bark. Some bark is marked by resin scars, where some sap has been emitted.

Broad-leaved trees, shrubs, and wildflowers reproduce by means of flowers. When flowers are present, they are usually of great use in identifying the plant. Many trees, however, bear small flowers that are hard to see and are not,

Orangy bark of Ponderosa Pine makes this species easy to identify.

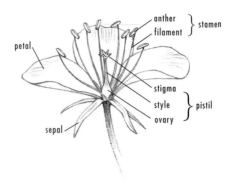

Figure 2. Parts of a flower

therefore, very helpful as field marks. In some cases, binoculars will help you see flowers located high on a tree well enough to identify the species. Even flowers in the hand can pose identification problems, and a hand lens is often quite useful, not only for identification but also for seeing the delicate structures of the flower. Petal color is important in identifying flowers. In many species *bracts* are important as well. Bracts are modified leaves that often resemble petals and grow from the flower base. Wildflowers tend to bloom throughout the summer in the West, and are especially abundant in mountainside meadows.

Please keep in mind that many of the most splendid wildflowers are vulnerable to human disturbance by trampling or picking. Treat flowers gently, and avoid picking them. A wise conservationist is willing to get down on hands and knees for the sake of the plant.

BIRDS

Birding has become a popular pastime because birds are generally conspicuous, both by sight and by sound. Birds tend to be brightly colored, vocal, and active during the daylight hours. It's fun to stop at a forest grove and see how many species of birds you can identify. At ground level you may find juncos and thrushes. In the shrubs and low trees might be some chickadees or a small flycatcher. By craning your neck and peering into the high canopy, you may locate a tanager or some warblers.

Birds abound in the West. From deserts to mountain meadows, colorful wildflowers attract hummingbirds. In the East, there is but one hummingbird species, the Ruby-throated. In the West you can find a dozen species, one of which, the Rufous, ranges north well into Alaska. Travel throughout the East and you can see 10 woodpecker species, exactly half the number of species you can see in the West. Out West, it's a good idea to have your binoculars with you always.

To identify birds, look for field marks such as overall size and shape. Is the bird sparrow-sized, robin-sized, or crow-sized? Note the bill size and shape. Is the bill chunky and thick, like that of a grosbeak, or slender, like that of a warbler or oriole? Note the color pattern. Does the bird have wing bars, wing patches, a white rump, or white outer tail feathers? Does it have an eye ring? Is its breast streaked or spotted? Behavior also helps with identification. When the bird flies, does it fly straight or tend to undulate? When on the ground, does it walk or does it hop? Is it with a flock of others of the same or different species, or is it solitary? What is it feeding on? How does it feed; does it glean its meal from the tree bark or flit around the outer branches? What is its habitat? Do you find it in a forest, a forest edge, or open brushy field? If in a forest, what kind of forest: pinyon-juniper, open pine, spruce-fir? What range does the species occupy? Some, like the Golden-cheeked Warbler, are found only in limited areas, in this case the

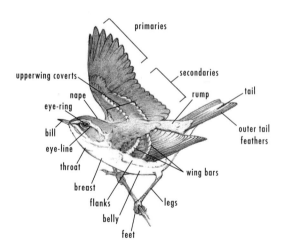

Figure 3. Anatomy of a bird

junipers and oaks of the Edwards Plateau in central Texas. Others, like the familiar American Robin, seem to be everywhere, from subalpine forests to backyards.

Bird identification is challenging, and you should be prepared to miss some. It's somewhat like the game of golf—you can get close but still miss the putt. That hummingbird on the columbine might be a female, and you just can't tell if it's a Rufous or a Broad-tailed. That thrush might have been a Swainson's, but you didn't see it that well and you just heard a Hermit Thrush moments before. Sometimes lighting conditions make it next to impossible to see color well. Often the bird is constantly active, and seeing it out in the open is more a wish than an actuality. Be patient, keep at it, and your skills will develop accordingly. *Birds are a major part of this guide,* and you should be able to identify most of the species you encounter.

MAMMALS

Mammals generally lack the bright colors of birds, but they are by no means dull. Their coat colors, often very subtle in tone, range from pure black or white to many shades of brown, gray, and reddish. Important field marks include overall size and shape, characteristics of the tail (ringed, bushy, naked, short, or long), and the markings on the face.

Many mammal species are most active at dawn or dusk, and some are entirely nocturnal. Many are fairly secretive. Seeing these elusive mammals poses a challenge; many furbearers are glimpsed when illuminated by headlights as they attempt to cross highways at night.

Large mammals like deer, Elk, and bears tend to be easy to identify, but smaller beasts are more challenging. Bats are very difficult to identify since they fly in the dark and move fast. Mice are mostly nocturnal and tend to stay out of sight. Chipmunks are diurnal and easy to see, but there are many different kinds, and they look very much alike. While any chipmunk you see in the east is the Eastern Chipmunk, there are 20 different species in the West. Range and elevation are important factors in chipmunk identification. Any given location will only have a few species.

REPTILES AND AMPHIBIANS

Reptiles are abundantly represented throughout the West by snakes, lizards, and, to a lesser extent, turtles. Amphibians are represented by salamanders, frogs, and toads. Both reptiles and amphibians are often quite colorful, but they can nonetheless be very well camouflaged in their environments. Many take refuge beneath rocks and logs, and thus you must search them out.

Amphibians tend to favor wet areas: ponds, streams, swamps, marshes, and wet meadows, though some do occur in deserts. Salamanders superficially resemble lizards, but salamanders have moist skin that lacks scales, and their toes are clawless. To identify salamanders, note the color pattern, the relative thickness of the hind limbs compared with the forelimbs, and the length of the tail. Frogs, treefrogs, spadefoot toads, and true toads are combined in a group called the anurans. To identify anurans, first look at the overall size, shape, and color. You can identify a treefrog by its toes, which have wide flattened tips, like suction cups. A toad will probably have dry, warty skin. Note the voices. Anurans are quite vocal during breeding season and are easily identified by voice.

Search for snakes during the daylight hours by carefully turning over rocks and other debris likely to shelter a resting serpent. (Stand *behind* the rock if you do this—*poisonous snakes are common in the West.*) Snakes are best identified by size, color, and pattern. Head shape (slender, wide, triangular) is also helpful in snake identification.

Lizards of many species are found throughout the West, usually in open, warm habitats, especially deserts. They are frequently seen sunning on rocks. Once warmed, lizards can move extremely quickly, scampering through dried leaves to shelter. Some lizards can even run on their hind legs for short distances. To identify lizards, note the overall pattern. Some lizards have boldly patterned heads and necks. Note the color and observe whether the scales look smooth or rough. The many kinds of spiny lizards that inhabit the West are, as a group, easily differentiated from the smooth-scaled species.

Turtles are slow-moving and thus easy to identify, unless the turtle slips into a pond and disappears.

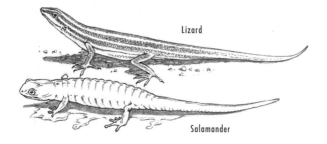

Figure 4. Lizard and salamander compared

You can see nature best when you learn a few simple techniques about how to observe.

VISIT DIFFERENT HABITATS

Plants and animals combine into natural groups called *communities*. These groups form recognizable *habitats*: open woodlands, mature forests, meadows, floodplains. To see diversity in nature, you must visit different habitats, because the residents of each habitat respond to different characteristics of the environment. American Dippers are birds well suited to living along fast mountain streams, but they have no place to dip in a closed pine forest. Moss Campion, a small, prostrate plant of the alpine tundra, would never be found among the junipers at lower elevations. Mountains, which are abundant in the West, provide a ready means of visiting several major habitats while driving only a short distance up or down the mountain.

VISIT DIFFERENT GEOGRAPHIC AREAS

In order to see all the forests described, you will need time, gasoline, and a love of the open road. Though many species, such as Ponderosa Pine, Elk, and Steller's Jay, range widely throughout the West, others, including the Black-Capped Vireo, Grizzly Bear, and Elegant Trogon, are much more restricted in range. This guide should help you better understand the distribution of plants and animals throughout the West, so that you can visit areas that host the species you most want to see.

KEEP A NOTEBOOK

Sooner or later, every naturalist learns the value of writing down his or her observations. Especially when traveling many miles in a few days, it becomes far too difficult and frustrating to try to remember just where you saw the Cooper's Hawk or in what kind of tree the Porcupine was perched (probably an aspen or a Lodgepole Pine). Notes taken afield help you hone your observational skills. It's surprising how uncertain you can be about whether or not the mystery bird had wing bars, or how long the needles were on an unidentified pine, when you try later to recall information consigned to memory. A pocket notebook can do wonders to help you organize your observations. Many naturalists carry pocket-sized tape recorders and make oral notes as they go. Some transcribe their notes into trip notebooks, but others simply replay the tapes later. Cameras, especially with macro and telephoto lenses, can be of great help as you can look again any time at what you saw. Many people carry camcorders to record animal behavior.

Don't Always Drive — Hike, Too

Automobiles can get you to many places, but seeing nature only from a car window will limit you immensely. Most animals avoid roads if at all possible, so you will both see and hear far more on foot. Allow enough time to take leisurely hikes through diverse habitats. National parks and forests abound with hikers' trails, and many are relatively uncrowded. Many national and state parks have well-marked nature trails, with printed guides to accompany the interested observer. Some even have some asphalt-covered trails accessible to everyone. Walk slowly, with binoculars ready. Be patient, taking time to identify what you see and make a few notes. Ask yourself, what trees are predominant? What species of predators might lurk in the forest? Should you come upon a mixed-species flock of birds, or perhaps a deer herd, take a few minutes to stop and watch what the animals are doing. Listen as well. Nature is rarely silent. There will be birds calling and singing, along with insects and maybe frogs and toads. Or there will be the tranquil sound of leaves moving in the breeze. Try to go beyond merely checking off the species you see and attempt to understand what the plants and animals are doing to stay alive. Ask yourself, "What's going on in this habitat?"

Don't Always Hike — Sit Still

A human is a large, conspicuous animal, and few of us go undetected as we make our way through a forest. By choosing a comfortable and interesting location in which to sit quietly and observe, we can often see more than by constantly moving. This is the best way to really begin to hear as well as see nature. You'll be much more aware of the sounds of the forest when you are still and quiet. Most experienced naturalists have had many memorable encounters with wildlife by sitting quietly and waiting to see what shows up.

Carry This Book

Field guides are exactly that—they are meant to be taken afield. This guide may provide the crucial point in identifying a tree or bird, or it may point out a behavior that you could look for. Because this guide treats both plants and animals, you can identify many different species with just one book. Take advantage and go to it.

FOREST ECOLOGY

There is an expression, oft repeated, about not seeing the forest for the trees. As with most venerable sayings, the statement has the ring of truth. As habitats go, forests present a complex picture. Trying to sort out the many impressions, the sights, the sounds, even the smells that one obtains when walking through a forest of stately Douglas-fir, Ponderosa Pine, or Engelmann Spruce can present a challenge. Forests are assemblages of many species, some of them interacting in most intimate ways, some not interacting at all. For the naturalist, the challenge is to observe enough about the habitat to understand something of what is happening there. Why is one forest dominated by Lodgepole Pine, while a nearby area consists almost exclusively of Rocky Mountain Juniper? Why are Quaking Aspens so patchily distributed among spruce stands? For that matter, why are spruce saplings growing beneath aspens? A good naturalist wants to inventory a habitat, learn what is there, in order to understand something of how the component species interact. Though forest habitats are complex, they do show certain patterns, forest "field marks" that can be your keys to understanding how the forest works. Ecology has sometimes been described as the search for nature's patterns and how to understand them. This chapter will help you to "read" a forest, recognizing its most significant patterns.

THE ECOLOGICAL COMMUNITY

Considered on the grandest of scales, there are two habitat types on Earth: terrestrial and aquatic. Seventy-one percent of Earth's surface is covered by water, most of it rather salty, some of it largely salt-free. The remaining 29 percent of the Earth is terrestrial, with a landscape of mountains, flat plains, or something in between. Living on land poses significantly different problems from living in water. On land, gravity is felt more strongly, temperature changes occur more rapidly, and water, perhaps the most vital resource for life itself, may be in short supply. Thus land organisms must have some support structure to resist gravity, must be physiologically able to cope with varying temperatures, and must be able to find water and use it judiciously.

Whether aquatic or terrestrial, no two habitats are alike: each presents unique challenges to living things. Aquatic habitats may be marine (from the intertidal zone to the deep abyss) or freshwater (from flowing rivers to standing-water ponds and lakes). Terrestrial habitats vary at least as much as aquatic habitats. Few plants can tolerate the desert heat and also thrive in the cool climate of a mountaintop. Few animals are equally at home in prairie grassland and dense coniferous forest. This array presents many challenges to which life must adapt if it is to persist. But it also presents opportunities, resources to be exploited for survival. Taken together, the living things that make up any habitat form an *ecological community*, a natural grouping of plants, animals, and microbes that are "solutions" to the challenges posed by the climate, geology, and other characteristics of the habitat.

Ecology is the study of organisms in relation to their environments: how they respond to and interact with the physical forces they encounter, such as temperature, precipitation, and soil, as well as the living forces, such as predators, competitors, or parasites. Ecologists try to figure out what factors are responsible for the distribution and abundance of all living things. That's a big job. It requires an understanding of the process whereby solutions for coping with varying environments are generated, called *evolution*. To a large extent, evolution is driven by the forces of *natural selection*.

WHAT IS NATURAL SELECTION?

Within any population, be it Golden-mantled Ground Squirrels in the Rocky Mountains or Green Ash along the Missouri River, no two members of the population are genetically identical. Consider humans. As you "people-watch" on the sidewalk, you notice many differences among your fellow pedestrians. Some folks are heavy, some thin. Some men have dense heads of hair, others are balding. Eye color, skin color, hair characteristics, even size of earlobes varies among humans. Some of these characteristics, among them eye color, are the work of the genes, the DNA that made the person. Only identical twins are genetically alike, and even they will show some differences due to environmental causes; for instance, most obese people are obese because they take in more calories than they use. And many, probably most, characteristics are influenced both by genetics and environment. A person may, for instance, be prone to develop diabetes, but only if exposed to a sugar-rich diet. In any case, most of us are in some small measure genetically unique.

Golden-mantled Ground Squirrels and Green Ashes show about the same genetic variability from individual to individual as do humans. Any naturalist who studies a wild population soon is able to recognize individuals. Just as we humans do not all look alike, largely because of genetic differences among us, so it is with all other forms of life.

Genetic variability is caused by random changes that occur on the genes themselves, the long molecules of DNA. These changes are called *mutations*. Through time, mutations accumulate, and thus so does genetic variability.

Although the creation of mutations is a random event—any gene may mutate at any time—the effects of mutations are anything but random. Some mutations, such as the gene for albinism in certain animals, are generally detrimental. An albino animal has a far less likely chance of escaping detection by predators than a normally pigmented animal. Imagine a pure white Golden-mantled Ground Squirrel scurrying about among a grove of Lodgepole Pines. A Great Horned Owl roosting in the pines would probably have little difficulty spotting what would soon become its next meal. An albino squirrel would be, on the average, far less likely to survive to reproductive age. Thus it would not pass on the gene for albinism. Albinism is almost always detrimental to the survival of the animal, and thus it remains a rare gene in natural populations. (But albinism is not detrimental in the confines of a research laboratory: most lab rats and mice are albinos. This observation helps underscore that it is the environment that determines whether a trait is beneficial or detrimental, not the trait itself.)

A mutation can be favorable to its carrier in a particular environment. Mutations that make individuals harder for predators to detect, or more tolerant of cold weather, or better able to detect food might, in certain environments, have very high survival value. Those individuals with such traits would have a much better chance of surviving to reproduce, thus passing the "favorable" genes to the next generation.

This natural process, whereby genetic variability is filtered at each generation through characteristics of the environment, is called *natural selection*. The term was invented and the process described by two 19th-century naturalists, Charles Darwin and

Alfred Russel Wallace. Their theory explains the mechanism by which evolution can occur. Populations of organisms—plants, animals, microbes—change genetically (evolve) because some in the population breed more than others. They are successful in breeding because their genes make them in some way better adapted than others to their environment. Many are born, hatched, or sprouted, but only a few live long enough to reproduce. The factors that determine who will survive are provided by the environment, including not only physical and chemical characteristics (rainfall, temperature, amount of calcium in the soil, etc.), but also biological characteristics (predators, parasites, competitors, etc.). Environmental characteristics, in the evolutionary sense, are *selection pressures* to which organisms must adapt or fail to survive. The popular phrase that describes natural selection is *survival of the fittest*.

WHERE DO NEW SPECIES COME FROM?

Throughout this guide the term *species* is used. But what, exactly, is a species? Darwin's most famous book, *On the Origin of Species*, was an attempt to explain how a single species could evolve into several new species. Darwin held that the process of natural selection, whereby adaptation occurred, also produced a gradual divergence of populations, such that new species evolved. Today most biologists agree that Darwin was essentially correct in linking adaptation with the emergence of new species, though there is a bit more to it than Darwin articulated at the time.

Species are populations that are *reproductively isolated* from other populations. In other words, the reason why a Ponderosa Pine is a different species from a Lodgepole Pine is that they are unable to reproduce successfully with one another. The same holds for why a Grace's Warbler is a species different from a Yellow-rumped Warbler. The assemblage of genetic material that makes up the gene pool of a Grace's Warbler is significantly distinct from that of a Yellow-rumped Warbler.

Each species is given a scientific name, or Latin name, that consists of two words. The first is its genus, or generic, name, and the second is its species, or specific, name. Ponderosa Pine is in the genus *Pinus* and has *ponderosa* as its specific name. Lodgepole Pine, in the same genus, is named *Pinus contorta*. Grace's Warbler and Yellow-rumped Warbler are both in the genus *Dendroica*, but Grace's is *Dendroica graciae* and the Yellow-rumped is *Dendroica coronata*.

Populations of the same species living in different areas may differ genetically because they have adapted to their different environments. A population high on a mountain may develop adaptations to cold not found in a population in the warmer foothills. These populations are usually referred to as *races* or *subspecies*. However, as long as two populations remain in at least some physical contact, they can probably continue to interbreed, and they remain a single, though racially diverse, species. Humans are a good example. Among western birds, Fox Sparrows exhibit strong racial variation, and Dark-eyed Juncos are even more racially distinct. For example, in the Black Hills of South Dakota the Dark-eyed Juncos are larger in body size than anywhere else, and most of them exhibit white wing bars. But these juncos, though they look relatively distinct, interbreed with juncos of the eastern "slate-colored" race. Because successful interbreeding occurs wherever two races of Fox Sparrows or two races of Dark-eyed Juncos meet, those races are not recognized as separate species.

Subspecies are also given scientific names. The subspecies name follows the species name. For example, the widely distributed Song Sparrow, *Melospiza melodia,* is distinctly pale where it occurs in southwestern deserts. The pale race, or subspecies, is named *Melospiza melodia saltonis*, distinguishing it from the more widely distributed *Melospiza melodia melodia*.

New species can arise when there is a sharp separation of the gene pools among populations. Some physical factor, some characteristic of geography may prevent individuals from one population from mating with those from another. If sufficient time elapses, the two gene pools will continue to diverge until they become incapable of forming hybrids, even if the two populations are eventually reunited. At this point, speciation is complete. The time required for speciation could be many millions of generations or relatively few. Much depends on population size, selection pressures, genetic characteristics, and other factors.

Sometimes speciation begins, but geographically isolated populations are reunited before speciation has been completed. In this case the two populations may look distinct but they are not reproductively isolated, so they still constitute a single species. Such is the case with the Red-shafted and Yellow-shafted races of Northern Flicker (see page 82).

The geography of the West is considerably more complex than that of the East. The high Rockies, Mexican Cordilleras, plus vast deserts have provided many possibilities for geographic isolation. This is probably the reason why there are some 15 chipmunk species in the West and only a single species in the East. The species richness of reptiles, amphibians, birds, mammals, and many plant groups is higher in the West than in the East.

In a dense forest in the Rocky Mountains stands an immense Ponderosa Pine. Its strong woody tissue and thick bark have enabled it to reach up to the light it needs to thrive and to resist the forces of wind, fire, and pathogens. On the orangy bark of the tree, a small bird, a Brown Creeper, hitches methodically upward, spiraling around the tall, straight trunk. Its streaked brown plumage lets the bird go undetected by a nearby Sharp-shinned Hawk that might make a quick meal of it. The creeper has stiffened tail feathers, enabling it to prop itself effectively while probing for insects and spiders hidden in the bark that it will eat or feed to its nestlings. Its thin, slightly curved bill is used like a delicate forceps to reach for food between bark fibers. Both the Ponderosa Pine and the Brown Creeper are well adapted to their environments.

The ongoing result of natural selection is to continually fine-tune organisms to their environments by means of *adaptations*. Most plants and animals are so well adapted that they seem to have been made specifically for their habitats. Should the environment change, as it did during the recent period of glaciation in the ice age of 20,000 years ago, plants and animals will tend to change, or evolve, as well—or become extinct, a frequent result of environmental change. This was the fate of the giant mastodon, the saber-toothed cat, and many other impressive animals that once roamed the American West.

Adaptations are characteristics of anatomy, physiology, or behavior that aid in survival. All evolutionary adaptations are genetic. They are coded in the DNA molecules that make up the genes of every organism. *For a trait to be adaptive, it must somehow aid, directly or indirectly, in promoting the ability of the plant or animal to reproduce.* The stronger the wood and bark of a Ponderosa Pine, the more likely it is to survive to produce seed-laden cones from which future generations of Ponderosa Pines will grow. The better a Brown Creeper is at both eluding predators and capturing food, the more young it can feed. Thus any genetic influence that makes Ponderosa Pine bark stronger or Brown Creepers more stealthful will tend to spread in those populations, because the individuals with such traits will leave more offspring, many of which will also carry the beneficial traits. In this manner, genes are selected over time as they adapt their living carriers to their particular environments.

Anyone who observes and studies nature sees adaptations everywhere. On the grandest of scales, major habitat types such as spruce-fir forests, grassland prairie, and scrub desert all reflect

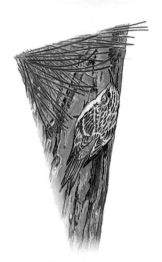

Brown Creeper on Ponderosa Pine

the adaptations that have evolved among the plants and animals to cope with the regional environment. Adaptation is the most powerful force in shaping species. It is an amazing process that has shaped all of the past and present diversity of life on Earth.

HOW BROWN CREEPERS GOT TO BE BROWN CREEPERS

Imagine an ancestral population of today's Brown Creeper, an ancestor that lived several million years in the past. What characteristics of this bird's environment selected for the adaptations that resulted in the evolution of the Brown Creeper?

Tree bark is a complex substrate, home to many hundreds of tiny insects, spiders, mites, and other invertebrates. Tall trees have many square feet of bark, most of it vertically oriented. Any bird that can manage to forage on a vertical surface has a fine source of potential food available to it. All birds have tail feathers, and among individuals from any given population, some might, by chance, have stiffer tail feathers than others. Slightly stiffer tail feathers would be of no value to most birds, but creepers are different from most birds because they cling to vertical bark to procure food. Among the ancestral creepers, stiffer tail feathers would be a real aid in propping the bird against the bark as it foraged. Those ancestral creepers with the stiffest tail feathers would tend to find the most food and thus leave the most offspring. The trait for stiff tail feathers, originally a genetic accident, would, in the environment of tree bark, be of great survival value.

One could argue that any bird making its living by hitching up tree trunks ought to do best with a stiff tail. Such is precisely the case for the world's 204 species of woodpeckers, most of which have stiff tails that are structurally very similar to creeper tails. Like creepers, woodpeckers search for food on vertical surfaces, but unlike creepers, woodpeckers drill into the bark and wood. Thus, although both groups have similar tails (because they have been naturally selected to perform the same function), their bills differ. Woodpeckers have straight, chisellike bills and long tongues for drilling and reaching deep within the bark and wood. Creepers have finely curved, forcepslike bills for probing into tight spaces and snagging tiny animals.

What would happen if some birds not closely related to Brown Creepers were to experience the same process of natural selection leading to adaptation as bark foragers and probers? In the American tropics there is such a group, the woodcreepers. There are 52 woodcreeper species, and each of them looks like a modified version of the Brown Creeper—to which none of them is closely related. The ancestors of woodcreepers were exposed to selection pressures similar to those of the ancestors of Brown Creepers, and the evolutionary result is strikingly similar. Biologists consider the similarity between Brown Creepers and woodcreepers to be an example of *parallel evolution.*

An adaptation need not be universal. Nature abounds with examples of how variety can succeed. Brown Creepers, woodcreepers, and woodpeckers all have stiff tail feathers, and all are bark

Figure 5. Woodcreeper (above) and Brown Creeper (below)

foragers, probing and hacking at the bark, seeking small animal prey. Nuthatches, however, are also bark foragers, and they do not have stiff tails. They move, however, quite differently from creepers and woodpeckers—they work their way headfirst *down* the tree trunk, rather than up. A stiff tail would be of little use to a bird moving in such a manner, and no such tail has evolved in nuthatches.

POLLINATION, A COMPLEX EXAMPLE OF ADAPTATION

Adaptation also explains some of the biggest questions in nature. For instance, why do many species reproduce sexually?

Most plants reproduce using pollen to fertilize an egg cell. Pollen is really a specialized form of the plant that has grown internally from a tiny spore. The pollen grain produces sperm cells, the male gametes that fertilize the egg cell. This process, whereby a small, mobile sex cell (sperm) fertilizes a large, energy-rich sex cell (egg), is called sexual reproduction. Obviously, sexual reproduction is not confined to plants; it is the primary form of reproduction in animals as well. What is said about the causes of plant sexual reproduction can just as easily be applied to animals. Sexual reproduction results in combining some of the genes of the male plant (or animal) with those of the female, creating a genetically unique offspring. Sexual reproduction developed billions of years ago. Today's plants and animals inherited the characteristic of sexual reproduction from their ancestors—a form of "evolutionary baggage," though baggage that is seemingly indispensable. We know, for instance, that humans must have sex in order to reproduce—there are no other options. But, why not?

One way to think about sex is to ask, what does it actually ac-

Dense clumps of aspen stems among older Ponderosa Pine. The aspens grew from root sprouts, the pines from seeds.

complish, and how important is that outcome? Most people answer that sex accomplishes reproduction—and it does. But, interestingly enough, sex isn't always essential for reproduction, especially in plants. The Quaking Aspen, an abundant tree throughout most of the West, is capable of cloning itself via root sprouts, a form of asexual reproduction. Exact copies of the mother plant grow from roots, producing a cluster of trees that, genetically speaking, is actually one individual. The next time you see a clump of Quaking Aspen, note the bunching of smaller plants that typically surround the main cluster, the clones, which are called *ramets*. Why should aspens reproduce without sex? Perhaps because they invade recently disturbed areas, and asexual reproduction provides the plant with a means of rapid colonization, before it is replaced by other plants such as spruces.

So plants can and do reproduce without sex, but they can only make genetic copies of themselves. What sexual reproduction accomplishes is genetic *variety*, because genes from the male sex cell (half of the male's total genes) combine with those from the female sex cell, creating an individual different from both parents. Myriads of different combinations are possible, so when a plant sets seed, it has produced a huge diversity of new genetic combinations—any one of which might be the most favorable one for the particular environment in which the seeds are dispersed. Why sexual reproduction? Not merely in order to reproduce, but in order to produce genetic variety, thus providing options for surviving in varying environments.

Pollination is the means by which male sex cells find female sex cells. Because plants are immobile and thus cannot move toward one another to engage in sex, some mechanism must intervene to disperse pollen. In many cases, that mechanism is wind, but in other cases, it is an animal of some sort. This suggests another question: Why are some plants wind-pollinated while others are animal-pollinated?

Wind-pollinated plants include all of the conifers, the pines, spruces, larches, firs, and others. Many broad-leaved trees, among them the oaks, elms, hickories, cottonwoods, and birches, are also wind-pollinated. Grasses and sedges, too, are wind-pollinated. Because no animal need be attracted to the plant to pollinate it, flowers of wind-pollinated species are small and inconspicuous (you don't send a bouquet of grasses on Mother's Day). Wind pollination is associated with two characteristics: either the plants live quite close to one another, or they live in open areas, where wind blows strongly. Pollen blown from nearby plants, such as within an Engelmann Spruce forest or a line of cottonwoods along a river bank, has a reasonable chance of reaching another plant. Wind does not blow pollen very far, often only to within a few hundred feet from the parent plant. However, that distance is sufficient if other plants are close by. Wind pollination also works well in exposed habitats, where winds blow strongly, as in open, grassy fields, meadows, or mountaintops. Wind pollination, being much like a lottery system, is not very efficient. Many tickets (pollen grains) are distributed, but very few win (succeed in reaching and fertilizing an egg). The important thing is that enough do succeed to make wind pollination adaptive for many plants.

Obviously, wind-pollinated species run the risk of merely pollinating themselves, hardly a way of accomplishing genetic diversity. That is probably why many wind-pollinated plant species, including the cottonwoods, have male flowers on separate plants from those with female flowers. Other plants, like the oaks, have adapted to be genetically unable to self-fertilize.

The inefficiency of wind pollination is largely corrected when animals are used as pollinators. Most shrubs and wildflowers are animal-pollinated, as are some trees. Animal pollination relies on the plant attracting an insect, bird, or, in some cases, a bat (or some combination of these) to visit a flower, collect pollen, and then visit a flower on a second plant, thus delivering the pollen. Animal pollination is more efficient than wind pollination because the animal makes specific choices from among plants and can deliver pollen accurately over fairly long distances. For instance, a Yellow Paintbrush growing in a high meadow in the Rockies is unlikely to be pollinated by wind, partly because the wildflower doesn't grow very tall. But a foraging Rufous Hummingbird can move easily from one Paintbrush to another, even if the plants are widely scattered.

Plants must invest energy in order to attract animal pollinators. First, the plants must signal the animals, and the signaling device used is a flower. Animal-pollinated plants tend to have bright, conspicuous flowers shaped in such a way that the anatomy of the pollinator is accommodated. For instance, flowers that attract hummingbirds tend to be bright red or yellow, usually rather large, and often tubular—a shape ideal for the hummingbird's long bill. Birds do not respond to smells very readily, and hummingbird-pollinated flowers tend to be relatively odorless. Some insects, such as the small flying beetles that pollinate Yellow Skunk Cabbage, use odor from the flower as the principal signal of attraction. Flowers with strong odors tend to be pollinated by moths and butterflies. Many insects, such as bees, can detect ultraviolet light, thus they see flowers differently from the way we do. Where they see a strongly patterned flower, we who cannot

Conspicuous color serves to attract hummingbirds and other pollinators to the Tiger-lily.

see in the ultraviolet wave-lengths see a uniform flower. For example, Marsh Marigold looks plain yellow to humans, but photographed under ultra-violet light, the center of the flower is a deep blue, forming a bull's-eye for foraging bees. Insects including ants, beetles, flies, and even mosquitoes can be pollinators for various flowers.

Animal pollination also requires a reward—the animal must, in effect, be bribed to visit the flower. The reward is sugar-rich nectar, expensive to make but essential for pollination to succeed. Some plants produce varying amounts of nectar from flower to flower. This forces animals to visit many flowers to gather enough nectar, thus insuring that pollen is distributed from one flower to another.

When you walk through a meadow in the high country and admire the many magnificent flowers before you, think about why they are so beautiful. Colorful flowers exist to bribe animals to carry sperm-containing pollen from one plant to another, in order to establish new genetic combinations that can cope with varying environments.

ADAPTATIONS IN THE WEST

Broadly speaking, there are three major habitat types in the West: forests, prairies, and deserts. You won't find spruce in the desert or cactus in the fir forest, because the plants and animals in each community are uniquely adapted to the demands and opportunities of that habitat. Although this guide is concerned mostly with forests, we note here the differences between these three habitat

A giant Saguaro cactus growing in the hot Sonoran Desert.

types as a way of introducing the broad factors that determine patterns in nature.

DESERTS

Three deserts in North America receive virtually all their precipitation in the form of rain, rarely snow, and are thus called "hot deserts": the Sonoran Desert (see Chapter 8, "Southwest Forests"), the Chihuahua Desert (treated briefly in Chapter 8), and the Mojave Desert (treated in our companion volume, *California and Pacific Northwest Forests*). Many of these desert areas receive under 10 inches of precipitation a year. Thus the species that live here must be able to survive on little water.

Hot deserts typically contain many succulent species, which

The Chihuahua Desert, with an abundance of Creosote Bush.

The Great Basin Desert, with Big Sagebrush. The Teton Mountains are in the background.

store water in their thick, fleshy leaves and stems. Cactus plants are common here, as well as a diverse array of yuccas and agaves. The Mojave Desert is dominated primarily by one species of yucca, the Joshuatree. Some hot deserts have areas where trees manage to survive, especially the various mesquites and palo-verdes. Most hot deserts receive enough water to support some woody shrubs, especially Creosote Bush.

Deserts vary with latitude. Those sufficiently far north receive some winter snow and are called "cold deserts." Lying between the Coast Ranges and the Rockies is the Great Basin Desert, the "big brown area" that air travelers see clearly from 30,000 feet. This vast desert exists because moisture is so efficiently blocked by the surrounding mountain ranges that very little is left to fall in most of eastern Washington, Oregon, Idaho, Utah, and Nevada. The Great Basin Desert is a "cold desert"—though tourists traveling through Nevada in the middle of summer might disagree. These deserts tend to be composed of scattered but hardy shrubs such as Big Sagebrush.

PRAIRIES

Natural grasslands abound on Earth throughout the temperate zone. They are referred to variously as *steppes* (Russia), *veldts* (southern Africa), and *pampas* (South America), but in this country they are called prairies. Grasses are the natural vegetation type of the Midwestern prairies extending from central Canada (Saskatchewan and Manitoba) southward through parts of central Mexico (Chihuahua, Durango, and Coahuila). Prairie is composed mostly of grass species but also includes many kinds of herbaceous plants, especially legumes such as the various clovers.

Side-oats Grama is one of many species of grasses that together make up the vast prairies of the Midwest.

Most natural prairie in North America has been taken into cultivation, making this area the "breadbasket" of the nation. Grassland prairie once covered 750 million acres in North America, but today more than half of the prairie lands have been lost. As a result, the traveler must visit a relatively few scattered natural reserves, such as Wind Cave National Park in South Dakota or the Pawnee Natural Grasslands in Colorado, in order to see what much of the Midwest once looked like.

Throughout North America, there is a general trend toward more precipitation to the east. Like all habitats, prairie is sensitive to moisture level. Thus the easternmost prairie was originally composed of tall grasses, while the westernmost was essentially desertlike short grasses. In general, prairies receive between 20

Much natural prairie has been eliminated by agriculture and grazing, but remnants remain, such as Lostwood National Wildlife Refuge in North Dakota.

Prairie Dogs, which are a species of ground squirrel, once existed in vast numbers in prairies.

and 50 inches of precipitation annually, depending upon whether they are located to the west or east. Another important factor in prairie ecology is periodic fire, usually set by lightning during summer storms. The combination of low moisture, periodic fire, and a history of grazing by animals such as Bison has helped prairie grasses (especially in the easternmost region) survive against invasions by less well adapted woody species, which would otherwise convert prairie into forest.

ADAPTATIONS IN THE FOREST

A traveler in the West encounters a diverse array of forest types. Some contain some of the world's tallest trees: Redwood, Giant Sequoia, Common Douglas-fir, and Ponderosa Pine, all giants capable of exceeding 200 feet in height. Other forests are composed mostly of small trees, junipers and pines that rarely grow taller than 30 feet. Most western forests are primarily made up of needle-leaved trees, the pines, spruces, firs, and junipers, but broad-leaved trees such as oaks, maples, cottonwoods, and aspens are also common, especially near water. And the desert forests of the Southwest, dominated by the giant Saguaro cactus, challenge most people's preconceptions about forests. This diversity reflects the ability of species to adapt to virtually any situation.

You can find numerous examples of adaptation in different tree species. When you look at a forest, ask yourself questions about what you see. Why do some trees have needles while others have broad leaves? Why do some trees drop their leaves every year while others do not?

NEEDLE-LEAVES AND BROAD LEAVES: Perhaps the first observation to make about a forest is whether it is composed primarily of needle-leaved evergreen species or broad-leaved species. Some forests, particularly those that range throughout most of eastern North America, are made up largely of broad-leaved species such as maples, oaks, and hickories. Forests in the West, however, tend to be mostly composed of needle-leaved trees such as firs, spruces, and junipers. In the West, broad-leaved species such as sycamores and cottonwoods are characteristic of moist areas typified by streamsides and river banks. There are many exceptions to this pattern, however. Quaking Aspen is a broad-leaved species that is abundant throughout the West, usually growing along mountain slopes among evergreen conifers.

Leaf shapes represent evolutionary responses to challenges posed by climate and other factors of the physical environment. Needle-shaped, evergreen leaves are adaptive in many environments, especially those in which the growing season is short and winter is long or the climate is hot and dry.

Almost all species of needle-leaved trees are evergreen (larches are the exception in the West), an adaptation for coping with a relatively short growing season. Leaves that are already present when snow thaws and temperatures warm in spring can begin photosynthesis immediately, thus taking full advantage of the limited time for growth. Each needle-leaf is, in itself, small and relatively "cheap" to produce. An injured needle is quickly replaced, whereas a large, broad leaf requires more energy to produce in spring and to replace if lost or badly damaged. Needle-leaves, by their density, also protect the tree well, and thus protect each other. The conical shape of spruces and firs, along with the flexibility of their boughs, makes it easy for snow to slide off the tree in the slightest breeze.

Needle-leaves are uniquely adapted to conditions in regions where winter is cold and long, such as northern or high mountain forests. Plant cells could be damaged by freezing, because water expands and forms ice crystals that could physically disrupt the delicate components of the cells. Some conifers, called hardy species, undergo cellular changes that permit their liquid contents to supercool, thus remaining liquid well below the temperature at which they would normally freeze. Some far northern species, such as White Spruce, are very hardy, meaning that they can endure extreme cold for prolonged periods. Very hardy species have empty spaces between cells that provide an area for liquid to freeze outside rather than inside the cell, thus saving the cell from destruction. Some hardwood species, including Quaking Aspen, are very hardy species.

Needle-leaves are also adaptive in moderately hot, dry regions, such as the western foothills, where pines and junipers are the predominant needle-leaved trees. Needles have a waxy coating that resists evaporation, helping retain water inside the leaf. The needle shape tends to minimize direct exposure to the sun's rays because clusters of needles help shade one another, which also helps hold in water. In hot, dry climates there is little winter snowfall, so a conical shape is no longer adaptive. Thus species such as pinyons have a broader, less conical look than spruces and firs.

Broad-leaved species succeed well where there is reasonably high moisture and a long growing season. Broad leaves are more apt to lose water in the sun's heat, thus the plant must have an adequate reservoir of ground water to pump into its leaves to make up for water lost through evaporation. Many broad-leaved species, such as the mesquites that live in dry desert washes, have deep tap roots that ensure a constant supply of water. And the long growing season permits the plant ample time to regrow leaves as the weather warms in spring.

DECIDUOUS AND EVERGREEN TREES: Only a few evergreen broad-leaved species live in North America, among them such species as Virginia Live Oak and oaks of the Southwest. These species are all confined to warm latitudes, where winters are gentle. Most broad-leaved trees and shrubs in the temperate zone are deciduous, dropping their leaves in winter. There is utterly no advantage to being deciduous if the climate is suitable for growing year-round; thus, in the warm and moist tropics, most broad-leaved species are evergreen. The cost of being deciduous is that the plant cannot photosynthesize while it is leafless. Since photosynthesis is the very lifeblood of the plant, there must be some other strong advantage to select for the evolution of deciduousness—and there is.

Mexican Blue Oak, a hardy evergreen oak.

In cold climates, winter presents two serious stresses for plants. First, days become shorter. Fewer hours of light mean less of the most essential raw ingredient for photosynthesis. The plant's ability to manufacture food is substantially reduced. Second, cold temperatures freeze water in the soil, making it impossible for plants to take up water through their roots. Therefore, water lost by evaporation cannot be replaced. The plant will eventually die from desiccation (water starvation).

By dropping their leaves in winter, deciduous plants avoid desiccation (since there is no leaf surface area from which to lose water) while at the same time not missing much opportunity for photosynthesis (since days are quite short). Also, the cold temperatures of winter slow down biochemical reactions—even if photosynthesis did occur, it would be far less efficient. As long as leaves can be rapidly regrown in spring, deciduous plants are not at a disadvantage.

Deciduousness is, therefore, adaptive throughout much of the temperate zone. In the far north and on high mountains, growing season is generally too brief for deciduous plants to succeed—these regions support needle-leaved evergreens. In equatorial regions, growing season is essentially year-round, so evergreen plants are the rule there as well. However, deciduousness also occurs in tropical areas where the dry season is severe, and many plants drop their leaves to avoid desiccation. Some desert plants have leaves only briefly during the short spring rainy season. In North America, the Ocotillo, a shrub of the hot southwestern deserts, is leafless most of the year but quickly grows small, waxy leaves whenever sufficient rain occurs. It is only then that the plant photosynthesizes.

FACTORS OF FOREST ECOLOGY

Students of natural history have long studied the factors determining which and how many species can coexist in a forest. Ecologists are now generally agreed that the major factors that determine species richness are climate, soil conditions, the effects of other species (including and perhaps especially humans), and disturbances such as fire and changes in geology.

CLIMATE

Some patterns of biodiversity are obvious: equatorial regions contain far more species than temperate regions, and temperate regions are much more species-rich than polar regions. In equatorial regions, hot savannas and even hotter deserts have far fewer species than nearby rain forests. This immediately suggests that species richness is linked with climatic factors. Climate includes such things as annual amount of precipitation, length of the growing season, annual temperature fluctuations, and number of overcast days. Perhaps the elaborate physiological adaptations necessary to exist in harsh climates (hibernation, long-distance migrations, a biochemistry tolerant of extreme heat or cold) present such a major challenge that relatively few organisms have been able to develop them.

Growth form of plants is highly affected by climate. As you move up a western mountain, you normally pass through an area consisting of short trees—a "pygmy forest" of junipers, pinyon pines, and often scrubby oaks, such as Gambel Oak. Higher in elevation, where temperatures are cooler and precipitation more abundant, trees are considerably taller. Finally, high atop some western mountains, trees such as Limber Pines and Bristlecone Pines become short and gnarled, seeming to show in the most literal sense the stresses of long winters and constant chilling winds. At mid-elevations, Engelmann Spruce is a tall, cone-shaped tree reaching a height of from 80 to 100 feet. On exposed mountaintops, however, where climate is especially severe in winter, Engelmann Spruce survives only as a prostrate, shrublike plant protected in winter by a blanket of snow.

SOIL

Soil characteristics exert a strong influence on what sorts of plants occur in an area. Soils that are acidic support different species of plants than do alkaline soils. Soils rich in calcium sup-

This aerial photo shows the dark soil characteristic of such places as North Dakota.

port certain plant species absent from calcium-poor soils. Prairie soils are typically dark, rich in calcium, and ideal for plants.

Soil texture is determined by the mixture of gravel, sand, silt, and clay particles present. Gravel consists of rock fragments and pebbles. Sand particles are smaller grains of rock. Silt particles are dustlike, and clay particles are so small that they can be differentiated only under a microscope. Soil texture strongly affects soil properties. Sandy soils hold water less efficiently than soils composed mostly of finer silts and clays. A soil with abundant clay may sometimes become waterlogged, actually drowning roots. And areas recently exposed to glaciation have very thin soils because there has not been sufficient time for soils to build up after being scraped away by the glacier.

THE EFFECTS OF OTHER SPECIES

No species is an island. Other species also present will likely be competitors, predators, or parasites. Some may be beneficial. All sorts of interactions among species are possible.

COMPETITION

Competition occurs when two or more species require the same resource and that resource is in limited supply. For example, there are many species of cavity-nesting birds throughout the West, including woodpeckers, chickadees, nuthatches, bluebirds, and certain swallows. Mammals such as the various squirrel species also live in tree cavities. Woodpeckers usually excavate these holes in dead trees, and their old nest holes are used in subsequent years by the other species. Thus the number of dead trees in a forest is important to cavity nesters, and the competition for good cavity snags is intense. This competition may be obvious to the birds but quite subtle to the human observer. Walking in a quiet aspen grove (Plate 11), we have no inkling that the Violet-green Swallow pair nesting in the aspen snag had to drive away a Tree Swallow pair and a male Mountain Bluebird to secure the cavity.

The long-term (evolutionary) results of competition may be reflected in broad patterns of distribution among species. In our aspen grove, we see a Red-naped Sapsucker, both Downy and Hairy woodpeckers, and a Northern Flicker. All four species are woodpeckers, and all share a similar anatomy. The Downy and Hairy are patterned almost identically but differ in size. This means that the little Downy selects smaller food items than the larger Hairy, thus they compete very little, if at all, for food. The sapsucker is similar in size to the Hairy Woodpecker but feeds entirely differently, by drilling rows of holes to get at the underlying cambium or sap. The Northern Flicker, largest of the four, also has a unique method of feeding. Flickers often forage on the ground, feeding on ant colonies. Indeed, one of the commonest ways of encountering a flicker is to have it fly up from the ground, revealing its bright white rump as it glides to a nearby tree trunk. Thus, four woodpecker species coexist in the same aspen grove, avoiding competition by feeding on different resources. This pattern is common in nature.

PREDATION

Predation is another prevalent pattern throughout all of nature. Each organism is a potential resource for another organism. Every school child learns about food chains: Plants are eaten by insects, insects are eaten by small birds, small birds are eaten by predators such as weasels, and weasels are eaten by hawks and owls.

Predation has caused the evolution of a host of adaptations. One is that of cryptic coloration, or camouflage. As you survey animal species, it soon becomes apparent that many are hard to detect, seeming to blend in with their surroundings. Examples can be found in nearly every animal group, from insects to mammals. Behavior is a critical component of good camouflage. The animal must know what background to choose and exhibit caution and alertness in its movements. Camouflage is of obvious importance to would-be prey species. The easier it is to avoid detection, the better the chances of not being captured and eaten. Camouflage is equally valuable to a predator, because if its prey sees it coming, the predator will likely miss its meal.

Another pattern associated with food chains and predation is that plants are much more numerous than animals, and prey are much more numerous than predators. If you were to weigh all of the plants and animals in a forest, you'd find that the plants vastly outweigh the animals. There may be many thousands of caterpillars in the cottonwoods lining a riverbed, but their combined weight pales compared with that of the trees they inhabit, upon whose leaves they feed. By this measure, plants are the most abundant living things on Earth, because they are "closest to the sun." This is because plants, not animals, photosynthesize. Plants are the direct recipients of the sun's energy. But plants must use some of that energy for their own support, meaning that there is less energy passed on to the animals that eat the plants. In fact, typically less than 10 percent of the energy captured by plants moves on in the food chain to the animals.

Herbivores are animals that feed on plants, and *carnivores* are animals that consume other animals. Most herbivores are insects (caterpillars, ants, beetles, bees), but many mammals ranging in size from deer mice to deer are also herbivores. Some birds (grouse, doves, thrushes, sparrows, finches) feed heavily on plant buds, seeds, and fruits, though not on leaves (some grouse do eat conifer needles). If plants are one energy step from the sun, herbivores are two energy steps from the sun. Thus herbivores are more numerous than carnivores.

Many insects, such as dragonflies, robber flies, and certain ants, are carnivores, and all spiders eat nothing but animal prey. All snakes and lizards, as well as salamanders, toads, frogs, and treefrogs, are carnivores. Many birds and mammals are also carnivorous. Every carnivore is at least three energy steps from the sun. Some, like the Mountain Lion, Wolverine, Great Horned Owl, and Northern Goshawk, are four or five energy steps from the sun.

Some animals are *omnivores,* capable of digesting both plant and animal food. Humans are an obvious example. Many bird species are omnivorous, including titmice, chickadees, orioles, thrushes, and grosbeaks. Among mammals, skunks, the Raccoon, foxes, and bears are omnivores. Even the Red Squirrel, though primarily a plant eater, will take nestling birds if it can. With their intermediate position on the food chain, omnivores are usually more abundant than strict carnivores but less abundant than herbivores.

Suppose you are very lucky and come upon a Northern Gos-

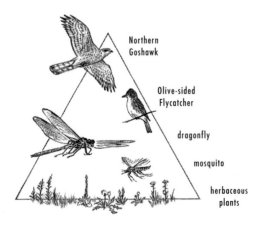

Northern
Goshawk

Olive-sided
Flycatcher

dragonfly

mosquito

herbaceous
plants

Figure 6. The ecological pyramid models the way energy is used in food chains.

hawk that has just captured an Olive-sided Flycatcher, caught napping on an open snag. Just a few minutes earlier, the flycatcher had consumed a dragonfly. The dragonfly's last meal had been several male mosquitoes, each of which had earlier dined on the juices of young plant sprouts. Thus some of the energy that will now sustain the Goshawk has already passed through four living things: a plant, a herbivorous sucking insect, a carnivorous insect, and a flycatcher. At each step in the food chain, some energy was lost as it was used by the various life forms. Precious little remained for the Goshawk. That's why there are a lot more mosquitoes, caterpillars, and ants in a forest than there are Goshawks, Wolverines, and Great Horned Owls.

ESSAY

PLANT-HERBIVORE WARS

Why don't herbivores eat all of the plants? Consider the fact that plants are incapable of escaping from their predators, the herbivores. Consider the fact that a herbivore—any one of billions upon billions of insects or millions of rabbits, hares, mice, deer, and gazelles—has but to walk up to a plant and consume it, lock, stock, and barrel. We all know how quickly rabbits can reproduce. It takes much longer to grow a spruce than a bunny, to say nothing of how quickly caterpillars can appear on the scene. Yet the world stays green. How do plants manage against the herbivore hordes (and herds)?

One possible answer is that predators control herbivores, preventing them from becoming so numerous as to pose a significant threat to the plants. But most predators do not exert strong effects on herbivore populations. Among large animals, for example, Gray Wolves rarely bring down a healthy Moose. They tend to kill only old, sick, or injured individuals no longer capable of reproducing. Calves would be easy prey, but they are usually well defended by the adults. Thus a Moose population is not normally controlled by predators. Tiny predators—the disease-causing bacteria and viruses and the many parasitic animals (tapeworms, roundworms, blood parasites)—may occasionally reduce populations. Epidemics can decimate animal populations (for instance, rabies can kill skunks, Raccoons, and foxes), but by and large the effect is temporary, and the population soon recovers.

Another possibility is that plants, even though they cannot run or hide, do successfully defend themselves. Plants have many defenses, from the obvious to the subtle. Among the obvious ones are the thorns and spines that cover stems and leaf edges of many species. A close look with a magnifying glass at the surface of a leaf will sometimes reveal tiny naillike structures, called *trichomes,* on which caterpillars can become stuck. And if a plant does get eaten, what then? Plants provide fiber, but what is fiber but indigestible material? Plants are largely composed of chemicals called cellulose, lignin, and tannin, all of which are extremely difficult to digest. Leaves and stems are often abundantly supplied with silica, an indigestible glasslike material.

And that's not all. Imagine sitting down to a salad made of some nice Skunk Cabbage leaves, a generous portion of Stinging Nettle, some Foxglove leaves, a sprinkling of Poison-oak, and perhaps a few juicy joints of Cholla cactus. No need to waste good croutons on that combination. If you ate such a salad, your mouth and throat would burn, sting, break into a rash, and bleed from the Cholla spines. You'd also be poisoned, probably fatally, by the Foxglove. Plant leaves are loaded with various kinds of poisons, among which are alkaloids, terpenoids, cyanide-containing chemicals, and poisonous amino acids. These substances can interfere with the production of DNA, stop respiration, cause glandular disorders, and prevent digestion.

Plants, quite simply, are for the most part biochemically hostile to animals. In fact, given the impressive diversity of plant chemical defenses, it is no small wonder that there are so many herbivores!

Of course, as plants can and have evolutionarily adapted to resist herbivory, so have herbivores been naturally selected to cope with plant defenses. Consider a cottontail rabbit eating leaves in a meadow. Were you to follow this animal closely you might be taken aback a bit to see it defecate and then turn around and consume its feces. Rabbits engage in a behavior called *coprophagy,* reingesting partially digested plant material. The second trip through the rabbit's intestinal system allows for more thorough digestion. Neat trick.

In mammals, the length of the digestive system is adapted to the difficulties associated with digesting food. Carnivores, which take in nonpoisonous, simple chemicals that make up the bodies of their prey animals, have short, uncomplicated digestive systems. The digestive system of some carnivorous mammals, if stretched out, would measure between 2 and 6 body lengths. Many large herbivorous mammals have digestive systems that measure 20 to 25 body lengths! Such a long system provides immense surface area for the chemicals of digestion to act on the difficult-to-digest plant substances.

Herbivorous mammals have other digestive adaptations. Many, including horses, have a large blind sac called a caecum at the juncture between the small and large intestine. The caecum provides additional space for breakdown of plant material. (Our appendix is all that remains of what was once a caecum.) Some large herbivorous mammals such as cows and sheep have a complex stomach divided into four chambers. Food is swallowed but later regurgitated and chewed as a "cud," then reswallowed. The elaborate stomach hosts billions of tiny microorganisms that actually do the difficult work of breaking up cellulose and other complex chemicals. Even the teeth of mammalian herbivores are especially adapted, with high crowns and complex cusps to cope with a difficult diet of coarse plant foods.

Insects, too, have at least to some degree met the challenges posed by plant defenses. Caterpillars, which exist in vast abundance in all forests, are notorious for the rate at which they can devour leaves, the photosynthetic surface of the plant. By consuming the plant's "solar panels," they cause it direct, sometimes irreversible harm. Caterpillars are constantly exposed to plant chemical defenses. The long-term result has been that various families of lepidopterans (butterflies and moths) have come to specialize on certain families of plants. In other words, the caterpillars are highly selective about which plants they eat. These plants are called host plants, because they are where the adults lay their eggs and where the caterpillars feed. For example, Monarch butterflies belong to a group called the milkweed butterflies; their larvae are among the only caterpillars that can tolerate cardiac glycosides, toxic chemicals that abound in many milkweeds (family Asclepiadaceae).

Insects have many ways to at least partially circumvent plant defenses. Some "mine" the leaves, visiting areas where defense

The bright colors of Monarch butterflies "warn" avian predators that the insects are toxic.

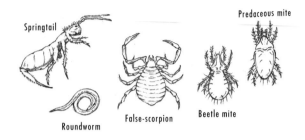

Springtail

Predaceous mite

False-scorpion

Beetle mite

Roundworm

Figure 7. Decomposer animals

compounds are least abundant. Others clip leaf veins, preventing the chemicals from reaching certain areas. The Western Pine Beetle, a serious pest on Ponderosa Pine, seems to turn a plant's defenses against it by using the pine's volatile terpenes as a signal to attract the female beetle to the tree.

For all their considerable efforts, herbivores have not really gotten the better of the plants. Consider what is beneath your feet as you amble through a quiet forest glade. The very existence of leaf litter means that those leaves were not eaten. In fact, the vast majority of the sun's energy collected by plant leaves never enters any animal while the leaf is alive. Most of the energy contained in a forest moves through what is called the decomposer food web. Leaves and branches drop off, collect on the ground, and are invaded by myriads of bacteria and fungi, as well as a host of beetles, mites, springtails, roundworms, rotifers, and earthworms, a list far from exhaustive. The colorful mushrooms of the forest floor are visible reminders of the largely microbial world through which most of the forest's energy flows. Decomposers are a vital part of forest ecology because they break down the elaborate plant chemicals into simple forms ready to be recycled back into the plants.

ALIEN SPECIES

When a species enters an area to which it is not native, it often cannot cope with its new environment and quickly dies out. If a species is well adapted to the new environment, however, it may succeed and exert a dramatic effect upon the ecology of that area. Without natural predators, parasites, and competitors to restrain

Figure 8. Kudzu-vine

it, the invading species may become disproportionately abundant.

The European Starling, introduced into Central Park in New York City in 1890, reached California by 1950. This aggressive species has probably contributed to the significant reductions in the populations of cavity-nesting birds such as woodpeckers and bluebirds. Likewise, the House Sparrow, introduced in 1850, quickly spread throughout North America. Kudzu-vine, a native of Japan, was brought to the United States in 1911. Since then it has rapidly spread throughout the Southeast and is now moving westward. Kudzu-vine can choke a woodland, draping the trees and blocking their sunlight. Other invader plant species, among them the Tamarisks from the Mediterranean region, were introduced as ornamental trees that, when planted in rows, could serve as windbreaks, but escaped from cultivation. These fast-growing, successful immigrant species now occur extensively along riverine thickets, outcompeting native species. Successful invasion by alien species may permanently change habitats, with the invading species replacing one or more of the native species.

HUMAN ACTIVITIES

Human activities are often linked with the invasion of alien species. In each of the examples above (European Starling, House Sparrow, Kudzu-vine, Tamarisk), humans brought the species to North America and purposefully introduced it. Humans have also reduced or eliminated many species. Predators such as Gray Wolf and Grizzly Bear have been hunted out of existence in most areas where they were once common. Coyotes and birds of prey fall victims to poisoned carcasses left out to eliminate "varmints." The majestic California Condor was entirely removed from the wild in an attempt to artificially breed it in captivity, in the hopes of saving the species. Recently, some offspring of the captive breeding program have been set free in the wild. Gray Wolves, long absent from their natural habitats throughout the Rocky Mountains, have been reintroduced into Yellowstone National Park in an attempt to restore the natural predators of this ecosystem.

Humans also affect habitats in many other ways. They bring in cattle and sheep, whose grazing transforms the landscape. Some southwestern regions have been changed from grassland to desert because cattle overgrazed the grasses until desert species, unpalatable to cattle, were able to invade and take over. Humans also cut forests for timber and to make room for agriculture and housing. Such activities result in forests becoming fragmented, so that small islands are all that remain of once-continuous forest acreage. The result is that large species such as the Bald Eagle and Black Bear are forced out because they cannot establish the large territories they need. Even smaller species often require large continuous forest in order to persist.

Timber practices also profoundly change the ecology of forests. Clear-cutting, in which hundreds of acres of mixed old-growth forest are simultaneously felled, results in the establishment of uniform-aged tree farms of young, fast-growing species. These areas support far fewer species than normal old-growth forest.

POLLUTION

In the strictest sense, pollution is the result of human activity. However, pollutants can affect forest habitats in ways that are subtler but more long-lasting than the effects of grazing and timbering. Acid rain can significantly change pond water, interfering with the reproduction of amphibians and other animals. Valuable minerals can be washed from the soil more easily when rainwater is of high acidity. Discharge of toxic metals from mine tailings are yet another way in which habitats can be disturbed by pollution.

MUTUALISM

All of the interactions among life forms thus far discussed have been basically antagonistic. Situations arise, however, where two or more species can exploit one another, to the benefit of each. Bees and many other insects feed on nectar, and in doing so promote cross-pollination. By feeding on the plant, the insect is unconsciously performing a service for it; the nectar is manufactured by the plant only to attract insects. This interaction is an example of mutualism, whereby two organisms act in a way that is beneficial to both. Some plants cannot be pollinated without in-

Figure 9. Bolete mushroom, a fungus

sects, but the insects would starve without the plants. Mutualism, though not rare, is generally far less common than antagonistic interactions.

One of the most significant cases of mutualism of western forests is one that occurs between certain fungi and many tree species. These fungi, called mycorrhizae, invade tree roots and consume some of the products of photosynthesis. The fungi also take essential minerals such as phosphorus into the tree, without which the tree couldn't survive.

ISTURBANCE

The species composition of any habitat is partly the result of chance factors. Nature is often unpredictable and even devastating. Disturbances such as flood, fire, volcanic eruption, pest outbreak, violent windstorm, or other natural acts can vastly and suddenly alter a habitat.

Natural disasters are large-scale ecological disturbances. No environment anywhere on the planet is immune from occasional disruption by some natural force or combination of forces. Ecologists once somewhat naively entertained a vision of the tranquil forest primeval, undisturbed and unchanging through the eons. Now that view has been largely abandoned. Forests, like any other habitat, are subject to nature's unpredictable furies. Forests can even suffer seemingly total destruction, yet eventually recover. Ecological disturbance is any event or combination of events, large or small, that affects habitats. Disturbance has three basic components—frequency, predictability, and magnitude.

Frequent disturbances often have the effect of maintaining a habitat that would otherwise eventually change into a different kind of habitat. Frequent fires in grasslands, for example, kill off invading woody species, but deep-rooted grasses quickly regrow.

Some disturbance factors are relatively predictable, while others are most unpredictable. Although climate is relatively predictable, there is variation from one year to another. Years of drought may occur in succession, imposing a change on the landscape as plants and animals suffer the effects of water shortage. It is safe to state that throughout the West, thunderstorms typify the summer months, and lightning will cause fires. However, it is not possible to predict exactly where a lightning fire will burn in any given season. Among the most unpredictable disturbance factors are volcanic eruptions. Fortunately, eruptions from volcanos are quite rare throughout the American West.

Obviously, the larger the magnitude of the disturbance, the more effects it will have, and the longer those effects will be felt. A forest may suffer many casualties among the canopy trees as a result of a violent summer windstorm. Or a single old tree may fall under milder conditions. Its downfall creates a small opening, a light gap in the canopy that permits light to enter and new plants, even new species, to thrive. The disturbances of largest magnitude in the West in recent years were the eruption of Mount St. Helens on May 18, 1980, and the devastating fires that occurred in Yellowstone National Park in the summer of 1988 (see Chapter 7). The effects from both of these events will be evident for many years to come. Small-magnitude disturbances also change the habitat, but for a much briefer time period.

Human activities, discussed above, are a major source of disturbance in western habitats. Of the many natural causes of disturbance, weather, fire, floods, and geology have perhaps the most profound effects.

Naturally set fire is the most common disturbance factor in both forests and prairies.

WEATHER

All organisms, whether plant, animal, or microbe, are subject to the constant effects of their external environments. Prolonged heat, cold, and drought can affect some species more than others. Throughout the West, many species of birds and mammals will migrate down from mountains to valleys, attempting to escape the severity of winter. In the temperate zone, weather is fickle— species ranging from Elk to the tiny Golden-crowned Kinglet may suffer periodic die-offs as a result of particularly severe winters. In forests, windthrow is an important disturbance factor, churning up the soil and providing new sites where seedlings and saplings can grow.

FIRE

Although most people think of fire as a catastrophe (and indeed some fires are), it is actually a vital part of western ecology. Most often, fires maintain habitats rather than destroy them. Frequent low-level fires give Ponderosa Pine forests in Arizona an open, parklike look, because the fires eliminate dense litter that could serve as the fuel for a large-scale fire. Prairie fires prevent the invasion of seedlings from various tree species, thus allowing the prairie grasses to remain dominant. Many tree species have adapted to the inevitability of fire. Jack Pine, common on poor soils throughout the boreal forest, requires heat for its cones to open and release seeds. The cones of Lodgepole Pine, abundant throughout western mountains, remain closed for years until the heat from fire opens them. Many herbaceous species, notably Fireweed, thrive in recently burned over areas.

Of course, some forest fires are destructive. When a forest goes

Figure 10. A charred stump sprouts new growth

Fireweed.

unburned for many years, litter can build up to such a degree that even a fire of natural cause results in a conflagration, a crown fire that utterly destroys the forest. Even then, however, the burned site will eventually recover.

FLOODING

Forests border rivers and streams. In spring, when winter snow melts and rains soak the landscape, flood waters rise and cover the forest adjacent to flooding rivers. Flooding may undercut soil and wash away areas of forest. But flooding is a dynamic process that establishes a rough balance between destruction and creation. Though they cause much damage, floods also deposit rich soils, which are quickly colonized by plants and animals. Sediment bars created during flooding provide a foundation for the eventual reestablishment of trees along the waterway. Many plant species are well adapted to withstand periods of immersion during the flooding season. In southwestern deserts, flooding may occur with frightening rapidity following heavy downpours in late summer. Arroyos, normally dry streambeds, become raging torrents of water.

GEOLOGY

Nothing is permanent. Over time periods measured in thousands and millions of years, climate and geology interact and change the landscape. Two hundred million years ago, the region that is now eastern Arizona supported a lush forest of conifers, among which scampered some of the first carnivorous dinosaurs. Now the area is desert, and the remains of those stately trees are randomly scat-

Dinosaur bones from Dinosaur National Monument, Utah.

tered on the desert floor in the Petrified Forest National Park. Just over 100 million years ago, some of the largest species of dinosaurs fed in herds along a tropical river in a valley in what is now Utah and Colorado; long-necked Apatosaurus fell prey to the ferocious Allosaur. Today the region is desert, with scattered small junipers. The dinosaurs remain only as fossils in the rocks at Dinosaur National Monument. The mountains throughout the West, but especially along the Pacific Coast, are not only geologically young but also active. In addition to Mount St. Helens, many other mountain regions show clear evidence of recent volcanic activity. Places like Craters of the Moon National Monument in Idaho still show disturbance effects from lava flows that occurred 2,000 years ago.

Lava flow at Craters of the Moon National Monument, Idaho.

All disturbances eventually end. Some types of disturbance, such as farming or ranching, may occur continuously on a single site for years. Eventually, however, the site may be abandoned. Other disturbances, like windstorm, flood, or fire, are over in a few hours. Once the disturbance has ceased, a process of ecological change begins. The disturbed area represents new habitat available for plants and animals to colonize. Often, the physical conditions of disturbed habitats are severe. A burned-over area may bake in the sun's heat with no shade to attenuate the scorching temperature. Winds, unimpeded by tree branches or blades of grass, cause high rates of evaporation, adding water stress to plants. Nonetheless, many species are well adapted to thrive under such challenging conditions.

Since newly disturbed areas are normally not hospitable, the first species to invade an area following disturbance tend to be quite hardy. They grow quickly and reproduce before other plant species enter and shade them out. These colonizing species, called pioneer plants but often referred to simply as "weeds," are eventually replaced by others that usually grow more slowly but remain longer. Finally, species move in that persist in the area indefinitely, until some further disturbance starts the process again. This process, the replacement of pioneer species by other species over time, is called *ecological succession*.

Succession is roughly but not precisely predictable in any given area. Certain fast-growing species, among them the Quaking Aspen, are clear indicators of recent disturbance followed by ecological succession. But if you look carefully at an aspen forest, you

Dwarf Buckwheat on volcanic rubble at Craters of the Moon.

will often note that trees such as Engelmann Spruce constitute the understory. The shade-tolerant spruces will grow up and eventually replace the aspens.

The pace of ecological succession in an area depends in part on how severely the area was disturbed. An abandoned farmstead or ranchland will tend toward a rapid succession, with woody shrubs and trees establishing themselves relatively quickly. Such will also be the case with lightly burned-over areas. The quick succession is possible because the soil is intact, mineral-rich, and loaded with seeds dispersed in the course of recent months or years. This seed bed represents the pioneer species that grow quickly, restabilizing the soil. On the other hand, areas subjected to major disturbances that have either destroyed the soil or otherwise disrupted the seed bed take much longer for succession to occur. The volcanic ash that resulted from the eruption of Mount St. Helens will persist for many decades, and succession, though it is occurring, will be slow. Craters of the Moon National Monument in Idaho still shows bare lava flows that date back 2,000 years. Plants such as lichens and Dwarf Buckwheat are among the few that can grow on essentially bare lava. Dwarf Buckwheat is a mere four inches tall, but it sends down roots to a depth of four feet, tapping into deep moisture that enables it to withstand the intense heat of the unshaded landscape.

3

LIFE ZONES

Mountain ranges have a major effect on climate, especially on rainfall patterns, because they force moisture-laden air to rise, cooling it and resulting in precipitation along the mountainside. These climatic effects are particularly great in the West because the western mountains are geologically young. The Rockies, Sierra Nevada, and Cascade Mountains are far younger than the eastern Alleghenys, Adirondacks, and Presidentials. Because of their comparative youth, western mountain ranges have not eroded very much and are thus characterized by peaks so tall they are snow-capped even in summer.

The mountains force air from the prevailing west winds upward along their steep slopes. As air rises, it cools, and the moisture in the air condenses into drops of rain or snow. Thus the western slopes of the mountains are cool and wet, while the eastern slopes are relatively dry. This phenomenon is called a *rainshadow,* or, more technically, orographic precipitation.

A good example is found in the Cascade Mountains of Oregon (described in more detail in our companion guide, *California and Pacific Northwest Forests*). Their western slopes are cool and wet, supporting lush temperate rain forests of Douglas-fir and other species. As the air moves eastward over the mountains, it drops most of its moisture. The mountaintop is misty and cool, and the trees are smaller, stunted by high winds causing wind chill and evaporation. On the leeward side of the Cascades, the air is much drier. Instead of rain forest, the eastern slopes are covered with a more arid forest of Ponderosa Pine and, in lower elevations, scattered junipers and sagebrush. The Great Basin Desert that covers much of Utah and Nevada, plus parts of Washington, Oregon, and Idaho, owes its existence in large part to the Pacific coastal mountains that capture moisture on their western slopes.

The major rainshadow cast by the Rockies extends from

Canada into Mexico and results in shortgrass prairie on the eastern side of the mountains. The grasses become progressively taller further eastward because moisture-laden air from Canada enters the central states. Much of the grasslands east of the Rockies would be far more lush—in fact, they would probably be forests—if the Rockies did not block moisture-laden air.

Different climates support different life forms. Thanks to changes in elevation and the rainshadow, mountains provide habitat for considerably more kinds of plants and animals than flatlands do. A ride over a western mountain will take you through several major habitat types called *life zones*.

The first explorer to comment on how nature changes as you climb a mountain was Alexander von Humboldt, a German who explored much of Amazonian and Andean South America between 1845 and 1862. Scaling the Andes in several places, von Humboldt documented how habitat changes from dense tropical rain forest, to cooler cloud forest, to even cooler alpine scrub and grassland as you climb ever upward on the mountainside. Humboldt related these altitudinal changes to those experienced when you traverse long distances north or south. For instance, at 70 degrees North latitude (in the Canadian Arctic), treeless tundra occurs at sea level. However, at 36 degrees North latitude (northern Arizona), you must be at an elevation of about 10,000 feet before encountering tundra.

In the 1890s, C. Hart Merriam described the same phenomenon for the San Francisco Peaks near Flagstaff, Arizona. Merriam's Life Zones, as they are often called, are still useful in describing much of the ecology of the West.

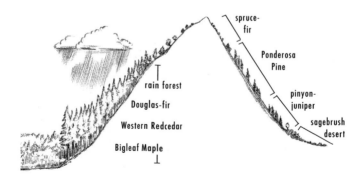

Figure 11. Rainshadow on the east slope of an Oregon mountain

Merriam noted that as one moves up a western mountain, the habitat changes from hot, arid desert to small forest and then to lush, mixed-species conifer forest. Go high enough and you will usually encounter an arctic environment of stunted trees, followed by the cold, treeless desert of alpine tundra.

Merriam thought that the divisions between the different altitudinal habitats were generally sharp, resulting in distinct vegetation belts around the mountain. Each of his life zones is defined as a vegetation belt encompassing a range of 4°C mean summer temperature (7.2 °F). Thus the average temperature drops 7.2 °F as you move up in altitude to the next life zone. You can begin your day in the desert, say at 90°F, and have your lunch at a picnic grove within a conifer forest with the thermometer registering around 60°F, just by driving up a mountain. Precipitation also varies, generally increasing with altitude. Rainshadows, however, can result in precipitation amounts being quite different on the east and west sides of a mountain.

Orientation on the mountain also affects life zones. South-facing slopes receive more summer sunlight than north-facing slopes. Therefore, life zones characteristic of arid, hot climates will occur further up the mountain on south-facing slopes. Likewise, life zones characteristic of cooler, less arid climates occur farther down the mountainside on north-facing slopes. This effect is particularly evident on mountains in the Southwest.

An altitude change of about 2,500 feet is roughly equivalent to a latitudinal move of about 400 miles. Thus a trip up a very high mountain is ecologically somewhat like going from, say, San Antonio to the tundra of Churchill, Manitoba.

There are six life zones in the western mountains. In general, these life zones can be observed throughout the West, though they are fairly variable, and there is often a gradual blending of one life zone into another, making it tricky to define where one zone leaves off and another begins. There is frequently much intermingling at the border between life zones (what ecologists call the *ecotone*). Usually you cannot walk from one life zone into another merely by taking a few steps. From lowest to highest elevation, the life zones are: *Lower Sonoran, Upper Sonoran, Transition, Canadian, Hudsonian,* and *Arctic-Alpine.*

Life zones are defined by the species that constitute them. Like any ecological community, it is the combination of species that is important in distinguishing one life zone from another, and many plant and animal species inhabit several life zones. For instance, Quaking Aspen is abundant both in the Transition and Canadian zones. However, when aspen is mixed with Ponderosa Pine, you are in the Transition Zone. When aspen is mixed with Douglas-fir,

The shrub desert of the Nevada Great Basin is a Lower Sonoran Zone ecosystem.

you're in the Canadian Zone. Engelmann Spruce is abundant in both the Canadian and Hudsonian zones, and many bird species, such as Red Crossbill, can be found in several life zones. Large animals such as Elk migrate seasonally from the high meadows of the Hudsonian Zone to the sheltered valleys of the Upper Sonoran Zone, a journey that takes them through four life zones. Following is a brief general description of each of Merriam's life zones, which will be treated in more detail as they occur in the regions discussed in later chapters.

LOWER SONORAN ZONE

This is a zone of desert or short grassland that consists of shrubs such as Big Sagebrush or various desert succulents, including the

This cactus desert in Arizona is also in the Lower Sonoran Zone.

Big Sagebrush, Pinyon Pines, and junipers share the Upper Sonoran Zone.

giant Saguaro cactus (Chapter 8). Cold-desert shrubs prevail to the north, hot-desert shrubs such as Creosote Bush, Blue Paloverde, and various succulents to the south. The temperature often exceeds 100°F in summer, and rainfall is minimal, about 10–11 inches annually in the driest locations.

Upper Sonoran Zone

Small, shrublike pinyon-juniper forests are indicative of this life zone. In parts of the Southwest, various shrubs such as manzanitas along with different yucca species are part of the zone as well. Pinyons and junipers are adapted to arid, semidesert conditions, where they occur along with shrubs such as Alderleaf Cercocarpus and Saskatoon Juneberry. Some cacti also survive in this

Junipers survive on arid hillsides of the Upper Sonoran Zone.

zone. In some Rocky Mountain areas, grassland prairie, with species such as Buffalo-grass and Blue Grama Grass, along with various wildflowers, are part of the Upper Sonoran Zone. In the Southwest, mixed oaks intermingle with pinyons and various junipers. Precipitation is generally 10–20 inches annually, and summer temperatures are often above 90°F.

TRANSITION ZONE

The name applies to the change from arid to lush, a transition from desert to real forest. Nonetheless, there often remains an arid look to the landscape. In some areas of the northern Rockies, high sagebrush country is considered a part of this zone. In other areas, oaks, especially Gambel Oak, often abound. But the trees

Stands of Ponderosa Pine (right) and Quaking Aspen (below) are indicative of the Transition Zone, where moisture is more abundant and temperatures are cooler.

Engelmann Spruce is an abundant indicator of Canadian Zone throughout the Rocky Mountains.

most indicative of the Transition Zone are Ponderosa Pine and Quaking Aspen. Open, parklike forests of stately Ponderosa Pine growing among tall grasses make this life zone among the most aesthetically pleasing. On south-facing slopes (which are hotter and drier because of high exposure to sunlight), Ponderosa Pine tends to mix with junipers from the Upper Sonoran Zone. On cooler, wetter, north-facing slopes, Douglas-fir often mixes with the pines and aspens. Annual precipitation tends to be between 20−25 inches.

CANADIAN ZONE

Named for its resemblance to the cool conifer forests of Canada, this life zone usually consists of a mixture of Douglas-fir, often the most abundant species, plus Engelmann Spruce, Subalpine Fir, Lodgepole Pine, and Quaking Aspen. The forest is usually dense, tall, and shady, with a thick bed of needles underfoot. On exposed ridges, you may find Limber Pine, Bristlecone Pine, or Whitebark Pine. Both Lodgepole Pine and Quaking Aspen are indicative of recent fires, but the aspen grows in areas of rich soil, while the pine frequents poorer soil. Depending upon the region, other conifers such as White Spruce (in the Black Hills) and White Fir (central and southern Rockies) may be common. Toward the Pacific Coast, the Canadian Zone includes such species as Grand Fir, Western Redcedar, Western Larch, Western Hemlock, and Western White Pine. Annual precipitation throughout the Transition Zone is from 25 to 30 inches, with snow falling throughout the winter. These mountainous regions are also often referred to as the Montane Zone.

Timberline in the Hudsonian Zone of the Central Rocky Mountains.

HUDSONIAN ZONE

Also called the Subalpine Zone, the name Hudsonian refers to Hudson Bay in Canada, a region where conifers are stunted and tundra takes over. The Hudsonian Zone is marked by timberline, where shrublike, wind-sculpted trees yield to alpine tundra. Species such as Engelmann Spruce and Subalpine Fir are the most common trees, but they scarcely resemble their counterparts from lower down in the Canadian Zone. Often they are shaped into "flag trees," with branches persisting only on the leeward side, those on the windward side having been killed by exposure. Spruce and fir may also spread to resemble dense shrubs that usually grow on the leeward side of a rock. This shrubby

Arctic-Alpine Zone in the Central Rocky Mountains.

Hardy species of perennial wildflowers, mosses, and lichens survive where trees cannot.

shape, called *krummholz,* is due to winter snow, which insulates the tree near ground level, protecting it from the wind chill that kills any branches protruding above the snow. Annual precipitation is about 30 inches or more, much of it as winter snow. Temperatures can be well below freezing, and winds are usually brisk.

ARCTIC-ALPINE ZONE

The Arctic-Alpine Zone is above the timberline and consists of grasses, sedges, and perennial wildflowers, with scattered rocks and boulders covered by lichens. Weather conditions are similar to the Hudsonian Zone, but maximum exposure prevents woody species from surviving. This zone occurs from the Central Rockies northward, as well as in the high Sierra Nevada and other Pacific Coast ranges, but is absent from most mountains in the Southwest.

WIDESPREAD WESTERN
MAMMALS AND BIRDS

MAMMALS

In general, the human population is far lower throughout most regions of the American West than in the eastern states, affording ample room for the buffalo to roam and the deer and the antelope to play (please—no discouraging words). In addition, the West's many mountain ranges provide ideal habitat to sustain a diversity of large mammals. Many of these are common in western national parks and forests. Often, local rangers can direct you to specific meadows, rivers, or mountainsides currently favored by various large mammal species. Keep a sharp lookout for Coyotes scampering across the road, or a herd of Bighorn Sheep trotting across a mountain crest. You don't want to miss them.

The large mammals described below are widely distributed in the western states, though some are not strictly forest dwellers.

ELK *Cervus canadensis*   PL. 1

Among deer, the majestic Elk, or Wapiti, is second only to the Moose in size. Males have a wide antler rack and a shaggy brown mane on the throat. A large bull may weigh just over 1,000 pounds and measure up to 5 feet tall at the shoulder, with a body length approaching 10 feet. Females are about 25 percent smaller than males. Both bulls and cows can be separated from other deer by their large body size and by their pale yellowish rump patch and short tail.

Elk frequent open meadows and forest edges at dawn and dusk, becoming most active at dusk and often foraging throughout the night. During the day, when they are resting, Elk are much less frequently seen. Look for wallows, shallow depressions made by scraping with hooves, where the odor of urine and feces is often strong. Also look for saplings stripped of bark by the chewing of cows marking territory or bark rubbed smooth by the bulls' antlers. Bulls also engage in "antler thrashing," essentially an attack on small trees and bushes. This behavior is thought to be part of preparation for sexual combat. Though Elk favor the high country in summer, they migrate to lower elevations in winter. Some places, such as Jackson Hole, Wyoming, attract large numbers of wintering Elk.

Elk feed on a diversity of plant material but are primarily grazers, feeding on grasses. In some areas, Elk will browse woody vegetation. They are also partial to the lichens that grow abundantly over rock surfaces on mountainsides.

For most of the year cows and calves stay together in herds, away from the mature bulls. During rutting season, however, which lasts from late August through November, adult bulls rejoin the herds and compete for mating privileges (see essay below). The gestation period is about nine months, so calves tend to be born in late June or early July. Normally, one calf is born per female, but sometimes a cow will give birth to twins. Calves weigh between 20 and 40 pounds at birth. Bears sometimes prey upon Elk calves, but normally the protection afforded by herding among adult females keeps the calves safe. Only the Mountain Lion, and occasionally the Grizzly Bear, is sufficiently robust to prey on adult Elk.

Elk live throughout the mountains of western North America, though they do not range into northern Canada and Alaska. They are most abundant in the northern Rockies, Sierra Nevada, Cascades, and Pacific Northwest. They are less abundant in the southwestern states. The Elk population of the Pacific Northwest is sometimes called the "Olympic elk" or "Roosevelt elk." These Elk frequent the lush rain forests of that region, as well as mountainous areas. Elk once ranged well east of the Appalachians, as far north as Vermont.

ESSAY

ADAPTATIONS: ELK AND SEXUAL SELECTION

In many animal species, the sexes look quite distinct. In birds, males are often larger and more colorful than females. In mammals, males also tend to be larger, and in many hoofed mammals, such as deer and antelope, males have impressive antlers that the females lack. Charles Darwin, famous for his concept of evolution by natural selection, conceived a theory to explain why, in some species, males are larger, more colorful, or carry more ornaments than females, a theory he called *sexual selection*.

Darwin argued that in sexually selected species, two forces affected the evolution of males that did not affect females. The first was female choice. Darwin mused that females may actively choose the largest, gaudiest males, thus selecting, generation after generation, for ever more elaborate male appearance. The largest, most colorful males would outbreed the least colorful, and thus bright coloration of males would spread rapidly through the species. In many bird species, for instance, males display before females, seeming to show off their bright patterns. The Sage Grouse and Greater and Lesser prairie-chickens are examples.

The second force was competition among males for access to females. Darwin believed that in some species, reproductive success was more a question of which male could ward off other prospective suitors and thus gain exclusive access to females. In species mostly affected by male-male competition, larger males would tend to have an advantage over smaller males, thus body size of males would tend to increase over evolutionary time. Any ornaments that could be useful in intimidating rivals or in actual combat would also convey an advantage.

Elk fit the Darwinian model of sexual selection based mostly on male-male competition. The large size, especially powerful neck muscles, and shaggy mane of bull Elk are all characteristics useful in intimidating other males and in combat. The wide antler rack is an obvious tool both for direct combat and for intimidation of rivals. During the rutting season, bull Elk have high levels of the male sex hormone testosterone in their bloodstream. They become aggressive, issuing vocal challenges to other males by "bugling." The bugle call consists of a bellow, followed by a shrill whistle and a series of grunts. Two males may engage in jousting contests, clashing antlers. This combat is essentially ritualized, and males are usually uninjured by it. However, occasionally a bull may seriously injure and even kill a rival. The bull most able to ward off other bulls wins the right to mate.

As is typical of sexually selected species, some bulls are extremely successful, while others are utter failures that never succeed in mating. A successful bull Elk may hold a harem of up to 60 cows. Highly polygynous and forming no real pair bonds, bull Elk do not remain with the female herds after the rut. Other deer are also sexually selected species, though to a somewhat lesser extent. Bison and Bighorn Sheep also fit the model.

WHITETAIL DEER *Odocoileus virginianus* PL. 1

The Whitetail Deer is the most widespread deer in the western hemisphere, its range extending from mid-Canada throughout the United States, and on into Mexico and Central and South

America. It is common mostly throughout the West, except in the Great Basin (Nevada, Utah, parts of Colorado and Arizona), and it is absent from California.

Whitetail Deer are well named, having a wide, flat tail that is held erect as the animal bounds away, flashing a bright white underside. Overall, this species is russet-tan in summer and grayish in winter. Only the male, or buck, has antlers. A large buck may weigh nearly 400 pounds and stand nearly 4 feet tall at the shoulder. Bucks are substantially larger than females, or does, which weigh only up to 250 pounds and stand 3 feet at the shoulder. Fawns are light tan with white spots.

This species is best described as a generalist. Whitetails occupy a diverse array of habitats and eat a wide variety of plant foods. You may encounter Whitetails in open fields, in pastures and agricultural areas, or in woodlands and forests. They are essentially browsers, feeding on leaves of many deciduous trees as well as numerous kinds of conifer needles. They are also fond of various nuts, including acorns and beechnuts. Around farmland, Whitetails favor cornfields. Because of elimination or reduction of predators over most of its range, as well as rigorous hunting restrictions, the Whitetail Deer is abundant in many areas. Local populations sometimes become too successful and overgraze, leading to higher disease rates and malnutrition in the herd.

During much of the year, bucks and does remain in separate herds, though they gather together at "deer yards" in winter. A buck may mate with several does or only one. A healthy doe will normally give birth to two fawns, occasionally to three. Newborn fawns avoid detection by predators such as Coyotes by crouching and freezing rather than trying to run away when a potential predator comes near.

Look for tree bark rubbed smooth by Whitetail Deer bucks vigorously scraping their antlers. When antlers grow in, they are initially covered with thin, hairy skin called velvet. The deer shed the velvet by scraping it off before the onset of rutting season.

MULE DEER or BLACKTAIL DEER　　　　PL. 1
Odocoileus hemionus

This deer is named for its ears, which tend to be larger than those of the similar Whitetail Deer. It is the only deer with black on the tail, from mid-tail to the tip. The tail color is the most reliable field mark in areas where this species occurs along with Whitetail Deer. Only bucks have antlers, and bucks range in weight from about 100 to 475 pounds. Does are smaller, weighing up to 160 pounds. In summer, Mule Deer are russet-brown, but in winter their coat color is grayish.

Mule Deer range throughout the West, from the southern areas of the Canadian provinces through northern Mexico and eastward as far as Texas and the Midwest. They are found in mountainous regions and flatlands but tend to prefer forested areas. In winter, high-country populations typically migrate down the mountain slopes to the lowlands. Like the Whitetail Deer, Mule Deer gather at "deer yards" in winter. Mule Deer are browsers, feeding on diverse plant foods including Big Sagebrush, Douglas-fir, junipers, and other conifers, and deciduous trees such as aspens and willows. They readily eat acorns.

During most of the year bucks remain away from does, but in rutting season the bucks are combative, and successful bucks join small herds of females for mating. A mature doe gives birth to twin fawns, which appear to recognize their mother by the scent from a small gland located just above the hooves of her hind legs. Bucks also have these glands, and when in herds, Mule Deer often sniff the glands of the other animals in the herd. Such behavior undoubtedly functions for individual recognition, but it might also signal aggression, tension, or some other emotional state.

PRONGHORN *Antilocapra americana* PL. 1

Sometimes called the "pronghorn antelope" or "American antelope," the Pronghorn is not an antelope at all, but rather the sole remaining member of the family Antilocapridae, a group of animals dating back some 20 million years. Pronghorns have true horns, not antlers (see page 66), and the horns are single-pronged, the field mark that gives the species its name. They are about 3 feet tall and weigh about 100 pounds.

Aside from the distinctive horn, present on both males and females (though larger on males), the Pronghorn's field marks are a white face, two wide, white neck stripes, and the large white rump, clearly visible as the animal bounds away. The white rump probably serves as a marker to help the animals remain together when fleeing and may also serve as a signal to flee. The long, white rump hairs stand erect when the animal becomes anxious.

Look for Pronghorns in open country such as prairie. The species ranges from west Texas north to the western Dakotas, Montana, and Wyoming, and west to the Great Basin, including most of Nevada, Utah, and Arizona. Like the Bison, Pronghorns have been much reduced by hunting and by fences, which inhibit their seasonal migrations. In recent decades, however, wiser range management practices have resulted in an increase in Pronghorns. They are not forest dwellers but are frequently seen by motorists who are driving across the country. Living in habitats where there is little or no opportunity to hide, the Pronghorn relies on its sharp vision and ability to detect the odor of potential predators. It is the swiftest mammal in North America, sprinting at speeds approaching 75 m.p.h. and able to sustain speeds of up to 40 m.p.h. An adept broad-jumper, the Pronghorn can easily leap 20 feet in one bound, though it cannot attain much vertical distance and so is unable to jump tall fences.

Pronghorns are grazers, feeding on grasses, herbaceous plants, sagebrush and other shrubs, and occasionally on cacti. They can get by on relatively little water. They tend to form large herds in winter, but in summer, herds are small, with does and yearlings remaining apart from bucks, which form bachelor herds.

Pronghorns breed in late summer and early autumn, and males form small territories, which are aggressively defended from intrusion by other males. After breeding season, horns are shed, to be regrown the following spring.

BIGHORN SHEEP *Ovis canadensis* PL. 1

Look for Bighorns in the high country, on alpine meadows, talus slopes, and cliffsides. They may also be observed occasionally in foothills. Bighorn Sheep, also sometimes called "Rocky Mountain sheep," range throughout the Rockies from southern British Columbia west to California and south to Arizona and New Mexico. The male, or ram, has robust coiled horns spiraling backward over his ears. He also has a thick neck and muscular body, and weighs up to 300 pounds. The female, or ewe, is smaller and has smaller, uncoiled horns. Bighorns are noted for their surefootedness. They are amazingly adept at negotiating narrow ledges and steep peaks.

Bighorns live in herds that may, in winter, number nearly 100 animals. Herds are typically led by an old ewe, the matriarch of the herd. Rams join ewes in herds during winter but normally confine themselves to bachelor herds in spring and summer. Herds range throughout high mountain regions, feeding in alpine meadows on grasses and herbaceous plants in summer and on shrubs in winter. Bighorns migrate to the valleys in winter.

In autumn comes mating season, and rams engage in butting contests to determine dominance and thus access to females. The size of the horns is critical to the success of a ram. Only rams with similar-sized horns clash, and the sharp report of their impact can be heard for miles. Butting contests often continue for many hours. Lambs, conceived in fall, are born the following spring. Lambs occasionally fall prey to Golden Eagles, Coyotes, and Bobcats, and adults can be slain by Mountain Lions, Wolves, and Grizzly Bears. Herding behavior and rough mountain terrain provide the Bighorn's best protection against predators.

ADAPTATIONS: PALE RUMP PATCHES

One characteristic that Pronghorns, Elk, and Bighorn Sheep share is the conspicuous pale rump patch. Whitetail Deer, while lacking a pale rump, show a broad white undertail, held high as they run. Each of these animals lives in herds, and each must be ever alert to the potential for danger. Their best defense is to detect a predator before it attacks and to flee from it. As the herd bounds away, the pale rump patches signal to each animal the whereabouts of others. Pale rump patches help keep the herd together.

Often, similar adaptations develop in very distantly related species. Juncos, Horned Larks, pipits, and longspurs all live in open areas and form large flocks. Each of these birds has white outer tail feathers, conspicuous only in flight, that help the flock stay together. Flickers are among the only woodpeckers to form flocks during their migration period. They, too, have a bright white rump patch, easily visible as the bird flies. The white rump of a Pronghorn and that of a Northern Flicker are each adaptive, and in virtually identical ways.

BISON *Bison bison* PL. 1

Victor H. Cahalane has touchingly described the Bison, or "buffalo": "A mountain of a beast, the buffalo seems to be perpetually brooding. The mighty head with its solemn short beard is low. The humped shoulders appear bowed with the sorrows and wrongs of a continent. It personifies in its vast, sombre hulk, and dull, inattentive eyes all the wildlife that was wastefully slaughtered in the Era of Exploitation." The Bison has, indeed, suffered a sad history at the hands of western settlers. Estimates vary, but most authorities agree that up to 60 million Bison once roamed North America, ranging from central Alberta and the Northwest Territories through the Great Plains as far east as the headwaters of the Potomac, central Georgia, and northern Florida. Persecution resulted in the near extinction of the species, but efforts both in Canada and the United States managed to avoid such a catastrophe. Today the best places to view wild Bison are Yellowstone National Park in Wyoming and Wind Cave National Park and Custer State Park in the Black Hills of South Dakota. In Canada, Bison can be seen at Wood Buffalo National Park in the Northwest Territories.

With fully mature bulls weighing up to a ton, the Bison is the largest land animal in North America. The bull has a huge rounded head and shoulder hump, and shaggy fur on the head, face, and shoulders. Both sexes have horns, but cows are considerably smaller than bulls. Calves are reddish brown, in contrast to the darker black-brown of the adults.

Bison herds can sometimes number well over 100 animals, though the normal herd size today is from about 5 to 25 animals. Of course, in the past, herds were immense. Bulls tend to remain separate from cow herds, except during breeding season in July, and small bachelor groups are not uncommon. Cows tend to remain in family groups with several generations of young. In former times, Bison made extensive seasonal migrations, traveling south in winter. Though large animals, Bison are swift, and can gallop at speeds approaching 35 m.p.h. Bulls are unpredictable and can be aggressive, especially during mating season when most tourists view them. *Never approach a bull closely, no matter how tempting the photo opportunity.* Bison often take dust baths, rolling in dry prairie soil and sending up clouds visible for a considerable distance.

Bulls bellow and butt heads during mating season, a practice that determines dominance among the animals. A successful bull may hold a harem of between 10 and 70 cows. When a cow is in heat, a bull will mate with her repeatedly.

Bison graze on a variety of grasses, sedges, and herbaceous plants, scraping away snow with their hooves in winter.

ESSAY

ADAPTATIONS: ANTLERS AND HORNS

Antlers and horns are ornaments used by a wide variety of hoofed mammals for defense and in courtship contests. Though somewhat similar in appearance, antlers and horns are fundamentally different. For instance, antlers tend to be branched, whereas horns are usually not branched. Antlers consist of bone, grown as outgrowths from the skull. Initially, antlers are covered with thin, hairy skin called velvet. As the antlers grow and mature, the velvet is shed, usually by the animal vigorously rubbing against bark. Antlers are normally grown only by males (the exception is the caribou, where both sexes have antlers), and are shed annually, after the breeding season.

Horns are made of both bone and skin. A horn has an inner core of bone that grows from the skull and an outer covering of solidified proteinlike material (horn cells) made from skin. Horns, which are found in African antelopes, sheep, goats, and cattle, are normally present on both sexes and are not shed. Rather, as the

Figure 12. Irish Elk, now extinct

outer covering of horn cells wears out, it is continually replaced. The Pronghorn is unique in that its horn has a single branch, and the outer covering of the horn is shed annually. Also unique is the rhinoceros horn, which is not bony but consists of a mass of solidified hairlike fibers.

Antlers probably evolved because of sexual selection (see page 60), since only males have antlers, and their function is primarily for male-male combat over access to females during breeding season. The animal with the largest known rack of antlers was the now-extinct Irish Elk (*Megaloceros*) that lived in Europe during the Ice Age, about 15,000–20,000 years ago. This huge deer carried antlers that weighed almost 100 pounds (nearly one seventh the animal's total weight) and measured 11 feet across. But the Irish Elk stag was a huge deer with very powerful neck muscles, and the weight of its antler rack was not overly burdensome. The antlers were most impressive when seen head on, with the animal's head slightly lowered. Dominant stags probably intimidated rivals by merely facing them, antler rack in full view.

Horns are probably not the result of sexual selection alone, since both sexes have horns. However, in many horned mammals, such as Bighorn Sheep, males have much larger horns than females. Horns probably evolved mostly for defense against predators, and in some species, evolved further in response to sexual selection.

COLLARED PECCARY *Tayassu tajacu*

PL. 1

The Collared Peccary, also called the Javelina, is America's "bristle pig." Though it resembles a pig, this stocky animal, which is covered with coarse bristly hair, is a member of the family Tayassuidae, a New World family quite distinct from Old World swine. Peccaries have several anatomical features that true pigs lack, the most unique of which is a musk gland located on the upper back, near the hips. Peccaries use their musk to identify each other, thus keeping the local herd together. The musk is most powerful, with a scent similar to but much stronger than human underarm odor. The scent is sometimes described as skunklike. Peccaries also have sharp canine teeth that are straight, like stilettos. Old World pigs, such as the Wild Boar, have tusks that curve outward.

The Collared Peccary is about 3 feet long and stands about 2 feet tall at the shoulder. A large peccary can weigh up to 65 pounds. Males, or boars, are larger than females, or sows. The grayish white "collar," or shoulder stripe, can easily be distinguished against the otherwise grayish black hair. Peccaries live in herds of up to 25, sometimes more, and constantly grunt softly as they forage for roots, cacti, and virtually anything they can find. When danger threatens, a peccary will erect its bristly hairs and utter a sharp, doglike "woof!"—an emphatic sound that alerts others in the herd. An excited peccary will also chatter its teeth and squirt musk from its musk gland. Peccaries have an undeserved reputation for aggressiveness. Though they can look intimidating, and, indeed, can bite ferociously if cornered, they are most unlikely to move in any direction other than away from potential danger. Should you come upon a herd, remain quiet and you can probably watch them with little difficulty.

The Collared Peccary ranges from the southwestern U.S. to Central and South America. In this country they favor deserts and wooded mountain slopes and are often found where oaks are abundant, as they are fond of feeding on acorns. They are particularly easy to observe at Big Bend National Park or Aransas National Wildlife Refuge, both in Texas, or in Cave Creek Canyon in southeastern Arizona.

MOUNTAIN LION *Felis concolor*

PL. 1

If you are remarkably fortunate, you may see this large, tawny cat. Known also as "cougar," "puma," and "panther," the Mountain Lion once ranged widely over the North American continent. Now its range is largely confined to the more remote areas of western mountains and forests, though scattered reports of sightings continue to come from eastern areas. In the West, Mountain Lions occur from Texas throughout the Rockies and Pacific coastal mountain ranges, including forests throughout the Pacific Northwest and north through British Columbia and southern Alberta. Mountain Lions also occur in Central and South America, but nowhere are they particularly common, mostly because of human persecution.

The Mountain Lion measures about 4.5 feet in length plus a tail up to 3 feet long. A large individual can weigh nearly 275 pounds, though most are smaller. Among the New World cats, only the Jaguar (*Felis onca*) is heavier.

Mountain Lions tend to be solitary, though mated pairs sometimes remain together until kittens are born. At that time, the female usually drives the male away, as males may kill and eat kittens. Like most large predators, Mountain Lions have extensive home ranges, often covering well over 20 miles in the course of an evening's hunting. Mountain Lions are excellent climbers and swift runners, and they can leap distances of up to 20 feet. They prey upon many species, including Porcupine, Raccoon, mice, and various birds, but prefer large mammals such as Mule Deer. They kill by leaping upon the victim's back and slashing the neck with their long, powerful canine teeth. They also use their sharp claws both to kill prey and to dismember it.

COYOTE *Canis latrans*   PL. 1

The plaintive, nocturnal howling and yapping of Coyotes is a western sound that bespeaks wilderness. The wide-ranging Coyote, also occasionally called "brush wolf," can be heard from Mexico and the Baja Peninsula throughout the western and midwestern states, and on up through the Canadian Provinces into Alaska. It is currently expanding its range eastward and is increasing in many areas in the West despite efforts to eradicate it through poisoning and trapping. Such success speaks highly of the species' apparent intelligence and adaptability.

Coyotes look like slender, thick-furred dogs. Their best field marks are the pointed snout and the bushy tail, black at the tip, which is held down between the legs, not horizontally, as the animal trots along. The overall coat color is gray, and legs, feet, and ears tend to be russet.

While they do not hunt in tight packs as wolves do, Coyotes do sometimes combine their efforts to kill large prey such as Pronghorns. Several Coyotes may take turns pursuing the prey while others rest. Coyotes eat a wide array of prey, almost any kind of animal, including carrion. They are swift runners, making speeds of up to 40 m.p.h., and they are skilled leapers.

Coyotes are relatively common throughout much of the West and can often be seen by day. Though usually wary, they are some-

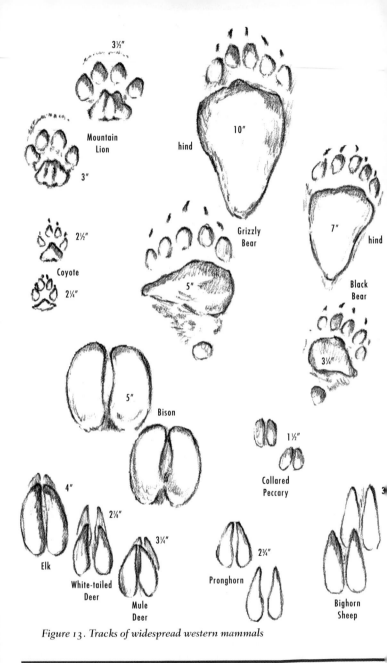

Figure 13. Tracks of widespread western mammals

times either bold or curious and will permit an observer to come quite close before scurrying away. As rabies is sometimes found in Coyote populations, beware of any Coyote that approaches you. Such behavior is most abnormal, and the animal should be avoided.

BLACK BEAR *Ursus americanus*

The Black Bear ranges throughout most of forested North America, extending north through Canada and Alaska. Though in most areas of its range it is uncommon, Black Bears are frequently sighted in big western national parks such as Yosemite and Yellowstone. It is always exciting to see a bear, but remember that *all bears are potentially dangerous* and should not be closely approached. This caution is especially advised should you come upon a mother with cubs. Resist the urge to get ever nearer for the sake of that perfect photograph.

The name Black Bear is descriptive over much of the animal's range (especially in the East), but many Black Bears in the West are brownish to cinnamon in color with white on the chest. Some far-northern populations are grayish. In general, bears resemble very large dogs, especially in their facial characteristics. Unlike dogs, however, bears walk on the soles of their feet, not on their toes. Black Bears can weigh anywhere from 200 to 600 pounds, and males are substantially heavier than females.

Anatomically, all bears are considered carnivores, because they have prominent canine teeth for puncturing, sharp incisors for nipping, and premolars adapted for slashing flesh. Actually, though, they are omnivores—they devour many kinds of food, ranging from fruit and berries to honey, sap, various insect grubs, birds, mammals, fish, and carrion. Black Bears are easily attracted to garbage dumps, where they can become nuisances, and they often enter campgrounds. When in a campground in bear country, you should store food safely in tightly sealed containers, because bears have a keen sense of smell. Black Bears are generally solitary, and an individual may have a home range of anywhere from 8 to 15 square miles.

In spring, Black Bears mate and eggs are fertilized, but the embryos are not implanted in the mother's uterus and development does not begin until the female bear is about to enter her winter den. Babies are born in the den during the winter, and the tiny creatures weigh as little as one-half pound at birth. Only the Opossum, which is a marsupial, gives birth to proportionally smaller young relative to the size of the adult.

Contrary to popular opinion, Black Bears do not hibernate, though over much of their range, they enter a deep sleep during winter. A bear will select a cave or some other protected place and fall very soundly asleep. During this period the bear does not eat or defecate. However, it maintains nearly normal body temperature, as well as normal heart and respiratory rates. True hibernators, such as the Woodchuck (*Marmota monax*), experience a precipitous drop in body temperature and metabolic rate.

You can sometimes tell if Black Bears are present in an area by noting such signs as claw and tooth marks on trees, bear hair rubbed off onto bark, disturbed vegetation, logs torn apart, and excavated rodent burrows.

GRIZZLY BEAR *Ursus horribilis* PL. 1

Weighing anywhere from 400 to 1,500 pounds or more, the Grizzly Bear ranks as the largest carnivore in the world. Though it is a magnificent animal, the sight of which provides an unforgettable thrill for anyone interested in natural history, it is a creature best enjoyed from a respectful distance.

The Grizzly Bear's name comes from the fact that the animal's brown and black hairs are tipped with white, giving them a "grizzled" look. Grizzlies are easily distinguished from Black Bears by their more humped shoulders and dish-shaped snout. Grizzlies are also considerably larger than Black Bears. A full-grown Grizzly, when standing on its hind legs, is over 9 feet tall. The largest Grizzlies are Alaskan Brown Bears, once considered a separate species but now regarded as a subspecies of the Grizzly Bear. Alaskan Grizzlies, such as those that inhabit Kodiak Island, can weigh up to 1,700 pounds.

The habits of Grizzlies are similar to those of Black Bears. Grizzlies have home ranges of many square miles, and tend to be most active at night. They are omnivorous, feeding on many kinds of plant materials as well as many animals, including such large species as Moose and Elk. Grizzlies are known to cache the carcasses of large kills, returning to feed until the prey is entirely consumed. In Canada and Alaska, Grizzlies tend to congregate, often with large numbers of Bald Eagles, along rivers when salmon are spawning. Adept at fishing, Grizzlies catch fish both by snapping them up in their powerful jaws and by trapping them with their huge claws. During the cold winter months Grizzlies sleep in dens, awakening periodically.

In addition to Alaska and parts of the Northwest Territories, Grizzlies can still be seen in parts of Montana, Wyoming, and Idaho, especially Yellowstone National Park. They once ranged much more widely in the lower 48 states.

Use extreme caution when hiking in backcountry frequented by Grizzlies. Grizzlies are swift runners over short distances (you won't be able to outrun one), but adult Grizzlies cannot climb, and trees have saved more than one hapless hiker who came too close to a Grizzly. Never leave food out at night where a foraging Grizzly could smell it. Food should be stored away from your sleeping quarters, placed in a sealed box, and hoisted by a rope high in a tree. Many backcountry hikers wear "bear bells," which alert Grizzlies that someone is approaching, giving the bear time to retreat. The most dangerous Grizzlies are those suddenly surprised at a food cache or awakened when asleep in the brush, or a mother with cubs.

WARNING: Grizzly Bears have killed people. NEVER approach a Grizzly, even if you think the distance between you is safe—it probably is not.

ESSAY

ADAPTATIONS: THE SELFISH HERD AND THE SOLITARY HUNTER

Many kinds of animals clump together in tight groups, called herds, flocks, or schools depending on whether the animals are mammals, birds, or fish. Herds of mammals are common, especially among hoofed mammals living in relatively open areas. In Bison, Elk, Bighorn Sheep, and other mammals, the herd, often led by a dominant female, is the normal unit of social organization. Why do such animals herd?

Herds provide protection from predators. In an open habitat there are few places for large animals to hide. Living in groups, with many individuals simultaneously on the lookout for danger, is an advantage to every member of the herd. Herds form among herbivorous mammals, where the various members of the herd are normally not in intense competition with each other for food. Because they eat plant material, there is usually sufficient food for all members of the herd. But grazing takes time, making feeding animals potentially more vulnerable to a predator. After eating, digestion of complex plant fibers also takes time. Again, with numerous eyes, noses, and ears on the alert, the would-be predator has a much more difficult time surprising a possible victim. Even when a predator attacks, it can rarely pick out a single victim among the swirling, galloping mass of animals, all moving as a unit. Consequently, predators usually take animals that are old, sick, or injured, and thus can't keep up with the rest of the herd.

Within the herd, each animal must focus on its own safety. An individual on the periphery of the herd is far more vulnerable to a quick predator attack than one in the center of the herd. Thus, animals constantly tend to move toward the herd's center. This behavior has led naturalists to label such a group the "selfish herd," because animals are acting in their own self-interest in attempting to be at the center. The tendency has been observed in mammals, birds, and fish. To be successful, a predator must manage to cut a would-be victim out of the herd, making the animal run in a direction different from the rest of the herd. A solitary animal can be run down far more easily than one in a herd, since the predator can focus sharply on this one particular animal. Animals on the periphery mistakenly bolt in the wrong direction more easily than those in the center of the herd.

Large predators such as Grizzly Bears and Mountain Lions are solitary hunters. Herding behavior would be of no use to these animals, which depend on stealth, cunning, and sudden attack in order to procure food and which, themselves, have little to fear from predators. Also, because they are carnivores, there is far less potential food available per square mile than if they ate only vegetation—another reason for being solitary, since competition for food could easily become a significant problem among predators in the same area. Even as solitary hunters, large predators tend to live "close to the edge," with the potential for starvation looming ever present. Large carnivores typically go for days with no food whatsoever, then stuff themselves when they finally do make a kill. Bears, because they are omnivorous and can exist on plant food, are always more abundant than strictly carnivorous species such as Mountain Lions. However, bears are many times less numerous than Elk, for instance, which eat only plant material, normally an abundant, easily procurable food source except in the deep snows of winter.

BIRDS OF OPEN AREAS

Several bird species are widespread and conspicuous in the American West. Some widespread species are not strictly forest dwellers but range into more open habitats. You see them in the skies, on fence posts and telephone poles, perched atop hay bales, or feeding on roadkills.

GOLDEN EAGLE *Aquila chrysaetos* PL. 2

Golden Eagles, with wingspreads of nearly 7 feet, are among the largest North American birds of prey—too large to be confused with hawks. In flight, they hold their wings horizontally, not tilted upward as vultures do. Eagles have large heads that project conspicuously forward as they fly, unlike the small heads of vultures.

The Golden Eagle is a year-round resident in all western states except for Alaska, where it is primarily a summer resident. The name refers to the golden sheen of its head feathers, visible only at close range when light is shining directly on it. Adults are uniformly dark, but immature birds have white patches on the undersides of the wings and white at the tail base.

Golden Eagles typically nest on high cliffs in mountainous regions, using the same nest every year. They range widely over forest, prairie, and grassland and hunt prey from the air, dropping abruptly at speeds approaching 200 m.p.h. (a behavior called "stooping") to make a kill. Food consists mostly of rabbits and rodents, especially larger species, though they are also known to take animals ranging from insects to magpies.

Golden Eagles have long been alleged to kill lambs and have been persecuted as a result. Biologists who have studied Golden Eagles in Montana have not found any evidence to suggest that eagles habitually kill lambs, though they may eat the carcass of a lamb or sheep already dead. Golden Eagles range into Europe, Asia, and Africa as well as North America.

URKEY VULTURE *Cathartes aura* PL. 2

A flock of Turkey Vultures, soaring slowly in high circles, borne by warm thermal currents rising from the ground, is a common sight in the West. You can identify Turkey Vultures at a considerable distance because they fly with wings tilted slightly upward. (The Northern Harrier also holds its wings this way, but harriers fly low and show a white rump.)

Turkey Vultures abound throughout the West and are also common throughout most of the East. Most are summer residents, migrating south to Mexico and Central America in winter. A successful species, the Turkey Vulture seems to be increasing its range northward and has occasionally been sighted in Alaska.

Turkey Vultures eat carrion, often supplied by roadkills, and thus vultures are commonly seen along roadsides and sitting on fence posts. An adult vulture has a naked red head; an immature one has a black head. The lack of head feathers is believed to be an adaptation for the vulture's feeding habits. Vultures probe their heads deeply into carcasses, and the decomposing flesh could easily foul feathers.

Turkey Vultures are reputed to have a keen sense of smell, an unusual characteristic for a bird. Being able to locate carrion by odor is certainly adaptive, if the carcass is, for instance, in a dense forest, where spotting it from the air would be difficult. Turkey Vultures, like all birds, also have keen vision. They will gather around a dying animal, circling overhead until the animal stops moving. Turkey Vultures have strong bills for tearing away flesh, but their feet and legs are weak compared with those of hawks and eagles. Though they can drag a carcass a short distance, they normally do not fly off with it, but consume it where it fell.

The Black Vulture, a primarily southeastern species, is seen in small numbers from western Texas to Arizona. It has a shorter, more widely spread tail than the Turkey Vulture and shows white outer wing patches in flight.

ESSAY

OLD WORLD AND NEW WORLD VULTURES: A CONVERGENCE?

If you travel to Africa or the Middle East you will see many kinds of vultures: Egyptian, Griffon, Hooded, Lappet-faced, White-backed, and White-headed—and this list is by no means comprehensive. In basic body structure these Old World vultures are quite similar to Turkey and Black Vultures, with naked heads, strong hooked beaks, and generally weak feet. A naturalist comparing a Turkey Vulture's anatomy with that of a Griffon could easily conclude that the two species were closely related and probably evolved from a recent common ancestor. But anatomy can be deceiving.

In recent years it has become possible to compare the DNA of species to determine the degree to which the molecules are similar. Because DNA is the actual chemical of heredity, the molecule containing the information that essentially defines the organism, DNA provides the most accurate means of comparing the evolutionary similarity of two species. Analysis of the DNA of Old World vultures shows that they are closely related to hawks and eagles. This is not particularly surprising, since vultures and birds of prey bear many anatomical similarities. It is surprising, however, to find that the New World Vultures, such as the Turkey and Black vultures, have DNA more distinct from that of both Old World vultures and birds of prey in general. New World vultures are genetically most similar to storks!

On the basis of the DNA comparison, some scientists now hold that New World and Old World vultures are only distantly related (they are, after all, both birds) and that their amazing anatomical resemblance is a case of *evolutionary convergence*. Convergent evolution occurs when two genetically distinct groups evolve a similar body form because each was exposed to similar selection pressures. This phenomenon helps demonstrate the power of natural selection to shape genetically distinct creatures into similar anatomical entities. No Old World vultures reached the New

World. Instead, the ancestors of New World vultures became genetically distinct millions of years ago from the group of birds to which storks belong, and evolved the vulturine body form. But why the vulturine body form?

Imagine you are a bird that eats decaying flesh from various sized carcasses. What would be the best body shape to have? Certainly you should be able to fly well enough to search for dead animals, a resource that may be scattered over many square miles. Wide wings and an ability to soar are both adaptive for such a lifestyle. You must have a strong bill, sharply hooked to tear away at dried, tough muscles and sinews. A naked head, as mentioned previously, avoids fouling head feathers as you plunge your head deeply into a rotting carcass. Big, strong talons are not of great use, since the prey animal is already dead and does not need to be subdued. Thus, the vulturine body form is ideal for such a way of life, and it has evolved independently in two groups, the Old World and the New World vultures. Though their anatomical similarities, in light of the genetic difference, are impressive, there are differences. For instance, some (but by no means all) Old World vultures have very long necks, adaptive for reaching into the carcasses of large mammals such as Water Buffalos or elephants. New World vultures have short necks.

Convergent evolution is not uncommon, and other examples are known for birds. Diving Petrels, which live in southern oceans, bear a striking resemblance to Dovekies, which are found only in north Atlantic seas and are genetically quite distinct. The African Yellow-throated Longclaw and Western (and Eastern) Meadowlark look very much alike, mottled brown with a yellow breast marked by a black V, and white outer tail feathers. But the longclaw belongs to the lark and pipit family, while the meadowlark is a member of the blackbird-oriole family.

A well-known case of convergence is that between Australian marsupial mammals and the placental mammals of other parts of the world. Australia has been long separated from the other continents, and evolution has proceeded there along unique lines. Hence, bandicoots resemble rabbits, sugar gliders resemble flying squirrels, and there is even a marsupial mole that looks almost exactly like our familiar placental moles. Virtually all Australian birds that look like European and Asian species are also cases of convergence. For example, Australian orioles are not closely related to European orioles but to crows.

ED-TAILED HAWK *Buteo jamaicensis*   PL. 2

Red-tails are buteos, large hawks with wide wings. They commonly soar high in the air, carried for hours by thermal currents.

Red-tails are year-round residents throughout the lower 48 states and are very common over most of their range. They perch atop telephone poles, in trees, even on roadside fence posts. Compared with other buteos, Red-tails look bulky, often hunched over. Red-tails can be challenging to identify because they occur in several color phases in the West. Typical adults have a white chest and an unbanded tail, reddish on its upper side. Seen soaring overhead, they have a dark band along the inner leading edge of their wings.

But some Red-tails are reddish brown overall or very dark. One race, Harlan's Red-tailed Hawk, is dark brown with white at the base of its upper tail. It is found in Alaska and migrates in winter south to Texas. Another race, Krider's Red-tailed Hawk, is very pale. It summers in Canada and migrates to Texas in winter.

Red-tails feed mostly on rodents such as ground squirrels, prairie dogs, and mice. They also take rabbits and some birds and will occasionally feed on fish, amphibians, reptiles, and insects. Red-tails sometimes hover over prey before dropping down on it.

Swainson's Hawk (*Buteo swainsoni*) is also a common summer resident throughout the West, particularly in the plains states. It is less bulky than the Red-tail, and adults have a brown (not white) breast and are buffy under the wings.

COMMON RAVEN *Corvus corax* PL. 2

The harsh croak of the Common Raven can be heard in all seasons wherever there are mountains or foothills in the West, including Alaska. Ravens are also common residents of deserts and the Pacific seacoast. Ravens are members of the crow family, and, at first glance, look like crows. However, in addition to being much larger (the size of a Red-tailed Hawk), Common Ravens have wedge-shaped tails, easily visible in flight. Ravens fly in a distinctive pattern, with several wing beats followed by a brief glide. A raven's bill is large and conspicuous, even at a distance. At closer range, look for the shaggy feathering of the throat. Ravens feed mostly on various forms of carrion scavenged from roadsides, beaches, garbage dumps, and other such places. Like gulls, ravens pick up shellfish and drop them from aloft, breaking the shells.

Most people who have observed ravens in detail comment on their apparent high degree of intelligence, which has been favorably compared with that of a dog. Members of the crow and jay families are considered, in general, to be among the most intelligent of birds. Like their close relative, the Black-billed Magpie, Common Ravens are cosmopolitan in distribution. They occur throughout Europe, Asia, and much of Africa.

WHITE-THROATED SWIFT *Aeronautes saxatalis* PL. 2

Streaking in noisy flocks through western canyons, the White-throated Swift is a summer resident in all of the far western states but does not range into Canada and Alaska. *Swift* is an appropriate term to describe these birds, which fly rapidly on stiffly held wings. One observer has reported seeing a White-throated Swift elude a stooping Peregrine Falcon estimated to be moving at 200 m.p.h.

The White-throated Swift is easily identified by its white underparts, which extend from its throat to its belly and contrast greatly with its otherwise black plumage. Like all swifts, this species spends most of its life in flight—it feeds, courts, and even copulates in midair. It nests along cliffs and mountainsides, usually in colonies. All swift species build nests that are glued in place with saliva (the basis for bird's-nest soup, an Asian delicacy).

Most White-throated Swifts migrate to Central America in winter, though some remain as permanent residents in southern California, Nevada, and Arizona. In cold weather when food is scarce, they have been observed to enter a state of torpor, a condition similar to hibernation in which the overall body metabolism slows greatly, allowing the animal to remain without food for longer periods. Some mountain-dwelling hummingbird species, which are closely related to swifts, also go into torpor on chilly nights. The Poorwill (*Phalaenoptilus nuttallii*), a desert nightjar closely related to the Common Nighthawk, is one of the few bird species that hibernates.

COMMON NIGHTHAWK *Chordeiles minor* PL. 2

The Common Nighthawk, or "bullbat," is a common summer resident throughout the western states and Canada, though not in Alaska. It is not a hawk but a member of the insectivorous nightjar family, to which the familiar Whip-poor-will belongs. Though mostly nocturnal, nighthawks are active at dusk and can often be observed flying during the day.

Nighthawks are identified by their coursing, purposeful flight and the white bars on their sharply pointed wings. Like all nightjars, the Common Nighthawk's mouth functions as a big insect trap. Nighthawks are often seen around street lights, snapping up insects attracted to the lights.

These birds nest on the ground in gravelly or rocky soil, or occasionally atop gravel roofs. The nest is a mere scrape in the surface, but both eggs and brooding birds are remarkably well camouflaged. Flocks of nighthawks fly to Central America to spend the winter months.

The similar but slightly smaller Lesser Nighthawk (*Chordeiles acutipennis*) occurs from southern Texas to southern California, largely replacing the Common Nighthawk in the Southwest. The Lesser Nighthawk's white wing bars are positioned farther toward the wingtips. Its voice is different from the Common Nighthawk's; the Lesser trills, suggesting the call of a toad. It also utters a dry, chucking note. Common Nighthawks make a loud and demonstrative *preent*.

BARN SWALLOW *Hirundo rustica*   PL. 2

Barn Swallows are abundant summer residents throughout North America. Along some stretches of western roadside, they are the most common birds.

All swallows are graceful and rapid fliers, with sharply pointed wings that they use to pursue insect prey. Barn Swallows are distinctive by their shiny blue and orange-red coloration and deeply forked tails (only in adults—juveniles have shorter tails, less deeply forked). They nest in colonies in the eaves of barns. Flocks feed aloft over pastures, prairies, grasslands, and along forest edges. Their loud, rapid, twittering notes are especially evident in spring when males pursue females in courtship flights. Males will occasionally fight while airborne, and the sight of two males, locked together in combat, falling like a broken pinwheel, attests to the intensity of their disputes. Barn Swallows winter as far south as Argentina.

CLIFF SWALLOW *Hirundo pyrrhonota*   PL. 2

Like the Barn Swallow, the Cliff Swallow is a common roadside bird throughout western North America, and Cliff Swallow flocks frequently can be seen flying in fields with Barn Swallows. The name describes their nest sites, though they may also nest under barn roofs and other such places. Cliff Swallows are highly colonial, and their nests are often very close together. Nests, which are made largely of dried mud, are shaped like bottles or gourds, with a small rounded opening and a wider base. Cliff Swallows are recognized by their square tails and buffy rump patch, both easily visible as the birds fly in quest of their insect prey.

BLACK-BILLED MAGPIE *Pica pica*   PL. 2

No western traveler fails to see magpies. They are permanent residents throughout most of the western states (including Alaska) and western Canada. Magpies are not strictly forest birds but prefer more open areas such as streamsides, pastures, and scrubby areas.

The Black-billed Magpie is unmistakable, with its boldly patterned plumage and long, streaming tail. Though the magpie looks essentially black and white, the shimmering blue iridescence of its wings and green sheen of its long tail feathers show up in good light. Like the Common Raven, the Black-billed Magpie is a member of the crow family. The family resemblance is evident in the shape of the head and bill and even in the way magpies walk.

Like the Common Raven, the Black-billed Magpie is also found throughout Europe and Asia, though the species is oddly absent from eastern North America. Magpies, like crows in general, are highly intelligent and quick to avail themselves of any opportunity to eat. They gather around camps, stockyards, and garbage dumps, and because they eat roadside carrion, they are frequently observed by motorists.

Like most crows, magpies tend to be gregarious, and they often nest in small colonies, building bulky nests of sticks along a stream or within a thicket.

A closely related species, the Yellow-billed Magpie, lives in California.

MOURNING DOVE *Zenaida macroura* PL. 2

The Mourning Dove is one of the most abundant and best known birds throughout North America, though its range does not extend into northern Canada nor Alaska. The dove's familiar pigeonlike shape can be spotted on telephone wires and fences in every western state. This is a species that has profited from the increase in agriculture accompanying the settlement of the West, and the birds abound in open fields where grain can be found. Mourning Doves are rich brown with long pointed tails. The name refers to their plaintive, mournful cooing, which is easy to mistake for the hooting of an owl.

In winter, Mourning Doves gather in large roosts, sometimes numbering in the hundreds. Though they feed in open areas, they are also seen in forests, particularly along forest edges, where they build their nests. Mourning Dove nests are rather small and crudely constructed of twigs and sticks. Mourning Doves feed their newly hatched young an exclusive diet of crop milk, a substance unique to doves and pigeons. These birds have a two-chambered crop, which is really part of the esophagus, the upper part of the digestive tube. Crop milk is a rather mucous substance, abundant with fats and proteins, that both males and females produce during breeding season. Young doves grow quickly on their rich diet. When the nestlings are about a week old, grains are mixed in with the crop milk.

Xanthocephalus xanthocephalus

The male Yellow-headed Blackbird is one of the most striking of western birds. Larger than the Red-winged Blackbird, with which it often shares habitat, the Yellow-headed male is glossy black with a bright yellow head and breast and a white patch on the leading edge of the wing. The female is smaller and brownish with a paler yellow breast. The species is found throughout the West and into southern Canada. Yellow-headed Blackbirds are colonial, nesting in freshwater marshes where there is standing water. They feed in open fields and along roadsides, seeking insects and various grains.

The Red-winged Blackbird (*Agelaius phoeniceus*), not illustrated, is another marsh-nesting blackbird that, because it is also abundant throughout the East, has a considerably wider range than the Yellow-head. Red-wing males are all black with red shoulder patches. Females, smaller than males, look like large, brown-striped sparrows.

Yellow-headed and Red-winged Blackbirds occasionally come into direct conflict over nesting sites. Red-wings nest in a variety of habitats, including marshes, grassy areas, fields, and streamsides. Yellow-heads nest only in wet freshwater marshes. Red-wings often return in spring before Yellow-heads and establish their territories throughout a marsh. However, when the larger, more aggressive Yellow-headed males return, they forcefully evict the Red-wings from the central, wettest part of the marsh.

BREWER'S BLACKBIRD *Euphagus cyanocephalus*   PL. 2

The Brewer's Blackbird is one of the most familiar western birds, common in open fields, pastures, farms, feedlots, ranches, cities, and towns. Males look black, but in good light they are seen to be iridescent glossy green, with yellow eyes. Females are brown with dark eyes. Brewer's Blackbirds are permanent residents in most of the West and summer residents in the northern states and Canada. Though normally birds of flatlands, they range into mountain meadows in the Central Rockies. They feed on grains and insects, which they find by methodically walking and searching. They nest in small colonies in fields and along marshes.

NORTHERN FLICKER ("Red-shafted" subspecies)   PL. 2
Colaptes auratus

Until recently, this bird was named the Red-shafted Flicker and considered to be a separate species. Three flicker species were recognized: the eastern Yellow-shafted, the western Red-shafted, and the Gilded Flicker of the southwestern desert. Because these three populations can and do hybridize where they meet, they have been "demoted" from species status and reclassified into subspecies or races. Thus, although the "Red-shafted" looks different from the "Yellow-shafted," they are not separate species, and the three races have been combined under the species name of Northern Flicker.

The "Red-shafted" race is identified by its red underwing and undertail feathers and its gray face. The male has a red "mustache" on his cheeks. "Yellow-shafted" Flickers have yellow underwings and tail, brown faces, and black mustaches. The "Gilded" Flicker, found only in the deserts of southeastern California and Arizona, has yellow underwings and tail but a face like the "Red-shafted" race. In the Great Plains states it is not uncommon to find hybrids between the "Red-shafted" and "Yellow-shafted" races. These birds have plumage that is a mixture of the two types.

Flickers are abundant throughout the West, occurring from sea level to alpine areas. They seem equally at home among deciduous trees of city parks or mountain conifers. Look for them anywhere. Though they are woodpeckers, flickers often descend to the ground and feed on ant colonies. They show a white rump patch when they fly up from the ground. The call of the Northern Flicker is an easily learned, strident *whicka, whicka, whicka.*

HOUSE FINCH *Carpodacus mexicanus* PL. 2

Put up a bird feeder anywhere west of the Rockies, from southern British Columbia to Mexico, and sparrowlike House Finches will be among the clientele. House Finches are also called Linnets but should not be confused with the European finch of the same name. Males are red (occasionally quite orangy) on the head, breast, and rump. Females and young males look much like sparrows, with brown streaking. House Finches usually live in flocks. Listen for their soft warble as they fly overhead.

House Finches seem to be expanding their population east of the Rockies. They have also been most successful at colonizing the far eastern states. In the 1940s, House Finches were abruptly released on Long Island, New York, because they had been illegally shipped to be sold as cage birds called "Hollywood finches." The released birds survived and eventually prospered so well that the species is now common from northern New England to the Carolinas, and it continues to spread. House Finches are birds of suburbia and farmland and are not common in forests. They feed mostly on weed seeds supplemented with some insects. They will readily nest in bird boxes.

Included here are a dozen bird species that range widely throughout western forests. These species will find their way to your bird list whether you are in the Sierra Nevada of California, the Santa Catalinas of Arizona, the Olympic Peninsula, or the Central Rocky Mountains. Get to know these, and you will have a base of knowledge that will help you identify the many other species you encounter.

WILLIAMSON'S SAPSUCKER *Sphyrapicus thyroideus* PL. 3

This western woodpecker is a bird of mountain coniferous and aspen forests (including burned areas), avoiding the Great Plains and deserts. When you see Ponderosa Pine, Lodgepole Pine, Douglas-fir, Western Hemlock, or Engelmann Spruce, look for Williamson's Sapsucker. And look closely—these birds can be quite unobtrusive as they quietly forage on tree trunks. Males are boldly patterned in black and white, with a yellow belly and red throat. In flight, they flash white wing patches and a white rump. Females are duller, barred on the back with a brownish head.

The name *sapsucker* refers to the habit of drilling into the cambium layer just beneath the bark of living trees, allowing sap to ooze. The woodpecker makes horizontal rows of holes and feeds on the sugar-rich cambial sap. Sap holes drilled by Williamson's and other sapsucker species often attract a crowd. Twenty-six species, from other woodpeckers to hummingbirds to nuthatches, are known to avail themselves of sap from sapsucker holes. In addition, birds such as flycatchers are attracted to the insects that gather around sapsucker holes. Williamson's Sapsucker also feeds heavily on ants, an important protein source. Like other woodpeckers, Williamson's Sapsucker nests in tree cavities.

HAIRY WOODPECKER *Picoides villosus* PL. 3

The Hairy Woodpecker also is boldly patterned in black and white, but the pattern is quite different from that of Williamson's Sapsucker. Hairies have white backs and no white wing patches. Male Hairies have a red patch on the back of the neck (the nape).

Hairy Woodpeckers feed mostly on insects obtained by drilling into dead trees, but they also are often attracted to the sap flows created by sapsuckers. They range widely and are permanent residents from Alaska through all the western states. They live in many kinds of forests, ranging from lowland deciduous woodlands and parks to montane coniferous forest, and they frequently visit bird feeders stocked with suet.

Eastern birders will notice that western Hairy Woodpeckers

look a bit different from their eastern counterparts. Western Hairy Woodpeckers have much less white spotting in the wings, the wings often appearing totally black. Hairy Woodpeckers in the Pacific Northwest are dusky, not white, on throat and breast.

WESTERN TANAGER *Piranga ludoviciana*   PL. 3

Tanagers, of which there are 242 species, are one of the most colorful groups of birds. Tanagers occur only in this hemisphere, and the vast majority live in equatorial rain and cloud forests. Only four species regularly reach North America, and the Western Tanager is the most western and northern of this group. Western Tanagers occur in forested areas throughout the western states and Canada, though they do not reach Alaska. They show a distinct preference for mountain coniferous forests and usually nest in conifers.

The male is brilliantly plumaged in yellow and black with a red head. Note his yellow shoulder patch and wing bar. The female can be identified by her yellow-green plumage and two wing bars. The song of the Western Tanager somewhat resembles that of a robin, though harsher. The call note, a staccato *pit-i-rik,* is easy to learn. Western Tanagers glean insects from tree branches and can often be observed darting out from a branch to snap up a fly in midair. They supplement their diet with fruit while migrating to winter in Mexico and Central America.

TOWNSEND'S SOLITAIRE *Myadestes townsendi*   PL. 3

This unique western thrush is identified by its gray plumage, its white eye ring and outer tail feathers, and orangy wing markings. Solitaires are mountain thrushes, and many species occur in the rich, moist cloud forests of Central and South America. Townsend's, however, is the only solitaire to reach North America. Like thrushes in general, solitaires are fine singers, and Townsend's sings its flutelike song from western conifers throughout the summer breeding months. Nests are well hidden, placed on the ground or in low conifer branches.

Townsend's Solitaire breeds as far north as Alaska and is a year-round resident throughout most of the western states. It is, however, an *altitudinal migrant,* a species that moves from higher to lower elevations in winter. An individual may nest in a forest of Engelmann Spruce and winter within a low-elevation forest of pinyons and junipers. One Arizona study has shown that Townsend's Solitaires feed almost exclusively on berries of the Oneseed Juniper (*Juniperus monosperma*), and each solitaire rigorously defends its winter feeding territory. In winters when berries are not plentiful, these territories may be quite large.

MOUNTAIN CHICKADEE *Parus gambeli*

PL. 3

The Mountain Chickadee is a common and conspicuous permanent resident throughout mountainous regions of the western states and most of British Columbia. It is similar in appearance to the closely related Black-capped Chickadee (*Parus atricapillus*), which ranges through the northeastern states, most of Canada, and Alaska. Both chickadees are active, big-headed grayish birds with black throats. The Mountain Chickadee has a white line above the eye and a sharply defined black stripe through the eye. Its call is a dry, buzzy *zee-zee-zee*.

Mountain Chickadees reside mostly in coniferous forests, ranging from Ponderosa Pine at middle elevations to higher-elevation spruce and fir forests. They nest in hollow trees, either using old woodpecker nests or hollowing out their own nests in dead snags. Mountain Chickadees often forage in mixed-species flocks along with Golden-crowned Kinglets and Pygmy Nuthatches. Chickadees are highly acrobatic, assuming many odd positions as they actively search conifer boughs for insects.

STELLER'S JAY *Cyanocitta stelleri*

PL. 3

Often called the "western blue jay," the Steller's Jay is a common resident of western forests, especially in conifers. It ranges throughout the western states and even reaches the Sitka Spruce forests of coastal Alaska. In the East, it is replaced by the familiar Blue Jay. Steller's Jay is a robust and conspicuous bird, deep blue with a dark head and large crest.

Steller's Jays frequent many forest types including oak-pine, Ponderosa Pine, and mixed conifers. During the summer breeding season, Steller's Jays feed mostly on insect and other arthropod food, supplementing their diets with acorns and pine seeds. In winter, when the birds often migrate to a lower elevation, the majority of their diet consists of acorns and pine seeds. Like other jays, Steller's will often cache seeds, and they sometimes help themselves to acorns stored by Acorn Woodpeckers. They are readily attracted to bird feeders and often congregate around campgrounds. Normally they are rather noisy, uttering a repetitive *sook-sook-sook* or *weck-weck-weck*. They also frequently mimic the calls of Red-tailed Hawks and, occasionally, Golden Eagles. Only during breeding season, when it stays close to the nest, does the Steller's Jay become quiet and secretive.

The eastern Blue Jay (*Cyanocitta cristata*), a species common to deciduous forests, is expanding its range westward. Like the Steller's, it feeds heavily on acorns, and the two species thus overlap in range and habitat. Hybrids have been observed in Colorado.

BAND-TAILED PIGEON *Columba fasciata*

PL. 3

This robust and wide-ranging pigeon can be found from coastal British Columbia south through the Cascades and Sierra Nevada, as well as throughout the southern Rockies and foothills. The species is found as far south as Argentina. The Band-tailed Pigeon is named for the pale band of gray at the tip of its tail. It is overall gray, but in good light look for a violet sheen on the breast and metallic green on the upper neck. There is a thin white band across the back of the neck.

Band-tailed Pigeons resemble Rock Doves (the familiar park pigeon) in both size and shape, but the two species occupy quite different habitats. Band-tails are birds of the forest, including oaks, pines, and mixed conifers. Flocks are often seen perched high in tall trees. The flocks range widely in search of pine seeds and acorns, and in winter they are often seen at low elevations in chaparral and, in some places, in city parks. Many people mistake their low *whoo-oo* call for that of an owl.

PINE SISKIN *Carduelis pinus*

PL. 3

This sparrowlike finch is often first noticed by its dry staccato chattering as a flock passes overhead. Siskins are heavily streaked, like sparrows, but up close you can see yellow feathering on the shoulder and at the base of the tail. A better name for this species would be "conifer siskin," since it is partial to spruce and fir forests as well as pine forests.

The Pine Siskin is closely related to the familiar American Goldfinch and is similar in size and in its undulating flight pattern. It is a fairly common permanent resident throughout western montane forests including southern Alaska. Siskins frequent both conifer and deciduous forests (especially birch and aspen) and feed on arthropods and seeds. In the West they often nest in loose colonies, with several pairs settling close together. In winter, siskins often become nomadic, suddenly becoming common, even abundant, in areas where they are seen infrequently. At these times they are easily attracted to bird feeders, especially if black thistle seed is offered.

BLUE GROUSE *Dendragapus obscurus*

PL. 3

This husky, chickenlike bird is a permanent resident of western montane forests from Arizona and New Mexico through British Columbia. Males are grayish blue, females mottled brown. The blue of the male is so dull that the species has been called "sooty grouse" (Pacific Coast) and "dusky grouse" (Rockies).

Two races occur, one in the Rockies and one along the Pacific coast. Rocky Mountain males have a yellow comb above each eye and a reddish pink neck sac, which are visible only when the cock bird is displaying. The white terminal tail band of the Rocky Mountain male is extremely narrow. Pacific males have bright orange combs, yellow neck sacs, and a broad white terminal band on the tail.

As shown on the plate, a displaying male fans his tail, inflates his neck sac, raises his eye combs, and struts before the female. The strut often follows a brief display flight during which the male drags his wings, cocks his tail, and draws his head in tightly. Males attract females with a deep hooting call (made with the aid of the expanded neck sacs), usually given from a high spot. The sound carries well, but humans often have difficulty finding the calling male, as the hooting has a ventriloquial quality (presumably female grouse do not have such difficulty). Breeding males are aggressive toward each other and can recognize each other's hooting. Male Blue Grouse take no part in nesting or raising young.

Many summer visitors to the West see Blue Grouse when they encounter a female leading her chicks across the road. In winter, Blue Grouse move up in altitude, occupying pine and spruce forests, where they feed on needles.

YELLOW-RUMPED WARBLER *Dendroica coronata* **PL. 3**

One of the most abundant North American warblers, the Yellow-rumped Warbler nests throughout both eastern and northwestern spruce-fir forests. Two races occur, and they are easy to distinguish in the field. The eastern race has a white throat. It was formerly called the "Myrtle Warbler." The western race, which has a yellow throat, was previously known as "Audubon's Warbler."

Though once considered to be separate species, the "Myrtle" and "Audubon's" warblers were recently lumped together as a single species because researchers learned that the two forms extensively hybridize where they meet in Canada. The hybrids seemed to succeed quite well, thus there was no justification for designating them as separate species.

Yellow-rumps are generalists, feeding from the treetops to the ground, equally at home on spruce boughs, aspen branches, or deciduous shrubs. They are among the largest of the wood warblers and are easily identified by the conspicuous yellow rump, apparent in both breeding and (duller) winter plumage. They also make a characteristic dry *chip* note when foraging in a flock. Flocks of Yellow-rumps are common during migration. The yellow rump may serve as a visual aid in keeping the fast-moving flock together.

DARK-EYED JUNCO *Junco hyemalis* PL. 3

Just as hybridization caused the lumping of the Yellow-rumped Warbler from two to one species, so it has caused the lumping of five juncos, each at one time considered to be a separate species. The "Oregon Junco," "Gray-headed Junco," "Pink-sided Junco," "White-winged Junco," and "Slate-colored Junco" have been combined into one species, the Dark-eyed Junco. Each subspecies is distinct in plumage and easily recognizable in the field, though hybrid birds and females can be tricky. The races generally occupy separate ranges but hybridize wherever they overlap. The "Oregon" subspecies is common throughout the Far West, whereas the "Gray-headed" subspecies occurs only in Arizona and New Mexico. The "Pink-sided" subspecies is found in the Central Rockies and the "White-winged" subspecies is found only in the Black Hills of South Dakota. The "Slate-colored" subspecies is eastern.

Dark-eyed Juncos breed in conifer forests, building a well-concealed nest in an embankment along the forest floor. Their song is a monotonous trilling, and their call note is an easily learned, sharp, one-noted, kisslike *smack*. Juncos frequent campgrounds, where they forage on or near the ground. In winter, large flocks are found at low elevations and they often frequent bird feeders. All juncos have white outer tail feathers, which, like the Yellow-rumped Warbler's yellow rump, probably serve as a signal to keep the flock together in flight.

WHITE-CROWNED SPARROW *Zonotrichia leucophrys* PL. 3

This species is a permanent or winter resident throughout the western states and a common, even abundant summer resident in Canada and Alaska. It is a large sparrow with a pink bill and a bold black and white head pattern, accentuated by the bird's characteristic upright stance. Several races occur, but they look generally quite similar. The Gambel's race, from Alaska and Hudson Bay, is most easily recognized by its distinctly yellowish bill.

White-crowned Sparrows are birds of boreal forest and bogs as well as high alpine tundra, where they can be seen along with American Pipits and Rosy Finches. The nest, of fine grasses, is always placed on or near the ground, often among low shrubs. In winter, flocks of White-crowned Sparrows are common throughout the West.

PLATE 1

WIDESPREAD WESTERN MAMMALS

These 11 large mammal species range widely through the national parks, forests, and prairies of the West. A few are common.

ELK *Cervus canadensis*
Large deer with a buffy rump. Male has a wide, many-pronged antler rack and brown, shaggy mane on the throat and neck. Female lacks antlers. Forests, mountain meadows.

WHITETAIL DEER *Odocoileus virginianus*
A common deer, russet-brown in summer, grayish in winter. White under the tail is conspicuous when the animal is bounding away. Only male has antlers. Forests, mountain meadows.

MULE DEER *Odocoileus hemionus*
Similar to Whitetail Deer but with somewhat larger ears and a black tip on the tail. Forests, mountain meadows. Common.

PRONGHORN *Antilocapra americana*
Rich brown with a white rump and white blazes on the neck and face. Both sexes have single-pronged horns, largest in males. Prairies, grassland, open country.

BISON *Bison bison*
Male is unmistakable with prominent humped shoulders, huge head, shaggy mane. Female is smaller, less humped. Horns occur on both sexes. Prairies, grassy meadows.

BIGHORN SHEEP *Ovis canadensis*
Dark brown sheep with a pale rump patch. Male has very large, curved horns. Female has smaller, straighter horns. Mountain meadows, peaks.

COLLARED PECCARY *Tayassu tajacu*
Piglike; grayish black with pale shoulder stripe. Low-elevation forests, deserts, grasslands. Southwest.

MOUNTAIN LION *Felis concolor*
A large cat, uniformly tawny to grayish, with a long tail. Forests, particularly in mountainous areas. Rare, infrequently seen.

COYOTE *Canis latrans*
Doglike; grayish with rusty legs, feet, ears. Bushy tail with black tip. Tail held between legs when running. Common at lower elevations throughout the West.

BLACK BEAR *Ursus americanus*
Color ranges from black to brown to cinnamon. Large; no tail. Widespread. Frequents campsites, garbage dumps.

GRIZZLY BEAR *Ursus horribilis*
Larger than Black Bear. Brown "grizzled" fur, humped shoulders, dish-shaped face. Uncommon except in Alaska, northwestern Canada. Potentially very dangerous.

PLATE 1

WHITETAIL DEER

ELK

MULE DEER

PRONGHORN

COYOTE

BISON

COLLARED PECCARY

MOUNTAIN LION

BIGHORN SHEEP

GRIZZLY BEAR

BLACK BEAR

PLATE 2

WIDESPREAD BIRDS OF OPEN AREAS

GOLDEN EAGLE *Aquila chrysaetos*
    43 inches. Large, dark, with big head. Wings held horizontally. Golden sheen on adult.

TURKEY VULTURE *Cathartes aura*
    32 inches. Large, black, soars with upturned (dihedral) wings. Tail long. Adult with red, naked head.

RED-TAILED HAWK *Buteo jamaicensis*
    25 inches. "Bulky" hawk with wide wings, rounded, spreading un-banded tail (reddish brown in adult). Upper breast unstreaked. Various color phases.

COMMON RAVEN *Corvus corax*
    27 inches. Hawk-sized but with large, straight (unhooked) bill and long, wedge-shaped tail. Soars. Often seen at roadkills.

WHITE-THROATED SWIFT *Aeronautes saxatalis*
    7 inches. Stiff, slender wings, white throat, chest, belly. Very rapid flier. Usually in flocks.

COMMON NIGHTHAWK *Chordeiles minor*
    9.5 inches. Pointed wings with white bars. White throat. Batlike flight, somewhat erratic.

BARN SWALLOW *Hirundo rustica*
    7.75 inches. Shiny blue above, reddish throat, rusty orange below. Forked tail. Usually in flocks.

CLIFF SWALLOW *Hirundo pyrrhonota*
    6 inches. Buffy rump, squared tail, pale whitish breast, white above bill. Usually in flocks.

BLACK-BILLED MAGPIE *Pica pica*
    22 inches with 12-inch tail. Black and white with long tail. Wings flash white in flight. Often seen at roadkills.

MOURNING DOVE *Zenaida macroura*
    12 inches. Pointed wings, pointed tail with white outer feathers. Small head. Often seen at roadsides, on wires and fences.

YELLOW-HEADED BLACKBIRD *Xanthocephalus xanthocephalus*
    11 inches. Males with yellow head, white wing patch. Females brownish, with yellow throat. Marshes, wet meadows.

BREWER'S BLACKBIRD *Euphagus cyanocephalus*
    9 inches. Males glossy black, females dark brown. Found near farms, fields, and towns.

NORTHERN FLICKER (RED-SHAFTED SUBSPECIES) *Colaptes auratus*
    14 inches. Brown woodpecker with white rump. Pale red under the wings and tail.

HOUSE FINCH *Carpodacus mexicanus*
    5.75 inches. Males streaked, rosy red to orange throat, breast, rump, head. Females streaked, resemble sparrows. Towns.

PLATE 2

TURKEY VULTURE

RED-TAILED HAWK

GOLDEN EAGLE

COMMON NIGHTHAWK

COMMON RAVEN

WHITE-THROATED SWIFT

BARN SWALLOW

CLIFF SWALLOW

BLACK-BILLED MAGPIE

MOURNING DOVE

YELLOW-HEADED BLACKBIRD

BREWER'S BLACKBIRD

NORTHERN FLICKER

HOUSE FINCH

PLATE 3

WIDESPREAD FOREST BIRDS

WILLIAMSON'S SAPSUCKER *Sphyrapicus thyroideus*
9.5 inches. A woodpecker. Male black with yellow belly, white wing patches, white rump. Female barred on back, lacks white wing patches.

WESTERN TANAGER *Piranga ludoviciana*
7 inches. Male yellow with black wings, tail, upper back. Red head. Female yellow with wing bars.

TOWNSEND'S SOLITAIRE *Myadestes townsendi*
8 inches. A brown thrush with an eye ring and white outer tail feathers, buffy orange on shoulders.

MOUNTAIN CHICKADEE *Parus gambeli*
5.75 inches. Active; gray with black cap, throat, and line through eye.

HAIRY WOODPECKER *Picoides villosus*
9.5 inches. Black and white, with unbarred white back. Males with red spot on head.

STELLER'S JAY *Cyanocitta stelleri*
13.5 inches. Large crest, black head and upper parts, otherwise deep blue.

BAND-TAILED PIGEON *Columba fasciata*
15.5 inches. Dark with lighter band at base of tail. White neck mark at close range.

PINE SISKIN *Carduelis pinus*
5 inches. Darkly streaked, pale yellow on wings.

BLUE GROUSE *Dendragapus obscurus*
21 inches. Male blue-gray with yellow "eyebrows." Females mottled brown.

YELLOW-RUMPED WARBLER (AUDUBON'S SUBSPECIES) *Dendroica coronata*
6 inches. Yellow rump and shoulder patch. Yellow throat.

DARK-EYED JUNCO (OREGON SUBSPECIES) *Junco hyemalis*
6.75 inches. Gray hood, rich brown back, flanks.

DARK-EYED JUNCO (GRAY-HEADED SUBSPECIES) *Junco hyemalis*
6.75 inches. Pale gray with reddish brown back.

WHITE-CROWNED SPARROW *Zonotrichia leucophrys*
7.5 inches. Large upright sparrow with bold white and black crown, pink bill (yellow in Gambel's race, not shown).

PLATE 3

WILLIAMSON'S SAPSUCKER

WESTERN TANAGER

TOWNSEND'S SOLITAIRE

MOUNTAIN CHICKADEE

STELLER'S JAY

HAIRY WOODPECKER

BAND-TAILED PIGEON

PINE SISKIN

YELLOW-RUMPED WARBLER

Oregon

DARK-EYED JUNCO

Gray-headed

WHITE-CROWNED SPARROW

BLUE GROUSE

WEST MEETS EAST:
GREAT PLAINS FORESTS

It is hard to say exactly where the West begins. For some New Englanders, the West begins at Albany. More realistically, most people associate the West with open spaces, flat, spacious plains with horizons interrupted by sharp mountain peaks, and sagebrush instead of maple trees. One definition holds that the West begins at the 100th meridian of longitude, a line running from western Manitoba south through the Dakotas, Nebraska, Kansas, the corner of Oklahoma, and the Edwards Plateau west of San Antonio in Texas. But such a definition overlooks the realities of natural history. East and West flow gradually into one another—there is a large, indistinct boundary to be crossed before leaving the broad-leaved eastern forests for the tall conifers of the West.

The most conspicuous distinction between eastern and western habitats is the transition from broad-leaved forest to grassland prairie. This boundary is dynamic, changing as climate has gradually changed over thousands of years. Studies of fossil pollen (which can be preserved surprisingly well for many thousands of years) have shown that trees such as American Basswood, American Elm, Eastern Hophornbeam, and American Hornbeam, all of which require moist soils, were common throughout northeastern Iowa from about 9,000 to 5,500 years ago. Beginning then, prairie moved eastward, replacing moist forests throughout northeastern Iowa until about 3,500 years ago, when the area became a dry oak savanna, a kind of mixture of forest and grassland.

The major climatic difference between prairie and broad-leaved forest is moisture. Prairie prevails in regions generally too arid to support the lush forests of the East. It is not surprising, therefore, that forests persevere along rivers throughout the Midwest. Rivers provide adequate moisture to support many species that cannot survive on arid prairie. These riparian forests are real oases of shade in the seemingly unending landscape of grasses.

Tall Cottonwoods are found in moist areas throughout the Prairie Region.

PRAIRIE RIPARIAN FOREST PLATE 4

INDICATOR PLANTS

CANOPY TREES: *Green Ash, Ashleaf Maple* (Box-elder), *Eastern Cottonwood, Peachleaf Willow, Water Birch,* Quaking Aspen, Bur Oak, Chinkapin Oak, Shin Oak, Post Oak, Blackjack Oak, American Elm, Bitternut Hickory, Shagbark Hickory, Northern Hackberry, Black Oak.

UNDERSTORY TREES AND SHRUBS: *Red-osier Dogwood,* Pussy Willow, Missouri Willow, Heartleaf Willow, Sandbar Willow, Desert Ironwood, Black Raspberry, Smooth Sumac, Common Buttonbush, Common Witch-hazel, Common Chokecherry, juneberries, hawthorns, Coralberry, Red Baneberry.

HERBACEOUS SPECIES: Virginia Creeper, Trumpet Creeper, Trumpet Honeysuckle, Winter Grape, Kudzu-vine (local), Globeflower, Stinging Nettle, Canada Violet, Cardinal Flower, Solomon's-seal, and various grasses and sedges.

INDICATOR ANIMALS

BIRDS: *Eastern Kingbird, Western Kingbird, Rose-breasted Grosbeak, Black-headed Grosbeak, Baltimore Oriole, Bullock's Oriole, Red-headed Woodpecker,* Green-backed Heron, Spotted Sandpiper, American Kestrel, Yellow-billed Cuckoo, Northern Flicker, Eastern Phoebe, Eastern Wood-Pewee, Tree Swallow, House Wren, Gray Catbird, Warbling Vireo, Yellow Warbler, Ovenbird, Common Yellowthroat, Red-winged Blackbird, Brown-headed Cowbird, Orchard Oriole, Northern Cardinal, American Goldfinch, Spotted Towhee, Song Sparrow.

MAMMALS: *River Otter, Mink,* Muskrat, Raccoon, Eastern Gray Squirrel, Eastern Cottontail.
REPTILES: *Painted Turtle,* False Map Turtle, Northern Water Snake.
AMPHIBIANS: Woodhouse Toad, Northern Leopard Frog.

DESCRIPTION

A forest that borders a river is called a *riparian* (riverine) or *gallery forest*. The prairie riparian forest is largely an extension of the eastern deciduous forest westward along the river systems that flow east, eventually to drain into the Mississippi. Moisture provided by the river enables the characteristic vegetation species to endure what would otherwise be far too arid circumstances. The riparian forest hugs the river and is bordered by prairie grassland beginning at the edge of the floodplain.

The dominant trees are willows, Green Ash, and Eastern Cottonwood (especially the subspecies Plains Cottonwood), along with various combinations of other water-loving species. Often there will be stately groves of widely spaced cottonwoods, with a rich understory of herbaceous wildflowers, but riparian forests may also consist mostly of dense, almost junglelike clumps of willows, especially Peachleaf Willow, along with Green Ash and Bur Oak and shrub thickets of Red-osier Dogwood, Smooth Sumac, and Buttonbush.

Riparian forests often are shrouded in vines such as bittersweet, honeysuckle, grape, and Virginia Creeper. The notorious Japanese Kudzu-vine is extending its range westward along riparian forests. Where rivers are wide and tend to wind, look for sandbars, accumulated sediment brought dur-

Cottonwood groves provide attractive habitat for many species otherwise absent from the open prairie.

ing the flooding cycle of the river. These bars are inevitably colonized by plants, especially Sandbar Willow and various sedges.

Both eastern and western species of birds live in the riparian forest. An Eastern Kingbird may share a tree with a Western Kingbird, and both subspecies of Northern Oriole, the eastern "Baltimore" and the western "Bullock's," may be found in the same grove of Eastern Cottonwoods.

SIMILAR FOREST COMMUNITIES: Eastern riparian forests (see *A Field Guide to the Ecology of Eastern Forests*) are generally similar, and the two have many species in common. Some characteristic eastern tree species, such as Silver Maple, American Basswood, Swamp White Oak, Eastern Sycamore, Red Maple, and Slippery Elm do not range to western river borders. There is a gradual transition from typically eastern riparian forest to prairie riparian, as species such as Peachleaf Willow, Green Ash, and Box-elder increase in abundance from east to west.

RANGE: From the prairie-forest border in Illinois, Iowa, Missouri, and Arkansas, extending along the major rivers through Oklahoma, Kansas, Nebraska, and the Dakotas. Most well developed along the Platte, Missouri, and Arkansas Rivers.

REMARKS

An *ecotone* is a boundary area between two kinds of habitats, or ecosystems. The transition between eastern deciduous forest and Great Plains prairie grassland forms one of the broadest and geographically largest ecotones in North America. The separation between forest and prairie is a gradual one. Remnant patches of

Figure 14. The ecotone, or boundary area, between a forest and a field

Cottonwood forest near Savory, Wyoming.

prairie exist in Mississippi, Ohio, Indiana, Illinois, Wisconsin, Minnesota, and other states, extending into southern Manitoba. The farthest route of penetration of eastern deciduous forest into the west is provided by rivers: the mighty Platte, Missouri, and Arkansas Rivers, and their many tributaries. The forests that line these rivers usually flood in spring when meltwater brings the river to crest. The floods are followed by summer drought, when evaporation tends to exceed precipitation, and the water level drops. Because of this annual cycle, western riparian forests tend to have broad, fertile floodplains, where sediment is deposited as waters recede.

As the settlers moved westward during the mid-19th century, they helped spread **EASTERN COTTONWOOD** along western rivers. **PLAINS COTTONWOOD** occurs throughout Kansas, Nebraska, the Dakotas, and eastern Colorado, Wyoming, and Montana. Most botanists believe Plains Cottonwood to be a subspecies of Eastern, and we describe it as such in this book, though others still treat it as a separate species. Groves of cottonwoods, some topping 100 feet tall, embrace the banks of much of the Platte River, and a drive across Nebraska on Interstate 80 means seeing a great many cottonwoods. A fast-growing tree, an Eastern Cottonwood can set seed within 10 years of germination and grow to full size within three decades. Cottonwood flowers are wind-pollinated and open early in spring, before leaves open, providing maximum potential for vernal winds to disperse pollen. Male flowers and female flowers are on separate streamerlike catkins. Female flowers are larger and contain seeds adorned with silky threads that help carry the seeds aloft. Seeds that fall in rivers are dispersed as they are deposited on floodplain. Cottonwoods thrive in moist soils, but because they have a long taproot that can reach a deep water table, they can also survive well on dry sandy soil.

ASHLEAF MAPLE (Box-elder) is the only maple with compound leaves. As its name suggests, it is sometimes mistaken for an ash. Largely midwestern in distribution, and most abundant along prairie rivers, Ashleaf Maple nonetheless can be found in many locations scattered throughout the Southwest, California, Mexico, and northern Central America. Like cottonwoods, Ashleaf Maples grow quickly, and thus are effective colonizers of riparian silt bars.

PEACHLEAF WILLOW is a small to medium-sized tree that is closely associated with streambanks and rivers throughout the Midwest, extending along rivers to the Pacific Northwest and south into Texas and New Mexico. Lewis and Clark were virtually never out of sight of the species as they navigated the Missouri and Columbia rivers. This is one of the first species to colonize recently formed bars, where dense stands of Peachleaf Willows act to stabilize the newly deposited soil. Other willow species and **WATER BIRCH,** though usually less abundant than Peachleaf, have similar colonizing abilities.

After the willows colonize an area, species such as **GREEN ASH** invade, gradually replacing the pioneer species. The natural history of Green Ash resembles closely that of Eastern Cottonwood. Both are wind-pollinated, and both utilize wind and water for seed dispersal. One difference between them is that ashes have male and female flowers on separate trees, not merely separate branches of the same tree, as cottonwoods do. The winged fruits of Green Ash mature in fall and are eaten by many species of birds and mammals. Green Ash enjoys a wide distribution, rang-

The seeds of the Green Ash attract many bird species.

ing from central Texas north to Manitoba and Saskatchewan.

For the birder, the prairie riparian forest offers a unique mixture of eastern and western species and subspecies. Both Rose-breasted and Black-headed grosbeaks may be encountered in the same cottonwood grove. Indigo and Lazuli buntings may sing from willows on opposite sides of a river. Eastern and Western kingbirds may sit side by side on utility wires. A pendulous oriole's nest may be inhabited by a pair of western Bullock's Orioles, or a pair of eastern Baltimore Orioles—or a female Baltimore and male Bullock's! A Northern Flicker may prove to be a member of the western "Red-shafted" subspecies, the eastern "Yellow-shafted" subspecies, or a hybrid between them.

Despite its name, the **EASTERN KINGBIRD** ranges widely into the western states, absent only from the Southwest. The **WESTERN KINGBIRD** occurs commonly in all western states and, during autumn migration, may turn up frequently along the eastern coastal states. Both kingbird species feed by flycatching from open perches, hence their preference for utility wires. Both build cup-shaped nests, often located near or over water. Both tend to be aggressive in defending their territories, harassing birds as large as crows and Red-tailed and Swainson's hawks.

ESSAY

THE EASTERN KINGBIRD'S DUAL PERSONALITY

If you pause for a spring or summer picnic among the stately cottonwoods, look for energetic Eastern Kingbirds that, in all likelihood, are somewhere around the cottonwood grove or perched on nearby roadside wires. This 8-inch flycatcher is among the most pugnacious of birds. Kingbirds will attack crows, hawks, vultures, owls, or any other birds, including one another. One observer even reports having witnessed an Eastern Kingbird attacking a low-flying airplane! Don't be surprised if you see kingbirds chasing after anything from a Red-winged Blackbird to a Red-tailed Hawk, chattering their high-pitched *bzeep, bzeep* call, sounding something like a bug light zapping insects. The Eastern Kingbird was once suggested as a good candidate to become the national bird, since the 13 colonies of the infant United States of America, a small but fearless lot, successfully drove out Great Britain, a much larger adversary. (However, the scientific name of Eastern Kingbird is *Tyrannus tyrannus,* meaning "tyrant of tyrants," perhaps not the best choice for a newborn democratic nation opposed to tyranny.)

Eastern Kingbirds are strictly territorial during breeding season. By attacking and harassing potential predators, the kingbirds may increase the probability of successfully raising young. By driving away other kingbirds, they make sure there will be enough insects to feed their brood.

But in other seasons, the Eastern Kingbird seems to undergo a personality change, at least with regard to fellow kingbirds. Beginning in late summer, when they prepare for migration, Eastern Kingbirds flock together. Just a few weeks earlier the sight of another Eastern Kingbird would inspire an aerial battle, but, as summer ends, it seems "the more the merrier." Together, they abandon the midwestern cottonwood groves and fly to their wintering grounds in Colombia, Ecuador, Peru, Chile, and northern Argentina.

The key to understanding why Eastern Kingbirds shift from being a territorial and aggressive species to a flocking, social one in winter is diet. Eastern Kingbirds feed heavily on various fruits while on their wintering grounds, just the opposite of their insectivorous summer diet. They move in flocks searching for fruiting trees and shrubs, descending on these plants to feed. Fruit is a "clumped resource," meaning that it is unevenly distributed in the environment. Once you find it, you usually find a tree full of it, too much for one individual bird to consume or defend. Flocking may help facilitate finding widely scattered fruiting trees, but it does more. Flocks of Eastern Kingbirds have a better chance of driving away larger fruit-eating tropical birds, like the Kiskadee (Plate 8) or the various toucans.

The plumage of the Eastern Kingbird reflects its dual personality. A small clump of red feathers on the top of its head, normally concealed, is raised when it becomes aggressive, such as in territorial battles. The Eastern Kingbird also has a white terminal tail band, quite conspicuous when it flies (and a good field mark for identifying the bird). The white tail band probably helps the birds easily keep track of each other in the moving winter flock. Two other flocking, fruit-eating species, the Cedar Waxwing and the Bohemian Waxwing (Plate 5) have yellow terminal tail bands that probably serve the same function.

Among the sweet sounds of the prairie riparian forest are the songs of the **ROSE-BREASTED** and **BLACK-HEADED GROSBEAKS**. Both species are fine singers with a rich, robinlike melody. Males of the two species look considerably different, but the females look generally alike, resembling oversized sparrows. The female Black-headed has a more orange-yellow breast, which lacks the streaking of the browner Rose-breasted female. The Rose-breasted

Grosbeak is generally confined to the East, except along western rivers, where it occasionally hybridizes with the Black-headed species. The Black-headed Grosbeak is widely distributed throughout the West, occurring in virtually all mid-elevation forests as well as along rivers and streams.

BULLOCK'S ORIOLE is also widely distributed throughout the West, including Canada and Mexico. Its preferred habitat is shady woodland groves, especially along streams. Its close relative, the eastern Baltimore Oriole, sometimes can be found in the same groves as Bullock's, and occasionally the two species hybridize. However, the hybrid birds fare worse than their parents and thus Bullock's and Baltimore are considered separate species (see essay below).

The **RED-HEADED WOODPECKER** is one of the most colorful inhabitants of gallery forests, as well as other deciduous woodlands throughout the midwestern and southeastern states. This boldly patterned bird is hard to miss as it flies from a dead snag or flycatches from the top of a utility pole. Because it frequently flies low and often nests in roadside utility poles, many birds are struck by automobiles. Also, over much of its range (especially in the East), the bird has probably been reduced in abundance through nest site competition with European Starlings. Redheads are still common, however, in gallery forest and burned-over areas. They are often locally abundant, living semicolonially.

The range of the **RIVER OTTER** extends throughout most of North America, and these delightful animals are occasionally sighted in the many rivers and streams that penetrate the Great Plains. Otters are aquatic members of the weasel tribe, making their homes by excavating dens in embankments. Otters are fairly social, so if you see one, there are undoubtedly others about. They are renowned for their apparent pleasure at frolicking, especially sliding down muddy banks. Their diet is carnivorous, consisting of fish, crayfish, frogs, and whatever other animals they can capture.

The **PAINTED TURTLE** is common in eastern streams, rivers, ponds, and lakes. One subspecies, the Western Painted Turtle, inhabits rivers from the midwestern states extending to British Columbia. It is the commonest turtle species in the prairie riparian habitat and can often be seen sunning itself on exposed logs and rocks.

WHERE TO VISIT: The best states in which to see prairie riparian forest are Oklahoma, Kansas, Nebraska, and the Dakotas, as well as the Canadian province of Manitoba. A drive along Interstate 80 in Nebraska from Grand Island to North Platte is recommended, for it affords an ideal view of the cottonwood-lined Platte River. In early spring, the Platte River is a major stopover point for Sandhill

Cranes migrating north to breed. Hundreds of these stately gray birds may be seen in fields and along the river at this time. From central Nebraska you might want to go northwest, following the North Platte River to Scottsbluff and on into Wyoming.

Farther south, the Kansas River, from Kansas City west past Topeka, affords excellent access to riverine habitat.

To the north, the long Missouri River winds through Montana, North Dakota, and South Dakota, south through Nebraska to eventually join the Mississippi River at St. Louis. In North Dakota and Manitoba, the Red River, draining from Lake Winnipeg, passing through Grand Forks and Fargo, is another excellent example of gallery forest.

Four national wildlife refuges, all in North Dakota, are worth a visit to see not only gallery forest, but also marshland, natural prairie, and prairie pothole lakes. These refuges, all in close proximity to one another in the northern part of the state, are Upper Souris, J. Clark Salyer, Des Lacs, and Lostwood. These wildlife refuges provide important habitat for breeding ducks, shorebirds, and grebes, and the surrounding prairie grassland is used by nesting Sharp-tailed Grouse and Greater Prairie-Chicken.

ESSAY

LUMPING AND SPLITTING ON THE GREAT PLAINS

For much of the past 65 million years, since the dinosaurs exited, the climate of North America has been mild and equitable. However, about 35–40 million years ago, a slow but steady change began toward a more arid and variable climate. The seasons became more pronounced, and grasslands flourished at the expense of forest. Part of this change was due to the uplift of the Rocky Mountains, which created a major rainshadow effect (see page 51). Then, beginning about 2 million years ago, climate changed more radically. This was the start of the Pleistocene, a time when glaciers moved south until they covered up to 32 percent of the world's surface (compared with about 10 percent at present). Glaciers expanded and contracted in North America perhaps as many as 20 times, causing significant displacement of forests and other habitats.

The combined effects of increasing aridity over the Great Plains plus the disruptions caused by glacial advance followed by warmer interglacial periods (such as the one we are in now) served to isolate eastern populations of many bird species from western ones. During these periods, which lasted thousands of years (thousands of bird generations), populations diverged and species split into new species. Where there had been one grosbeak, there was now the eastern Rose-breasted Grosbeak and the western Black-headed Grosbeak. Where there had been one meadowlark, there were now the Eastern Meadowlark and the Western Meadowlark. And where there was one oriole, there were now the Baltimore Oriole and Bullock's Oriole.

Many of the bird species that seem to have eastern and western counterparts are thought to have arisen from speciation during climatic changes over the past several million years. These include, in addition to the ones named above, the Eastern and Western wood-pewees, Eastern and Western screech-owls, Indigo and Lazuli buntings (plus the southwestern Varied Bunting and southeastern Painted Bunting), the Blue and Steller's jays, and the Red-bellied and Golden-fronted woodpeckers.

In some cases, however, the eastern and western populations were not geographically isolated long enough to result in the populations becoming genetically incompatible. Also, many range expansions have occurred in recent years, bringing separated eastern and western populations together, often in the same habitat. The Eastern Towhee encountered the western Spotted Towhee (which, until recently, were considered separate species, the eastern "Rufous-sided" and western "Spotted" Towhees). The Tufted Titmouse encountered the southwestern Black-crested Titmouse —and interbred. The Baltimore Oriole encountered Bullock's Oriole—and interbred. And the Yellow-shafted Flicker encountered the Red-shafted Flicker—and interbred. These Great Plains hybrids pose a problem because it is difficult to know if they should be treated as separate species or as races of the same species. In the case of the orioles, some years ago they were "lumped" into one species, the Northern Oriole. However, the hybrid birds are so much less successful than the nonhybrids that the orioles have recently been reassigned to separate species. The same is true for the towhees. However, some Great Plains hybrids are as fit as their parents and thus what was once two or more species are lumped into but one. An extreme case is the five formerly separate junco species that have now been lumped into one.

However, the process of species designation can work the other way—a single species may be taxonomically split into two. Speciation can be surprisingly difficult to detect. In recent years the Western Flycatcher has been recognized to be actually two species, the Pacific-slope Flycatcher of the West Coast and the Cordilleran Flycatcher of the interior. Though the two species look virtually identical, they sound different, and more important, they do not interbreed. Likewise, the Brown Towhee has recently been split into the coastal California Towhee and the interior Canyon Towhee.

Many hours of dedicated field work are required to collect enough information to say with certainty whether two bird populations are interbreeding and to know if hybrids can successfully breed. But the difficulties encountered in trying to determine when to lump and when to split demonstrate that species do, in fact, evolve.

LACK HILLS FOREST PLATE 5

NDICATOR PLANTS

NOPY TREES: *Ponderosa Pine, White Spruce,* Lodgepole Pine (local), Rocky Mountain Juniper, Quaking Aspen, Paper Birch, Bur Oak, American Elm, Green Ash, Eastern Hophornbeam, Ashleaf Maple, Eastern (Plains) Cottonwood, Water Birch, Peachleaf Willow, and other willows.

DERSTORY TREES AND SHRUBS: Alderleaf Cercocarpus, Common Juniper, Kinnikinnick, Mountain Snowberry, Shrubby Cinquefoil, Redosier Dogwood, and various sumacs and currants. In grasslands: *Big Sagebrush,* Canada Buffaloberry, Rubber Rabbitbrush, Tall Rabbitbrush.

RBACEOUS SPECIES: Red Fireweed, Striped Coralroot, Green Gentian, Yellow Lady's-slipper, many others.

ASSLAND SPECIES: Many *grasses,* including Slender Wheatgrass, needlegrass, Needle-and-thread, Junegrass, and Blue Grama. Also Eastern Prickly-pear, Leadplant, Partridge Pea, Scarlet Globemallow, and many composites and legumes as well as other prairie wildflower species.

DICATOR ANIMALS

DS: *Blue Jay, Dark-eyed Junco* ("White-winged" form), *Gray Jay,* Lewis's Woodpecker, Bohemian Waxwing (winter), Rock Wren, Ruffed Grouse, Northern Flicker, Western Wood-Pewee, Black-capped Chickadee, White-breasted Nuthatch, Red-breasted Nuthatch, Black-billed Magpie, American Dipper, Townsend's Solitaire, Mountain Bluebird, Cedar Waxwing, Yellow-rumped Warbler, Ovenbird, Northern Oriole, Western Tanager, Black-headed Grosbeak, Lazuli Bunting, Indigo Bunting, Red Crossbill, Chipping Sparrow.

MMALS: *Red Squirrel, Blacktail Prairie Dog, Bison,* Least Chipmunk, Northern Flying Squirrel, Porcupine, Beaver, Coyote, Bobcat, Black Bear, Elk, Mule Deer, Whitetail Deer, Pronghorn, Mountain Goat, Bighorn Sheep.

REPTILES: Prairie Rattlesnake, Bullsnake, Black Hills Red-bellied Snake, Western Wandering Garter Snake.

AMPHIBIANS: *Great Plains Toad*, Southern Chorus Frog.

DESCRIPTION

Situated amid the high plains of the Midwest, the Black Hills is an area of low mountains surrounded by prairie grassland. The name refers to the dark look created by dense stands of Ponderosa Pine and White Spruce, the dominant trees, as they appear against the lighter background of waving prairie grasses. The forest, though not particularly tall, is dense, and the understory is generally poorly developed. The forest floor is mostly dried pine needle litter. Ponderosa Pine predominates in most places, replaced by White Spruce on northern exposures and moist areas. At higher elevations, shrubs such as Alderleaf Cercocarpus abound. Along streams and rivers, deciduous trees such as willows, cottonwoods, Bur Oak, Green Ash, and American Elm can be found. At lower elevations, the Black Hills forest is punctuated by one of the few remaining areas of natural prairie grassland, with an abundance of native grass species as well as many wildflower species. Shrubs, such as Big Sagebrush, Tall Rabbitbrush, and Buffaloberry, also are common. Ponderosa Pine stands often encroach on grassland but are periodically burned back; thus natural fires are essential to maintenance of healthy grassland. Evidence of fire is common in the Black Hills, such as the dense stands of Red Fireweed that dot the landscape.

Many bird species occur throughout the Black Hills, some typically western, some more eastern in range. Large mammals such as Elk, Mule Deer, and Whitetail Deer are common, and small

Figure 15. Blacktail Prairie Dogs

The forests of Ponderosa Pine and White Spruce that border the prairies are called the Black Hills.

herds of Bison and Pronghorns may be viewed on the grasslands, along with colonies of Blacktail Prairie Dogs. The highest point in the Black Hills is Harney Peak, at 7,242 feet, which is also the highest elevation east of the Rocky Mountains. It is inhabited by Mountain Goats, recently reintroduced into the region.

SIMILAR FOREST COMMUNITIES: Ponderosa Pine forests throughout the West are generally similar, though the Black Hills hosts a unique mixture of western and eastern species. Ponderosa Pines in the Black Hills are somewhat smaller in stature than those in most other areas where the species is abundant.

RANGE: Southwestern South Dakota, extending slightly into eastern Wyoming. The total area ranges about 70 miles wide and 110 miles long.

REMARKS

The Black Hills is a rich area, in both natural history and human history. Gold was discovered here in the 1870s, leading quickly to the eviction of the Lakota Sioux Indians from their historic lands and eventually resulting in the Battle of the Little Bighorn (which occurred in southern Montana), where Sitting Bull soundly defeated General George A. Custer. Situated within the Black Hills are the historic frontier towns of Sundance, Custer, Lead, and Deadwood, where Calamity Jane rode the Deadwood Stage and Wild Bill Hickok was gunned down at the #10 Saloon.

Two detailed studies of Black Hills plant species showed that 30 percent come from the Rockies, 17 percent are from the Great Plains, 9 percent are eastern deciduous species, 6 percent northern boreal species, and 4.5 percent southwestern species. **WHITE SPRUCE** occurs in the Black Hills, 600 miles south of its main

range, and **LODGEPOLE PINE** is found here, more than 200 miles east of the nearest stand, in the Big Horn Mountains of Wyoming. **BUR OAK** reaches its westernmost range in the Black Hills. Some herbaceous species, such as **TWINLEAF** and **NORTHERN MAIDENHAIR FERN,** also reach their range limits in the Black Hills.

Fire is frequent in the Black Hills and surrounding prairie. Without periodic burning, the more slowly growing **PONDEROSA PINES** would gradually but continuously encroach on the seas of grassland. Indeed, as you look upon a vista of forest and grassland, you are seeing a natural struggle among different vegetation forms, played out over a long time period. Lightning-set fires have long influenced this struggle, maintaining grassland where forest would otherwise prevail. Prescribed (intentional) burning is necessary for the continued welfare of natural prairie grasslands.

Burned-over Ponderosa Pine stands provide habitat for **LEWIS'S WOODPECKER,** a husky dark-green bird with a pink underbelly and red face. In flight, the bird is crowlike, with slow and steady wingbeats. Mostly a foothill species and found throughout the West, Lewis's Woodpecker is particularly attracted to the snags of recently burned pines, ideal for both nest excavation and foraging.

Besides Lewis's Woodpecker, 138 other bird species occur regularly in the Black Hills, including some that reach either their extreme eastern or extreme western breeding ranges. The **AMERICAN DIPPER, MOUNTAIN BLUEBIRD, TOWNSEND'S SOLITAIRE, WESTERN TANAGER, SAY'S PHOEBE, CASSIN'S FINCH, ROCK WREN,** and **LEWIS'S WOODPECKER** breed no further east, while the **OVENBIRD** and **INDIGO BUNTING** breed no further west. **BLUE JAYS** search for acorns among the groves of Bur Oak, while boreal **GRAY JAYS** skulk among the boughs of White Spruce. Nomadic species such as **RED CROSSBILL** and **BOHEMIAN WAXWING** are often present in substantial numbers, the latter only in winter, when it feeds on berries of Western Red-cedar and fruits of mountain-ash.

One bird unique to the Black Hills is the "White-winged" form of the **DARK-EYED JUNCO**. Once considered a separate species, this population, easily recognized by varying amounts of white barring on the upper wing, is now considered a variety of the widely varying Dark-eyed Junco species.

Among mammals, the **RED SQUIRREL** abounds in the Black Hills along with the **LEAST CHIPMUNK** and the **NORTHERN FLYING SQUIRREL**. Because the flying squirrel is totally nocturnal, you are unlikely to see it, though you should have no difficulty finding the other two rodents. In addition, **PORCUPINES** are not uncommon, nor are **BEAVER**. Large hoofed mammals can be found at all elevations: **BISON** and **PRONGHORN** on the grasslands, deer and **ELK** at middle elevations, and **MOUNTAIN GOATS** and **BIGHORN SHEEP** on the steep slopes and granite ridges. Look for Mountain Goats on Harney Peak near Mt. Rushmore. **COYOTES** occur on the grasslands and in open pine forests, and **BOBCATS** are common throughout the Black Hills, especially along streams and at lower elevations.

A unique part of Black Hills natural history is its grasslands complex, a true remnant of the vast prairie that dominated the Midwest during centuries past. Today this diverse habitat, which harkens back to the romance of the pioneer days, has largely been eliminated to make room for wheat and corn. Many of the approximately 2,000 species of flowering plants that occur among the Black Hills are grassland

Among the many wildflower species of the Black Hills prairie are these Gayfeathers.

species, now protected as part of the nation's ecological heritage. Among them are several species of cacti, especially the prickly-pears, many kinds of composites, such as coneflowers, gumweeds, gayfeathers, thistles, daisies, sunflowers, asters, and goldenrods, and an abundance of legumes, such as clovers, bush-clovers, vetches, **LEADPLANT,** and **PARTRIDGE PEA.** Yuccas rise above the waving grasses, adding relief to a monotonous but nonetheless pleasing landscape. Identifying the many grass species found on the prairie poses a challenge for any botanist.

In addition to forest and grassland, the Black Hills feature rocky outcrops and cliff faces, arid lands where species such as **ROCKY MOUNTAIN JUNIPER** and **ROCK WREN** are common. Shrubs, among them the colorful yellow **SHRUBBY CINQUEFOIL,** as well as **ALDERLEAF CERCOCARPUS,** are also prevalent in such areas.

Among the common snakes of the Black Hills are two forms largely restricted to the region, the **WESTERN WANDERING GARTER SNAKE** and the **BLACK HILLS RED-BELLIED SNAKE.** The former is a race of a species widely distributed in the West, and the latter is the westernmost race of an eastern species. **PRAIRIE RATTLESNAKES** are most common on the grassy plains but are not uncommon among the foothills of the Black Hills region. Among the larger serpents, the **BULLSNAKE,** which can reach a length of 9 feet, is the most common. About 18 other snake species are known to occur in the Black Hills.

Amphibians also can be found in the Black Hills, including the **SOUTHERN CHORUS FROG,** a small green frog with brown stripes that is common in ponds, and the **GREAT PLAINS TOAD,** a husky gray toad with brown blotches, common on the plains and foothills. The toad's strident, metallic trill can be heard throughout its spring breeding season.

WHERE TO VISIT: Both Wind Cave National Park and Custer State Park afford ideal areas in which to experience the Black Hills. Wind Cave, comprising just over 28,000 acres, is one of the smaller national parks, but it provides the visitor an opportunity to experience both natural grassland and coniferous forest, as well as to explore some 53 miles of caves. There is a colony of Blacktail Prairie Dogs and a Bison herd, both easily seen. Pronghorn are not uncommon, and a Coyote can often be spotted by the keen observer. Custer State Park, located just to the north of Wind Cave, supports a somewhat larger Bison herd and is a good area to observe Elk, especially at twilight, when they descend from the forests to feed along the forest-grassland edge. Black Hills National Forest, which surrounds Mt. Rushmore National Memorial, consists of 1,233,000 acres extending from just west of Rapid City, S.D., into eastern Wyoming. In addition to Mt. Rushmore, there are many trails along which to birdwatch and botanize. At the extreme western border of the Black Hills, in eastern Wyoming, is Devil's Tower National Monument, an 865-foot column of hardened volcanic magma. About 50 miles east of the Black Hills is Badlands National Park, an excellent place to observe natural prairie grassland as well as deposits of huge fossil mammals. Badlands also has a re-created prairie homestead of historical interest. The Black Hills are most easily reached via Interstate 90.

ESSAY

WHAT IS A COMMUNITY?

Throughout this guide I have arranged western forests as though they form integrated, clearly recognizable ecological communities. The Black Hills forest, the prairie riparian forest, and all the others described in these pages are separated by the distinctly different combinations of species they comprise. You can easily distinguish between prairie riparian forest and Black Hills forest — one is a broad-leaved forest of ash and cottonwood, the other is a coniferous forest of Ponderosa Pine and White Spruce. One has kingbirds, the other juncos.

The fact that ecological communities are, indeed, recognizable clusters of species has led some ecologists, particularly those living earlier in this century, to claim that communities are highly integrated, precisely balanced assemblages. This claim harkens back to even earlier arguments about the existence of a balance of nature, where every species is there for a specific purpose, like a vital part in a complex machine. Such a belief would suggest that to remove any species, whether it be plant, bird, or insect, would somehow disrupt the balance, and the habitat would begin to deteriorate. Likewise, to add a species may be equally disruptive.

One of these pioneer ecologists was Frederic Clements, who studied ecology extensively throughout the Midwest and other areas in North America. He held that within any given region of climate, ecological communities tended to slowly converge toward a single endpoint, which he called the "climatic climax." This "climax" community was, in Clements's mind, the most well-balanced, integrated grouping of species that could occur within that particular region. Clements even thought that the process of ecological succession was somewhat akin to the development of an organism, from embryo to adult. Clements thought that succession represented discrete stages in the development of the community (rather like infancy, childhood, and adolescence), terminating in the climatic "adult" stage, when the community became self-reproducing and succession ceased. Clements's view of the ecological community reflected the notion of a precise balance of nature.

Clements was challenged by another pioneer ecologist, Henry Gleason, who took the opposite view. Gleason thought that every ecological community was, in some way or another, significantly distinct from all others, a notion he termed the "individualistic" concept. Gleason viewed the community as largely a group of species with similar tolerances to the stresses imposed by climate and other factors typical of the region. Gleason saw the element of chance as important in influencing where species occurred. His concept of the community suggests that nature is not highly integrated. Gleason thought succession could take numerous directions, depending upon local circumstances.

Who was right? Many ecologists have made precise measurements, designed to test the assumptions of both the Clements and Gleason models. For instance, along mountain slopes, does one life zone (see Chapter 3, "Life Zones") grade sharply or gradually into another? If the divisions are sharp, perhaps the reason is that the community is so well integrated, so holistic, so like Clements viewed it, that whole clusters of species must remain together. If the divisions are gradual, perhaps each species is responding individually to its environment, and clusters of species are not so integrated that they must always occur together, as Gleason suggested.

It now appears that Gleason was far closer to the truth than Clements. The ecological community is largely an accidental assemblage of species with similar responses to a particular climate. Green Ash associates with Plains Cottonwood because both can

A single Ponderosa Pine among prairie in the Black Hills. Is it a member of the prairie community? The forest community would gradually "invade" the prairie were it not for fire.

survive well on floodplains and the competition between them is not so strong that only one can persevere. One ecological community often flows into another so gradually that it is next to impossible to say where one leaves off and the other begins. Communities are individualistic.

This is not to say that precise harmonies are not present within communities. Most flowering plants could not exist were it not for their pollinators—and vice versa. Predators, disease organisms, and competitors all influence the abundance and distribution of everything from oak trees to field mice. But if we see a precise balance of nature, it is largely an artifact of our perception, due to the illusion that nature, especially a complex system like a forest, seems so unchanging from one day to the next.

Nature does change, it is dynamic, and the model of the ecological community is but a generalized way of describing a group of plants, animals, and microbes. Few examples illustrate this notion as well as the odd mixture of eastern and western species that make up the Black Hills, or the primarily eastern species that invade the West by following the courses of the major rivers through the arid prairie.

Though each community is individualistic, in any given locale they have enough in common that we can meaningfully describe a "Black Hills Forest." But look closely from one forest to another in the Black Hills. You'll see all sorts of differences, once you really look.

PLATE 4

PRAIRIE RIPARIAN FOREST

GREEN ASH *Fraxinus pennsylvanica*
> To 70 ft. Opposite leaves, compound, with 7–9 leaflets per leaf. Leaflets slightly toothed near apex, smooth at base. Bark grayish brown, occasionally reddish. Fruits slender and winged, in clusters.

ASHLEAF MAPLE (BOX-ELDER) *Acer negundo*
> To 65 ft. Opposite leaves, compound, with 3–5 leaflets per leaf. Bark grayish, deeply furrowed. Fruits winged, in pairs, clustered.

PEACHLEAF WILLOW *Salix amygdaloides*
> To 65 ft., usually smaller. Alternate leaves feel papery and are lance-shaped with fine teeth. Bark is brown, ridged.

EASTERN COTTONWOOD *Populus deltoides*
> To 100 ft., occasionally taller. Open crown. Leaves alternate, heart-shaped, toothed. Bark grayish, smooth in young trees, dark and deeply furrowed in older trees. Fruits with feathery fibers, in capsules on stalk.

RED-OSIER DOGWOOD *Cornus stolonifera*
> Small tree or shrub, usually with multiple trunks. Leaves opposite, elliptical, edges smooth. Bark is thin, usually quite reddish. Fruits are white, in clusters.

WATER BIRCH *Betula occidentalis*
> Shrub or small tree. Leaves alternate, somewhat heart-shaped, toothed. Bark black and smooth in young trees, reddish in older trees. Fruits in small cones.

RED-HEADED WOODPECKER *Melanerpes erythrocephalus*
> 9 in. Entire head bright red. Conspicuous white wing patches visible in flight and when at rest. Sexes alike, juvenile brownish.

ROSE-BREASTED GROSBEAK *Pheucticus ludovicianus*
> 8 in. Chunky. Male (shown) black and white, red on breast. Female sparrowlike, brownish with streaks on breast. Beak is white.

WESTERN KINGBIRD *Tyrannus verticalis*
> 8 in. Gray above, yellow belly, black tail with white outer tail feathers. Sits upright. Sexes are alike.

BULLOCK'S ORIOLE *Icterus bullockii*
> 8 in. Slender. Male (shown) with bright orange breast, black above with white wing patch and black line through eye. Female grayish with yellow throat.

BLACK-HEADED GROSBEAK *Pheucticus melanocephalus*
> 8 in. Chunky. Male (shown) dark russet on breast, sides, rump, otherwise black. White on wings. Female sparrowlike, with orangy breast.

EASTERN KINGBIRD *Tyrannus tyrannus*
> 8 in. Slate gray above, white below, with a white tail band. Perches in the open. Sexes are alike.

RIVER OTTER *Lutra canadensis*
> Long shape, with thick tail. Total length about 40 inches. Dark brown above, silvery below.

WESTERN PAINTED TURTLE *Chrysemys picta belli*
> Upper shell (carapace) black with red lines, including netlike lines over entire surface of carapace.

PLATE 4

ROSE-BREASTED GROSBEAK

GREEN ASH

RED-HEADED WOODPECKER

ASHLEAF MAPLE

WESTERN KINGBIRD

BULLOCK'S ORIOLE

WATER BIRCH

PEACHLEAF WILLOW

BLACK-HEADED GROSBEAK

EASTERN KINGBIRD

EASTERN COTTONWOOD

RED-OSIER DOGWOOD

fruit

WESTERN PAINTED TURTLE

RIVER OTTER

PLATE 5

BLACK HILLS FOREST

WHITE SPRUCE *Picea glauca*
> Cone-shaped conifer with dense, 1-in., blue-green needles. Bark gray-ish to brownish, somewhat scaly. Needles distinctly 4-sided.

PONDEROSA PINE *Pinus ponderosa*
> Straight conifer growing up to 100 ft. in Black Hills. Bark reddish or-ange, especially on mature trees. Needles 4–10 in., in bundles of 2 or 3. Abundant in Black Hills.

AMERICAN ELM *Ulmus americana*
> Deciduous tree up to 120 ft., with symmetrical, elliptical crown. Leaves alternate, toothed; may be rough above, smoother below. Common along streams and rivers.

BUR OAK *Quercus macrocarpa*
> To 100 ft. or more, with alternate, smoothly lobed leaves and often deeply furrowed bark. Acorn has a "burred" cap.

ROCKY MOUNTAIN JUNIPER *Juniperus scopulorum*
> A dense, shrubby juniper, usually not more than 30–35 ft. tall, with scalelike leaves and bluish gray, waxy, fleshy cones. Dry soils.

BIRCHLEAF CERCOCARPUS (MOUNTAIN-MAHOGANY) *Cercocarpus montanus*
> Shrub growing to 6 ft. tall, with small leaves slightly toothed along the upper margin. Flowers in spring are pinkish and inconspicuous. Fruits up to 3 inches long, hang as fuzzy streamers in fall. Dry soils.

SHRUBBY CINQUEFOIL *Potentilla fruticosa*
> Dense shrub with bright yellow, 5-petaled blossoms and small silver-gray, hairy leaves. Grows to 3 ft. Forms a shrub zone between forest and grassland at higher elevations.

LEWIS'S WOODPECKER *Melanerpes lewis*
> 11 in. Iridescent green back and head, appearing black in low light. Pink breast, red face. Flight somewhat crowlike, with steady wingbeats. Often flycatches from exposed snag. Somewhat colonial.

BOHEMIAN WAXWING *Bombycilla garrulus*
> 8 in. A husky gray bird with a crest. Cinnamon under tail helps separate it from similar Cedar Waxwing. Large flocks attracted to berries in winter.

BLUE JAY *Cyanocitta cristata*
> 12 in. Bright blue above and white underneath, with a black bib, black barring, and white on the tail and wings. Crested. Often noisy, calling *jay, jay!* Prefers oaks.

DARK-EYED JUNCO *Junco hyemalis*
> 6 in. Sparrowlike; gray above, white below, white outer tail feathers. "White-winged" form of the Black Hills has white wing bars. Call con-sists of sharp twittering. Often feeds on ground beneath pines.

RED SQUIRREL *Tamiasciurus hudsonicus*
> An 8-inch tree squirrel, usually rusty red, with small ear tufts. Abun-dant in conifers. Often vocal, a sharp, scolding chatter.

ROCK WREN *Salpinctes obsoletus*
> 5 in. A streaky brown wren, grayish brown with a cinnamon-buffy rump. Rocky outcrops and cliffsides.

PLATE 5

6

SOUTH TEXAS FORESTS

Texas is a vast state with a bounty of habitats. If you enter the Lone Star State in the northeast, say from Texarkana, and drive south to the Lower Rio Grande Valley, then northwest to San Antonio and the Edwards Plateau, and finally west to the Trans-Pecos, you will pass through vastly different ecological communities, each of which contains some of North America's most interesting species. The mixed pine and broad-leaved forests of eastern Texas are quite different from the rugged pinyon pine and juniper forests of the western Trans-Pecos, along the Rio Grande. Southern Texas has a natural history very much like Mexico, with Mexican species of plants and birds that occur nowhere else in the United States. The Gulf Coast, known for its rich marine life, boasts a landscape of picturesque Virginia Live Oak groves, often joined by other coastal species. A drive across Texas will take you from the ecology of the East to that of the West, with Mexico in between!

This chapter focuses on the forests of southern Texas, including the Lower Rio Grande Valley. Some, such as the dry mixed pine forests and the rich bottomland swamp forests typical of the Big Thicket area of northeastern Texas, are more characteristic of the East than the West. The rich ecology of Gulf Coast forests is also included. In Central Texas, one finds the scenic Edwards Plateau forests, rich in oaks and junipers, abundant with wildflowers, and nesting grounds for two endangered bird species. Finally, the forests of the Lower Rio Grande Valley, discussed in detail in this chapter, are unlike any others in the United States because of the strong influence of Mexican species.

The western parts of Texas, including Big Bend and Guadalupe Mountains National Parks, are discussed with southwestern forests in Chapter 8.

GULF COAST LIVE OAK FOREST

INDICATOR PLANTS

TREES: *Virginia Live Oak, Laurel Oak, Blackjack Oak, Netleaf Hackberry,* Durand Oak, Post Oak, Southern Hackberry, Redbay, Anacua, Black Willow, Honey Mesquite, Retama, Huisache, Spanish Buckeye, Salt-cedar, Southern Prickly-ash. Introduced palms such as Sago Palm.

SHRUBS: *Yaupon, Waxmyrtle,* Common Buttonbush, Groundsel-tree, Texas Forestiera, American Beautyberry, Marsh-elder, Southeastern Coralbean, Spiny Hackberry, Texas Torchwood, Spanish Dagger. Vines: Bullbrier Greenbrier, Trumpet Creeper, Dewberry, Pepper Vine, Poison-ivy.

HERBACEOUS SPECIES: *Spanish Moss, Ball Moss,* American Mistletoe, Spreading Dodder, Texas Lantana, Wild Indigo, Texas Pricklypear, Red Prickly Poppy, Daisy Fleabane, Meadow Pink, Sharp Gayfeather, American Germander, Texas Bluebonnet, Drummond's Phlox, Goldenwaves, Square-bud Primrose, Redspike Mexican Hat.

INDICATOR ANIMALS

LAND BIRDS: *Red-bellied Woodpecker, Scissor-tailed Flycatcher, Loggerhead Shrike, Northern Parula, Painted Bunting,* American Kestrel, Red-tailed Hawk, Turkey Vulture, Black Vulture, Northern Bobwhite, Wild Turkey, Eastern Screech-Owl, Barred Owl, Yellowbilled Cuckoo, Common Nighthawk, Chimney Swift, Ladderbacked Woodpecker, Barn Swallow, Cliff Swallow, Purple Martin, Carolina Wren, Northern Mockingbird, Brown Thrasher, American Robin, White-eyed Vireo, Yellow Warbler, Common Yellowthroat, Northern Cardinal, Red-winged Blackbird, Great-tailed Grackle, Boat-tailed Grackle.

WATER BIRDS: *Whooping Crane* (winter only), Anhinga, Double-crested Cormorant, Brown Pelican, American White Pelican, Great Blue Heron, Little Blue Heron, Tricolored Heron, Green-backed Heron, Reddish Egret, Snowy Egret, Great Egret, Cattle Egret, Black-crowned Night-Heron, White Ibis, White-faced Ibis, Roseate Spoonbill, Osprey, Laughing Gull, Caspian Tern, Forster's Tern, Gull-billed Tern, Black Skimmer, Killdeer, Willet, American Avocet, Black-necked Stilt, Black Oystercatcher, Belted Kingfisher. Many duck species in winter.

MAMMALS: *Armadillo, Wild Boar,* Opossum, South Texas Pocket Gopher, Eastern Fox Squirrel, Nutria, Blacktail Jackrabbit, Eastern Cottontail, Raccoon, Collared Peccary, Whitetail Deer.

REPTILES: *Gulf Coast Ribbon Snake, American Alligator,* Rough Green Snake, Speckled Kingsnake, Texas Rat Snake, Eastern Hognose

Snake, Cottonmouth, Western Diamondback Rattlesnake, Ground Skink, Southern Fence Lizard, Green Anole.

DESCRIPTION

The Texas Gulf Coast, from Galveston to Brownsville, is habitat for a picturesque forest of spreading Virginia Live Oaks draped in dense cloaks of Spanish Moss. Mixed among the live oaks are other oak species as well as hackberries and various other trees. This forest is subject to coastal weather, especially winds (including occasional hurricanes) and salt spray. Often the vegetation seems sculpted by wind. The forest is always close to salt meadows and salt marshes, and there is frequently a gradation from salt marsh to shrubby meadow to woodland. The moist air makes ideal conditions for epiphytes, plants that live on the branches of other plants. Epiphytes thickly cover the arching oak branches. Parasitic plants such as American Mistletoe and Spreading Dodder also commonly grow in the oak branches. Spring and summer are times of abundant wildflowers. Shrubs, ranging from desert-like yuccas to Waxmyrtle and Yaupon Holly, abound in the understory and open areas. Grasses are also common. Soils tend to be sandy. Water birds are conspicuous, and salt marshes support herons and egrets, including the Roseate Spoonbill. Land birds are similar to those from the mixed pine forest but also include

some from the Texas savanna. Mammals are often sighted because of the openness of the woodlands. Whitetail Deer may be abundant, and in some areas, Wild Boars and Collared Peccaries are common.

Virginia Live Oaks form an attractive canopy over the road.

REMARKS

The Texas Gulf Coast has been densely developed for tourism, and much of the natural ecology has given way to marinas, condominiums, beach houses, and motels. Nonetheless, the naturalist can still enjoy the sight of pristine live oak groves, the Spanish Moss–draped trees lined up against a beach like dignified sentinels guarding the coast.

VIRGINIA LIVE OAK reaches the westernmost part of its range in eastern and central Texas. It is really a tree of the southeastern coastal plain, ranging as far north as southeastern Virginia. Because of its spreading shape and usually heavy burden of veillike **SPANISH MOSS,** the coastal live oak ranks as among the most photogenic of trees. Rarely exceeding 65 feet in height, live oak more than makes up for its small stature by having a wide-spreading crown and a thick trunk, often buttressed, which gives the tree an almost tropical look. Leaves are simple, unlobed, and waxy, and the tree is evergreen. Acorns are sharply pointed at the tip and are much sought after by many bird and mammal species. The live oak is an essential species to the coastal ecosystem not only as an important food plant but because its roots aid immensely in stabilizing the soil against the often harsh elements of weather.

Other oak species, especially the **LAUREL OAK** and **BLACKJACK**

Spanish Moss, an air plant related to the many Bromeliad species of the American Tropics, is abundant throughout the coastal forest.

Exposure to salt spray denudes the branches. Understory of Spanish Dagger.

OAK, are common components of coastal forests. Blackjack Oak is deciduous, its leaves turning reddish brown in fall.

YAUPON HOLLY is a common shrub that often dominates the understory. It has evergreen leaves with stiff, wavy margins. The red berries, which often cover the bush in late summer, are an important food for many species of migrating birds.

Birds are a major feature of Gulf Coast ecology. The Texas Gulf Coast makes a natural highway to and from Central America for several hundred bird species ranging from rails to warblers. In spring, immense waves of migrating warblers, orioles, grosbeaks, thrushes, tanagers, and others sometimes seem to cover trees, shrubs, and even manicured lawns in Rockport or High Island. At such times, birds such as the **BAY-BREASTED** and **BLACKBURNIAN WARBLERS,** which nest amid the cool spruces of the Canadian boreal forest, hop along beaches snatching up midges and other insects.

During most of the year, water birds, by their very conspicuousness, attract most attention. Stately Brown and American White pelicans glide effortlessly along the shoreline, their wings almost touching the water. **BROWN PELICANS** dive in head first, plunging beneath the water to scoop up fish in their saclike lower jaw. **AMERICAN WHITE PELICANS** forage from the surface, sweeping tiny fish and shrimp into their huge bills. Several heron and egret species are common and easily seen. Among them, the **REDDISH EGRET** is perhaps the most interesting because of its distinctive feeding behavior. Reddish Egrets open their wings a bit and seem to dance in shallow water, stirring up the bottom with one foot to

Figure 16. Reddish Egret feeding

expose fish, shrimp, crabs, and other morsels. This vigorous style of feeding makes the Reddish Egret resemble a huge windup toy bird, moving erratically round and round. Reddish Egrets are dull brownish red on the head and neck; the body is slate blue. A snow-white form is found in the East. Either color phase can be identified as a Reddish Egret by the ragged, shaggy head feathering and the long pale pink bill, black at the tip.

Another wading bird not to be missed is the **ROSEATE SPOONBILL,** whose name describes both its overall color and its most distinctive field mark. The pale green bill is widened and flattened at the tip, and does indeed look much like a large spoon attached to the bird's face. Flocks of spoonbills feed in shallow water, sweeping their bills from side to side as they search for small marine animals.

The most sought-after bird of the Texas Gulf Coast is probably the magnificent **WHOOPING CRANE,** which winters at Aransas National Wildlife Refuge near Corpus Christi. From a low of 15 birds in 1941, the population of this endangered species has risen to the current number of approximately 150, virtually all of which winter on the marshes of the 54,829-acre Aransas Refuge. The Whooping Crane stands at 50 inches, making it North America's tallest bird species. Its wingspread is nearly 7 feet. In fall, these huge black and white cranes travel here in family groups from their breeding grounds in Wood Buffalo National Park in northern Canada, 2,600 miles to the north. Fully protected on the

Family of Whooping Cranes at Aransas Refuge.

large Aransas refuge, their numbers, while still precarious, have made a modest recovery over the years.

Less awe-inspiring perhaps than Whooping Cranes but interesting nonetheless are the two similar grackle species whose ranges overlap along the Gulf Coast. You cannot help but see **BOAT-TAILED** and **GREAT-TAILED GRACKLES,** conspicuous residents of coastal marshes, fields, city parks, lawns, and even parking lots. The male is glossy black (really iridescent purple), like a slender crow, with an outrageously long and wide tail. Females, smaller than males, are rusty brown. The two species look quite alike, except that Boat-tails have dark-colored eyes and Great-tails have pale or yellow irises. Don't try to identify them until you look them in the eye! The two species also sound different. Neither is musical; their calls are about as pleasing as harsh static on a radio. Courtship behavior (males fluff their feathers, bend their necks, and spread their tail feathers), vocalizations, and eye colors vary between the two species, and each is capable of recognizing and mating only with others of its kind. Great-tails are western in distribution, ranging across Mexico and north to central Arizona and southern California. Boat-tails are southeastern, ranging north to salt marshes in New Jersey and New York. They overlap only in westernmost Louisiana and along the Texas Gulf Coast.

Among mammals, **WHITETAIL DEER** are common, and **EASTERN FOX SQUIRRELS, ARMADILLOS,** and **OPOSSUMS** can seem to be everywhere. One animal can be cantankerous and even dangerous. This is the **WILD BOAR,** or Feral Hog, not native to the region but a descendant of the European Hog. Established as a breeding species at Aransas National Wildlife Refuge, the Wild Boar is a rugged-look-

American Alligator basking in the sun.

ing animal, with shaggy, coarse hair and a long, down-pointing snout. Native **COLLARED PECCARIES** are smaller and, compared with Wild Boars, much cuter. Wild Boars are considered a nuisance species because their rooting activities and big appetites have a substantial effect on the ecology of the oak forests.

AMERICAN ALLIGATORS, once considered a threatened species, have rebounded with protection and are common in many swamp forests along the Texas coast, especially around Aransas Refuge.

WHERE TO VISIT: Aransas National Wildlife Refuge, north of Corpus Christi, is perhaps the best example of the ecology of the Gulf Coast. The refuge contains Virginia Live Oak forest, thickets, and fresh- and saltwater marshes. Tour boats from Rockport operate in winter, taking birders to see Whooping Cranes. Other national wildlife refuges include Anahuac and San Bernard, both near Galveston. These refuges are sparsely forested but are ideal places to see waterbirds, especially wintering rails. Padre Island National Seashore is beautiful, and both Rockport and High Island (just north of Galveston) host remarkable numbers of migrating birds, especially in spring.

EDWARDS PLATEAU FOREST   PLATE 6

INDICATOR PLANTS

CANOPY TREES: *Ashe Juniper, Lacey Oak, Cedar Elm, Pinchot Juniper,* Virginia Live Oak, Post Oak, Texas Oak, Bigelow Oak, Chinkapin Oak, Honey Mesquite, Gregg Catclaw, American Baldcypress, Southern Hackberry, Texas Ash, Eastern Cottonwood, Texas Persimmon, Pecan, Netleaf Hackberry, Eastern Sycamore, Texas

Walnut, Florida Linden, Texas Madrone, Ashleaf Maple, Bigtooth Maple, Coastal Plain Willow.

UNDERSTORY TREES AND SHRUBS: *Agarito, Texas Butterflybush,* Inland Ceanothus, Scarlet Leatherflower, Texas Mulberry, Blanco Crabapple, Escarpment Black Cherry, Mexican Plum, Pink Mimosa, Huisache, Sensitive-brier, Eastern Redbud, Mountain Laurel, Littleleaf Sumac, Twistleaf Yucca.

HERBACEOUS SPECIES: *Eastern Prickly-pear, Firewheel,* Ball Moss (epiphyte), Goldenwaves, Greenthread, Prairie Larkspur, Engelmann's Sunflower, Square-bud Primrose, Prairie Brazoria, Redspike Mexican Hat, Texas Lantana, Texas Bluebonnet, Dakota Vervain, Scarlet Penstemon, Texas Milkweed, Cedar Sage, Texas Toadflax, Prairie Goldenrod, plus about 400 other species including several endemic to the region. Grasses, especially *Prairie Three-Awn* (Needlegrass), are often abundant. Vines include Western White Honeysuckle, Bullbrier Greenbrier, Winter Grape, and Sweet Mountain Grape.

INDICATOR ANIMALS

BIRDS: *Golden-cheeked Warbler, Black-capped Vireo, Cave Swallow,* Ladder-backed Woodpecker, Northern Bobwhite, Wild Turkey, White-winged Dove, Mourning Dove, Inca Dove, Yellow-billed Cuckoo, Greater Roadrunner, Eastern Screech-Owl, Great Horned Owl, Chuck-will's-widow, Black-chinned Hummingbird, Green Kingfisher, Golden-fronted Woodpecker, Eastern Kingbird, Western Kingbird, Scissor-tailed Flycatcher, Ash-throated Flycatcher, Acadian Flycatcher, Eastern Phoebe, Scrub Jay, Common Raven, Tufted Titmouse (Black-crested), Carolina Chickadee, Verdin, Bewick's Wren, Carolina Wren, Canyon Wren, Cactus Wren, Blue-gray Gnatcatcher, Eastern Bluebird, Long-billed Thrasher, White-eyed Vireo, Bell's Vireo, Yellow Warbler, Yellow-breasted Chat, Northern Cardinal, Blue Grosbeak, Indigo Bunting, Painted Bunting, Canyon Towhee, Rufous-crowned Sparrow, Lark Sparrow, Bronzed Cowbird, Brown-headed Cowbird, Hooded Oriole, Summer Tanager, Lesser Goldfinch.

MAMMALS: *Mexican Freetail Bat,* Armadillo, Eastern Fox Squirrel, Eastern Cottontail, Blacktail Jackrabbit, Raccoon, Collared Peccary, Whitetail Deer.

DESCRIPTION

The Edwards Plateau, part of the Texas Hill Country, is a land of juniper-covered hillsides, limestone soils, scrubby oaks, diverse wildflowers, and canyons rich with riverine species such as Cedar Elm and Baldcypress. The plateau is located in central Texas, from Austin and San Antonio west to Fort Stockton and Midland.

Annual rainfall is about 30 inches in the easternmost part of the plateau but decreases to 10–15 inches in the western parts. Because of low rainfall, the forests of the Edwards Plateau consist for the most part of small trees and scattered shrubs. Predominant among the trees are Ashe Juniper and Virginia Live Oak, which often form dense stands, especially on hillsides. The Edwards Plateau is ecologically unique, supporting at least seven endemic wildflower species (species found nowhere else) as well as two endangered bird species, one of which, the Golden-cheeked Warbler, nests nowhere else. The Black-capped Vireo, also an endangered species, is common in parts of the Edwards Plateau.

The region abounds in hills, on the slopes of which grow Ashe Junipers, locally called cedar. Several oak species, particularly Virginia Live Oak, are common among the cedar, especially at the bases of hills. These small, widely spreading trees are densely laden with Ball Moss, an air plant (epiphyte) related to the tropical bromeliads. River valleys and streambeds are bordered by Baldcypress as well as Cedar Elm, Pecan, sycamores, and other species. Some groves of Bigtooth Maple, relict populations stranded at the close of the most recent period of glaciation, can be found on the plateau. The area is generally quite hot in summer, and many desert plants and wildflowers occur, including many legumes.

Many bird species are present, especially during breeding season in the summer months. These include two endangered species, the Golden-cheeked Warbler and Black-capped Vireo. Other birds include a combination of eastern and western species, as well as some species, such as the Green Kingfisher, most characteristic of Mexico and the Lower Rio Grande Valley.

Spring wildflowers abound among the dense oaks and shrubs of the Edwards Plateau.

Often-seen mammals include the Armadillo, Whitetail Deer, and Eastern Fox Squirrel. The region contains several scattered limestone caverns that support huge populations of Mexican Freetail Bats.

SIMILAR FOREST COMMUNITIES: The Edwards Plateau shares many plant and animal species with the lower Rio Grande forest.

RANGE: Limited to central Texas, from Austin and San Antonio west to Fort Stockton and Midland. Best seen in Kerr, Uvalde, Real, and Bandera counties.

REMARKS

The Edwards Plateau is one of the most scenic and ecologically interesting areas in Texas, a state with no shortage of good areas for naturalists. The well-eroded limestone that makes up much of the geology forms diverse landscapes of hills, flatlands, and sheltered river valleys. Waters are cool and clear, densely shaded by overarching **AMERICAN BALDCYPRESS** and **CEDAR ELM.** Exposed hillsides bake in summer's heat, and much of the forest seems stunted. Only the hardy Ashe Juniper and some associated shrubs can thrive. Ashe Juniper and robust oaks of several species abound. The forest is generally open and easy to walk through, though some areas of dense Ashe Juniper and oaks can be essentially impenetrable. Terrain is almost always uneven, except in areas largely given over to ranching.

The most characteristic tree of the Edwards Plateau is the **ASHE JUNIPER,** commonly called Mexican, mountain, or blueberry cedar. This tree ranges northward into Oklahoma, Arkansas, and Missouri, but it is most abundant throughout the Hill Country of central and northeastern Texas. It shows a high affinity for limestone soils; in fact, its presence indicates underlying limestone. Ashe Juniper is quite similar to Oneseed Juniper, which is common in Mexican Madrean foothill forest (page 275). The tree is bushy, almost shrublike, and often grows in dense, clumped stands called cedar brakes. Ashe Juniper can survive for up to 350 years, producing abundant cones every two or three years. Many bird and mammal species feed on juniper cones. The tree is tolerant of natural fires, and fire suppression, as well as clear-cutting, has led to a reduction in Ashe Juniper in many places on the plateau.

Several oak species form a major part of the vegetation of the Edwards Plateau. Two species, **VIRGINIA LIVE OAK** and **LACEY OAK,** are common, but other species such as **POST OAK, TEXAS OAK, BIGELOW OAK,** and **CHINKAPIN OAK** are often seen as well. Lacey Oak is essentially confined to the Edwards Plateau, but live oak is common throughout the Southeast, especially along coastal regions. Oaks of the Edwards Plateau tend to be small, rarely reaching 50 feet, but widely spreading, somewhat like large shrubs. Oaks seem to attract air plants, or epiphytes, and the inner branches in particular are frequently lined with them. Most prominent on the Edwards Plateau is **BALL MOSS,** which looks at first glance like a thick hairball but is a close relative of Spanish Moss as well as the many bromeliad species that characterize tropical rain forests. Ball Moss grows densely on oak branches but can also attach to telephone wires.

Leguminous plants, including trees, shrubs, and wildflowers, abound on the drier slopes of the Edwards Plateau. **HONEY MESQUITE** is common, as are **PINK MIMOSA, GREGG CATCLAW, HUISACHE, TEXAS REDBUD,** and **SENSITIVE-BRIER.** This latter species is one of several plants whose compound leaves fold up instantly when touched. The colorful **TEXAS BLUEBONNET,** which blooms from March through May, is one of the many leguminous wildflowers.

AGARITO is among the most commonly encountered shrubs of the plateau. At first glance this plant appears to be a small species of oak. The leaves are sharply lobed and oaklike. However, Agarito is a desert-adapted shrub that blooms with yellow flowers from February to April, followed by bright red berrylike fruits. Leaves are compound, with 3–7 very sharply pointed leaflets—so sharply pointed, in fact, that they remind the careless walker of cactus.

One bird species, the colorful **GOLDEN-CHEEKED WARBLER,** which nests only in central Texas and mostly on the Edwards Plateau, depends on Ashe Juniper for nesting material. This warbler uses bark strips taken from Ashe Juniper to line its nest. Indeed, the bird often places its nest in a juniper. The best places to search for the Golden-cheeked Warbler (which arrives in Texas in March and remains until breeding is completed in July) are among mixed oaks and Ashe Juniper, often near water. The bird frequently forages among broad-leaved trees such as **ARIZONA WALNUT, CEDAR ELM,** and **BIGTOOTH MAPLE.** You may have to search—a Golden-cheek pair can have a territory as large as 25 acres, though in more food-rich habitats territory size is closer to 3 acres. After breeding season, Golden-cheeks migrate along the Mexican Sierra Madre Oriental mountains to their wintering range in Nicaragua, Honduras, and Guatemala.

The Golden-cheeked Warbler is an endangered species that has seriously suffered from habitat loss due to land clearing and from nest parasitism by **BROWN-HEADED COWBIRDS** and **BRONZED COWBIRDS,** both of which abound in the region. Female cowbirds build no nests of their own; they are skilled at locating other birds' nests and quickly depositing an egg. The nestling cowbird hatches sooner, grows quicker, and is more aggressive than its brood-mates. In extreme cases, a Golden-cheek pair may raise more cowbirds than warblers!

The **BLACK-CAPPED VIREO** is another bird species that has been victimized by habitat reduction and cowbird parasitism. It, too, is listed as an endangered species. Black-capped Vireos range from Mexico and southern Texas north to parts of Oklahoma and Kansas, especially on the Edwards Plateau, particularly among the dense oaks. Unfortunately, much of this favored habitat has been cleared to make room for ranching and, more recently, for housing developments. The vireo is an active bird, singing its harsh warbling song while foraging. It can be hard to see, as it is often hidden among the dense, shaded branches of thick oaks.

Many other bird species occur on the Edwards Plateau. The small southwestern **LADDER-BACKED WOODPECKER** may be seen foraging on an oak at the foot of which stands a **NORTHERN BOBWHITE,** a quail basically eastern in distribution. Taken together, the bird community is a mixture of eastern and western species, plus several species, such as the **GREEN KINGFISHER** and **LONG-BILLED THRASHER,** that are more typical of the Lower Rio Grande Valley. One species that has increased dramatically in recent years is the **CAVE SWALLOW.** This bird, which resembles the more widespread Cliff Swallow (Plate 2), can be identified by its pale throat and dark chestnut forehead (exactly the opposite of the Cliff Swallow's pattern). Cave Swallows nest in many places on the plateau including roadside culverts, picnic shelters, and, of course, caves.

The swallows sometimes share caves with a much more abundant species, the **MEXICAN FREETAIL BAT.** Two caves on the plateau each support in excess of 10 million of these flying insectivorous mammals. At dusk the bats begin to stream out in numbers so vast that from a distance they appear to be smoke trails. The bats range widely over central and southern Texas, foraging on flying insects and returning to their cave at dawn. Despite their seemingly vast numbers, Texas populations of Mexican Freetail Bats are vulnerable to habitat loss (the caves) and the effects of pesticides sprayed on fields and picked up by the bats' insect prey.

The sharp geological relief of the Edwards Plateau includes valleys where clear streams and rivers flow. The vegetation along these riverine areas includes an abundance of Baldcypress, Cedar Elm, **TEXAS WALNUT, TEXAS ASH, SOUTHERN HACKBERRY,** and **EASTERN COTTONWOOD.** River banks are often draped with vines such as **WESTERN WHITE HONEYSUCKLE, BULLBRIER GREENBRIER, WINTER GRAPE,** and **SWEET MOUNTAIN GRAPE.** In the quiet shade of the river's edge you may find a Green Kingfisher or hear a **YELLOW-BILLED CUCKOO** singing its soft *chaow-chaow-chaow.*

Figure 17. Mexican Freetail Bat

Another great attraction of the Edwards Plateau is the amazing diversity of wildflowers that carpet the plateau every spring. From colorful cactus, like the **EASTERN PRICKLY-PEAR,** to the unmistakable **FIREWHEEL,** the field botanist has an embarrassment of riches to sort through. Over 400 species of wildflowers have been found on the plateau including several endemics. These include **SYCAMORE-LEAF SNOWBELL, TEXAS BARBERRY, CANYON MOCK-ORANGE, SCARLET LEATHERFLOWER, BRACTED TWIST-FLOWER, PLATEAU MILKVINE,** and **TWO-FLOWER ANEMONE.**

The **ARMADILLO** is one of the commonest mammals on the Edwards Plateau. Related to the anteaters and sloths of South America, armadillos are ground-dwelling mammals that probe the vegetation in search of worms and insects. Mostly hairless, their skin is hardened and bonelike. When threatened, the animal curls into a tight ball, protected by its bony armor. Armadillos make burrows, often along stream banks. Armadillos forage both night and day but are more often seen after dark.

Other common mammals include the colorful tan **EASTERN FOX SQUIRREL** and **WHITETAIL DEER. EASTERN COTTONTAIL** rabbits are frequently sighted, and in more desertlike regions on the plateau, **BLACKTAIL JACKRABBIT** can be seen.

WHERE TO VISIT: Several state parks across the Edwards Plateau afford ideal opportunities to see the natural history of the region. These include Garner, Meridian, Pedernales Falls, and Lost Maples parks and the Kerr Wildlife Management Area. Lost Maples is particularly recommended as it is home to all of the species discussed above and also contains a relict population of Bigtooth

Maple, a close relative of the eastern Sugar Maple. Bigtooth Maple is widely distributed in the Far West, but only a few small relict stands, believed to be remains of the Ice Age, occur in Texas and Oklahoma.

ESSAY

MEXICAN BIRDS

Many of the resident bird species of the Lower Rio Grande region are essentially Mexican (or tropical American) in origin and distribution. These include such species as Least Grebe, Green and Ringed Kingfishers, Groove-billed Ani, White-tipped Dove, Kiskadee, Green Jay, Altamira and Audubon's orioles, and Olive Sparrow. In recent years, as increasing numbers of birders have visited the Lower Rio Grande Valley, there have been more frequent sightings of rare bird species of Mexican origin. Some of these species are now becoming established residents of the Brownsville region, while others, which in this area are called *extralimitals* because they are beyond their normal ranges, are seen only occasionally.

There are probably two reasons why increasing numbers of typically Mexican species are showing up on south Texas bird lists. One is that there are simply more birders looking. The number of active field birders has increased steadily in recent decades, as have the numbers of books on how to find and identify birds. Many field guides to American birds now include illustrations of extralimital Mexican species, so birders know what to look for. In addition, excellent bird-finding guides now exist that tell exactly where to search for choice species. So birders can maximize the number of exotic species they encounter. Telephone hotlines and rare bird alerts keep birders informed on the latest rarities being seen in the area. Many natural history tours led by expert naturalists feature trips to the Lower Rio Grande region.

A second reason for the influx of Mexican bird species across the U.S. border may have to do with reduced habitat in Mexico. As habitat declines, bird species must range more widely to find suitable habitat. Ironically, however, this lack of habitat is one reason so many bird species are seen in the Lower Rio Grande region. Birds are forced into a few forest areas, and the birder visiting these areas can be relatively confident of seeing the desired species.

The following primarily Mexican or Central American bird species are occasionally seen in the Lower Rio Grande region:

MASKED DUCK, a small, reddish brown, black-faced duck with a spiked tail, shaped like a Ruddy Duck.

MUSCOVY DUCK, a large black duck with white wing patches. Often domesticated. Seen regularly at Salineño.

NORTHERN JACANA, a dark reddish marsh bird that can walk on lily pads. Has long slender toes and bright yellow wing patches.

HOOK-BILLED KITE, a dark bird of prey with a banded tail and a sharply hooked beak. Feeds on large snails.

APLOMADO FALCON, a large slender falcon, brownish gray above, reddish below. Recently reintroduced at Laguna Atascosa National Wildlife Refuge.

RED-BILLED PIGEON, a dark pigeon with a red bill. Frequent around Bentsen State Park.

RUDDY GROUND-DOVE, a plain-breasted, chunky dove. Males are reddish.

GREEN PARAKEET, a long-tailed, all-green parrot. Now established in Brownsville.

RED-CROWNED PARROT, a chunky parrot, short-tailed, with red on wings and head. Now established in Brownsville, but may be escaped cage birds.

YELLOW-HEADED PARROT, a chunky parrot with an all-yellow head and red on shoulders. Virtually all sightings attributed to escaped cage birds.

FERRUGINOUS PYGMY-OWL, a small, hawklike, reddish owl, often observed in daytime. Occasionally seen in forest below Falcon Dam.

PAURAQUE, a large nightjar with white wing patches and white outer tail feathers (most conspicuous on males). Common in dry washes and on roads at night.

GREEN VIOLET-EAR, a dark green hummingbird with deep blue patches on its face and breast.

BUFF-BELLIED HUMMINGBIRD, light green with buff belly and red bill. Relatively common around Brownsville, Santa Ana National Wildlife Refuge, and Sabal Palm Sanctuary.

COUCH'S KINGBIRD, very similar to Western Kingbird but with notched tail lacking white outer tail feathers. Recently separated as a species from Tropical Kingbird, which occurs in the U.S. only in southern Arizona.

NORTHERN BEARDLESS-TYRANNULET, a small, active, gray flycatcher often found near water.

ROSE-THROATED BECARD, a chunky, dark gray flycatcher with a rosy throat. More common in southern Arizona.

BROWN JAY, a very large and conspicuous all-brown jay, usually in flocks. Young birds have all-yellow bills. Increasingly common along Rio Grande (especially Falcon State Recreation Area below Falcon Dam).

MEXICAN CROW, a sleek, shiny, small crow, seen at Brownsville dump.

CLAY-COLORED ROBIN, an all-brown robin with a buffy breast. Skulks in dense brush.

RUFOUS-BACKED ROBIN, reddish brown (rufous) on back and flanks, gray on head, wings, and tail. More often seen in southern Arizona.

TROPICAL PARULA, a warbler, similar to widespread Northern Parula but more yellow below. Occasional at Sabal Palm Sanctuary and elsewhere.

GOLDEN-CROWNED WARBLER, olive above, yellow below, with a yellow crown. Usually seen in winter.

BLUE BUNTING, similar to Indigo Bunting but more deeply colored and bill more rounded. Usually seen in winter at Bentsen State Park.

WHITE-COLLARED SEEDEATER, a small brown finch with black and white wings. Has been a highly local Lower Rio Grande region resident (i.e., San Ygnacio, Texas) in small numbers for many years.

LOWER RIO GRANDE FOREST   PLATES 7, 8

INDICATOR PLANTS

CANOPY TREES: *Texas Ebony, Cedar Elm, Retama, Great Leadtree, Sabal Palm, Anacua, Huisache, Berlandier Ash,* Black Willow, Honey Mesquite, Texas Persimmon.

UNDERSTORY TREES AND SHRUBS: *Brasil, Spiny Hackberry, Lime Prickly-ash (Colima),* David's Milkberry, Brush Holly, Snake-eyes, Guayacan, Lotebush Condalia, Coyotillo, Mexican Buttonbush.

HERBACEOUS SPECIES: Spanish Moss, American Mistletoe, Texas Pricklypear, bunch grasses, vines such as greenbrier.

INDICATOR ANIMALS

BIRDS: *Plain Chachalaca, Ringed Kingfisher, Golden-fronted Woodpecker, Kiskadee, Green Jay, Altamira Oriole, Brown Jay, Longbilled Thrasher, Olive Sparrow, Audubon's Oriole,* Least Grebe, Black-bellied Whistling-Duck, Mottled Duck, Gray Hawk, Black-shouldered Kite, Ferruginous Pygmy-Owl, Red-billed Pigeon, Common Ground-Dove, Inca Dove, White-winged Dove, White-tipped Dove, Groove-billed Ani, Pauraque, Buff-bellied Hummingbird, Green Kingfisher, Ladder-backed Woodpecker, Northern Beardless-Tyrannulet, Couch's Kingbird, Brown-crested Flycatcher, Tufted (Black-crested) Titmouse, Verdin, Hooded Oriole, Bronzed Cowbird.

MAMMALS: Ocelot, Jaguarundi, Eastern Fox Squirrel, Armadillo, Coyote, Eastern Cottontail, Collared Peccary, Whitetail Deer.

REPTILES: *Texas Tortoise,* Texas Spiny Lizard, Speckled Racer, Texas Indigo Snake.

ANTS: Texas Harvester Ant, Texas Leaf-cutter Ant.

DESCRIPTION

This forest is semiarid, with 18–25 inches of rainfall annually and summer temperatures often in excess of 100°F. Because of the overall aridity of the climate, the forest generally consists of small trees and shrubs, often dense, many of which are spiny and desertlike. Trees are tallest along rivers, but even here trees rarely exceed 75 feet in height. In many places trees are abundantly laden with Spanish Moss as well as other epiphytes. Mistletoe is common. Shrubs, especially spiny species, as well as shrub-sized prickly-pears, are often abundant, so bushwhackers should beware. Many trees and shrubs (Honey Mesquite, Huisache, Guayacan) are leguminous, with delicate compound leaves and seeds in conspicuous pods. Open areas abound with bunch grasses. This forest attracts numerous birders because only here can such Mexican "specialties" as Plain Chachalaca, Ringed Kingfisher, Kiskadee, Altamira Oriole, and Green and Brown jays be encountered within the borders of the United States. The most abundant mammals are Eastern Fox Squirrels, Eastern Cottontails, Armadillos, and Whitetail Deer, though three elusive cats, the Ocelot, Jaguarundi, and Bobcat, occur sparingly. Ocelot and Jaguarundi are both endangered species.

SIMILAR FOREST COMMUNITIES: See Edwards Plateau forest; also arroyo and desert scrub.

RANGE: Extreme south Texas from Harlingen to Brownsville.

Subtropical forest of the Lower Rio Grande Valley.

Visitors to the southernmost part of Texas need not cross the border to experience a bit of Mexican natural history. Today, only about 5 percent of the natural habitat of the Lower Rio Grande Valley remains, and these tracts of Lower Rio Grande forest are but remnants.

The forest is most lush along the Rio Grande. This subtropical riparian forest is best seen along the edges of *resacas*, oxbow lakes that were once part of the flowing waters of the Rio Grande. It is along the *resacas* that species such as Cedar Elm, Retama, and Anacua abound, along with Rio Grande Ash and various willow and vine species. **CEDAR ELM**, a deciduous species, reaches heights of 75–80 feet and is best identified by its arrow-shaped, toothed leaves, which are smaller than any other North American elm species. The bark has scaly ridges and deep fissures. **RETAMA**, also called Jerusalem-thorn, is instantly recognized by its smooth green bark and long sharp thorns. The slender whiplike branches are lined with tiny leaflets. Flowers are yellow and resemble the flowers of peas. Pods are long and straight.

In the quiet waters of the *resacas*, the diminutive **LEAST GREBE** dives from the water's surface in pursuit of fish, while overhead the 8-inch **GREEN KINGFISHER** plunges from the air with equal purpose. The slate blue and reddish **RINGED KINGFISHER**, twice the size of the Green Kingfisher, is unmistakable as it courses along uttering its harsh rattling call. Both kingfisher species are widely distributed and common throughout Central and South America. Other *resaca* inhabitants more characteristic of equatorial latitudes include the rather drab **MOTTLED DUCK** and the colorful **BLACK-BELLIED WHISTLING-DUCK**.

One unique species dependent on *resacas* is **SABAL PALM**. This plant is the only palm native to the Rio Grande delta. All others, such as the species commonly planted around hotels and along roadsides, are nonnative, introduced species. Sabal Palm once ranged more widely, from northeastern Mexico well into southern Texas. However, the plant requires substantial amounts of moisture, and the climate here has become drier than in previous times. This, plus loss of natural habitat as agriculture grew, has made Sabal Palm an endangered species. The current U.S. population, confined to one sanctuary (see below, **WHERE TO VISIT**), is now utterly separated from the nearest Mexican population. Sabal Palm has wide spiky fronds that hang loosely from the tree.

Upland forest is drier and shorter in stature than riverine forest and consists of numerous leguminous trees and shrubs, many of which are thorny. This forest is called *monte* or *matorral* in Spanish, and can be generally thought of as a subtropical thorny wood-

Figure 18. Sabal Palm

land. In many areas, elements of the riverine and *matorral* forest intermingle, adding to the diversity of this unique natural area.

TEXAS EBONY, a member of the huge family of legumes, is characteristic of *matorral* forest. Named for its dark-colored wood, which is used in cabinetmaking, this tree is recognized by its spreading crown and evergreen compound leaves with oval leaflets. When in bloom during the summer months, the tree is covered with light yellow flower clusters, attracting many insect pollinators. The seed pod is dark brown, curved at the bottom.

GREAT LEADTREE, also called Tepeguaje, has feathery, fernlike compound leaves and smooth, grayish brown bark. Its white flower clusters mature into long, thin, flattened seed pods, with pealike seeds bulging within. Great Leadtree is a fast-growing species that quickly invades recently disturbed land. Because it grows rapidly, it reestablishes ground cover essential to wildlife species such as Plain Chachalaca, White-tipped Dove, and Collared Peccary.

The **TEXAS PERSIMMON** is one of only two members of its tropical plant family to reach the U.S. This deciduous species is a close relative of the more widely distributed Common Persimmon. Not confined to the Lower Rio Grande Valley, Texas Persimmon grows across the Trans-Pecos. Its rounded fruits, 1 inch in diameter, turn black when ripe in August and are an important food for many wildlife species.

SPANISH MOSS is often abundant, draped from the boughs of many tree species, providing the forest with an ethereal look. This plant, which is a member of the tropical pineapple family, is an epiphyte, or air plant. It grows upon other plants (and occasionally on utility wires), but it uses its host only for attachment, not for nutrition. Spanish Moss obtains its food through photosynthesis, as do other green plants, and takes nutrients (nitrogen, calcium, etc.) from rainfall. Flowers are tiny and vary in color from tan to yellowish white.

Many shrub species occur along the *resacas* and within *matorral* forest, including **BRASIL** and **SPINY HACKBERRY**. Brasil, which can grow as a small tree as well as a shrub, has extremely sharp thorns. Thickets of Brasil are essentially impenetrable, making ideal areas of protection for wildlife. Leaves feel quite leathery. Many bird species feed heavily on the black berries, which mature in summer. Spiny Hackberry, also called Granjeno, is identified by its dark, evergreen, toothed leaves that feel rather rough. Like Brasil, Spiny Hackberry is well endowed with sharp thorns and forms dense thickets. Its small orange fruits are also an important wildlife food.

Two ant species are conspicuous forest residents. Look for **TEXAS LEAF-CUTTER ANTS** moving in narrow columns, each carrying a piece of freshly clipped leaf. These ants, which are among the northernmost representatives of an abundant group of tropical ants, take the leaves into a large subterranean colony, where the leaves serve as food for a fungus that forms the ants' only food. Another name for these ants is Fungus Garden Ants. Leaf-cutter Ants are most commonly observed in shady areas. In more open, drier areas, you might see the **TEXAS HARVESTER ANT,** often simply called red ants. These ants collect seeds from grasses and herbaceous plants and carry them to their underground colony, where they are a major food source. The ants also feed on other insects and can give a painful sting. Many species of harvester ants occur throughout the West, especially in prairie and desert habitats.

Many naturalists visit the Lower Rio Grande Valley to see birds. Many of the most common species are Mexican in distribution, reaching the United States only in the Lower Rio Grande Valley. Among these are the Plain Chachalaca, Ringed Kingfisher, Kiskadee, Green Jay, and Altamira Oriole.

The **PLAIN CHACHALACA,** at first glance, resembles a large, slender, long-tailed, olive-brown chicken. When it flies, which it seems to do reluctantly, it reveals a white outer tail band. The Plain Chachalaca is not a chicken or quail, but a member of the tropical bird family Cracidae, which includes 44 species of guans, curassows, and chachalacas, all from Central and South America. Only the Plain Chachalaca reaches Texas. Named for its loud, unmusical *cha-cha-lac* call, often given simultaneously by a flock of a dozen or more birds, this species is a common inhabitant of thickets and often visits bird feeders. Though most often seen on the ground foraging for food, chachalacas fly well and roost among the tree branches.

The husky **RINGED KINGFISHER** has become increasingly common along the rivers of the Lower Rio Grande Valley since it first appeared back in the late 1960s. Larger than the similar and much more widely distributed Belted Kingfisher, the Ringed can be identified by the reddish breast of both males and females. In the Belted Kingfisher, only females have a reddish breast band, and female Ringed Kingfishers also have a white band between their blue upper breast and reddish lower breast and belly. The Ringed Kingfisher feeds on large fish it captures by plunging into the water. Look for it perched in the open, over a pond or river.

The **KISKADEE,** which, like the chachalaca, is named for its loud, ringing voice *(kisk-a-dee!)*, is, at nearly 10 inches long, the largest tyrant flycatcher to reach North America. Formerly called Derby Flycatcher, this species is widespread and abundant throughout tropical America. It is unmistakable, with bright yellow underparts, bold black stripes through the eyes, and bright reddish brown on the wings. Look for the Kiskadee near water, such as around *resacas*. In addition to flying from a perch to capture airborne insects, Kiskadees will often snatch fish, kingfisher style, from the water. The Kiskadee makes a very bulky nest of grasses and other plant materials, usually placed deep inside a thorny mesquite or similar tree.

Despite its brilliant color, the **GREEN JAY** can be difficult to see when it is perched deep within dense green foliage. This jay lacks a crest. It is identified by its overall green color and yellow outer tail feathers, which are conspicuous in flight. The head is blue, the throat black. Green Jays range south into Ecuador but cross the U.S. border only in the Lower Rio Grande Valley. During breeding season Green Jays are somewhat reclusive, but they are otherwise gregarious, noisy, and easily attracted to bird feeders.

The 10-inch **ALTAMIRA ORIOLE** (formerly called Lichtenstein's Oriole) is an almost electric orange alternating with black. Adults have an orange shoulder patch, separating them from the much smaller but similarly patterned Hooded Oriole. Like other oriole species, Altamiras build long basketlike nests that are suspended from a branch, often overhanging water. Cedar Elms are popular nest trees. Another oriole species that is found only along the Lower Rio Grande is Audubon's Oriole (formerly named Black-headed Oriole). Almost as large as the Altamira, this species is not orange but bright yellow, with a black head.

Many other bird species inhabit *resaca* floodplain forests and *matorral* woodland, and many are uniquely Mexican in origin. Five species of doves and pigeons, among them the **RED-BILLED PIGEON** and **WHITE-TIPPED DOVE,** feed on fruits and seeds, often flying off in a whirr of wings when flushed from the ground. The inconspicuous **OLIVE SPARROW,** another Mexican species, skulks within the thickets. Its odd song has the unmistakable cadence of a ball bouncing and slowly coming to rest. The Black-crested race of **TUFTED TITMOUSE** is abundant and conspicuous. In winter, foraging flocks of titmice are joined by **ORANGE-CROWNED** and **YELLOW-RUMPED WARBLERS, RUBY-CROWNED KINGLETS, LADDER-BACKED** and **GOLDEN-FRONTED WOODPECKERS,** and other species. The Golden-fronted Woodpecker ranges from Mexico into northern Texas, being replaced to the east by the similar Red-bellied Woodpecker and in the Southwest by the Gila Woodpecker. Golden-fronted Woodpeckers have bright gold napes and a small patch of yellow above the bill. Males have a small red cap. They are often seen on utility poles and fence posts and are abundant throughout Lower Rio Grande forests.

Three mammal species, **EASTERN FOX SQUIRREL, EASTERN COTTONTAIL,** and **ARMADILLO,** are common and often seen throughout Lower Rio Grande forests. Eastern Fox Squirrels are grayish brown above but bright reddish below, often almost orange. Cottontails are instantly identified by their puffy white tails and their general cuteness. Armadillos are the closest relatives of tropical anteaters in North America. Armadillos dig for insects with their sharp claws. As they probe and dig, they are apt to hop up and down on their front legs. When threatened, they curl into a ball, protecting their soft underparts with their bony plated skin. The armadillo is also a skilled burrower and, despite its size and appearance, a swift runner.

Two tropical cats, **OCELOT** and **JAGUARUNDI,** are native to the Lower Rio Grande region, but today they are endangered species. Ocelots, which resemble small Jaguars, once ranged throughout Texas into southernmost Oklahoma, and also into central Arizona. They have been drastically reduced by habitat loss and persecution, though now they are protected by law. However, only about 20 to 120 Ocelots still prowl southernmost Texas. Efforts are under way to buy thousands of acres of land to add to the Lower Rio Grande National Wildlife Refuge, in part so that Ocelots will have suitable habitat. Ocelots are stealthy foragers, hunting for mammals, birds, and other prey in typical catlike manner. Ocelots are skillful climbers and prey on both adult birds and nestlings. The Jaguarundi is a slender unspotted cat, usually dark-colored, with a long tail. Three color phases, gray, reddish, and black, are known. While many cats are nocturnal, Jaguarundis are sometimes active in daylight. They are rare throughout Lower Rio Grande forests.

The **TEXAS TORTOISE**, a member of the terrestrial Gopher Tortoise family, is apt to be encountered munching on a tuft of grass or a pad of prickly-pear cactus. Its domed shell is yellowish. Usually active at night, the tortoise spends most of the hot daytime hours in a burrow.

The **TEXAS SPINY LIZARD** is a pale, long-legged lizard covered by rough spines. Sixteen species of spiny lizards occur within the United States, and most are found in the Southwest, some with rather limited ranges. This species ranges from eastern Mexico into northern Texas. All spiny lizards eat insects and other arthropods.

The colorful greenish **SPECKLED RACER** is a Mexican snake species that reaches the United States only in southernmost Texas. Racers are active during the day and can move with great speed. This species feeds primarily on frogs. The Texas race of **INDIGO SNAKE**, though similar in length and habits to the Speckled Racer, is colored differently. It is brownish black around its head, becoming more bluish toward the tail. Racers and Indigo Snakes are nonpoisonous and are not constrictors. They capture small prey, kill it with pressure from their jaws, and swallow it whole.

HERE TO VISIT: There are three national wildlife refuges that preserve tracts of the Lower Rio Grande Forest. Laguna Atascosa National Wildlife Refuge, near the town of Rio Hondo, consists of 45,000 acres of coastal wetland, brushland, and dry forest. In addition to forest species, the refuge provides habitat for numerous waterfowl, herons and egrets, and shorebirds. Flocks of Sandhill Cranes can be found in migration and during the winter months. Santa Ana National Wildlife Refuge, located near Brownsville along the Rio Grande, is a 2,080-acre remnant tract of subtropical riparian forest. Dense stands of Texas Ebony, Cedar Elm, and Honey Mesquite, draped in Spanish Moss, provide habitat for 377 bird species, including most of the Mexican rarities. The National Audubon Society's Sabal Palm Grove Sanctuary is located adjacent to the Lower Rio Grande Valley National Wildlife Refuge, also near Brownsville. The 172-acre sanctuary protects a unique 32-acre grove of Sabal Palm and features a 1-kilometer self-guided nature trail. Other areas of interest include Bentsen-Rio Grande Valley State Park and Falcon State Recreation Area. Bentsen encompasses 588 acres and includes many trails through *matorral*, or thorn-scrub subtropical forest typical of Mexico. Along the river below Falcon Dam, look for Ringed Kingfisher, Ferruginous Pygmy-Owl, Brown Jay, and Audubon's Oriole.

ESSAY

LOWER RIO GRANDE VALLEY WILDLIFE CORRIDOR

A wildlife sanctuary is a form of habitat security. An area is set aside in perpetuity so that native wildlife species may have adequate and suitable habitat, and so that we humans can see what the natural ecology of an area is all about. We visit sanctuaries, refuges, and state and national parks to see nature as it no longer is in most areas frequented by humans, where development has taken over.

How effective are wildlife sanctuaries? Two factors weigh heavily. One is size, the other is access.

If a wildlife sanctuary is tiny, a small natural island in a sea of farmland, parking lots, or housing developments, its effectiveness in providing habitat will be compromised. Many species require large ranges. Large mammals, birds of prey, and others are lost from small sanctuaries.

An isolated sanctuary also poses severe potential problems for wildlife. Many species move around, hunting in a variety of habitats. Many are migratory and must move from one place to another. Isolated refuges may be too isolated to be of any substantial use to migrating animals. It won't do any good to have habitat if the creatures can't get to it or if it is too small to hold them.

The Lower Rio Grande Valley, as mentioned in the text, has experienced about a 95 percent loss of natural habitat. Sanctuaries such as Bentsen and Falcon Dam Parks, Sabal Palm, Santa Ana, and Laguna Atascosa are essentially well separated from one another, small islands in a huge sea of alien landscape. They stand to suffer from the effects of isolation. For this reason, there is an ambitious land acquisition program now in progress to create a wildlife corridor along the southern portion of the Rio Grande, including a large area of land in the Lower Rio Grande Valley now given over to farming and ranching.

This corridor, to be called the Lower Rio Grande Valley National Wildlife Refuge, would encompass about 107,500 acres and include 10 important habitat types. The refuge would supply adequate habitat for migrating species as well as 115 vertebrate species currently listed as endangered, threatened, or on the extreme periphery of their ranges. Species such as Ocelot and Jaguarundi will be among the prime beneficiaries of this extensive refuge, if its founders succeed in creating it. Because much of the land to be purchased is currently being used, generally as farmland, the natural ecology will have to be reestablished by careful reintroduction of selected native plant species, creating suitable habitat for animals. That such a bold plan exists for taking land out of the human domain and putting it back in a natural state is testimony to our changing view about the true value of nature.

EAST TEXAS PINE FOREST

INDICATOR PLANTS

TREES: *Longleaf Pine, Slash Pine, Shortleaf Pine, Loblolly Pine,* Turkey Oak, Southern Red Oak, Post Oak, Laurel Oak, Pecan, Beech, Red Maple.

SHRUBS: *Dwarf Palmetto,* Southern Bayberry, Winged Sumac.

HERBACEOUS SPECIES: Spanish Moss (epiphyte), Colicroot, Yellow Star Thistle.

INDICATOR ANIMALS

BIRDS: Turkey Vulture, Black Vulture, Red-shouldered Hawk, American Kestrel, Wild Turkey, Northern Bobwhite, Chuck-will's widow, Mourning Dove, Common Ground-Dove, Red-bellied Woodpecker, *Red-cockaded Woodpecker, Brown-headed Nuthatch,* Eastern Bluebird, Brown Thrasher, Loggerhead Shrike, Northern Parula, Yellow-throated Warbler, Prairie Warbler, Pine Warbler, Northern Cardinal, Painted Bunting, Spotted Towhee, *Bachman's Sparrow.*

MAMMALS: Opossum, Armadillo, Bobcat, Gray Fox, Raccoon, Whitetail Deer.

REPTILES: Common Garter Snake, Eastern Hognose Snake, Common Kingsnake, Rat Snake, Copperhead, Ground Skink, Eastern Fence Lizard, Eastern Box Turtle, Western Box Turtle.

DESCRIPTION

The "piney woods" is a generally open forest dominated by one or several pine species, especially Longleaf and Slash Pine. There is usually a well-defined shrub layer consisting mostly of Dwarf Palmetto but with other species as well. Because light is usually abundant, many grasses and wildflowers may be found among the shrubs. Soils tend to be sandy; the forest is generally restricted to the Gulf coastal plains, where the landscape is generally flat or gently sloping, rarely exceeding 300 feet above sea level.

Many bird species are common and easily observed in the pine forest, including several, such as the Brown-headed Nuthatch, Bachman's Sparrow, and Red-cockaded Woodpecker, that are unique to this habitat. Small bands of active, noisy Brown-headed Nuthatches, which closely resemble the western Pygmy Nuthatches (Plate 10), search for animal food among flakes of pine bark and needle clusters. Pine and Yellow-throated warblers sing melodious trills along with the buzzy-sounding Northern Parula as all three glean insects in the higher branches, while Prairie Warblers sing their high buzzy trill from the understory shrubs. Eastern Bluebirds nest in decaying pine snags, and Loggerhead Shrikes pursue insects, which they often then impale on barbed wire or thorns. At night, the Chuck-will's-widow, a nightjar with an immense mouth adapted for capturing large moths, repeatedly whistles its name. Bachman's Sparrow, a species in decline that is restricted to southern pine woods, may be found among the shrubs. The most endangered bird of the piney woods is the Red-cockaded Woodpecker, identified by the black and white ladder stripes on its back and bold white cheek markings. Small groups of Red-cockaded Woodpeckers nest exclusively among old-growth pines.

Opossums and Armadillos are abundant throughout the east Texas pine forests. Both species are most active at night (and are most frequently seen crossing roads) but are nonetheless often encountered by day. An Opossum may sometimes be found hanging from a tree, suspended by its muscular, prehensile tail, which functions as a fifth limb. If threatened, an opossum will hiss, but if that counterthreat fails, it will usually collapse and remain immobile, a behavior that mimics death. Much less frequently seen than Opossums are Bobcats and Gray Foxes, both relatively common throughout much of the pine forest.

Many reptiles frequent the piney woods, including the Eastern Hognose Snake, a species that, like the opossum, may feign death when severely threatened. One poisonous species, the Copperhead, is both common and well camouflaged among the dry leaves of the litter layer. Copperheads, like rattlesnakes, are pit vipers. They locate potential prey by detecting its body heat with heat-sensitive organs located in pits near their eyes. More abundant, and much less dangerous, the Eastern Fence Lizard is usually first observed when it scurries through dry leaves.

SIMILAR FOREST COMMUNITIES: None in this region.

RANGE: From eastern Texas east to Florida and the coastal Atlantic states. It tends to merge with southern oak forests (see *Field Guide to Eastern Forests*).

REMARKS

The mixed-pine forest is characterized by frequent natural fires, a factor probably responsible for the persistence of pines as the dominant species. In areas protected from fire, oaks tend eventually to replace pines. However, oaks are more easily damaged by fire than pines. Thus oak seedlings and saplings are destroyed by periodic fire, while pines survive. Indeed, one species, **LONGLEAF PINE,** is splendidly adapted to withstand ground fires, even as a seedling. The seedlings are often mistaken for tufts of grass, which they closely resemble. In its first 3–7 years, a Longleaf Pine devotes most of its energy to growing a long taproot, storing energy for subsequent rapid growth. While in this so-called "grass stage," it is protected by a dense cluster of long, drooping needles. After the grass stage, the young tree grows quickly until it exceeds the height where a ground fire could do extensive damage.

The bird species most closely associated with the mixed pine forest is the **RED-COCKADED WOODPECKER,** which has become an endangered species over most of its range. This species requires old-growth pines and dead and decaying trees invaded by heart fungus in which to excavate nest holes. The U.S. Forest Service has, in many areas throughout the woodpecker's range, controlled fire (which kills some old pines and makes it possible for the fungus to invade) and promoted cutting of old trees to make room for younger, more rapidly growing trees. These practices have drastically reduced habitat suitable for Red-cockaded Woodpeckers. Red-cockaded Woodpeckers live in small colonies, foraging together over an area of several hundred acres. Their nest cavities are characteristically smeared with pine resin, which may help protect the nest from predators. Rat Snakes, normally adept at climbing trees and highly predatory on nestling birds, have been observed to drop from a pine trunk housing a Red-cockaded nest once they encounter the sticky resin.

WHERE TO VISIT: The Angelina National Forest, located near Lufkin in east-central Texas, provides a good example of mixed-pine forest. Also near Lufkin, the Davy Crockett National Forest represents a forest showing the transition from pines to oaks. Red-cockaded Woodpeckers nest in both forests and can also be found in the Sabine National Forest on the border between Texas and Louisiana, near Hemphill.

PLATE 6

EDWARDS PLATEAU FOREST

ASHE JUNIPER *Juniperus ashei*
> To 40 ft. A shrubby tree, with dark evergreen, scalelike leaves. Bark peels in strips. Cones berrylike, blue-black.

AGARITO *Berberis trifoliata*
> Dense shrub with sharp-pointed leaves, somewhat oaklike. Flowers yellow, fruits berrylike, red.

LACEY OAK *Quercus glaucoides*
> Small tree, spreading crown. Leaves bluish green, leathery, gently lobed. Bark gray with deep fissures.

VIRGINIA LIVE OAK *Quercus virginiana*
> Small, spreading tree with small, unlobed, evergreen leaves. Acorns sharply pointed at tip. Bark dark brown to reddish, furrowed.

EASTERN PRICKLY-PEAR *Opuntia compressa*
> Shrubby cactus with wide pods, large yellow-orange flowers.

FIREWHEEL *Gaillardia pulchella*
> Abundant wildflower in roadsides and fields. Flower heads have red rays tipped with yellow. Blooms April–June.

GOLDEN-CHEEKED WARBLER *Dendroica chrysoparia*
> 5 in. Active; bright yellow face, black on back, top of head and wings. Song somewhat buzzy.

BLACK-CAPPED VIREO *Vireo atricapillus*
> 4.5 in. Males with black cap, white "spectacles," green above with wing bars. Females with grayish head. Active; sings while foraging.

LADDER-BACKED WOODPECKER *Picoides scalaris*
> 7 in. Small woodpecker with black and white patterning. Males with red on top of head. Call is a loud *pik!*

NORTHERN BOBWHITE *Colinus virginianus*
> 10 in. Chunky, usually seen on ground. Rusty bars along sides. Males with white on face, buffy in females. Call is a strident, whistled *bob-white!*

ARMADILLO *Dasypus novemcinctus*
> To 2.5 ft. Unmistakable. Small head with pointed face, armorlike "shell," tail. Active mostly at night.

PLATE 6

GOLDEN-CHEEKED
WARBLER

AGARITO

ASHE
JUNIPER

BLACK-CAPPED
VIREO

VIRGINIA
LIVE OAK

LACEY
OAK

LADDER-BACKED
WOODPECKER

EASTERN
PRICKLY-PEAR

NORTHERN
BOBWHITE

FIREWHEEL

ARMADILLO

PLATE 7

LOWER RIO GRANDE FOREST I

TEXAS PERSIMMON *Diospyros texana*
Small (to 50 ft.) tree with rounded crown. Leaves alternate, deciduous (though persistent), oblong, leathery, dark green, slightly hairy above, quite hairy below. Bark varies from smooth to scaly, light gray to reddish. Flowers are white, fruits are black.

TEXAS EBONY *Pithecellobium flexicaule*
Small (to 40 ft.) tree with thorny branches. Leaves evergreen, compound, dark green. Flowers are light yellow, in clusters. Seeds in dark heavy pods, curved at the tip.

CEDAR ELM *Ulmus crassifolia*
Up to 80 ft. Leaves are simple, alternate, deciduous, and dark green, and feel leathery. Bark is deeply furrowed, variable in color from gray to reddish.

BLUEWOOD CONDALIA (BRASIL) *Condalia hookeri*
An evergreen thorny shrub. Leaves are smooth and oblong. Berries are black.

PLAIN CHACHALACA *Ortalis vetula*
24 in. Slender, chickenlike, brownish olive, long tail tipped with white. Usually in flocks.

GREEN JAY *Cyanocorax yncas*
10–11 in. Overall green, with yellow outer tail feathers. Head is blue, throat black.

GOLDEN-FRONTED WOODPECKER *Melanerpes aurifrons*
10 in. Black and white barred back, wings, tail, golden orange nape. White rump is visible in flight.

JAGUARUNDI *Felis yagouaroundi*
To 50 in. Slender, dark, with long tail. Coat is unspotted black, gray, or reddish.

TEXAS SPINY LIZARD *Sceloporus olivaceus*
11 in. Pale with black markings on upper back. Rough, pointed (keeled) scales.

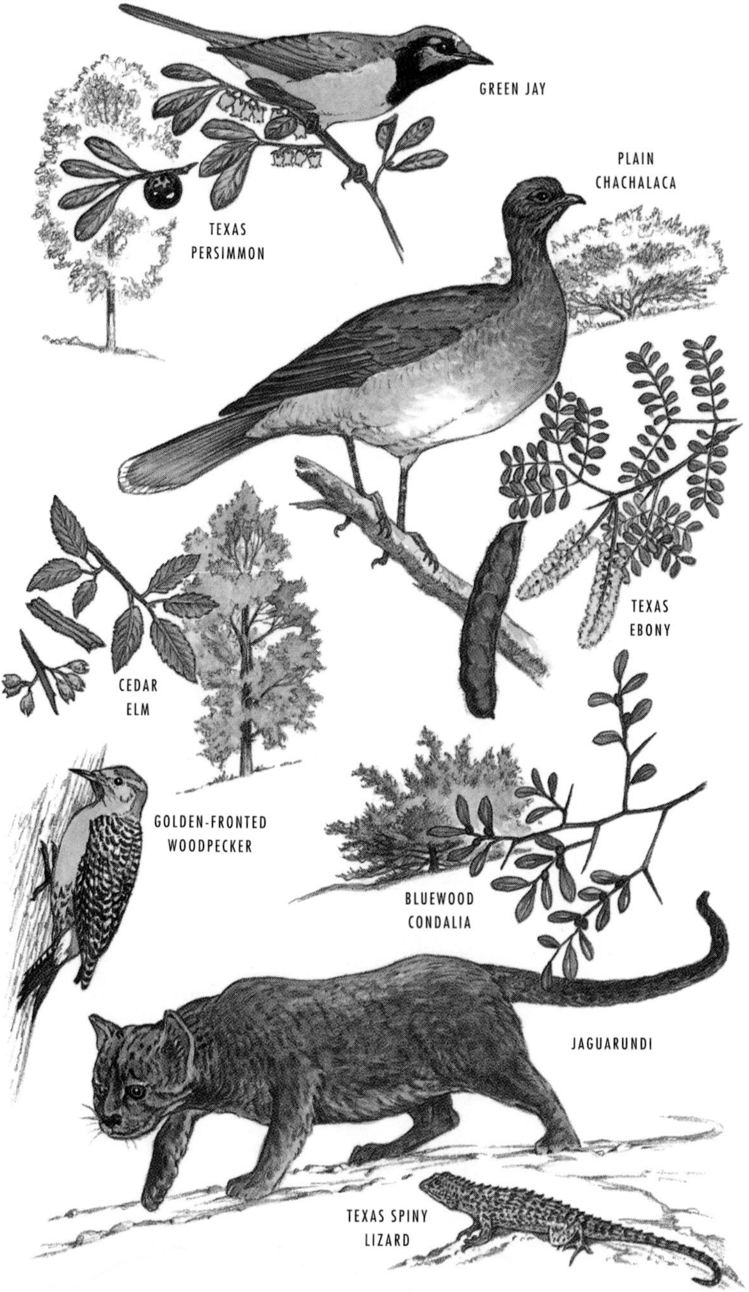

PLATE 7

GREEN JAY

TEXAS
PERSIMMON

PLAIN
CHACHALACA

TEXAS
EBONY

CEDAR
ELM

GOLDEN-FRONTED
WOODPECKER

BLUEWOOD
CONDALIA

JAGUARUNDI

TEXAS SPINY
LIZARD

PLATE 8

LOWER RIO GRANDE FOREST II

JERUSALEM-THORN (RETAMA) *Parkinsonia aculeata*
Small (to 40 ft.), green-barked (but reddish brown in old trees), and thorny. Spreading branch pattern. The alternate compound leaves hang whiplike, with 22 – 30 pairs of small (0.1 – 0.3 in.) deciduous leaflets. Has yellow, pealike flowers and long seed pods.

GREAT LEADTREE *Leucaena pulverulenta*
Up to 50 ft. Featherlike compound leaves. Flowers white, tiny, in dense globular heads. Seeds in flattened, dark pods.

SPINY HACKBERRY *Celtis pallida*
Densely branched, thorny, spreading shrub. Leaves alternate, toothed, feel coarse. Fruits are orange.

RINGED KINGFISHER *Ceryle torquata*
16 in. A large, crested bird, slate blue above and reddish brown below.

KISKADEE *Pitangus sulphuratus*
9.75 in. Bright yellow breast, reddish brown wings, striped head.

ALTAMIRA ORIOLE *Icterus gularis*
10 in. Glowing orange with black wings, tail, throat, upper back. Small orange patch on shoulder.

OCELOT *Felis pardalis*
To 53 in. Grayish to tawny with large, black-bordered brown spots.

TEXAS TORTOISE *Gopherus berlandieri*
To 8.5 in. A terrestrial reptile with a domed yellowish shell and stumpy legs.

SPECKLED RACER *Drymobius margaritiferus*
To 100 in. A glossy black snake with yellowish speckling above, greenish yellow belly.

PLATE 8

RINGED
KINGFISHER

ALTAMIRA
ORIOLE

JERUSALEM-THORN

GREAT
LEADTREE

KISKADEE

OCELOT

SPINY
HACKBERRY

SPECKLED
RACER

TEXAS
TORTOISE

7

ROCKY MOUNTAIN FORESTS

An immense ridge of rock spans the continent of North America. It runs from southern Alaska, central Alberta, and British Columbia south through Idaho, Montana, Wyoming, Utah, Colorado, New Mexico, and the Big Bend region of Texas, then continues into Mexico, where it joins the Sierra Occidental range. This geological wall that divides the entire continent is called the Rocky Mountains. It is a continental divide in the most literal sense: Water striking the western slopes of the Rocky Mountains will drain eventually to the Pacific Ocean, while that falling on their eastern slopes will drain to the Gulf of Mexico. Approximately 5,000 miles long, the Rockies are a young range, with many sharp, jagged peaks in excess of 14,000 feet, topped by Mt. McKinley in Alaska, which reaches 20,320 feet. Approached from the east, the Colorado Front Range of the Rockies forms an imposing wall of snow-capped peaks, in sharpest possible contrast to the short, arid grasslands that lie within the Rockies' rainshadow. Mt. Elbert (14,433 feet) looms straight ahead, Pikes Peak (14,110 feet) just to the south, Longs Peak (14,255 feet) in Rocky Mountain National Park to the north. Farther north in the Rockies, in extreme northwestern Wyoming, is Yellowstone National Park, the oldest national park in the United States, established in 1872, as well as nearby Grand Teton National Park. Still further north is Waterton-Glacier International Peace Park, which crosses the Canadian border, as well as Banff and Jasper national parks and scenic Lake Louise. In the south, Big Bend National Park in southwestern Texas is still part of the Rocky Mountains, though the peaks are no longer snow-covered, by virtue of their smaller size and more southerly location. Here, along the bend of the Rio Grande, the mountains mingle closely with the desert.

Imagine early settlers first encountering this massive wall of rock. The westward movement might have ceased altogether were

The northern Rocky Mountains presented a formidable obstacle to early westward travelers.

it not for the discovery of passes, such as Berthoud Pass and Loveland Pass, west of Denver. Virtually all of the passes through the Rockies were discovered by fur traders. The rugged nature of this endeavor is reflected in historic location names such as Hole-in-the-Wall, Hell's Half Acre, and Devil's Gate. Most settlers passed through the Rockies on the Oregon Trail, crossing the Continental Divide at South Pass near Lander, Wyoming. South Pass, discovered by a fur trader in 1812, is at only 7,550 feet elevation, affording a relatively easy passage with a longer snow-free period than other passes through the central Rockies. Meriwether Lewis first laid eyes on the Rockies in what later became the state of Montana. In a journal entry dated Sunday, May 26, 1805, he wrote that the mountains were "covered with snow and the sun shone on it in such manner as to give me the most plain and satisfactory view." Sacagawea, the Shoshoni woman who accompanied Lewis and Clark, is buried on the Wind River Indian Reservation in central Wyoming, surrounded by the Rocky Mountains.

Geologically, the story of the Rocky Mountains begins about 70 million years ago, when dinosaurs still inhabited lush green forests of giant conifers that covered a very different-looking landscape. At that time, a vast sea covered much of what was to eventually become the Rocky Mountains and Midwest. This was the onset of the Laramide Orogeny, a period of intense volcanic activity, mountain building, regional uplift, and erosion that continued virtually to the present day. Along with this geologic activity, the climate was changing, becoming less tropical and more arid. Grasslands began to take over lands that had been forested.

Beginning about 2 million years ago, frequent bouts of glaciation were added to the already volcanically active geology, produc-

The Grand Teton Range of the central Rockies, among the most frequently visited of the Rocky Mountains.

ing the rugged look of the Rockies today. Many of the mountain valleys are actually *cirques,* bowls carved by mountain glaciers that have since largely receded. The dinosaurs are long gone, having become extinct about 65 million years ago, but their fossil remains are still being exhumed in areas such as Dinosaur National Monument in Utah, Como Bluff in Wyoming, Hell Creek in Montana (where the first tyrannosaur was discovered), and Dinosaur Provincial Park in Alberta, Canada.

Throughout the Tertiary Period, from 65 million years ago to the present day, the region has become increasingly arid. The lush conifer forests remain only on the mountain slopes. Hundreds of mammal species, including odd, knobby-headed uintatheres, rhinoceroslike arsinotheres, long-necked camels, various-sized horses, and immense mastodons, have lived and become extinct,

Rugged terrain at Dinosaur National Monument, where the fossils of giant dinosaurs have been unearthed.

their fossil remains still abundantly represented in places like the Badlands in South Dakota. During the time the Rockies were forming, a terrier-sized animal named Hyracotherium, sometimes called Eohippus, fed tentatively on the early grasses, ever watchful of swift attacks by predatory diatrymas, ostrich-sized, flightless birds with huge hawklike beaks that were the legacy of the dinosaurs. Little Hyracotherium was the first of many in a lineage that would eventually produce the domestic horse, so much a symbol of the American West. Though horses evolved in North America, they became extinct there and were later reintroduced by Spanish *conquistadores.* Descendants of those horses, the wild mustangs, still run free today.

The natural history of the Rocky Mountains is a story of elevation and latitude. Rocky Mountain ecology forms much of the basis of the concept of life zones (see Chapter 3). Beginning in the Lower Sonoran Zone, essentially a grassland desert, the landscape changes as you climb through the Upper Sonoran pinyons and junipers into the transition-zone forests of Ponderosa Pine and up into the cool, moist Canadian-zone forests of aspen, Lodgepole Pine, spruce, and fir. At the highest elevations, you enter the climatically rigorous Hudsonian zone, a landscape of stunted trees in alpine tundra. Some of the world's oldest living things, the Bristlecone Pines, survive atop some of the Rocky Mountains.

The highest elevation zones are found mainly in the central and northern regions of the Rockies. This chapter will focus mainly on the region from Colorado and Utah northward. The next chapter, "Southwest Forests," will include the southernmost components of the Rockies, from Big Bend in Texas to the Grand Canyon in Arizona.

The Badlands of South Dakota.

INDICATOR PLANTS

TREES: *Gambel Oak.*

SHRUBS: *Big Sagebrush, Antelopebrush, Rubber Rabbitbrush, Black Greasewood,* Prairie Sage, Four-wing Saltbush, Shadscale, Winter Fat, various cercocarpuses.

HERBACEOUS SPECIES: Golden Aster, Scarlet Gilia, Sego Lily, various penstemons, paintbrushes, delphiniums, and other wildflowers; also various cacti and grasses, including Cheatgrass, Junegrass.

INDICATOR ANIMALS

BIRDS: Turkey Vulture, Red-tailed Hawk, Swainson's Hawk, *Ferruginous Hawk, Golden Eagle,* Prairie Falcon, *American Kestrel, Sage Grouse, Burrowing Owl,* Mourning Dove, Greater Roadrunner, Common Poorwill, Common Nighthawk, Eastern Kingbird, Western Kingbird, Black-billed Magpie, Common Raven, Barn Swallow, Rock Wren, *Sage Thrasher,* Mountain Bluebird, Loggerhead Shrike, Horned Lark, Western Meadowlark, Brewer's Blackbird, Vesper Sparrow, *Sage Sparrow,* Lark Sparrow.

MAMMALS: *Whitetail Prairie Dog,* Richardson Ground Squirrel, Sagebrush Vole, Blacktail Jackrabbit, Whitetail Jackrabbit, Coyote, Badger, *Pronghorn.*

REPTILES: Eastern Fence Lizard, Sagebrush Lizard, Bullsnake, Western Rattlesnake.

DESCRIPTION

The Great Basin Desert is a Lower Sonoran Zone community of shrubs, grasses, and wildflowers that, in various assemblages, covers the vast region between the Pacific Coast mountain ranges and the Rocky Mountains. Depending upon soil moisture, soil chemistry, and altitude, a given area may be dominated by Big Sagebrush (or another sagebrush species), various species of saltbushes and greasewood, or short-statured Gambel Oaks and various cercocarpuses.

The Great Basin is often termed a "cold desert" because, though precipitation is limited (10 to 20 inches annually), it often falls as winter snow. Soils in natural areas of drainage may be relatively moist, in which case a diverse group of shrubs and wildflowers is usually present. Drier soils, and soils that are highly saline or alkaline, support far fewer species, often only one or two shrub species.

Many of the more rugged sites are dominated by saltbush species (*Atriplex*), usually along with Black Greasewood. These shrubs are not aromatic, and flowers tend to be inconspicuous.

Less rugged sites are the haunts of the various aromatic sagebrush species, especially Big Sagebrush, which is abundant at low elevations, where soils are suitable for the deep sagebrush taproots to penetrate. Rubber Rabbitbrush and Antelopebrush usually can be found among the Big Sagebrush. Sagebrush also can be found at elevations of between 7,000 and 10,000 feet, where sagebrush species intergrade with Gambel Oak, various cercocarpus species, and various serviceberries. The higher elevation sagebrush communities include Mountain and Hoary sagebrushes.

Shrublands, sometimes also called *shrubsteppes,* impress many observers as largely a two-dimensional habitat, perhaps not very interesting, with little structural diversity. Nonetheless, the careful birder is rewarded with many species ranging from Burrowing Owls to the specialized Sage Sparrow and Sage Thrasher, both found nowhere else but the shrublands. Various species of western hawks search from the skies for prey ranging from grasshoppers to lizards to jackrabbits, depending upon whether the raptor is an American Kestrel, a Ferruginous Hawk, or a Golden Eagle. In early spring, groups of Sage Grouse gather in areas called leks, where males engage in an elaborate courtship display.

Sagebrush shrublands are ideal habitats for Pronghorn, as well as colonies of Whitetail Prairie Dogs.

SIMILAR FOREST COMMUNITIES: See pinyon-juniper forest.

RANGE: Both eastern and western sides of the Rocky Mountains and throughout the Great Basin, between the Rockies to the east and the Cascades and Sierra Nevada to the west.

Figure 19. Sage Grouse in courtship display

Late afternoon sun turns Sagebrush golden in color.

REMARKS

Recent studies of shrubsteppe bird communities have added to our knowledge of what factors determine how many species, and how many individuals, can live within any given habitat. The studies have also changed our view of precisely how nature is balanced.

Many ecologists assumed that availability of food or some other essential resource such as nesting sites ultimately determined bird species richness and abundance. They felt that each habitat contained essentially as many species as there were resources available. If a given community contained more or less species than another, it was because resources were greater or less. Part of this view of nature included the assumption that bird species were constantly actively competing for resources and that the long-term result of this persistent competition was that only certain combinations of species could coexist. Nature was ultimately balanced through the process of competition.

Research on Great Basin shrubsteppe bird communities revealed otherwise. The abundance of various bird species changed from one year to the next but not in accordance with abundance of resources or the presence of other bird species. There was no clear-cut pattern to the changes. Nature did not appear to be carefully balanced, at least not in this particular habitat. The researchers suggested that in habitats such as the Great Basin shrubsteppes, climate may occasionally be so severe and unpredictable that some bird species, often by chance, suffer serious declines when others, again largely by chance, fare better. A wintering flock of sparrows may be largely killed off by a sudden severe winter storm, for instance. Another flock, some distance

Pronghorn trot among the Sagebrush and other shrubs of the Great Basin Desert.

away, may be largely spared. Because environmental factors having to do with climate are exerting strong effects, shrubsteppes are not filled to capacity with as many bird species as they can hold, but are more accurately described as being in a constant state of flux, with some species temporarily thriving while others are reduced in population. Any given area may be inhabited by rather different bird assemblages from one year to the next. Nature is not precisely balanced but is instead much more subject to the laws of chance.

WHERE TO VISIT: The Great Basin shrubland communities are abundant at low and moderate elevations from Montana and Wyoming through Idaho and eastern Washington, south through Utah, Colorado, and Nevada. Great Basin National Park, a national park established in 1986, is about 300 miles from Las Vegas. Also recommended is Grand Teton National Park in Wyoming, especially the area around Jackson Hole.

SHORTGRASS PRAIRIE

INDICATOR PLANTS

TREES: Essentially none.

SHRUBS: *Big Sagebrush, Rubber Rabbitbrush,* Black Greasewood, Prairie Sage, Four-wing Saltbush, Spanish Bayonet.

HERBACEOUS SPECIES: *Blazingstar, White Prickly Poppy,* Common Sunflower, *Russian-thistle* (tumbleweed), prairie-clovers, Prairie Aster, plus many other wildflowers, various cacti, many grasses including Blue Grama, Side-oats Grama, Junegrass, Buffalograss, Cheatgrass.

INDICATOR ANIMALS

BIRDS: Turkey Vulture, Red-tailed Hawk, Swainson's Hawk, Golden Eagle, Prairie Falcon, American Kestrel, Killdeer, *Mountain Plover,* Burrowing Owl, Mourning Dove, Greater Roadrunner, Common Poorwill, Common Nighthawk, Eastern Kingbird, Western Kingbird, Black-billed Magpie, Common Raven, American Crow, Barn Swallow, Rock Wren, Western Bluebird, Loggerhead Shrike, Horned Lark, Western Meadowlark, Brewer's Blackbird, Lark Bunting, Vesper Sparrow, Grasshopper Sparrow, Brewer's Sparrow, Lark Sparrow, *Chestnut-collared Longspur, McCown's Longspur.*

MAMMALS: *Blacktail Prairie Dog, Thirteen-lined Ground Squirrel, Blacktail Jackrabbit,* Whitetail Jackrabbit, Coyote, Badger, Pronghorn.

REPTILES: Eastern Fence Lizard, Lesser Earless Lizard, Short-horned Lizard, Many-lined Skink, Coachwhip, Bullsnake, Western Rattlesnake, Western Box Turtle.

AMPHIBIANS: Plains Spadefoot Toad, Great Plains Toad.

DESCRIPTION

The shortgrass prairie is a rather flat and monotonous landscape lying in the rainshadow east of the Rocky Mountains. It is part of the Lower Sonoran Zone, a desertlike habitat of high winds, often severe fluctuating temperatures, and limited precipitation. When precipitation does occur, it is often in the form of hail or blizzards, and tornados and dust storms are also frequent. No trees grow in this habitat (except along watercourses), but extensive stands of shrubs, especially Big Sagebrush and Rubber Rabbitbrush, can be found, along with many grasses. Buffalo-grass is one of the commonest of about 25 grasses that populate the prairie. It is a short,

Pawnee Grasslands east of the Rocky Mountains.

Figure 20. Badger

gray-green grass that grows in dense clumps forming a thick sod.

Several short cacti species grow among the grasses, particularly the prickly-pears, and many wildflower species bloom in spring and summer. The delicate lavender Blazingstar and bright White Prickly Poppy are usually abundant, especially along roadsides. The alien Russian-thistle, also known as tumbleweed, is sometimes so abundant as to be a nuisance.

Two bird species are unique to the shortgrass prairie, the Mountain Plover and McCown's Longspur. Mountain Plovers resemble the more widely spread Killdeer but lack the two breast bands and bright orange rump characteristic of the Killdeer. Instead, this plover is uniformly brown above and clear white on the neck and breast. Mountain Plovers live in small flocks and are often seen feeding in freshly plowed fields. McCown's Longspurs resemble husky sparrows in size and shape. Males are brightly colored when in summer breeding plumage, with a white face and throat, black cap, and black chest. Females are sparrowlike, and both sexes have chestnut on the shoulders. In autumn and winter, large flocks of McCown's, Chestnut-collared, and Lapland longspurs are joined by Horned Larks and American Pipits in foraging for seeds on the vast, windswept prairie.

Jackrabbits are perhaps the most commonly sighted mammals of the shortgrass prairie, though colonies of Blacktail Prairie

Dogs are not uncommon. A similar species, the Thirteen-lined Ground Squirrel, is often seen scurrying across the road—those that fail to avoid being struck by automobiles are fed upon by Black-billed Magpies. Badgers are predators of both ground squirrels and prairie dogs, but are not frequently seen because they are active mostly at night. Badgers are aggressive and are skilled diggers, often pursuing rodents into their burrows.

SIMILAR FOREST COMMUNITIES: On low-elevation slopes and protected ridges, the grasses and shrubland plants of the Lower Sonoran Zone intermingle with pinyons and junipers. See also Great Basin Desert.

RANGE: East of the Rocky Mountains in Montana, Wyoming, Colorado, and New Mexico. Eastward, this habitat intermingles with medium- and tallgrass prairie.

REMARKS

Much of the prairie habitat is gone, converted to rangeland or agriculture. Since the latter part of the last century, this entire region has been extensively grazed by cattle, often resulting in a deterioration of habitat from overgrazing. The area was formerly populated by extensive herds of Bison, which were extirpated in the last century. Bison also grazed extensively on prairie grasses, but they would simply move to greener pastures when they had consumed most of the grass in a given area. Cattle are normally fenced, forcing the animals to overgraze their range.

Many ecologists believe that Bison, over the course of many millennia, affected the evolution of shortgrass species through their grazing activities. Unlike most plants, grasses grow from the base of the stem, not the tip, thus grass can be eaten down to the base and still easily and quickly regenerate. Some prairie grasses

Pawnee Grasslands in the rain shadow of the Colorado front range of the Rockies.

are adapted to intensive grazing by means of a system of underground stems called rhizomes, which allow the grass to store much energy below grazing level and to continually send up new sprouts that replace those eaten away.

Though the shortgrass prairie may look relatively monotonous, a closer examination reveals that this habitat is complex, populated by a considerable number of grasses and wildflowers, and the exact composition of species varies with soil moisture conditions. The shortest grasses, Blue Grama and Buffalo-grass, are most widespread, and tolerate the driest conditions. Other grass species become increasingly common when soil moisture increases. Alkaline areas support still another assemblage of species, so the prairie is best thought of as a mosaic of different grassland communities. Wildflower abundance and diversity is also moisture-dependent, and years of abundant moisture usually produce spectacular wildflower displays, which change as spring-blooming species give way to those that blossom in late summer and fall.

WHERE TO VISIT: The best area for seeing shortgrass prairie is the Pawnee National Grassland, an area of approximately 775,000 acres northeast of Denver, Colorado, accessible from Interstate 76. Several roads take the visitor directly through ideal shortgrass habitat.

PINYON-JUNIPER FOREST   PLATE 9

INDICATOR PLANTS

TREES: *Two-needle (Colorado) Pinyon, Utah Juniper, Rocky Mountain Juniper, Gambel Oak,* Oneseed Juniper.

SHRUBS: *Big Sagebrush, Alderleaf Cercocarpus,* Curlleaf Cercocarpus, Bitterbrush, Desert Buckbrush, Saskatoon Juneberry (Western Serviceberry), Utah Juneberry, Apache-plume, Rubber Rabbitbrush, Mountain Spray, Cliffrose, Four-wing Saltbush, Mormontea, Spanish Bayonet.

HERBACEOUS SPECIES: *Sego Lily, Indian Paintbrush, Scarlet Globemallow,* various lupines including *Bluebonnet (Silky Lupine),* Golden Aster, Wild Zinnia, Scarlet Gilia, New Mexico Thistle, Little Sunflower, Prairie Sunflower, milkvetch, Skeleton Mustard, Tansy Mustard; various cacti including prickly-pears, Claret Cup and other hedgehogs, Candelabra; various grasses including Blue Grama, Side-oats Grama, Junegrass, Muttongrass, Cheatgrass.

INDICATOR ANIMALS

BIRDS: *Bushtit, Pinyon Jay, Juniper Titmouse, Black-chinned Hummingbird, Blue-gray Gnatcatcher, Rock Wren, Canyon Towhee,* Turkey

Vulture, Red-tailed Hawk, Swainson's Hawk, Golden Eagle, Prairie Falcon, American Kestrel, Great Horned Owl, Western Screech-Owl, Mourning Dove, Greater Roadrunner, Common Poorwill, Common Nighthawk, White-throated Swift, Downy Woodpecker, Ash-throated Flycatcher, Gray Flycatcher, Scrub Jay, Sage Thrasher, Clark's Nutcracker, Black-billed Magpie, Common Raven, Mountain Chickadee, Bewick's Wren, Canyon Wren, Western Bluebird, Mountain Bluebird, Virginia's Warbler, Black-throated Gray Warbler, Chipping Sparrow, Lark Sparrow.

MAMMALS: *Blacktail Jackrabbit, Ringtail, Colorado Chipmunk, Rock Squirrel,* Long-legged Myotis, Pallid Bat, Least Chipmunk, Rock Mouse, Pinyon Mouse, Mountain Cottontail, Spotted Skunk, Coyote, Gray Fox, Longtail Weasel, Mountain Lion, Mule Deer.

REPTILES: *Collared Lizard,* Eastern Fence Lizard, Side-blotched Lizard, Northern Tree Lizard, Short-horned Lizard, Bullsnake, Western Rattlesnake.

DESCRIPTION

The slightest rise in elevation from flat grassland and shrubland will take you into a world of small pines and junipers, often termed the pygmy forest. The only common conifers are Two-needle Pinyon and three juniper species: Oneseed, Rocky Mountain, and Utah. These needle-leaved trees are often joined by Gambel Oak. This is the dominant forest of the upper Sonoran zone, a forest of short, shrubby trees that are usually widely spaced, living on gentle, arid slopes throughout the southern and central Rocky Mountains. In summer, the pinyon-juniper forest is hot, with desert shrubs such as Big Sagebrush, cercocarpuses, and Rabbitbrush interspersed among the small trees. Gambel Oak may form dense thickets in certain areas. Ground cover is often sparse, though wildflowers such as Scarlet Globemallow and Bluebonnet (Silky Lupine) add color to the parched-looking landscape. Russian-thistle, often called tumbleweed, an invader plant from Eurasia now considered to be a nuisance, grows abundantly, and dead stalks often collect in big, loose balls along fences. The plant is an annual, and as the wind blows, the broken stalks are thrown along the ground, distributing the seeds of the next generation.

Skies are usually hot and clear above the diminutive stands of pines and junipers, and Turkey Vultures, Red-tailed Hawks, and Swainson's Hawks soar high on the midday thermal currents rising from the hot ground. The vultures are often seen along roadsides competing with Black-billed Magpies and Common Ravens for a recently run-over jackrabbit or skunk. Utility poles are used as perches by huge Golden Eagles. A Greater Roadrunner may be taking shelter from the intense sun under a pinyon.

Pinyons and junipers dominate the slopes, while Sagebrush inhabits the flat area in a pinyon-juniper forest.

The most characteristic bird of the pinyon-juniper forest is the Pinyon Jay, a raucous blue bird that is normally found in flocks of up to 50 or more. These nomadic jays roam the pines in search of the large pinyon seeds or pine nuts, which are a principal food source for them. The small trees also are habitat for the Juniper Titmouse and Black-throated Gray Warblers, as well as foraging flocks of Bushtits.

Because the upper Sonoran zone is still largely a desertlike habitat, various cacti are common, especially the prickly-pears. Also characteristic of deserts, many lizard and snake species can be found, including the poisonous Western Rattlesnake. More common, however, are Collared Lizards, Eastern Fence Lizards, and the Short-horned Lizard, often called the "horned toad."

SIMILAR FOREST COMMUNITIES: The grasses and shrubland plants of the lower Sonoran zone intermingle extensively among the pinyons and junipers. Also see Chihuahua Desert.

RANGE: Best developed in Utah, southern Colorado, New Mexico, and Arizona at elevations of 5,000–7,000 feet, rising as high as 9,000 feet on some south-facing slopes where temperature and evaporation rate are high.

REMARKS

It is not possible for a visitor to the southern Rocky Mountains to miss pinyons and junipers. The most widely distributed of the three species of pinyon is **TWO-NEEDLE PINYON,** the species illustrated on the plate. This species is largely replaced by Singleleaf Pinyon in Nevada and the southern Sierra Nevada in California, and by Mexican Pinyon in Texas. All pinyons are short and somewhat shrubby, rarely exceeding 30 feet in height. As the name implies, Two-needle Pinyon has its stiff, dark green, short (1−2 inches) needles in clusters of 2 (but occasionally 3). Cones are also small, only about 2 inches in length, with open scales that lack sharp tips. The name pinyon, from the Spanish word *piñon* meaning nut, refers to the large seeds within the cones. The scientific species name *edulis* refers to the fact that the pine nut is edible. The cones take three years to mature, and each cone contains only about 10−20 seeds. Abundant seed crops in any given area tend to occur about every 5−7 years, a factor that keeps the flocks of Pinyon Jays nomadic, as they must find locations where cones are mature and plentiful. The nutritious seeds are also eaten by Native Americans. Pinyons can live up to 350−400 years, though ages of between 80 and 200 are much more common. Pinyons survive well on arid, rocky soils because they have deep taproots and wide-spreading surface roots, enabling them to take in the maximum amount of available moisture.

Pinyons share the upper Sonoran zone with junipers. Three species, the **ROCKY MOUNTAIN, ONESEED,** and **UTAH JUNIPERS** are common, and, like the Two-needle Pinyon, these are replaced by other species in the extreme Southwest and in Texas. There are actually 10 juniper species found throughout the West, a contrast with the East, where there is only one juniper species, the (misnamed) Eastern Redcedar, a common successional species. Junipers are characterized by their two types of foliage: one type is scaly, often prickly, and the other consists of small needles. Another easy way to identify a juniper tree is by its fruits, modified cones that are not dry but rather are fleshy and berrylike. They are blue to brownish red, usually with a fuzzy whitish covering.

Rocky Mountain Juniper is common throughout the Upper Sonoran Zone of the central Rockies.

Many animal species ranging from thrushes, waxwings, and grouse to chipmunks, foxes, and deer feed on the often aromatic berries. Like the pinyons, junipers produce an abundance of berries only periodically, usually every 2 – 5 years.

The three juniper species of the central and southern Rockies do not normally occur together. Oneseed Juniper is most common among the pinyons, whereas Rocky Mountain Juniper (Plate 10) occupies slightly higher elevations, often in pure stands beyond the altitudinal range of pinyons. Rocky Mountain Juniper is also abundant in the north-central Rockies, particularly on eastern slopes. There is some evidence that this species is expanding its range, invading grasslands, perhaps because of overgrazing by cattle. Cattle do not eat juniper, but they do consume a lot of grass, so young junipers can spread where cattle help suppress the grasses. On the other hand, some researchers believe that junipers were once much more common among the grasses, but that Indian-set fires reduced its abundance in favor of grasses. If this is the case, Rocky Mountain Juniper is merely reclaiming lost ground, not invading new territory. Utah Juniper occurs only on the west slopes of the mountains, often among pinyons. The three juniper species are much alike in appearance but can be separated by their fruit colors: pure blue for Rocky Mountain, reddish blue for Oneseed, and dull red-brown for Utah. Juniper berries have the odor of gin, an aroma that often permeates juniper stands.

GAMBEL OAK, a small, often shrubby oak, can be abundant in the upper Sonoran zone. Leaves feel very leathery and are deeply lobed and smooth, with no points. Gambel Oak frequently hybridizes with other oak species (Havard, Gray, Mohr, Chinkapin, Turbinella, Arizona), producing a hybrid commonly called Wavyleaf Oak. Acorns are eaten by Scrub and Steller's jays, as well as deer and various rodents.

ALDERLEAF CERCOCARPUS, also called **MOUNTAIN-MAHOGANY,** is one of several shrubs in the genus *Cercocarpus* that abound throughout western mountains. The small greenish flowers mature into seeds that have long, feathery tails, and the name cercocarpus means "tailed fruit." Leaves are oval, with small teeth, hairy underneath, and, in this species, closely resemble alder leaves.

BIG SAGEBRUSH is one of the most abundant plant species in the West, carpeting dry, hot flatlands in parts of every western state except Texas. It is particularly characteristic of the Great Basin Desert in Idaho, Utah, Nevada, and southeastern Oregon, but it is no stranger to the upper Sonoran zone throughout the Rocky Mountains. It is an easy plant to identify, both by sight and smell. Always a shrub, the leaves are quite small and gray-green, with three little lobes at the tip (hence the species name *tridentata*—3 teeth). The plant is highly aromatic; crushing some leaves to keep in your car as you travel adds a pungent freshness to the air. Flowers are small and yellowish and are wind-pollinated. Big Sagebrush is an extremely important food plant for birds, especially Sage Grouse. Deer and Bighorn Sheep also feed extensively on the plant.

When the **PINYON JAY** is around, you can't miss it, though be warned that it is often not around. Many birders are frustrated by how such a seemingly obvious bird can be so difficult to locate in thousands of acres of pinyon-juniper forest. The fact is that these birds are almost always in flocks, and the flocks move around a lot in search of a locally abundant pinyon crop. Anywhere from 30 to 50 birds, sometimes up to 150 birds, all steely blue, all noisy, all active, can suddenly descend on an area, only to depart a few minutes later when they discover that there are too few good seeds to be had. They breed in colonies of up to 150 and gather in winter flocks that can approach 1,000 individuals. The welfare of the jay is closely tied to the natural history of the pinyon pines. In winter, Clark's Nutcrackers, also in the jay family, descend from higher elevations to partake of pinyon nuts.

Like the Pinyon Jay, the small, gray **JUNIPER TITMOUSE** is very much a bird of the upper Sonoran zone, a species closely tied to pinyons and junipers over most of its range, though it does occur in broad-leaved forests as well. Once called Plain Titmouse, this little relative of chickadees is all gray. It sounds a bit like a chickadee, making a wheezy *dee-dee-dee* call that reveals its presence usually before you find it foraging in the pine or juniper foliage. Like all titmice and chickadees, this species is a cavity nester, excavating its nest site in an old pine or juniper. Pairs remain together all year and usually join mixed foraging flocks, especially in winter.

BUSHTITS look somewhat like slender versions of Juniper Titmice, and indeed are closely related. They do not nest in cavities, however, but build a gourd-shaped nest made of leaves, grasses, lichens, and other material skillfully woven together with spider silk. Bushtits range throughout the West, occurring in broad-leaved forests as well as pinyon-juniper habitat. They are immensely gregarious—if you see one Bushtit, you'll soon see more, often up to 30 or more in a single flock. These small, seemingly hyperactive birds make loud contact notes as the flock moves quickly through an area, rather like small, insectivorous versions of the Pinyon Jays. Even during nesting season, Bushtits have a high tolerance for each other, and unmated birds are reported to occasionally help feed nestlings of other birds. In parts of their range, especially in the Big Bend area of Texas, some Bushtits have black on the side of the face, and were formerly called Black-eared Bushtits. This variety was once considered to be a separate species, but now all are lumped together merely as Bushtits.

Many colorful wildflowers, among them **SEGO LILY, SCARLET GLOBEMALLOW,** and **BLUEBONNET,** grow in the arid, rock-laden soils of the upper Sonoran zone. Brightly colored flowers attract numerous bees, butterflies, and hummingbirds, all of which act to cross-pollinate the plants, though their actual motive in visiting the flower is a search for nectar. Sego Lily has broad white petals and brightens the dry soils throughout most of the West. It has been chosen as the state flower of Utah. Scarlet Globemallow is unmistakable, with five bright orangy red petals. It is common among the pinyons and junipers, one of several globemallows widely distributed in the West. Lupines of many species can be found in the West and, depending on the species, they live anywhere from arid grasslands to high alpine meadows.

The **BLACK-CHINNED HUMMINGBIRD** is the commonest low-elevation hummer, often seen among the pinyons and junipers. It ranges throughout the West and is not at all confined to the upper Sonoran zone, occurring anywhere from backyards to riverine forests. The male has a black chin with a purple throat below, but the purple color is hard to see unless you have the bird in excellent light.

Though not uncommon, the **RINGTAIL** is nocturnal and not often seen. It is closely related to the Raccoon, a fact revealed by its bushy, ringed tail. It's never difficult to separate a Ringtail from a Raccoon, however, as the Ringtail is smaller and more slender, and lacks the black mask so characteristic of the more widely distributed Raccoon. Primarily southwestern in distribution, Ringtails range from Texas to California. They prefer rocky areas to closed forest and can also be found in deserts. Ringtails eat many kinds of animals and plants including a large number of rodents, and they are sometimes called ringtail cats. Another name for the animal is "cacomistle," a name apparently derived from an Indian term for "half mountain lion."

Among the numerous lizard species that scurry among the dried needles shed by the pinyons, the **COLLARED LIZARD** is certainly worth a look. This 14-inch lizard is named for its black collar, visible as the animal is sunning on a rock. Its body color is mostly green, unusual for an aridland lizard; most other species are primarily brown. When in a considerable hurry, it can stand up and run on its hind legs. Be glad it runs away, as it is capable of a nasty bite if you grab it. Collared Lizards occur throughout the Central

Rockies and Southwest, south into Mexico. There are five sub-species.

WHERE TO VISIT: This forest type is most characteristic of the central and southern Rocky Mountain foothills. Pinyon-juniper forests can be found from Colorado Springs southward all along Interstate 25 south past Walsenburg. West of the Rockies, the southern half of Mesa Verde National Park has outstanding examples, and many stands can be found outside the park around Durango, Colorado. There is also much pinyon-juniper at Dinosaur National Monument and Colorado National Monument and in the Uncompahgre National Forest (south-central Colorado). The largest Two-needle Pinyon known, with a trunk circumference of about 12 feet, is in Manti-LaSal National Forest in southeastern Utah. The largest Rocky Mountain Juniper, named the "Jardine Juniper," is at Wasatch and Cache national forests in north-central Utah. This tree, estimated to be about 3,000 years old, has a trunk diameter of 8 feet.

ESSAY

COEVOLUTION: THE INTERLOCKING FATES OF JAYS AND PINYONS

Would there be pinyons without Pinyon Jays? Would there be Pinyon Jays without pinyons? Organisms frequently evolve adaptations that make them utterly and specifically dependent on other organisms for resources—and the other organisms become dependent upon them. For example, most western trees must have mycorrhizal fungi living in their root systems, fungi that are indispensable to the tree because they facilitate mineral uptake from the soil. Kill the fungi, and you kill the trees. In turn, the fungi rely on the trees to photosynthesize; they use some of the tree's chemical food as their only energy source. Kill the trees, and you kill the fungi. Such intimate relationships are examples of *coevolution*, where two species become so interdependent that they can thrive only in the presence of each other.

Pinyons throughout the Southwest produce cones and seeds that seem to attract potential seed predators, especially the Pinyon Jay. A seed, of course, contains an embryonic plant. Why sacrifice it to an animal? Some plants have poisonous seeds, an obvious adaptation to reduce loss to animals. Pinyons, however, have an array of characteristics that combine to encourage jays to visit the pines and help themselves to the seeds. Cones are positioned upward and outward on the tree, so the seeds inside are in plain sight of the jays, essentially inviting them to partake. Pinyon seeds are unusually large for pine seeds, and each seed is high in energy. The seed coat is thin, meaning that birds can not only ingest the seeds but also digest them. In many plants, an indigestible seed coat permits the seed to pass unharmed through the bird's alimentary system. Pinyon seed coats differ in color between edible and nonviable seeds, signaling the jays as to which they should select.

Now suppose a single pinyon is loaded with seed-containing cones, while most of the other pinyons in the stand are devoid of cones. A flock of Pinyon Jays, anywhere from 50 to several hundred of them, happen by. Because the Pinyon Jay has an expandable pouch in its throat, each bird can gather up to 56 seeds. At that rate of seed consumption, a flock of 250 birds could consume about 30,000 seeds per day. Obviously, in a very short time the tree would have lost all of its seeds to jays, not a promising reproductive future for the tree. Suppose, however, that the jays were behaviorally adapted to bury any seeds in excess of their immediate survival needs. Suppose the jays behaved in a way that helped insure that they would have food during winter, providing they could find *some* of their buried seeds. For these two suppositions to be correct, there must be an abundance of seeds far beyond the jays' immediate needs. One tree could never produce so many seeds, but if *all* the pinyons in a region produced heavy seed crops at once, they would indeed "flood the market" with vastly more pinyon seeds than any flock of jays could hope to consume. In fact, there would be more seeds than all the jays, Clark's Nutcrackers, Cliff Chipmunks, Pine Cone Moths, and Pine Cone Beetles combined could eat. In fact, that is exactly what the trees do.

It requires a great deal of energy to make so many seeds, so much energy that it is unlikely that a pinyon population could produce such a bumper seed crop every year. More important, however, it would be to the severe disadvantage of the trees to produce huge seed crops annually, even if they could. Doing so would make the resource not only abundant but predictable. Seed predators could, over the years, steadily build their populations, eventually increasing so much that they could, indeed, consume virtually all of the seeds. It is much more adaptive for the plants to produce seed cornucopias irregularly. Doing so has several major advantages: First, energy can be stored for some years and then devoted to cone and seed production, insuring adequate energy to produce a huge seed crop. Second, seed predator populations will decline in years of low seed production, either through starvation, reduced reproduction, or emigration. At one well-documented site in the Southwest, pinyon seed bonanzas occurred in

1936, 1943, 1948, 1954, 1959, 1965, 1969, and 1974. In intervening years, seed crops were dramatically less. Pinyons in most areas have this roughly 6-year interval between heavy seed crops.

Many other species of trees have similarly synchronous but irregular bumper crop years, including other conifers and oaks. Even animals employ this evolutionary survival strategy. Mayflies emerge synchronously from ponds in numbers far more than all the birds and other predators could possibly consume. Grunion breed synchronously, slithering from the water to the beaches in numbers far in excess of what predators could deal with. The well-known periodical cicada, too, emerges synchronously in vast numbers.

Pinyon Jays have so successfully adapted to the cycle of the pinyons that their reproduction is tied to it. Most species of birds mature sexually in response to changes in day length, or photoperiod. In Pinyon Jays, however, photoperiod is only one stimulus for reproduction. The other cue is availability of pinyon seeds. When seeds are abundant, jays can breed very early in spring, continue breeding through summer, and re-enter breeding condition as early as winter solstice.

Jays bury pinyon seeds—lots of pinyon seeds. In one study it was estimated that from September through January, a flock of 250 pinyon jays buried about 4.5 million pinyon seeds! They do not bury the seeds just anywhere. The jays tend to cache seeds in open areas, selecting sites near brush piles or fallen trees. Such sites are ideal for germination and growth since they are protected and are away from other trees with which they would compete for scarce water. Jays may also enjoy an advantage in caching seeds away from pinyon stands. Fewer potential competitors, such as woodrats and Scrub Jays, occur in open areas. The jays nest near their caching sites, often in Ponderosa or pinyon stands. Throughout the winter months, they succeed in finding some of their cached seeds but by no means all. Nor do they need to; they store far more than their needs demand. Thus many seeds have an opportunity to germinate.

PONDEROSA PINE FOREST   PLATE 10

INDICATOR PLANTS
TREES: *Ponderosa Pine, Quaking Aspen, Lodgepole Pine,* Common Douglas-fir, Gambel Oak, Rocky Mountain Juniper, Limber Pine.

SHRUBS: *Antelopebrush,* Alderleaf Cercocarpus (mountain-mahogany), Desert Buckbrush, Snowbrush, Wax Currant, Common Juniper, Kinnikinnick, Big Sagebrush, Waxflower.

HERBACEOUS SPECIES: *Curlycup Gumplant (Gumweed),* various paint-brushes, Blanketflower, Miner's Candle, Wild Geranium, Arrowhead Butterweed (Groundsel), Heartleaf Arnica, Silky Pasqueflower, Wallflower, Spring-beauty, One-seeded Penstemon, Small-flowered Penstemon, Dwarf Mistletoe, grasses including Blue Grama, Side-oats Grama, Junegrass, Needle-and-thread, Arizona Fescue, Mountain Fescue, Spike Fescue, Aridland Sedge.

INDICATOR ANIMALS

BIRDS: *Hepatic Tanager, Western Bluebird, Pygmy Nuthatch, Band-tailed Pigeon, Steller's Jay, Dark-eyed Junco,* Northern Goshawk, Cooper's Hawk, Sharp-shinned Hawk, Great Horned Owl, Northern Saw-whet Owl, Northern Pygmy-Owl, Flammulated Owl, Common Nighthawk, Broad-tailed Hummingbird, Downy Woodpecker, Hairy Woodpecker, Northern Flicker, Williamson's Sapsucker, Western Wood-Pewee, Cordilleran Flycatcher, Lewis's Woodpecker, Black-billed Magpie, Mountain Chickadee, White-breasted Nuthatch, Red-breasted Nuthatch, Brown Creeper, Rock Wren, Mountain Bluebird, American Robin, Townsend's Solitaire, Plumbeous Vireo, Yellow-rumped Warbler, Grace's Warbler, Western Tanager, Black-headed Grosbeak, Evening Grosbeak, Pine Siskin, Chipping Sparrow.

MAMMALS: *Tassel-eared (Abert) Squirrel, Golden-mantled Ground Squirrel,* Colorado Chipmunk, Least Chipmunk, Porcupine, Mountain Cottontail, Black Bear, Grizzly Bear (local), Longtail Weasel, Coyote, Elk, Mule Deer.

REPTILES: Eastern Fence Lizard, Many-lined Skink, Sagebrush Lizard, Short-horned Lizard, Northern Tree Lizard, Milk Snake, Bullsnake, Western Rattlesnake.

AMPHIBIANS: Woodhouse Toad.

DESCRIPTION

Ponderosa Pine is the most widely distributed and probably the most abundant tree in the West. Throughout the Rocky Mountains, Ponderosa Pine is the indicator tree for the Transition Zone, a mid-elevation region where the aridity of the grassland and shrubby desert yields to a cooler, moister climate. Low-elevation Ponderosa Pine forests and those on south-facing slopes are quite dry, and Rocky Mountain Juniper is usually mixed among the pines. At higher elevations, Ponderosa Pine intermingles with Quaking Aspen and Lodgepole Pine, and shrubs are much more dense than at lower elevations. Throughout the Transition Zone, soil is sandy, rather dry and acidic, rainfall is low, usually no more than 25 inches annually (increasing with altitude), most of it in the form of spring snow.

Ponderosa Pine forests are typically open. Plenty of sunlight reaches the ground, supporting a ground cover of grasses and wildflowers. The forest is often described as parklike, as though the trees were arranged to allow lots of room for hiking and picnicking. The open look, when it occurs, is usually due to periodic fire, which reduces litter buildup, destroys competing species, and permits the pine and grass to persist. Mature Ponderosa Pines are stately trees, reaching heights of over 150 feet. Needles are long, and bark is yellowish, often orangy red, in flat scales. A Ponderosa Pine forest not only looks good, it smells good, with the aroma of fresh pine needles. Get up close and press your nose right into a furrow of the bark; it often has a vanilla scent.

Many Ponderosa Pines are victims of Dwarf Mistletoe, a parasitic plant that grows in clumps among the pine boughs. The mistletoe invades the pine tissue and often causes it to form "witch's brooms," odd bursts of branches that disrupt the normal shape of the tree. Pines significantly weakened by mistletoe can succumb more easily to fungal invasion as well as attacks by Mountain Pine Beetles.

The openness of Ponderosa Pine forests makes birdwatching immensely pleasant. Though the needles are long, they usually don't hide the Hepatic Tanagers, Western Bluebirds, and Western Tanagers foraging in the canopy. American Robins, Chipping Sparrows, the "Gray-headed" race of Dark-eyed Juncos, and Mountain Bluebirds are often on or near the ground. Don't be surprised if a red-shafted Northern Flicker flies up from the ground, for the moment abandoning its lunch of ants. Speaking

Figure 21. Mistletoe ("witch's broom") on Ponderosa Pine

Tall Ponderosa Pines often allow little understory, creating a park-like stand.

of lunch, there are usually Steller's Jays near picnic tables. A close search among the pine branches may reveal the presence of a roosting Great Horned Owl, or perhaps the very hard to find Flammulated Owl. With an abundance of small birds occur the bird hawks. Northern Goshawks, Cooper's Hawks, and Sharp-shinned Hawks all lurk among the pines, each awaiting its opportunity to swiftly strike at some luckless junco or thrush. Among the vertical foragers, Williamson's Sapsuckers are common, as are Downy and Hairy woodpeckers and the Brown Creeper. All three nuthatch species occur, and Pygmy Nuthatches in particular can be abundant and vocal.

The Tassel-eared Squirrel is one mammal especially partial to Ponderosa Pine forests. Other mammals, from Least Chipmunks and Golden-mantled Ground Squirrels (check the picnic areas) to Elk and Mule Deer, live among the pine parks.

SIMILAR FOREST COMMUNITIES: See Black Hills forest, Arizona Madrean foothill forest, Southwest Mountain forest.

RANGE: Throughout the central and southern Rocky Mountains on both sides of the continental divide, usually at elevations of 5,600 – 9,000 feet. Especially on gentle slopes, will mix extensively with Rocky Mountain Juniper, Quaking Aspen, Lodgepole Pine, Douglas-fir. Northward in the Rockies it is replaced by forests dominated by Douglas-fir. In addition, Ponderosa Pine forests occur at appropriate elevations throughout the Southwest, the Sierra Nevada, the Pacific Northwest, and the Black Hills of South Dakota. The species is absent from the Canadian Rockies.

Pinus ponderosa, as botanists refer to this magnificent tree, is as typical of the West as any tree could possibly be. Probably more picnics have been held in the shade of **PONDEROSA PINE** than any other western tree. The tree is very easy to identify, with long (5 – 10 inches) needles in clusters of 3 (though clumps of two occur rather frequently among the threes). The bark is unmistakable, yellowish to reddish, and in large flakes. Cones are prickly, 3 –6 inches long. Ponderosas grow fast and may live for up to 600 years. Root systems are extensive, with taproots that can penetrate to depths of over 30 feet, as well as a wide-spreading shallow root system that may extend over 100 feet from the tree trunk. Such root area gives the tree an advantage during dry periods.

Ponderosa Pines require an abundance of sunlight to germinate and prosper, so fire is important to their ecology. Without periodic fire to clear out competing species, the saplings eventually die from lack of light. Many Ponderosa Pine stands are rather crowded with mature trees that cast too much shade for the good of future generations. In addition, crowded trees create intense competition for nutrients, water, and sunlight, often weakening the trees in general, making them more susceptible to disease, fungus, or insects. The main reason for crowded stands is probably fire suppression. Normally, fire starts by lightning, usually from late summer storms. The fires burn leaf litter, release nutrients to the upper soil, and destroy competing species, allowing pine seeds to sprout and the young trees to prosper in an abundance of sunlight. Adult Ponderosa Pines have corky bark that is resistant to ground fires. Fire suppression over an extended time period leads to a huge litter buildup, creating ideal conditions for

Transition Zone in the Colorado Rockies, with Ponderosa Pine among Big Sagebrush.

catastrophic crown fires that can devastate the forest. Periodic burning by native Indians in past centuries may have also contributed to the openness of Ponderosa Pine forests. In the last century, increased cattle grazing may also have affected Ponderosa Pine abundance. Cattle reduce competing grasses, allowing the sun-seeking young pines to grow.

The Upper Sonoran and Transition zones often intermingle, thus **ROCKY MOUNTAIN JUNIPER** and **GAMBEL OAK** are commonly associated with Ponderosa Pine at lower elevations. Low-elevation forests also have sparse shrub cover, though **BIG SAGEBRUSH** and **ANTELOPEBRUSH** are anything but uncommon. Antelopebrush is a spreading shrub that reaches a height of about 3 feet. Like its cohort, Big Sagebrush, Antelopebrush has long, narrow leaves with 3 small teeth on the ends. Flowers are yellowish, with 5 petals, surrounded by 5 white sepals. It is also called bitterbrush for the taste of the leaves and twigs, though the shrub is browsed heavily by deer and Elk.

At higher elevations, or on north-facing exposures, where the Transition Zone grades into the Canadian Zone, **COMMON DOUGLAS-FIR** moves in, along with aspens and often **LODGEPOLE PINE.** Areas such as these are often patchworks of stands, some mostly of Ponderosas, some entirely of aspens, some only Lodgepoles, some mixtures. Middle- to higher-elevation Ponderosa Pine stands have a substantial understory of shrubs, including **WAX CURRANT** and **DESERT BUCKBRUSH.** Wax Currant is easily identified by its pink trumpetlike flowers that give way to sticky-haired, orange-red berries. Its small leaves are unevenly lobed. Buckbrush is one of many *Ceanothus* species that cover the West. This species is a thorny spreading shrub with small oval leaves.

CURLYCUP GUMPLANT (GUMWEED) is a common wildflower not only in Ponderosa Pine forests but in other mountain forests as well. The bright yellow flower is daisylike, and the buds are quite rounded and sticky. The plant, though once chewed as gum by Native Americans, can be toxic because it thrives on soils containing the toxic metal selenium.

The **HEPATIC TANAGER** is common in pines from southwestern North America through Central America and southward to Argentina. The name comes from the color of the female, a liver yellow. Males are dull red, with a brownish bill and brown patch aside the face.

GRACE'S WARBLER may be found foraging for insects in the canopy, a small bird among the long pine needles. Like the Hepatic Tanager, it is a bird of southwestern pine forests that migrates to Mexico for the winter. The bird looks quite similar to the eastern Yellow-throated Warbler, with a yellow face and two distinct wing bars, but it lacks the black face markings of the eastern species. Listen for its trilling song, a *cheedle-cheedle-chee-chee-chee*.

WESTERN BLUEBIRDS are common in the central and southern Rocky Mountains and range westward to the Pacific Northwest, absent only from the Great Basin Desert. Males have blue throats and rusty backs, field marks that separate them from the similar Eastern Bluebird (their ranges overlap in the Rockies). Bluebirds need tree cavities in which to nest, so they prefer older Ponderosa Pine forests that contain dead snags. One detailed study of the birds of Ponderosa Pine forests concluded that the Western Bluebird was one of the most successful species in the forest, along with the **NORTHERN FLICKER, PLUMBEOUS VIREO, DARK-EYED JUNCO,** and **WHITE-BREASTED NUTHATCH,** based on their overall abundance and reproductive success.

The **PYGMY NUTHATCH** can be found throughout western mountains, always in Transition Zone forests. These diminutive nuthatches feed on the outer parts of branches much more than the other two nuthatch species. Pygmys are noisy, and they travel in flocks, so you know when they are around. Their high-pitched, excited, piping keeps the flock together as they fly from tree to tree in search of food. Like the Grace's Warbler, they have an eastern counterpart, the Brown-headed Nuthatch of southeastern pine forests.

The **TASSEL-EARED SQUIRREL,** as squirrels go, is just plain elegant. Larger than most tree squirrels, up to 23 inches long, the Tassel-eared Squirrel is dark gray with an immaculate white belly and a salt-and-pepper bushy tail. Its rusty-colored ears are outrageously long for a squirrel, tipped with long hairs. Tassel-eared Squirrels feed on quite a variety of foods including mistletoe, inner bark of trees, and selected wildflowers, as well as more traditional squirrel food, namely nuts. In this case, the nuts are pine nuts from Ponderosas and, occasionally, from pinyons. The Tassel-eared Squirrel ranges throughout the central and southern Rockies. Its cousin, the Kaibab Squirrel, occurs on the Kaibab Plateau on the North Rim of the Grand Canyon. It is darker overall than the Tassel-eared.

The **COLORADO CHIPMUNK** is one of 15 species of chipmunks found in the West, of which six occur within the Rockies. As the name implies, this species is partial to the state of Colorado, though it occurs in Utah, Arizona, and New Mexico as well. It closely resembles the **LEAST CHIPMUNK** but is a bit larger and slightly reddish, whereas the Least is grayer. Both species are frequent visitors to picnic sites, so why not feed them both? Good luck in telling them apart.

MOUNTAIN COTTONTAIL ranges throughout the West, absent only from the Pacific Coast. It is common throughout the Lower Sonoran and Upper Sonoran zones and can be found well into the Transition Zone. It has much shorter ears than a jackrabbit and a puffy white tail, and is an overall rich brown color. Compared with jackrabbits, cottontails are cuter. Like all rabbits, Mountain Cottontail is strictly herbivorous, feeding on a variety of herbaceous vegetation.

WHERE TO VISIT: Excellent stands of widely spaced Ponderosa Pines are seen at Rocky Mountain National Park near Estes Park, Colorado, and throughout the foothills to Boulder and Denver. In addition, the species is abundant in many areas in the central and southern parts of the Rockies. San Juan National Forest in southwestern Colorado has large Ponderosa Pines. Several national forests in Arizona (Coconino, Coronado, Kaibab, Prescott, and Tonto) contain extensive Ponderosa Pine stands. Santa Fe National Forest in New Mexico is also recommended. Ponderosa Pine forests are not well represented in the northern Rockies.

ESSAY

BIRD GUILDS: PICKERS AND GLEANERS, HAMMERERS AND TEARERS

When you look at the structure of the Ponderosa Pine forest, you see lots of tall pine trees, an understory of grasses, and not much in between. In overall structure, the habitat seems, at least at first glance, relatively simple. Yet it is home to many bird species. How do so many different species coexist without suffering severe competition for space and food? Though it sometimes happens that two species will directly confront each other, one eventually driving away the other, open aggression as evidenced by physical encounter is rare among birds. Two ornithologists, Robert C. Szaro and Russell P. Balda, made a detailed study of what they called bird community dynamics in Ponderosa Pine forests within the Coconino National Forest in Arizona. They learned that the habitat looks a bit more complex to the birds than it does to us. The researchers determined that 20 species bred in mature Ponderosa Pine forests. They further determined that each species fit into one of four distinct "foraging guilds" and one of four different "nesting guilds."

A guild is a general category for how some important ecological activity is done. For example, one way of feeding is to pursue and capture prey in the air. Several birds do this, including Broad-tailed Hummingbirds (when they feed on insects rather than nectar), Western Wood-Pewees, Violet-green Swallows, and Western

Bluebirds. These species are thus placed together in the "aerial feeders guild." Another way of feeding is to search the ground for food, as do Chipping Sparrows, Dark-eyed Juncos, and Rock Wrens, all members of the "ground feeders guild." Nesting location varies as well, and three guilds are recognized: the cavity and depression nesters (woodpeckers, chickadees, nuthatches, Western Bluebird), the foliage nesters (Plumbeous Vireo, Grace's Warbler, Western Wood-Pewee), and the ground nesters (Rock Wren, Hermit Thrush, Dark-eyed Junco). Of the 20 species nesting in mature Ponderosa Pine forest, eight were cavity nesters, eight were foliage nesters, and four were ground nesters.

Ecologists have long known from studies in many different kinds of habitats that each bird species seems to feed in a certain way and in a certain location within its habitat, a behavior that acts to minimize competition among species. Szaro and Balda recognized four feeding guilds for the Ponderosa Pine forest: pickers and gleaners, hammerers and tearers, ground feeders, and aerial feeders. They studied each of the guilds and learned that within each guild, bird species are rather different in how they go about the important business of finding and capturing a day's rations. The result is what ecologists term species segregation, with each species competing little, if at all, with others in the same guild.

For example, pickers and gleaners search the foliage for caterpillars and other small animal food. Each picker/gleaner has several choices of possible feeding sites. It could feed high in the tree, in the middle, or near the ground. It could feed on outer branches or inner branches. It could probe into needle clusters, hang from the branches, or methodically search the branches for food. Szaro and Balda found that Plumbeous Vireos preferred to feed in small, shrubby pines and in lower areas of mature pines, whereas Mountain Chickadees tended to feed fairly high in tall pines. Grace's Warblers fed higher still, and Pygmy Nuthatches tended to forage most commonly at the treetops. Thus the feeding activities of these four species are separated vertically. Feeding methods also result in species segregation. Grace's Warblers spent considerably more time in the outer foliage than did the Plumbeous Vireos. Pygmy Nuthatches spent much more time hanging beneath needle clusters and buds than did Grace's Warblers. Plumbeous Vireos differed considerably from Mountain Chickadees because they spent much more time on open branches and much less in needle clusters.

Similar general tendencies were evident for species in the guild called hammerers and tearers, which forage on tree trunks and large branches. Northern Flickers spent much more time on the ground than did Hairy Woodpeckers. White-breasted Nuthatches differed from Hairy Woodpeckers in that they spent much more time in Gambel Oaks than in pines. Another important point is that the body size of these three birds is quite different, so on that basis alone they tend to select different sized food.

The three ground feeders also differ in body size: the smallest is the Chipping Sparrow, the largest is the Dark-eyed Junco, and the Rock Wren is in between. Szaro and Balda found that Chipping Sparrows tended to probe more than juncos, which spent most of their time picking.

When you visit a Ponderosa Pine forest, or any other forest for that matter, take a close look at just what each bird species is doing. You should be able to find several examples of vertical segregation and different feeding behaviors.

ASPEN GROVE   PLATE 11

INDICATOR PLANTS

TREES: *Quaking Aspen,* Lodgepole Pine, Common Douglas-fir, Blue Spruce, Subalpine Fir, White Fir, Engelmann Spruce, Gambel Oak.

SHRUBS: *Roundleaf Snowberry, Rocky Mountain Maple, Common Chokecherry,* Common Juniper, Kinnikinnick, Ninebark, Snowbrush, Common Gooseberry, Red-osier Dogwood, Red Raspberry, Saskatoon Juneberry (Western Serviceberry), Thimbleberry, Wild Rose, various blueberries (Vaccinium).

HERBACEOUS SPECIES: *Colorado Columbine, Showy Daisy,* Red Fireweed, *Showy Loco,* Common Lupine, Sego Lily, Globe Anemone, Trumpet Gilia, Wild Geranium, Heartleaf Arnica, Black Coneflower, Cow Parsnip, Black-eyed Susan, False-hellebore, Harebell, Common Yarrow, Orange Sneezeweed, Monkshood, Giant Red Paintbrush, Prairie Sage, various larkspurs (delphiniums), various valerians, Pussytoes, American Vetch, Bracken Fern, various grasses, especially Thurber Fescue, Blue Wild-rye, Slender Wheatgrass, Purple Onion-grass.

INDICATOR ANIMALS

BIRDS: *Violet-green Swallow, Mountain Bluebird, Red-naped Sapsucker, Broad-tailed Hummingbird,* Red-tailed Hawk, Northern Goshawk, Cooper's Hawk, Sharp-shinned Hawk, American Kestrel, Ruffed Grouse, Lincoln's Sparrow, Great Horned Owl, Northern Pygmy-Owl, Western Screech-Owl, Hairy Woodpecker, Northern Flicker, Williamson's Sapsucker, Tree Swallow, Cordilleran Flycatcher, Western Wood-Pewee, Western Kingbird, Steller's Jay,

Black-billed Magpie, Black-capped Chickadee, Mountain Chickadee, White-breasted Nuthatch, Pygmy Nuthatch, House Wren, Western Bluebird, American Robin, Warbling Vireo, Plumbeous Vireo, Black-headed Grosbeak, Dark-eyed Junco, Song Sparrow.

MAMMALS: *Beaver, Porcupine,* Masked Shrew, Dusky Shrew, Long-legged Myotis, Northern Pocket Gopher, Golden-mantled Ground Squirrel, Least Chipmunk, Red (Pine) Squirrel, Longtail Weasel, Coyote, Black Bear, Elk, Mule Deer.

REPTILES: Smooth Green Snake, Western Terrestrial Garter Snake.

AMPHIBIANS: Boreal Toad.

DESCRIPTION

Quaking Aspen is the deciduous equivalent to Ponderosa Pine in that it is abundant throughout the West, a tree that any observer interested in natural history will surely see. Aspens occur in dense groves that are often pure stands but, because the species is successional, may be mixed with firs, spruces, Douglas-fir, and occasionally junipers. Aspen groves can be found throughout the Rocky Mountains, ranging from the low Transition Zone through the Canadian Zone, normally from 7,500 feet up in elevation. In northern areas, aspens reach 10,000 feet elevation, and they get to 11,500 feet in the southern Rockies. At the highest sites, they are usually on south-facing slopes. On moist, protected sites, aspen groves can occur as low as 5,600 feet. Most areas where aspens prosper have lots of snow in winter and at least 25 inches of precipitation annually.

Aspen groves have great natural beauty. The trees themselves are welcoming, with light yellow-green, heart-shaped leaves that flutter in the slightest breeze. The name Quaking Aspen (the scientific name is *Populus tremuloides,* which means "trembling poplar") is a reference to the oscillating leaves. The groves are bright with dappled sun but just shady enough to be an inviting place to cool off during a long hike or horseback ride. Depending on local soil and moisture conditions, an aspen grove may have an understory of shrubs such as Chokecherry or Rocky Mountain Maple plus numerous wildflowers, or it may be drier, with many grasses and perhaps some Bracken Fern. Because aspens are largely a successional species destined to be replaced by more shade-tolerant conifers, many aspen groves have an understory of young spruces, firs, or Douglas-firs.

Many bird species use aspen groves. On the smooth trunks, look for the horizontal rows of holes made by Red-naped Sapsuckers, the Rocky Mountain species that is closely related to the more northern and eastern Yellow-bellied Sapsucker. Mountain Bluebirds nest in aspen snags, as do Violet-green Swallows and

Aspens are among the most distinctive of western trees, easily identified by the pale bark and broad, often "quaking" leaves.

House Wrens. The persistent, gurgling song of the House Wren is characteristic of aspen groves, as are the melodious offerings of Warbling Vireos and Black-headed Grosbeaks. A loud, somewhat hysterical trill is probably a territorial Broad-tailed Hummingbird defending its exclusive access to a particularly desirable clump of Colorado Columbine.

Two big rodents are especially fond of aspens. Look for Porcupines up in the canopy and Beavers on the ground. Both enjoy a good meal of aspen bark, and Beavers also use aspens extensively to build their dams and lodges.

SIMILAR FOREST COMMUNITIES: See also Lodgepole Pine forest.

RANGE: Quaking Aspen is the most widely distributed tree species in North America. Aspen groves can be found from the Brooks Range in Alaska throughout Canada and the northern United

States and south into northern Mexico. Aspen is absent from the middle Atlantic states, the Southeast, and Texas but is present to some degree in all western states, and it is particularly abundant throughout the central and northern Rocky Mountains.

REMARKS

The wide distribution and overall abundance of **QUAKING ASPEN** tell us immediately that natural disturbance is a frequent and important component of the western ecology. Nature is dynamic, with windstorms, fire, avalanches, and other events that quickly alter the landscape. Trees that have stood for hundreds of years are suddenly downed and the landscape opened, an opportunity for other species to invade and, at least for a time, to prosper. Throughout the Rockies, and, for that matter, throughout most of the West, two species, Quaking Aspen and Lodgepole Pine, are the first woody invaders, following quickly on the heels of Red Fireweed to colonize newly opened sites. Both of these species rely heavily on periodic disturbance, often by fire, for their continued prosperity. Aspens are important resources for many Rocky Mountain species. One enterprising researcher has suggested that about 500 different plant and animal species, from fungi to deer, are directly dependent on aspens.

Quaking Aspens look beautiful in full sunlight, and indeed, they need sunlight to thrive. Easily identified by their broad, heart-shaped leaves on long petioles and by their smooth, yellowish green bark, these are the only abundant deciduous trees in the high Rockies. Aspen leaves are dark above, light below, and when blown in the breeze they seem to shimmer, making the grove look like glimmering silver. In fall, aspens turn brilliant yellow or or-

An aspen grove forms part of a narrow Transition Zone. Sagebrush dominates lower elevation, while Ponderosa Pine and Engelmann Spruce replace aspen on the slopes.

ange, adding a dramatic touch of gold to an otherwise monotonous green landscape. In winter their bare branches stand out in stark contrast with the needle-covered conifers. In spring, some trees develop male catkins, some female catkins, and pollination occurs by wind. Female catkins mature to hold many tiny, hairy seeds that are also wind dispersed. Abundant seed crops occur only about every 4–5 years, and a tree does not produce seeds until it is 15–20 years old.

Though aspens can produce an abundance of seeds, they propagate mainly by sending up shoots from their root systems. When you see a small aspen grove, note that it is often somewhat circular in shape, with the smallest trees on the edges, the largest in the middle. This pattern is the result of the emergence of root shoots, not seed germination. This sort of spreading, by asexual rather than sexual reproduction, is quite common in plants, though not generally among trees.

So how many aspens are in the grove? You might count hundreds of trunks, but they could all be from the same root system. All the trees in the grove are really from the same root system—in fact, they are genetically identical and thus technically are really part of the same tree! Botanists call each trunk or stem a *ramet* and refer to the entire cluster as a *genet* (genetically identical unit). Another somewhat mind-boggling aspect of aspen natural history is that when a tree dies, perhaps from a too-heavy accumulation of snow or insect invasion, is it really dead? Probably not. That particular ramet is gone, but the roots survive below ground. The roots might live to be many hundreds of years old, continually sending up new ramets when conditions are suitable. Aspen roots are generally fire resistant, and an aspen canopy can reform quickly after a fire.

As for the seeds, aspens do not seem to germinate well in the Rockies. The seeds are short-lived, and some researchers believe that all of the aspens in the Rockies today are derived from root shoots of aspens that germinated from seed hundreds of years ago, when the climate was wetter.

Many aspen groves are on moist sites where shrubs and wildflowers also thrive. **ROCKY MOUNTAIN MAPLE,** or Western Mountain Maple, occurs throughout the Rockies, Cascades, and Sierra Nevada, reaching north through British Columbia. It grows as a shrub or small, spreading tree. It is identified as a maple by its opposite leaves, and as Rocky Mountain Maple by the fact that leaves are strongly toothed.

CHOKECHERRY is often common in the shrub layer beneath a canopy of aspen. Leaves are oval and toothed, white flowers are on long clusters, and fruits are in the form of black cherries.

Chokecherry is common throughout northern North America and ranges into the southern Rockies. The berries are an important food source for many animals from grouse to Bighorn Sheep.

ROUNDLEAF SNOWBERRY, like aspen, is usually one genet comprising a cluster of ramets. In other words, it reproduces primarily by root shoots. Snowberry has grayish, oval leaves and small, paired, pinkish, bell-like flowers that become shiny white berries (the source of the plant's common name).

Aspen groves make ideal habitats in which to search for wildflowers. Colorado's colorful official state flower, the **COLORADO COLUMBINE,** often blooms among the aspens. This member of the buttercup family can grow to 3 feet high, with flowers that have 5 large, cream-colored petals alternating with 5 violet-blue sepals. **SHOWY DAISY** is also common in aspen groves. It closely resembles fleabane, with a flowerhead containing a yellow disk surrounded by rays that range in color from pink and lavender to white. Showy Daisy ranges widely throughout western mountains. **SHOWY LOCO** is recognized by its fuzzy pink flowerheads and delicate compound leaves, which have a silvery tone. A member of the large legume family, locos are close relatives of clovers, and, like clovers, they attract many bees.

The **BROAD-TAILED HUMMINGBIRD** is common in aspen groves, feeding on columbines, paintbrushes, gilias, and other flowers. Broad-tails closely resemble the eastern Ruby-throated Hummingbird. The male is green with a brilliant red throat. However, Broad-tails are exactly that, having a wider, broader tail than Ruby-throats, which have a distinct notch in their tails. Broad-tails occur throughout the central and southern Rockies but are absent from the Pacific Coastal mountains.

The Broad-tailed Hummingbird is especially fond of Colorado Columbine because the long spurs are vessels that often hold an abundance of nectar. Probing deep within the flower, the hummingbird picks up pollen from the yellow anthers and distributes it to other flowers as it makes its rounds. At least that's the idea. However, the bird occasionally cheats. Broad-tailed hummers have been seen to poke a hole directly in the flower's spur, gaining access to the nectar without touching the pollen. Some bees do the same trick. Such actions show that different species, in spite of what some people would like to believe, do not really cooperate. The so-called cooperative mutualism between pollinator and plant is much more accurately described as reciprocal parasitism. When one party can "cheat" and get away with it, it does.

The **VIOLET-GREEN SWALLOW** is one of the most beautiful of the world's swallows, and it occurs only in western North America, nesting well up into Alaska. Seen closely and in full sunlight it reveals an iridescent violet tail and wings, a deep green iridescent back, and a brownish head. Its breast is pure snowy white. This bird can be confused only with the Tree Swallow, a species common both in the East and West. Violet-green Swallows are most easily distinguished by the white feather ovals at the base of their wings, lacking on the Tree Swallow. Violet-green Swallows are not confined to aspen forests, though they are certainly common there. They nest in tree cavities. Some observers have noted these swallows aiding Western Bluebirds in rearing young, then taking over the bluebird's nest cavity after the young bluebirds have fledged. (Just how manipulative are birds, anyway?)

MOUNTAIN BLUEBIRDS are on the must-see list of any western birder. The males are exquisite birds, a true turquoise color shown off to full advantage in bright sunlight. They can be found throughout western mountains, almost always above 7,000 feet elevation, but not along the Pacific Coast. Mountain Bluebirds are aggressive at defending both their nest cavities (always in demand by swallows, wrens, woodpeckers, and the much despised Starling) and their young. Ornithologists have noted that the closer the young are to fledging, and thus the higher the parental investment in reproduction, the more vigorously the adult Mountain Bluebirds defend their young.

The **RED-NAPED SAPSUCKER** was, for many years, believed to be a subspecies of the widespread Yellow-bellied Sapsucker. They certainly look alike, except that the Red-naped has a little red patch on the back of its head. Ornithologists have recently "split" the sapsuckers and now recognize three species, including the Red-breasted of the Pacific Northwest, rather than one.

PORCUPINES are common in aspens as well as in most western conifers. These husky, prickly rodents, which range throughout western North America as well as the Northeast, may weigh up to 40 pounds, but they seem unhindered by their bulk. They are excellent climbers and enjoy feasting on leaves and buds from many tree species. Porcupines are active all year, and in winter their diet usually turns to bark. They concentrate on eating the cambium layer immediately beneath the outer bark. In doing so, they can strip a tree severely enough to kill it. Bark is generally difficult to digest, and like many herbivores such as horses, Porcupines have a long digestive system that includes a large blind sac, the caecum, at the juncture of the large and small intestines. The caecum permits additional time for the coarse plant material to ferment and thus provides for more efficient digestion.

Of course Porcupines are best known for their body armor, a coat of modified hair called quills. Quills are hollow and have tiny barbs that expand when the quill is implanted beneath the skin of any animal (including humans) that happens to come too close to the Porcupine. Quills cover the rump and tail of the otherwise grizzled yellowish animal. One zoologist reported that the average Porcupine has somewhere around 30,000 quills (this information seems of dubious value, but since it is known, I thought I should report it). Porcupines are mistakenly believed to "shoot" their quills. The quills are easily dislodged, however, and the Porcupine, if threatened, will shake itself, greatly enhancing the probability that the quills will come in contact with its tormentor — and the quills stick. Imbedded Porcupine quills are not only painful but potentially lethal. Animals such as foxes, Bobcats, Coyotes, or Fishers, all frequent predators of Porcupines, usually cannot remove all the quills after an encounter with a Porcupine. The wounds can fester and become infected, until finally the animal succumbs to bacterial poisoning. Fishers are reported to be the most effective predators of Porcupines, as they quickly turn a Porcupine on its back and attack its soft, unprotected belly, but this tricky maneuver does not always work.

Porcupine love is also tricky. Mating season is in late fall, a time when Porcupines are quite vocal. Females who wish to mate raise their potentially lethal tails well above their backs, making life, and love, much safer for male Porcupines. Young are born in late spring with soft quills that harden within minutes after birth. Porcupines require 3 years to mature and can live up to 8 years in the wild. Many are killed by automobiles.

The **BEAVER** is arguably the most historically important animal in North America. Though Bison roamed the Great Plains in immense herds, Bison were not the reason the West was explored. It was the search for Beaver pelts that really opened the West, bringing the fur trappers who discovered the passes through the Rockies and thus prepared the way for the settlers who followed on their heels.

The Beaver, weighing in at an average of 50 pounds (but sometimes reaching 100 pounds), is the largest rodent in North America and the second largest in the world, exceeded only by the South American Capybara, which reaches 120 pounds. Beavers are widespread throughout North America, absent only from the sparsest parts of the Great Basin. They are aquatic animals, well known for their engineering activities that involve creating impoundments by the ambitious building of dams. Beavers create habitat for many kinds of plants and animals. They often use aspens in their dam and lodge building, and they are fond of eating aspen bark as well. Active all year, Beavers collect food for winter and store it in their lodges. They are mostly nocturnal, so the best time to look for them is at dawn or dusk. They are wary animals;

Aspens among the Douglas-firs add fall color to mid-elevation Rocky Mountain forests.

when a Beaver detects danger, it is apt to slap the water with its tail, a warning to its nearby relatives to take cover.

Beavers are quite unmistakable, as there is no other rodent of such large size with a naked, scaly, flat tail. Their hind feet are webbed, an obvious adaptation for efficient swimming, and membranes protect their nostrils, ears, and eyes when they are swimming beneath the water's surface. Beavers can remain underwater for up to 15 minutes. They waterproof their thick fur with oil (castoreum) taken from glands near the anus and applied with comblike nails on the hind toes. Beavers live in family units and are thought to pair for life. Young are born in late spring.

WHERE TO VISIT: Aspen groves occur at appropriate elevations on disturbed sites throughout the Rocky Mountains. Good stands are present at most of the national parks and national forests, as well as in the vicinity of well-named Aspen, Colorado. U.S. Highway 550 over the Red Mountain Pass in Colorado is recommended, as is the San Juan National Forest near Durango, Colorado. Targhee National Forest in Idaho, on the western side of the Grand Tetons, has extensive aspen groves. Try to see aspens in the fall, when the leaves have turned brilliant gold. They are spectacular.

LODGEPOLE PINE FOREST   PLATE 12

INDICATOR PLANTS
TREES: *Lodgepole Pine, Quaking Aspen,* Common Douglas-fir, Western White Pine, Whitebark Pine, Limber Pine, Engelmann Spruce, Subalpine Fir.

SHRUBS: *Snowbrush (Sticky Laurel), Kinnikinnick,* Grouse Whortle-berry, Red Elderberry, Canada Buffaloberry, Wild Rose, Bush Honeysuckle (Twinberry), Scouler Willow, Rocky Mountain Blue-berry, Common Juniper, Mountain-lover.

HERBACEOUS SPECIES: *Heartleaf Arnica, Wyoming Paintbrush, Pinedrops, Red Fireweed,* Pipsissewa, Mountain Pussytoes, Orange Sneeze-weed, Common Yarrow, Sego Lily, Green-flowered Wintergreen, One-sided Wintergreen, Drop-pod Locoweed.

INDICATOR ANIMALS

BIRDS: *White-breasted Nuthatch, Blue Grouse, Western Wood-Pewee, Steller's Jay,* Red Crossbill, Pine Grosbeak, Northern Goshawk, Cooper's Hawk, Sharp-shinned Hawk, Northern Saw-whet Owl, Northern Pygmy-Owl, Pine Siskin, Calliope Hummingbird, Townsend's Solitaire, Downy Woodpecker, Hairy Woodpecker, Black-backed Woodpecker, Three-toed Woodpecker, Lewis's Woodpecker, Gray Jay, Clark's Nutcracker, Common Raven, Mountain Chickadee, Red-breasted Nuthatch, Brown Creeper, Ruby-crowned Kinglet, House Wren, Hermit Thrush, Yellow-rumped Warbler, Evening Grosbeak, Cassin's Finch, Dark-eyed Junco.

MAMMALS: *Red (Pine) Squirrel,* Marten, Hoary Bat, Least Chipmunk, Uinta Chipmunk, Uinta Ground Squirrel, Boreal (Southern) Redback Vole, Porcupine, Snowshoe Hare, Mountain Cottontail, Longtail Weasel, Coyote, Black Bear, Bobcat, Elk, Mule Deer.

Dense stands of Lodgepole Pine are indicative of natural fires and their influence in structuring ecosystems.

Lodgepole Pine forests in the Rocky Mountains are typically rather monotonous, with dense stands of straight pines and little understory. The name "lodgepole" is a reference to the straightness of the tree trunks, which were indeed used as poles for lodges and tepees. Depending upon the history of the site, Lodgepole Pines may occur in essentially pure, even-aged stands or be well mixed with other species. When shrubs are present, species such as Kinnikinnick, Sticky Laurel, and Common Juniper tend to prevail. The forest is usually quite shady and often shows signs of fire: charred stumps, fire-scarred trunks, ashy soil. The lower branches of many trees are usually dead from lack of light, and the density of these dead branches can make it difficult to walk through the forest. Litter is mostly acidic pine needles, slow to decompose. When seedling and sapling trees are present, they may be Lodgepoles or other species, most often spruces, firs, and Douglas-fir, though Ponderosa Pine may occur on some sites. Lodgepoles are abundant in the upper Transition and Canadian life zones, at elevations of between 8,500 feet and 10,000 feet. Below 9,000 feet they are most common on cooler north-facing slopes. Lodgepoles occur at the same elevations as Quaking Aspen, and, like aspens, they are usually successional trees, occupying a site after fire or some other environmental disturbance. It is not clear why a disturbed site is dominated by aspen rather than Lodgepole Pine (or vice versa), but both types of stands often occur in close proximity.

Note sapling trees in the understory of this Lodgepole Pine forest.

Many of the bark-foraging birds use Lodgepole stands, including several nuthatch and woodpecker species. Three woodpecker species that specialize in burned stands, the Black-backed, Three-toed, and Lewis's woodpeckers, all occur in recently burned Lodgepole Pine stands. Owls and hawks of various species both roost and nest within the dense pine needle canopies. Insect foragers include the ubiquitous Mountain Chickadee, Ruby-crowned Kinglet, Yellow-rumped Warbler, and Western Wood-Pewee. House Wrens and Hermit Thrushes select nest sites in the undergrowth, and Dark-eyed Juncos peck in the pine litter.

The most frequently sighted mammal is probably the Red Squirrel, also called the Pine Squirrel, though both Least and Uinta chipmunks are common as well. Much less frequently seen is the Marten, sometimes called Pine Marten, which preys not only on these rodents but also on Boreal Redback Voles, Mountain Cottontails, and Porcupines. The pale-colored Hoary Bat can sometimes be seen at dusk flying above the forest.

SIMILAR FOREST COMMUNITIES: See aspen grove.

RANGE: Lodgepole Pine forests are abundant within the upper Transition and Canadian zones from the central Rocky Mountains northward. They also occur, to various degrees, in the Sierra Nevada and Cascades, and along the Pacific Coast ranging into central Alaska.

REMARKS

The scientific name of **LODGEPOLE PINE,** *Pinus contorta,* seems at odds with its common name. The scientific name probably applies to a variety of Lodgepole called Shore Pine that can be found on the Pacific Northwest coast. Shore Pine is short and often shrubby. Rocky Mountain Lodgepole Pines are quite straight, reaching heights of up to 115 feet. The needles have a distinctly yellowish tinge and are shorter (1–2 inches) than those of Ponderosa Pine, though needles of both species occur in bundles of two. Lodgepole bark is somewhat yellowish and slightly furrowed, not in large scales. Cones are small (1–2 inches) and prickly. Because many Lodgepoles have serotinous cones (capable of opening only when exposed to fire), the cones may remain on the tree for years. Female cones take about two years to reach maturity, and good seed crops occur every two to three years. A single tree may live for several hundred years.

Unlike aspens, which reproduce mostly asexually through root sprouts, Lodgepole Pines rely on seeds. The windblown seeds are released from the cones following exposure to heat from fire, and the seeds quickly germinate in the newly burned, mineral-rich soil. On some sites the young pines grow very quickly, and a dense, even-aged grove results. After the initial period of rapid growth, growth can be quite slow as competition for sun and water causes the stand to thin out, and only a few of the original trees reach adulthood. On other sites, seed germination is slower, and a more mixed-age stand results.

Serotiny is a cone characteristic, whereby cones remain closed on the trees indefinitely until heated by fire, at which point they open and release the still-viable seeds. Lodgepole Pine is often considered the archetypal serotinous tree, a species that is utterly dependent on fire for reproduction. Indeed, one researcher has suggested that the very high flammability of Lodgepole Pines is itself an adaptation to spread fire and thus insure reproduction. But studies have shown that not all Lodgepole Pines are serotinous. Those that occur where fire is frequent are strongly serotinous, but those that occur in less fire-prone areas are not. Stands that have been reduced by insect invasion, avalanche, or wind are replaced largely by nonserotinous Lodgepoles.

Both Lodgepole Pine and **QUAKING ASPEN** are usually successional trees, destined to be replaced eventually by firs, spruces, or Douglas-fir. When a site is disturbed, what determines whether it will be occupied by Lodgepoles or aspens? Research on soils and climate suggests that Lodgepoles do best in coarse soils with a high granite content, while aspens thrive on fine soils high in calcium, a subtle but important difference. In the southern Rockies, where Lodgepoles do not occur, aspens occur on any soil type. It is possible that where they both occur, they compete, and Lodgepole "wins" only on coarse, granite-rich soil. Studies also show that Quaking Aspen tolerates a wider range of moisture and temperature than Lodgepole Pine. On some sites, especially those in which seed sources of spruce and fir are poor to unavailable, aspens or Lodgepoles can exist indefinitely.

SNOWBRUSH and **KINNIKINNICK** are abundant shrubs, not only in many Lodgepole Pine forests but among aspens, Ponderosa Pine, and spruce-fir. Snowbrush, also called Sticky Laurel, is in the genus *Ceanothus,* of which there are about 60 species. This shrub produces masses of small, snowy white flowers with 5 petals, 5 sepals, and 5 stamens. The alternate name Sticky Laurel refers to the evergreen, oval-shaped, fine-toothed leaves, which are a bit sticky on their upper surfaces. Snowbrush is most abundant on recently burned mountain slopes up to elevations of around 8,500 feet. It is capable of fixing atmospheric nitrogen (with the aid of bacteria in root nodules) and thus helps fertilize the soil. Leaves and twigs are important winter foods for deer and Elk.

Kinnikinnick is in the genus *Arctostaphylos,* the same genus as the numerous manzanitas that characterize chaparral habitats in the Southwest and in California. It is a prostrate, rambling shrub easily recognized by its small, dark green, oval, leathery leaves and bright red, pea-sized berries. Flowers are shaped like tiny bells and are pink or white. Another name for Kinnikinnick is bearberry, a reference to its species name, *uva-ursi,* which translates to "bear's grape." The evergreen leaves are important winter food for deer, Elk, and Bighorn Sheep, and the berries, which remain throughout the winter, are fed upon by numerous mammals and birds including bears and grouse. The species ranges very widely throughout northern North America, Europe, and Asia. In North America it ranges from sandy beaches to high mountains and is found throughout the West. It is most common from the Transition Zone upward, usually on gravelly soils.

HEARTLEAF ARNICA looks like a big yellow daisy or sunflower. Several arnica species occur throughout the Rockies and other western mountains. This species, common among aspens and Lodgepole and Ponderosa pines, grows about 2 feet tall, with large, heart-shaped basal leaves.

WYOMING PAINTBRUSH, also called Narrowleaf Paintbrush, is one of 24 species of paintbrush, all in the genus *Castilleja,* found within the Rockies. This species is the Wyoming state flower, though it is found in most other western states as well as Mexico. It is not confined to Lodgepole Pine forests, but occurs from sagebrush flatlands to elevations of around 9,000 feet. Nearly 200 paintbrush species occur throughout all of western North America, and many are prone to hybridize, making identification frequently problematic. Many paintbrushes look much alike and the common names themselves are confusing. This species is often mistakenly called Indian Paintbrush, but that common name properly belongs to a different species entirely. Wyoming Paintbrush is recognized by its long, slender leaves with three forklike lobes. Paintbrushes are colorful, adding great beauty to the West, but the flower is not the source of the color. Look closely and you will see that the flowers are actually small, greenish yellow structures located within bright red bracts and upper leaves. The red color attracts hummingbirds, butterflies, and bees. Many paintbrushes are root parasites; their root systems will penetrate root systems of other plant species, obtaining some nutrition from them.

WHITE-BREASTED NUTHATCHES are found throughout most of the United States and southern Canada. Among the four nuthatch species, White-breasts are by far the most common in broadleaved trees. However, in the West, their nasal *yank-yank* is frequently heard in Lodgepole Pine forests, as well as Ponderosa

Pine, Douglas-fir, and even pinyon-juniper lands. All nuthatches are bark foragers, with bills slightly upturned (you must look closely to see this), an adaptation for probing under bark scales. The White-breast's usual mode of foraging is to hitch head first down the tree trunk, though the birds often conduct their searches for food on thick horizontal branches as well. This species is much less likely to explore cones and needle clusters than are Pygmy or Red-breasted nuthatches. All nuthatches eat much animal food (insects, spiders) but are also partial to pine nuts. This species frequents bird feeders, especially those that offer sunflower seeds. White-breasts normally forage as pairs and often join chickadee flocks. They nest in tree cavities.

The **RED CROSSBILL** is a nomad. It is found wherever there are abundant cones, throughout mountain and northern regions of North America, well into the Mexican mountains and as far south as Nicaragua. You are as apt to find them in the pines at Big Bend in Texas as in the spruces of Colorado or the Western Hemlocks of Washington. This species is also present in northern Eurasia. One researcher, on the basis of DNA studies, has suggested that the odd Hawaiian Honeycreepers may have originally derived from Red Crossbills. If you are to see crossbills, cones must be present, and lots of them. Because cone crops are irregularly abundant, so are crossbills. The name crossbill refers to their odd crossed mandibles, an adaptation that helps them extract seeds from cones. In this species, males are brick red with dark wings and tail. Females are dull yellow, also with dark wings and tail. Crossbills usually travel in flocks and are quiet feeders, often remaining high atop a cone-laden tree, where they climb parrotlike over the cone clusters extracting seeds. You could easily overlook them, but listen for their dry, chattering call as they fly from one tree to the next. Red Crossbills can breed anytime during the year.

The **PINE GROSBEAK** looks a bit like a large Red Crossbill. Males are robin-sized, rosy red with black wings (note the two white wing bars) and notched, black tail. The bill is thick and dark. Females are yellowish gray where the males are red, and young males are like females but with bright yellow-orange rumps and heads. Pine Grosbeaks range throughout northern North America, usually in spruce and fir. In the West, they also frequent Lodgepole Pine forests, occurring throughout the Rockies and the northern Cascades and Sierra Nevada. They enjoy ash seeds as well as conifer seeds and often frequent apple orchards in winter, feeding on the downed fruits. Pine Grosbeaks are known for their tameness. If you see a small flock, walk slowly and quietly towards them, and you'll be surprised how close they will allow you to come. The species experiences irregular population explosions over much of its range, moving south in large numbers in winters when food sources are poor in their normal range.

It's difficult to miss the **RED SQUIRREL,** or Pine Squirrel, in a Lodgepole Pine forest. This little squirrel of the conifers is common in its range from the Northeast through the north-central states and all of Canada up into Alaska. It is abundant throughout the Rocky Mountains, always in needle-leaved trees. It is curious and noisy and often comes to picnic areas. It eats anything from insects and birds' eggs to seeds, nuts, and even fungi. It often caches food, as it remains quite active throughout the cold, snowy months. The common name refers to the rusty coat color, often most evident in winter. Note also the relatively small size and bright white eye ring. The most common vocalization is a low, growling *chuck* or *churr*. A similar species, the Douglas Squirrel, is found in the Sierra Nevada and Pacific Northwest. Both the Red and Douglas squirrels are commonly called Chickaree, a reference to their vocalizations.

The **MARTEN,** or Pine Marten, is a 40-inch member of the weasel family that ranges throughout the boreal forest. In the West, it occurs in the mountains of the Pacific Northwest and Sierra Nevada as well as the central and northern Rockies. The Marten has a doglike face with small ears. Its coat color is dull yellowish brown and its throat is buffy. The tail is long and rather thick. A similar species, the Fisher, is larger and darker, though otherwise similar. Martens frequent conifer forests, where they prey on Red Squirrels. They are usually nocturnal, but you might see them in early morning or late afternoon, particularly on overcast days. They run well and are skilled climbers, mostly staying in trees. A single pair of Martens may have a territory that ranges over as much as 15 square miles. Like many furbearers, they have been persecuted for their pelts and have been much reduced over certain parts of their range.

WHERE TO VISIT: Lodgepole Pine forests are well developed throughout the Medicine Bow Mountains (particularly Medicine Bow National Forest) and Laramie Mountains of Wyoming. Good stands are present in Yellowstone National Park. Waterton-Glacier International Peace Park also is recommended. Other areas include Shoshone National Forest in Cody, Wyoming; Flathead National Forest in Kalispell, Montana; and Lewis and Clark National Forest in Great Falls, Montana. Many other national forests in the central and northern Rockies have good stands of Lodgepole Pines. In Colorado, they are best developed in the northern and central areas. South of Colorado, they are widely scattered and not well developed.

WAS SMOKEY WRONG?
THE ECOLOGICAL ROLE OF FIRE

In 1950, an abandoned and forlorn-looking bear cub was rescued following a large fire in Lincoln National Forest in New Mexico. This little creature instantly was selected as a living symbol for a cartoon character created by the National Park Service five years earlier. The cub was named Little Smokey, after the gentle, overalls-wearing symbol of forest fire prevention, Smokey the Bear. Smokey the Bear remains a symbol for ecological responsibility. A historical park created in his honor describes the history of fire prevention. The park is in Capitan, New Mexico, near the site where Little Smokey was rescued.

Smokey is one of the most widely recognized symbols in the United States. Almost everyone has seen and heard from the serious, brown-eyed bruin in a ranger hat who looks deeply and appealingly at you and says, "Only *you* can prevent forest fires." But should you? More importantly, should the National Park Service? The answer to the first question is an unequivocal yes. But the answer to the second is a definite, and perhaps surprising, no.

Smokey's campaign against fire was excellently promoted and well conceived. Many catastrophic wildfires were documented to have been accidentally set by careless campers or cigarette smokers. There is simply no excuse for carelessness with fire in natural areas, just as there is no excuse for it in the home. Fire has the capacity to destroy with stunning fury. But fire is also a natural and

Fire-scarred Lodgepole Pines in Yellowstone National Park.

Vast aspen stands owe their existence in large part to periodic natural fires.

necessary occurrence. From the Florida Everglades and the southern Longleaf Pine forests to the eastern coastal plain, north to the boreal Jack Pine forests, west through the prairie grasslands, and into the Ponderosa Pine forests, Lodgepole Pine forests, California chaparral—even the stately groves of Giant Sequoias and Redwoods—fire is an indispensable part of the ecology.

Fire is dramatic and frightening. It seems that we ought to do everything in our power to stop it, to put it out. But such a belief is mistaken. Years of careful ecological study have shown how fire affects various habitats and why these areas actually need to experience periodic fire.

In 1972, on the basis of substantial research on the ecology of fire, the National Park Service adopted a policy that gave park officials the power to choose whether to quell a fire. When fire did not occur, foresters could prescribe burning in certain areas. These decisions were made because of increased understanding of how the plants in various habitats have, over the millennia, adapted to natural fires.

The park service's policy was put to a severe test in the summer of 1988, when over 700,000 acres in and around Yellowstone National Park were ablaze. Many people were outraged that park service officials were not more aggressive in the early stages of the fires. Where was Smokey when we needed him? At the peak of the conflagration in early September, eight immense fires burned out of control in various areas at Yellowstone. The extent of the fires in Yellowstone and surrounding areas far surpassed anything previously recorded. More acres burned in 1988 than the totals from the previous 116 years taken together.

Kilpecker Burn, a large fire that was caused by human accident.

KILLPECKER FIRE JUNE 12,1978
1,200 ACRES MAN CAUSED

Lightning-set fires occur every summer throughout the West. In Yellowstone in 1988, however, conditions were unusual. There was a dry spell, with almost no rain in July and August. Relative humidity was amazingly low, at times only 6 percent. The ground litter—fallen logs, twigs, needles, etc.—was in some cases drier than kiln-dried lumber. And because there had been no fire for considerable periods in many parts of Yellowstone, there was a lot of ground litter. Some of the Yellowstone fires, including the one that threatened the Old Faithful Inn, resulted from human carelessness. Others, however, were set by lightning, some of which struck without accompanying rainfall. Once the fires were ignited, they devoured the tinder with a greed that in some cases produced full-fledged firestorms, with tornado-force winds driving walls of flames as much as 14 miles in a day.

The Yellowstone fires were *crown fires,* moving across the canopy treetops with great speed, burning everything down to the ground. Virtually all trees, shrubs, and herbaceous plants die in crown fires. Animals have little choice but to try to flee. Everything from Redback Voles and pocket gophers to Bison and Great Gray Owls must move ahead of the flames. Some don't make it, though direct loss of animal life from fire (at least among birds and mammals) is surprisingly low. For instance, a survey conducted shortly after the fire indicated that only 246 Elk died in the Yellowstone blazes, though the total population in the park was around 32,000. Also killed were two Moose, four Mule Deer, and nine Bison. However, many animals may perish after the fire from lack of food and shelter.

Crown fires depend on litter accumulation to supply fuel for the fire. When litter is sparse, or when the ground is relatively moist, most fires tend to be either *ground* or *surface fires*. Ground fires burn only the litter, while surface fires consume litter, seedlings, saplings, and shrubs but only singe the mature trees. Ground and surface fires move relatively slowly, and they do not create their own winds; consequently, they are relatively easy to control. All prescribed burns, each one set after careful analysis of conditions, are limited to surface fires. The longer an area goes without fire, the more dry litter there will be, and a fire is more likely to become a crown fire. The way to prevent catastrophic fires is to have regular noncatastrophic fires.

Fire creates conditions ideal for certain species, including some of the most treasured trees in the West. Burning releases minerals and reduces populations of competing seedlings, generally acting to prepare the soil for rapid seed germination. Some tree species such as Lodgepole Pine and Jack Pine have serotinous cones (see page 194), which remain closed on the tree until the heat of fire opens them, releasing seeds long dormant to sprout in the newly mineralized soil. Some herbaceous species, such as the well-named Fireweed and various lupines, thrive in areas opened by fire. Would Fireweed exist without periodic fire? Probably not. Seedlings of species such as Ponderosa Pine require nearly full sun. In a shady, closed forest, future generations of Ponderosas are doomed by darkness. The largest single organism in the world, the Giant Sequoia of the Sierra Nevada Mountains, is dependent on fire for successful reproduction. Fire opens its cones and eliminates seedlings of competing species, opening the groves so that the light-demanding young Sequoias can grow. Though long lived, Sequoias would all be eventually replaced by White Fir were it not for fire.

Fireweed is often among the first plants to invade following a fire.

When a fire sweeps through a stand, it leaves scars on the trees that are evident on the growth rings decades later. It is therefore possible to analyze old trees to determine the frequency of fire in any given region. There is much regional variability. The open Ponderosa Pine stands around Flagstaff, Arizona, burn as frequently as every 2 to 5 years. In contrast, Lodgepole Pine stands at Yellowstone average 300 to 400 years between large fires (so the 1988 fires were really not out of the ordinary, considering the time scale). California coastal Redwoods, which are normally bathed in moist summer mist, tend to burn at intervals of 250 to 500 years, but inland stands can experience fire as frequently as every 50 years. Even the temperate rain forests of the Pacific Northwest experience fire, though up to 2,000 years can go by without a serious burn.

Recent research of fire scars and tree growth from 1700 to 1905 has shown that extensive fires in the Southwest, which typically occur after an abnormally dry spring, are strongly correlated with the Southern Oscillation, a short-term climatic shift originating in the South Pacific. This shift is linked with the occurrence of El Niño, a climatic event resulting, among other things, in abnormal rainfall in many places worldwide. Thus events occurring thousands of miles away in the Pacific Ocean can strongly influence the ecology of western forests.

Native Americans routinely used fire, to drive game or to make hunting easier. Lewis and Clark described how Indians drove Bison with fire. There is no evidence that this practice was ecologically harmful. On the contrary, the indigenous peoples were unwittingly doing a bit of applied ecology.

Yellowstone is no longer black with the soot of destruction but is instead green with new life. Ecological succession is occurring in earnest, and the legacy of the 1988 fires will not be one of tragedy, but one of ecological renewal. Even Smokey would probably agree.

PARIAN FOREST PLATE 13

DICATOR PLANTS

ES: *Eastern (Plains) Cottonwood, Narrowleaf Cottonwood, Fremont Cottonwood, Black Cottonwood,* Peachleaf Willow, Ashleaf Maple (Box-elder), Green Ash, Netleaf Hackberry, Russian-olive, Tamarisk, Beaked Hazelnut, Sitka Mountain-ash, Balsam Poplar, Quaking Aspen, Blue Spruce, White Fir, Water Birch, Scouler Willow.

SHRUBS: *Common (Whitestem) Gooseberry,* Wild Rose, Mountain Maple, *Chokecherry,* Snowberry, *Mountain (Thinleaf) Alder,* Utah Juneberry, Saskatoon Juneberry (Western Serviceberry), hawthorn, Four-lined Honeysuckle, American Plum, Wax Currant, up to 10 willow species including Bebb, Blue, Sandbar, and Subalpine.

HERBACEOUS SPECIES: *Cow Parsnip,* Star Swertia, White Marsh Marigold, Yellow Monkeyflower, Yellow Pond Lily, Globeflower, Chimingbells, Giant Angelica, Bittercress, Western Shooting Star, Twisted-stalk, Northern Bog-orchid, Brook Saxifrage, Parry's Primrose, Common Woodrush, Bulrush, Common Horsetail (Scouring Rush), and vines such as grape, Virginia Creeper, and *White Clematis.*

INDICATOR ANIMALS

BIRDS: *Cordilleran Flycatcher, American Dipper, MacGillivray's Warbler,* Common Merganser, Ring-necked Duck, Mallard, Blue-winged Teal, Green-winged Teal, American Coot, Spotted Sandpiper, Common Snipe, Killdeer, Cooper's Hawk, Northern Harrier, Great Horned Owl, Western Screech-Owl, Belted Kingfisher, White-throated Swift, Broad-tailed Hummingbird, Downy Woodpecker, Northern Flicker, Willow Flycatcher, Dusky Flycatcher, Western Wood-Pewee, Tree Swallow, Violet-green Swallow, Bank Swallow, Cliff Swallow, Black-billed Magpie, Mountain Chickadee, Black-capped Chickadee, House Wren, Bewick's Wren, Marsh Wren, Swainson's Thrush, American Robin, Warbling Vireo, Orange-crowned Warbler, *Yellow Warbler,* Wilson's Warbler, Common Yellowthroat, Black-headed Grosbeak, American Goldfinch, Song Sparrow, White-crowned Sparrow, Fox Sparrow, Lincoln's Sparrow, Red-winged Blackbird, Yellow-headed Blackbird.

MAMMALS: Opossum, Little Brown Myotis, Northern Water Shrew, Least Chipmunk, Beaver, Longtail Vole, Meadow Vole, Eastern Fox Squirrel, Deer Mouse, Muskrat, Eastern Cottontail, Mountain Cottontail, Coyote, Red Fox, Raccoon, Black Bear, Mink, Striped Skunk, Elk, Whitetail Deer.

REPTILES: Western Terrestrial (Wandering) Garter Snake, Smooth Green Snake, Bullsnake.

AMPHIBIANS: *Tiger Salamander,* Boreal Toad, Striped Chorus Frog, Northern Leopard Frog.

DESCRIPTION

Aside from aspen groves, the only Rocky Mountain forest communities dominated by broad-leaved trees are riparian, or riverine, habitats. These forests, especially at low to middle elevations, are dominated by cottonwoods, which, like aspen, are in the genus *Populus*. East of the Rockies, the riverine forest is really a continuation of the prairie riparian forest and is dominated by stately Plains Cottonwoods. On the western slopes, especially in the southern Rockies, Fremont Cottonwood dominates, and is replaced by Narrowleaf Cottonwood from about 7,000 feet upward. From the northern Rockies to Alaska, Black Cottonwood prevails. At lower elevations, cottonwoods are joined by Ashleaf Maple, Peachleaf Willow, Green Ash, Russian-olive, and occasionally Tamarisk. At middle elevations, cottonwoods share the river bank with Balsam Poplar, and Quaking Aspen, as well as two conifers, Blue Spruce (Plate 14) and White Fir. Both of these picturesque conifers occur along mountainside watercourses, and both are commonly planted as ornamentals. White Fir (not illustrated) is identified by its long, upcurved, flattened needles, which have a powdery look, and its smooth, light gray bark. At high elevations, cottonwoods are replaced by Water Birch, Mountain Alder, and various willows.

Shrubs can be extremely dense along riverine areas, dominating on sand and gravel bars, where shrubby willows usually abound. At high elevations, alder thickets prevail. The abundance of sunlight along river banks often stimulates an abundance of vines, especially Wild Grape and Virginia Creeper.

Wildflowers are also abundant, including such tall species as Cow Parsnip, Common Woodrush, and Bulrush. These are joined by smaller and more delicate shooting stars, twisted-stalks, and gentians. On the eastern side of the Rockies, some eastern wildflowers such as Wild Sarsaparilla can be found.

Riverine areas are oases for birds. Vireos, warblers, goldfinches,

Riverine forest of Narrowleaf Cottonwood in southwestern Colorado.

and grosbeaks sing from the cottonwood canopy, and Red-tailed Hawks and Cooper's Hawks perch in the tall, spreading trees, which also form ideal nesting sites for both Western Screech-Owls and Great Horned Owls. Belted Kingfishers emit their dry, rattling calls as they dive for fish. The more methodical Great Blue Heron stands stock-still at the water's edge, not moving a muscle, then suddenly striking at a fish or frog with its long neck and bill. Flowing waters may harbor pairs of Common Mergansers or Ring-necked Ducks, both of which dive for their food, while quiet, bulrush-lined pools are nesting grounds for dabbling ducks such as Blue-winged and Green-winged teals. Two species, MacGillivray's Warbler and American Dipper, are both riverine specialists. The warbler favors the dense shrubs that line the river's edge, while the dipper can be found in clear, fast-flowing mountain streams.

The Beaver is the most important riverine mammal, since its activities can alter the very flow of the river. In some areas, humans disagree with the engineering decisions of the Beaver, preferring to keep the river undammed, and the robust rodents are unwelcome. Making far less impact on the habitat, the Muskrat is easily distinguished from the Beaver by its narrow tail and smaller body size. Minks patrol the river banks in quest of voles and other warm-blooded fare, and Raccoons wash their food by moonlight in the cool, flowing waters. The Opossum, a southeastern mammal and North America's only marsupial, is expanding its range along rivers and has reached the eastern side of the Rockies.

SIMILAR FOREST COMMUNITIES: See prairie riparian forest, Arizona canyon riparian forest.

RANGE: Throughout the Rocky Mountains at all elevations, though species composition changes with elevation. On the eastern slope, this forest community is essentially a continuation of the prairie riparian forest.

REMARKS

Four cottonwood species dominate riverine communities in the Rocky Mountains, and they are sometimes difficult to distinguish. Fortunately, the species tend to occur in different areas or at different elevations. However, there are places where their ranges overlap, and occasionally they hybridize. A tree called Lanceleaf Cottonwood, once thought to be a separate species, is in fact a hybrid between Plains Cottonwood and Narrowleaf Cottonwood.

All cottonwoods have leaves on long petioles, as do aspens and poplars. Cottonwoods also tend to have deeply ridged bark, usually light in color. **PLAINS COTTONWOOD**, a subspecies of Eastern

Cottonwood, has broad, heart-shaped, toothed leaves that are larger than those of the otherwise similar **FREMONT COTTONWOOD.** **NARROWLEAF COTTONWOOD** is well named, as it has either lance-shaped or long leaves with tiny teeth. **BLACK COTTONWOOD** leaves have more of an arrowhead shape than a heart shape. All cotton-woods produce wind-dispersed seeds with feathery attachments that help the seed "fly." All cottonwoods have deep taproots that enable the tree to survive during periods of little rainfall, and all are relatively short-lived.

Narrowleaf is the smallest species, rarely topping 50 feet, while Black Cottonwood (not in the Rocky Mountains) is the tallest, sometimes reaching 165 feet. Plains and Fremont cottonwoods rarely exceed 100 feet, but both have wide trunks and spreading crowns, making them among the most picturesque of trees.

NETLEAF HACKBERRY is a tree of the southern Rockies and the Southwest, ranging into Mexico. Hackberries are related to bass-woods and redbuds. Leaves are long, unlobed, and untoothed, with asymmetrical bases. The netlike veins on the leaves give this species its name. Bark is smooth but with numerous warty growths. This species produces a smooth, red, cherrylike fruit often eaten by Native Americans and by many wildlife species.

MOUNTAIN ALDER, as the name implies, grows at higher eleva-tions throughout western mountains as far north as central Alaska. Leaves are oval and double-toothed, and branches are reddish. As with all alders, this species has seeds in small, cone-like female catkins. Male catkins are slim and drooping, and catkins of both sexes occur on the same tree. Mountain Alder grows no taller than about 30 feet, usually smaller. In the south-ern Rockies it can be found at elevations of about 10,000 feet, but it moves progressively lower with higher latitude. In Alaska, it is found on flat tundra at sea level. Mountain Alder is quite simi-lar to other alder species, and identification can be difficult.

CHOKECHERRY, with its sprays of white flowers that become dark blue fruits, often forms thickets along streams and rivers.

COMMON GOOSEBERRY, also called Whitestem Gooseberry and Gooseberry Currant, is one of several species in the genus *Ribes* that occur in various habitats from the Lower Sonoran Zone to the Canadian Zone. Gooseberries are members of the saxifrage family. All are spiny shrubs with pinkish flowers. Berries are sticky and heavily fed upon by birds. Deer and Elk browse the leaves.

COW PARSNIP, a member of the parsley family, is a huge wild-flower capable of attaining a height of 8 feet under favorable con-ditions. It thrives in moist areas such as streambanks and moun-tain meadows and is widely distributed in North America. Hundreds of tiny white flowers form flat umbels that attract numerous pollinating insects. In this large plant, an umbel may measure fully a foot in diameter. Leaves are compound, with 3 deeply toothed leaflets per leaf. Cow Parsnip is so named because it is eaten by animals ranging from deer and sheep to humans (and, of course, cows). It is reputed to be bad-tasting, and the stem hairs are extremely irritating to soft mouth tissues. Experienced people peel the stems before attempting to consume the plant. They also identify the plant carefully, because its close relative the Water Hemlock is extremely poisonous, and they do look a bit alike. Another relative is Poison Hemlock, the plant reputed to have terminated Socrates.

From the canopy of a cottonwood, you may hear a sharp two-note sound, something like *pit-wheep*. The bird making this sound is a nondescript, greenish brown, 5.5-inch flycatcher called the **CORDILLERAN FLYCATCHER.** If you see it well, note its eye ring and two white wing bars, and a yellow wash on its breast. This little bird and the very similar Pacific-Slope Flycatcher were recently "split"; both were formerly called Western Flycatcher. The Cordilleran and Pacific-Slope flycatchers are in the genus *Empidonax*, a group of 10 species that look very much alike. The best way to separate the various species is by range, habitat, and especially voice. The Pacific-Slope Flycatcher is found in the far West, and its note is an upward-slurred *tsleep*, distinct from the note made by the Cordilleran species. To confuse matters, however, these two flycatchers share a similarly variable, rather unmusical, three-note song. In other words, they look alike, and, except for the call notes, they sound alike, but they do not share a range. The Cordilleran occurs only in the Rockies.

Much easier to identify is the **AMERICAN DIPPER** (or Water Ouzel), which can be found along fast-running, rock-strewn mountain streams throughout the West, ranging well into Alaska and as far south as southern Mexico. One of only four dipper species worldwide, this chunky, 8-inch, wrenlike bird is uniformly slate gray with a short tail and faint eye ring. Look for it standing on a boulder or rock wherever there is swift current, including rapids. Like most songbirds, dippers are territorial, but because they stay close to streams, their territories are linear. Each dipper pair has its own stretch of stream. The mossy nest is placed on a cliff or big rock, usually over the water, where it would be difficult for predators to reach. The most remarkable characteristic of dippers is their ability to swim underwater, where they forage for the aquatic insect larvae that are their principal food source. Dippers have a strong preference for streams with a lot of rubble on the bottom, and they are reputed to swim without difficulty in currents too strong for a human to stand upright.

Singing from an alder or willow thicket, the **MACGILLIVRAY'S WARBLER** is recognized by its gray hood, bright yellow breast, and split eye ring. This husky, 5.5-inch warbler is a summer resident throughout the West, ranging as far north as southern Alaska. Its melodic song is a rolling *tweedle-tweedle-tweedle-tweet-tweet*. This is a bird of the dense undergrowth, but it is worth the patience required to stalk it for a good look. It closely resembles the more eastern Connecticut and Mourning warblers, but neither of those nests in the Rocky Mountains. The grassy nest is usually deep in a thicket, close to the ground.

Perhaps easier to see than MacGillivray's, the **YELLOW WARBLER** alights to sings its loud *wheet-wheet-wheet-wee* song anywhere from the high cottonwood canopy to the head of a Cow Parsnip. Yellow Warblers are among the most widespread and common wood warblers, ranging throughout all of North America into northern Alaska. Males are bright yellow with red stripes on the breast. Females are duller yellow. In spring, male Yellow Warblers engage in territorial disputes among themselves, and it is not uncommon to see them chasing each other as they try to sort out the real estate. Yellow Warblers are often parasitized by cowbirds, which lay their eggs in the warblers' nests. If the warbler detects the strange egg, it may abandon its (and the cowbird's) eggs and build a new nest atop the old one.

The 13-inch **TIGER SALAMANDER** is one of the largest salamanders in North America and the largest found on land. Various races of this species can be found anywhere from damp cellars to wet woodlands from eastern North America throughout the West into central Canada. It is not uncommon in wet Rocky Mountain forests and along rivers and streams. It breeds in ponds and can be found from the Lower Sonoran Zone through the Canadian Zone, up to 11,000 feet. The Rocky Mountain subspecies, called the Blotched Tiger Salamander, is pale yellow-brown with black stripes, often blotchy. Tiger Salamanders are carnivores, eating earthworms, insects, other amphibians, and an occasional mouse.

WHERE TO VISIT: Riverine areas abound throughout the Rocky Mountains. Nearly all the national parks and national forests have at least some riverine habitat. Lots of picnic groves and campgrounds are located near riparian areas. Dippers are relatively easily seen at Rocky Mountain, Grand Teton, Waterton-Glacier, Banff, and Jasper national parks. The Colorado River, running from Rocky Mountain National Park through the Grand Canyon in Arizona, affords particularly impressive riverine habitat. Farther north, visit the riparian areas in Yellowstone National Park.

INDICATOR PLANTS

TREES: *Engelmann Spruce* (White Spruce in far north), *Subalpine Fir* (Balsam Fir in far north), Corkbark Fir (a variety of Subalpine Fir), Blue Spruce, White Fir, Lodgepole Pine, Quaking Aspen, Common Douglas-fir.

SHRUBS: *Grouse Whortleberry,* Myrtle Blueberry, Tundra Dwarf Birch, Canada Buffaloberry, Colorado Currant, Red Elderberry, Common Juniper, Mountain-lover, Snowbrush, Kinnikinnick.

HERBACEOUS SPECIES: *Jacob's Ladder (Skypilot),* Explorer's Gentian, Broadleaf Arnica, Heartleaf Arnica, Pipsissewa, Orange Sneezeweed, Colorado Columbine, Western Bistort, Alpine Avens (Dryad), Monkshood, Twinflower, Starflower, Globeflower, Northern Bogorchid, Aspen (Five-veined) Sunflower, Wood Nymph, Falsehellebore (Cornlily), Showy Daisy.

INDICATOR ANIMALS

BIRDS: *Gray Jay, Ruby-crowned Kinglet, Golden-crowned Kinglet, Redbreasted Nuthatch, Black-backed Woodpecker, Hermit Thrush, Yellow-rumped Warbler,* Northern Goshawk, Sharp-shinned Hawk, Blue Grouse, Northern Saw-whet Owl, Boreal Owl, Hairy Woodpecker, Three-toed Woodpecker, Williamson's Sapsucker, Olivesided Flycatcher, Steller's Jay, Clark's Nutcracker, Common Raven, Mountain Chickadee, Brown Creeper, Townsend's Solitaire, Wilson's Warbler, Pine Siskin, Red Crossbill, Pine Grosbeak, Cassin's Finch, Dark-eyed Junco, White-crowned Sparrow.

MAMMALS: *Snowshoe Hare, Red (Pine) Squirrel,* Least Chipmunk, Golden-mantled Ground Squirrel, Porcupine, Mountain Vole, Boreal Redback Vole, Longtail Weasel, Ermine, Marten, Lynx, Bobcat, Black Bear, Grizzly Bear, Red Fox, Elk, Mule Deer, Bighorn Sheep.

DESCRIPTION

Two tree species, Engelmann Spruce and Subalpine Fir, dominate the Canadian and Hudsonian zone forests throughout the central and southern Rockies. Each of these species is gradually replaced by White Spruce and Balsam Fir in the northern Rockies. This is a dark forest of tall, spired evergreens, interspersed among aspen and Lodgepole Pine stands, often with areas of mountain meadow. At lower elevations, Douglas-fir forests are not uncommon. The interior of a spruce-fir forest is dark, with a soft bed of slowly decomposing needles. Lots of fallen, decomposing trees and an abundance of dead branches make foot travel difficult. Wildflowers are often sparse, but a few, including Twin-

Figure 22. Boreal (left) and Saw-whet owls

flower, Pipsissewa, and various arnicas, can be common. The most abundant shrubs are usually in the genus *Vaccinium*, the blueberries and whortleberries.

The shady, fragrant forest of "Christmas trees" hosts many bird species. Perhaps most characteristic is the husky Gray Jay, sometimes called Whiskeyjack or Camp Robber for its habit of boldly landing on picnic tables and helping itself. Much more secretive are the Boreal and Northern Saw-whet owls, two small owls that are not uncommon nesters in the spruce-fir forest. Woodpeckers are also common, including both the Three-toed and Black-backed woodpeckers, but they are often quiet and easily overlooked. If you see areas of stripped bark, especially in recently burned areas, listen for the soft tappings of these woodpeckers. More easily heard are the sharp nasal calls of the Red-breasted Nuthatch, one of the most abundant Canadian Zone birds. Often in company of kinglets, the nuthatch searches the conifers for insects and spiders. In a forest of cone-producing trees, the seed eaters are also there, especially Pine Siskins and Red Crossbills. The melodious Cassin's Finch, splendid in its raspberry plumage, often sings from a treetop.

Red Squirrels noisily move from tree to tree, often searching for a bird's nest to rob, while on the ground the Snowshoe Hare nibbles on various wildflowers. Picnic grounds are usually the haunts of Least Chipmunks and Golden-mantled Squirrels, but every now and then a Black Bear may pay a visit. The much more dangerous Grizzly Bear also roams the spruce-fir forest and adjacent meadows.

A high-elevation lake in the spruce-fir forest.

SIMILAR FOREST COMMUNITIES: See timberline-alpine tundra and high pine forest.

RANGE: Canadian and Hudsonian zones throughout the Rocky Mountains, usually beginning at about 9,000 feet in Colorado; at lower elevations farther north, higher ones in the south, continuing to the tree line. Extends south to the Sangre de Cristo Mountains in New Mexico, and the Chiricahua Mountains and Santa Catalina Mountains in southern Arizona.

REMARKS

The spruce-fir forest of the Rockies is a sharp contrast to the Upper Sonoran pinyon-juniper forest. High in elevation, the climate is no longer hot and dry, but is instead cool and moist, with an average yearly temperature of just under 35°F and frost possible any month of the year. Winter snowfall is heavy, with about 5 feet or more on the ground throughout the winter, some of it remaining in isolated snowfields throughout much of the summer. Total annual precipitation, depending on location, is 28–40 inches.

Spruce and fir trees look alike in general shape but are nonetheless easily differentiated. Spruce needles are prickly, with sharp points, while fir needles are considerably softer. Both spruce and fir cones are usually on the uppermost branches, but spruce cones are brown and dangle downward, whereas fir cones are usually purplish in color and upright. Fir cones disintegrate on the tree, leaving pencillike, upright sticks. Spruce cones drop off and accumulate on the forest floor, often in large numbers.

ENGELMANN SPRUCE occurs abundantly at appropriate elevations throughout the Rockies and much of the Cascades, ranging well into British Columbia. Needles are dark bluish green and are not

Engelmann Spruce is extremely abundant throughout much of the Rocky Mountains.

quite as prickly as other spruces. Bark is brown and scaly. Cones are brown, with nonprickly scales. While Engelmann Spruce can reach nearly 200 feet tall, heights of around 80 feet or less are more common. At timberline, Engelmann Spruce forms shrublike *krummholz* (page TK).

SUBALPINE FIR ranges throughout the Rockies, Cascades, and Olympic Mountains, north to the Yukon and southern Alaska. The needles are flat, but their bases are curved, making them turn upward on the branch. Each needle usually has a thin white stripe on its upper surface, though you will need to look closely. Bark is pale and smooth, with resin blisters. Cones are purple, upright, and rarely found on the ground.

CORKBARK FIR is a variety of Subalpine Fir, named for its somewhat soft, corky-feeling bark. It replaces Subalpine Fir in the southern end of the Sangre de Cristo Range in New Mexico.

The Canadian Zone spruce-fir forest is an extension of the boreal forest that characterizes much of Canada and, for that matter, northern Eurasia. The most abundant boreal forest trees are **WHITE SPRUCE** and **BALSAM FIR.** Engelmann Spruce is a close relative of White Spruce, is replaced by it in many places in the northern Rockies, and often hybridizes with it. Likewise, Subalpine Fir is closely related to Balsam Fir and tends to be replaced by it in the northern Rockies. Balsam and Subalpine firs also occasionally hybridize. Another pair worth mentioning is **JACK PINE** and **LODGEPOLE PINE,** which, like the pairs of spruces and firs, are considered to be "sister species." Such close genetic similarity is not unexpected considering that the Rocky Mountains did not even begin to form until 70 million years ago (that sounds like a long time but, in terms of tree evolution, it's really rather brief—

trees have long generation times). Engelmann Spruce, Subalpine Fir, and Lodgepole Pine are newly evolved species derived from the boreal species that are their near relatives.

Glaciation has probably strongly affected the distribution of Engelmann Spruce, Subalpine Fir, and Lodgepole Pine, especially in the southern Rockies. For instance, neither Engelmann Spruce nor Lodgepole Pine are present on Pike's Peak in central Colorado. Pike's Peak is just east of the main Colorado Front Range and is thus somewhat isolated. Following glacial retreat, neither species has been able to colonize, probably simply because their seeds have not blown there. In the Chiricahua Mountains in southeastern Arizona, only Engelmann Spruce occurs, but in the Santa Catalina Mountains near Tucson, Engelmann Spruce is absent, but Subalpine Fir is present.

Throughout most of the central and northern Rockies, both Engelmann Spruce and Subalpine Fir occur in the Canadian Zone. Why? Usually the majority of the large trees in a stand, often up to 75 percent, are spruces, but the understory of seedlings and saplings may be 50 to 90 percent fir. Is fir destined to replace spruce? Did spruce enjoy some initial advantage? These questions, as yet, lack answers. One possible contributing cause is that spruce lives longer than fir. And at least one ecologist has suggested that spruce seedlings survive best under a canopy of fir,

and vice versa. Each species may be a bit different from the other in its ideal habitat requirements. Spruce seems more able to withstand extremes than fir, dominating on really wet sites as well as really dry sites. Engelmann Spruce is the "tree-line tree," the one

Short cones with distinctive bracts help identify Common Douglas-fir.

that makes it to the timberline, but fir drops out at lower elevations. Fir seems to thrive best on moderately moist sites. Spruce tends to establish itself much more quickly than fir on newly opened sites following fire, whereas fir seedlings are apt to invade shady forests with a good organic litter layer.

BLUE SPRUCE, a well-known ornamental tree, is native to elevations of between 6,000 and 11,000 feet, with a limited range from eastern Idaho and southern Wyoming south to scattered locations in New Mexico. It is most common along streams and in wet meadows, where it is often scattered among meadow sedges and wildflowers. Named for the distinctly blue-gray look of its needles, this tree is nonetheless often difficult to distinguish from Engelmann Spruce. Blue Spruce has darker, more furrowed bark than Engelmann Spruce, probably the most helpful field mark in separating the two. Its needles are also a bit more prickly. Blue Spruce grows quite slowly but is long lived, up to 800 years old. Though it produces dense seed crops, the seeds germinate only on sites disturbed by landslide or fire.

The Canadian Zone conifers are subject to various serious pest species. Western Spruce Budworm, actually the caterpillar of a moth species, can defoliate both Engelmann and Blue spruces. If the infestation is protracted, the trees will die. The Engelmann Spruce Beetle can also do severe damage.

Forests dominated by **DOUGLAS-FIR** are common throughout the Rockies, usually from about 5,600 feet up to 9,000 feet. Douglas-fir seems to require more moisture and shade than Ponderosa Pine but less than Canadian Zone spruces and firs. Douglas-fir forests in

This mixed stand is dominated by tall Douglas-firs.

the Rockies are similar to those found in much of the Pacific Northwest.

GROUSE WHORTLEBERRY, in the genus *Vaccinium* along with the blueberries, is one of the most abundant understory shrubs in the Canadian Zone. Approximately 15 *Vaccinium* species occur in the Rocky Mountains, all of them shrubs with elliptical, untoothed leaves and large berries. Whortleberry fruits are bright red. All *Vacciniums* thrive best in the acidic soils of conifer forests.

EXPLORER'S GENTIAN is one of the showiest of the Canadian Zone wildflowers. It is common along streams at elevations of between 7,000 and 10,000 feet. The plant is about 12 inches tall. Each stem terminates in a single blue flower, spotted inside with little greenish dots. The leaves are opposite and not toothed.

JACOB'S LADDER, also known as Skypilot, produces a large lavender flower with yellow anthers. Look for it at high elevations, usually between 9,000 and 12,000 feet, anywhere in the Rocky Mountains. There are several other similar species, all commonly called Jacob's Ladder. This species is interesting for its odor, which is remarkably like that of a skunk. Should you crush the leaves, either by choice or by stepping on them, you will probably wish you hadn't, as the odor is often quite strong. The disagreeable smell presumably means a disagreeable taste, perhaps an adaptation to reduce grazing pressure. Leaves are compound and, in addition to being smelly, they are a bit sticky.

The **GRAY JAY** is, indeed, just that. This stocky, 11.5-inch, crestless jay is gray above and pale below. Birds in the southern Rockies have whiter heads than those to the north. The former name for Gray Jay was Canada Jay, because the bird is abundant throughout the Canadian boreal forest. It is common throughout the Rockies and Pacific Northwest but is absent from the Sierra Nevada. Gray Jays are opportunists, and, like most jays, rather bold and curious. They will gather at campsites or picnic areas and even land on your hand if you offer food. Immature birds, which often accompany a parent, are dark slaty gray. Gray Jays cache food but are reported to be frequent victims of robbery by Steller's Jays. In winter, Gray Jays sometimes migrate to lower elevations seeking warmer climes and increased food resources.

The **RED-BREASTED NUTHATCH** ranges throughout North America, wherever there are spruces and firs. Over much of its range it is irruptive and migratory, but it is essentially a permanent resident in Rocky Mountain forests. Unlike Pygmy Nuthatches, Redbreasts do not travel in single-species flocks, though they sometimes join chickadees in mixed-species foraging flocks. The bird is easy to identify, as it is the only nuthatch with a black line through the eye. It forages in traditional nuthatch fashion, hitching head first down tree trunks, but it also explores outer branches and cones. The voice of this little upside-down bird of the conifer trunks is a sharp, nasal *yank-yank*, a sound that has been compared to a tin horn. Like other nuthatches, this species nests in tree cavities, usually in a spruce. During nesting, the parent birds may get a lot of spruce resin on their feathers. Red-breasts feed on both animal food and pine seeds.

Two kinglet species, the **RUBY-CROWNED KINGLET** and the **GOLDEN-CROWNED KINGLET,** can be found throughout western mountain forests, though the Ruby-crowned is but a summer resident over most of the northern Rockies. Kinglets, at 3.5 to 4 inches, are among the tiniest of birds, larger only than hummingbirds, none of which winters in areas as cold as the ones kinglets call home. The Golden-crowned Kinglet is smaller and more hardy than the Ruby-crowned. The Golden-crowned actively forages for overwintering insect eggs, cocoons, and spiders throughout the snowy winter months. Kinglets are "flitters." They scoot from tree to tree, often hovering momentarily at a promising needle cluster or cone. Kinglets, along with chickadees, seem to have developed a strong "search image" for stationary animal food. This means that unlike wood warblers, which seem to have to see movement to know that food is in the offing, kinglets and chickadees know how to distinguish animal food, even if it does not move in any way. This adaptation may be one possible reason why kinglets, and not wood warblers, live in winter woods. Another probable reason is that physiologically, kinglets simply can withstand cold better than wood warblers. Kinglets are genetically related to Eurasian warblers, which evolved in colder climates than American wood warblers, a group that almost certainly originated in the tropics. The Golden-crowned Kinglet is named for its yellow head, which includes brilliant orange in males. The Ruby-crowned has a red topknot, usually concealed but visible if the bird is particularly excited. Both are small, olive green birds with wing bars.

The **SNOWSHOE HARE,** often called the Varying Hare, ranges throughout northern North America, from northern Alaska and Canada south to the northernmost states. It occurs in all major mountain ranges, including the eastern Appalachians as well as the Rockies, Cascades, and Sierra Nevada. The Snowshoe's most notable characteristic is that its color changes with the seasons. It is quite white in winter and mottled brown in summer. At all seasons its feet are white (pale in summer), and its ears have black tips. The only other rabbit to occur in the Canadian Zone is **MOUNTAIN COTTONTAIL,** which lacks black ear tips and has a puffier, whiter tail. Mountain Cottontails do not become white in winter. The color change undergone by the Snowshoe Hare is determined by day length, with shorter days in fall triggering the change to white and longer days in spring stimulating the change to brown. Spring hares are conspicuous if snow persists longer than usual, but when this occurs, the animals themselves seem more wary, as though they know they are uncamouflaged. Snowshoe Hares are known for their extreme population cycles. Peak populations occur, on average, every 9 to 10 years, followed by a major population crash. Snowshoe Hares are heavily preyed upon by foxes, Bobcat, Lynx, and other predators. Predator populations crash as well after their food source is so seriously reduced. These events are thought to stimulate southward irruptions of certain birds such as Great Gray Owls and Rough-legged Hawks. Snowshoe Hares eat a variety of vegetable foods and will eat meat if they can get it. When excited, they tend to run wildly in circles.

WHERE TO VISIT: The spruce-fir forest covers the higher elevations of the Rocky Mountains like a blanket. Waterton-Glacier, on the Canada-U. S. border, and Banff and Jasper national parks in Canada have extensive spruce-fir stands. In southern Wyoming, try the Medicine Bow National Forest, and in northwestern Wyoming, take the road northeast (Scenic Highway 212) from Yellowstone through Shoshone National Forest across Beartooth Pass. In Idaho, the Boise National Forest provides access to the picturesque Sawtooth Wilderness Area. Cache and Wasatch national forests in northern Utah are recommended. Rocky Mountain National Park and Trail Ridge Road in particular are strongly recommended. Also in Colorado, the roads across Berthoud Pass and Loveland Pass provide ideal looks at spruce-fir forest. Roosevelt, Arapaho, Routt, White River, Gunnison, San Juan, and Rio Grande national forests, all in Colorado, are recommended. The drive from Durango to Silverton in southwest Colorado will take you through plenty of nice spruce-fir. Carson and Santa Fe national forests in New Mexico are also recommended.

HIGH PINE FOREST   PLATE 15

INDICATOR PLANTS
TREES: *Rocky Mountain Bristlecone Pine, Limber Pine, Whitebark Pine,* Subalpine Larch, Subalpine Fir, Engelmann Spruce.
SHRUBS: *Canada Buffaloberry, Grouse Whortleberry, Kinnikinnick, Common Juniper,* various blueberries, Red Raspberry, Wild Rose, Mountain Snowberry, Shrubby Cinquefoil, Mountain-lover.
HERBACEOUS SPECIES: *Lanceleaf Sedum (Yellow Stonecrop), Rock Cress,* Alpine Pussytoes, Rocky Mountain Loco, Alpine Clover, Alpine Thistle, Alpine Phacelia (Purple Fringe), Wallflower, Alpine Pen-

stemon, Mountain Muhly, Common Alumroot, Mountain Candytuft, Spotted Saxifrage, Antelope Sage (Alpine Buckwheat), Muttongrass, Junegrass.

INDICATOR ANIMALS

BIRDS: *Clark's Nutcracker,* Three-toed Woodpecker, Golden Eagle, White-tailed Ptarmigan, Hairy Woodpecker, Gray Jay, Common Raven, Horned Lark, American Pipit, Yellow-rumped Warbler, Wilson's Warbler, Pine Grosbeak, Red Crossbill, Pine Siskin, Cassin's Finch, Dark-eyed Junco, White-crowned Sparrow.

MAMMALS: *Least Chipmunk, Bushytail Woodrat,* Porcupine, Red (Pine) Squirrel, Golden-mantled Ground Squirrel, Yellowbelly Marmot, Snowshoe Hare, Longtail Weasel, Ermine, Elk, Mule Deer, Bighorn Sheep.

DESCRIPTION

Though spruce and fir dominate the Canadian and Hudsonian zones throughout the Rockies, these trees fare badly on high mountain sites that are dry and windswept, as is typical of many south-facing slopes. Here they are largely replaced by a forest of small, twisted, gnarled trees, most of which belong to the white pine group, five-needled pines adapted to withstand harsh, dry conditions. Two species, Rocky Mountain Bristlecone Pine and Limber Pine, predominate throughout the central and southern Rockies. Farther north, these species are replaced by Whitebark Pine and Subalpine Larch. The look of these high pine forests is open and rugged. Rarely do any of the trees exceed 30 feet in height, and most are smaller. Many have unique twisted shapes, molded by hundreds, in some cases thousands, of years of essentially uninterrupted exposure to wind and snow. There is rarely a closed canopy. Instead, these stocky pines are widely spaced on uneven, rocky terrain, sometimes among patches of Kinnikinnick or Common Juniper, often just on bare rock and dry, gravelly soil. Wildflowers grow sparsely as well, though Rock Cress and Lance-leaf Sedum manage to gain a roothold among the rocks.

The large and formidable Golden Eagle often looks down on the old pines as it searches from the sky for unsuspecting marmots or hares, and Common Ravens may cavort together in the high air. Water Pipits and Horned Larks fly by, though they will not land until they reach the alpine tundra. A few Dark-eyed Juncos join White-crowned Sparrows in the shrubby undergrowth, and a Red Crossbill flock may stop momentarily to check the pine cones for seeds. The most characteristic bird of the high pines is Clark's Nutcracker, a bold gray and white member of the crow and jay family, named by Meriwether Lewis in honor of his part-

Bristlecone Pines show effects of extreme exposure.

ner. Nutcrackers range upward from the Upper Sonoran Zone, but at heart they are birds of subalpine lands, and the wind-sculpted boughs of the ancient pines are their chosen perches.

A few mammals are at home in the high pines, especially Bighorn Sheep, Yellowbelly Marmots, and Least Chipmunks. The Bushytail Woodrat diligently attends its midden, a nest or pile that it fills with whatever suits its fancy.

SIMILAR FOREST COMMUNITIES: See timberline-alpine tundra.

RANGE: Throughout the central and southern Rocky Mountains on dry, windswept, exposed high-mountain sites, typically above 9,000 feet, though the range can be from 7,500 feet up. Limber Pine occurs at lower elevations than Bristlecone Pine. In the northern Rockies, Whitebark Pine and Subalpine Larch replace Limber and Bristlecone pines.

REMARKS

The high pine forest is a land of extremes—of extreme temperatures, frequent drought (usually less than 30 inches of annual precipitation), high winds, severe ice and snow, intense summer sunlight, hard, dry soils, and an abundance of rocks. The cool, moist climate that supports the spruce-fir forest is not found here—and neither are the spruces and firs.

LIMBER PINE is the most widely distributed tree in this forest, occurring from 5,000–12,000 feet throughout the Rocky Mountains, much of the Great Basin, and the Sierra Nevada. The scientific name *flexilis* and common name "limber" refer to its flexible twigs, adapted for bending in the intense winds. Limber Pines rarely exceed 50 feet in height, but their trunks may mea-

The needles of Bristlecone Pine grow in clusters of five that tightly hug the branch.

sure as much as a yard in diameter. The yellow-green needles are in clusters of 5, and usually are 2–2.5 inches long. Cones measure 3–6 inches and open at maturity, releasing seeds. Trunks are quite dark, usually deeply furrowed. Though Bristlecone Pines are better known for their Methuselan life spans, Limber Pines can survive for nearly 2,000 years.

ROCKY MOUNTAIN BRISTLECONE PINES are found on scattered mountains in Colorado, northern New Mexico, and the San Francisco Peaks just north of Flagstaff, Arizona. Some botanists lump them with Great Basin Bristlecones, which occur on widely scattered peaks in Utah, Nevada, and eastern California. The two species are very similar except that the Rocky Mountain Bristlecone has abundant resin dots (little white specks) on its needles and only one resin duct (thin line) on the upper needle surface. Great Basin Bristlecones live to be considerably older, some exceeding 4,000 years. By comparison, Rocky Mountain Bristlecones are a mere 1,500 to 2,000 years old. Identify a Bristlecone Pine by its short (less than 2 inches), dark green needles in clusters of 5 that tightly hug the branch. Cones are short, only about 3 inches, and are, as the common name suggest, really prickly. Bark is pale brown and not deeply furrowed. Bristlecones rarely reach more than 30 feet in height.

Bristlecone Pines are elegant old trees. They aren't big, in fact they're quite small compared with such giants as Douglas-fir, Giant Sequoia, and Redwood. They're more the size of pinyons. It is their shape, not their size, that makes them an art form. Many have stood firm against time's arrows for 10 times as long as there has been a United States, their history seemingly etched on their twisted trunks and bare limbs. Clumps of dense needles, many of which have remained on the tree for a dozen years or more, tightly hug a few surviving branches, capturing just enough sunlight to keep the old tree alive. Roots twist down among the boulders, penetrating deeply, keeping the tree firmly anchored. Bristlecones grow very, very slowly. A look at a cross section of trunk will reveal scores of growth rings far more densely packed than in other, larger, younger trees. Such a growth pattern helps protect the tree against the ravages of insects and fungi, since the wood is so dense it is virtually impenetrable. As the centuries pass, Bristlecones tend to die slowly, in stages, perhaps losing some bark to fire, then a little more to the appetites of Porcupines, then suffering damage from wind, ice, or occasional lightning strikes. Finally the tree is finished, but its wood is so resistant to decay that its bare-branched skeleton remains standing for decades after its last needles have dropped forever.

SUBALPINE LARCH is found in the northern Rockies in Idaho, Wyoming, Alberta, and British Columbia, and the Washington Cascades. It is usually at high elevations, though on exposed sites with poor soils it may occur as low as 5,500 feet. Needles are in clumps, and each needle is distinctly 4-sided. Cones are about 2 inches long, and the scales have long bracts. Twigs are whitish and quite hairy, and the bark is grayish. Like the nine other larch species in the world, Subalpine Larch is a deciduous conifer, dropping its needles in fall and growing new ones in spring. This species tends to share the northernmost high pine forest with Whitebark Pine, another of the 5-needle pines.

COMMON JUNIPER is indeed common, not only on exposed sites in the Rocky Mountains (and all other western mountains) but also throughout northern North America and Eurasia. It is the only juniper to have a shrubby growth form, and large thickets of it carpet exposed sites, forming mats up to 10 feet in diameter. Needles are in whorls of 3, and seeds are contained in juicy, dark blue "berries," actually modified cones, that give off the scent of gin.

ROCK CRESS is one of a few wildflowers able to thrive in the rugged, dry soils of the high pine forest. It is an upright plant, from 1–2 feet tall, with 4-petaled white flowers. As with other members of the mustard family, seeds are contained in upright pods. Leaves are long and hug the stem tightly.

LANCELEAF SEDUM, also known as Yellow Stonecrop, is recognized by its characteristic basal rosettes of thick, fleshy, wax-coated leaves, adapted to retain moisture in the drought-prone environment. Flowers are yellow, borne on stalks that stand 1–2 feet tall. Both Rock Cress and Lanceleaf Sedum are found on exposed sites at high elevations throughout the Rockies.

The unmistakable **CLARK'S NUTCRACKER** is a permanent resident throughout all western mountains, ranging north to central British Columbia and Alberta. It is one of the birds that virtually every visitor to western national parks gets to see, because it often seeks handouts at picnic areas, mountain overlooks, or other places where tourists gather. In flight it looks like a small (13-inch) crow, but it has a long bill, a gray body, and black wings and tail. The outer tail feathers and rear edge of the wings are bright white. It is a noisy bird, often calling a loud, somewhat crowlike *craah-craah*. Nutcrackers normally travel in small flocks, moving up and down mountain slopes in search of their two preferred foods, pinyon seeds and Limber Pine seeds. Both the pinyons and Limber Pines produce large pine nuts that are rich in fat and relatively high in protein. Nutcrackers are real specialists when it comes to harvesting pinyon and Limber Pine seeds. Using their long bills, they probe deep inside the cone, and each seed that is removed is carefully shaken to determine if it is satisfactory. If not, the nutcracker discards it on the spot. If the seed is acceptable, the nutcracker will appear to swallow it, but, in reality, the seed is being placed in an expandable pouch beneath the bird's tongue (the sublingual pouch, found only in nutcrackers). This pouch can hold over 100 Limber Pine seeds or up to 95 pinyon seeds. When the bird has filled its pouch, it flies away—to bury the seeds. Nutcrackers fill their late summer and early fall days by collecting seeds and taking them to certain preferred areas, usually south-facing slopes relatively devoid of snow in winter, where they carefully dig little holes and deposit one or two seeds in each hole. In other words, they spend their summers planting pine trees. The cached seeds are the nutcrackers' winter larder, an insurance that food will be available during the short, cold days to come. Nutcrackers are enthusiastic about caching seeds. Some birds have been estimated to cache anywhere from 20,000 to 33,000 pinyon seeds in the course of a summer. Each bird must be able to relocate and devour somewhere in excess of 1,000 seeds to make it through the winter. This means that each bird must relocate about 5 percent of the seeds it buries. Nutcrackers, indeed, have demonstrated remarkable memories for relocating cached seeds. The birds use landmarks such as positions of boulders and trees to find the seeds. Nutcrackers also use cached pine seeds to feed their young, as they breed in early spring, before many other food sources are available. Seed caching is obviously good for the pines. Given the number of seeds eaten by nutcrackers, usually far fewer than were cached, and even given losses to woodrats and other seed predators, many buried seeds eventually sprout and grow. Further, they are planted in exactly the sites where the trees thrive, south-facing slopes. Biologists consider the relationship between Clark's Nutcrackers and Limber and pinyon pines to be one of *coevolution,* in which both animal and plant have evolved an intricate interdependency. A similar situation occurs with Pinyon Jays and pinyon trees. The world is rarely perfect, however, and in some years the pine seed crop fails. At those times, nutcrackers often become irruptive, flying long distances from the mountains to winter in lowland areas, where possibilities for finding food are greater.

The 10-inch **THREE-TOED WOODPECKER** sometimes ventures into the high pines, though it is more common in the denser spruce-fir. It is recognized by its all-black back and barred sides, and the male has bright yellow atop his head. This species and the similar Black-backed Woodpecker, occur throughout western mountains, but the Black-backed is found mostly from the central Rockies northward. Both species are often overlooked because they forage quietly, lightly tapping the tree, often stripping dead bark. They are fond of newly killed trees, and a good place to look for them is in groves that have recently burned.

The **LEAST CHIPMUNK** is, at most, 9 inches long including its tail, making it the smallest of the chipmunks. It is appropriate to illustrate it with Clark's Nutcracker, since, like the nutcracker, this little chipmunk sooner or later makes the acquaintance of virtually every human visitor to any western national park or forest. It enjoys the widest geographical and altitudinal range of any of the western chipmunks and is equally at home on the sagebrush flats, in Ponderosa Pine, among the spruces and Douglas-fir, or climbing up into a Limber Pine to get a seed or two. Least Chipmunks are found in every western mountain range and are common throughout the Canadian provinces and into southern Alaska. They vary in color from bright rusty brown in moist areas to more yellowish gray on drier sites. Like other chipmunks, this species consumes a diversity of foods ranging from insects and other invertebrates to seeds, fruits, acorns, and fungi. They often raid the seed caches of other animals to add to their own stores.

The Clark's Nutcracker certainly caches seeds, but the **BUSHY-TAIL WOODRAT** caches virtually everything. Woodrats are commonly called packrats because of their curious hoarding behavior. Woodrats construct middens, large nests where they store food and other objects. There are eight species in North America, all in the genus *Neotoma,* and seven of the eight occur in the West. The Bushytail is the most widely distributed species, ranging throughout the western mountains and British Columbia and into southern Alaska. Most of the other species are southwestern. Woodrats are as large as Norway and Black rats but are differentiated by the fact that their tails are hairy, not naked and scaly. The Bushytail's tail is much more densely furred than any other woodrat. Bushy-tails like mountains, where they construct their middens under rocks or logs. For reasons yet unknown, Bushytail Woodrats accumulate not only sticks, nuts, mushrooms, seeds, and leaves, but also shiny objects like coins and bottle caps. Bushytail Woodrats are good climbers and sometimes build their middens in dense pine trees. Woodrat middens from many years past still can be found in the West, and the objects in them are of great interest to anthropologists and ecologists. For instance, seeds in old middens provide clues to what type of vegetation covered the region well before the present day.

WHERE TO VISIT: Limber Pines are present on exposed sites at high elevations throughout the central and southern Rockies. They can be found abundantly at the southern end of the Sangre de Cristo Range in New Mexico. Craters of the Moon National Monument near Arco, Idaho, is an ideal place to see Limber Pine because it is the only trees growing on the black, basaltic, lava rock that covers the region. Rocky Mountain Bristlecone Pine can be found at many places in Colorado and New Mexico. Recommended are Clayton Pass – Bristlecone Pine Research Area in Carson National Forest (northern New Mexico); Spanish Peaks, San Juan National Forest, Colorado; Highway 82 between Twin Lakes and Independence Pass, Interstate 70 near Silver Plume, Colorado; the Sawatch Range near St. Elmo, Colorado; Pike National Forest (Windy Ridge – Bristlecone Pine Scenic Area); and the Mount Goliath Natural Area near Echo Lake on the Mt. Evans road in Colorado. Bristlecones are also present at timberline on the four San Francisco Peaks that are part of Coconino National Forest north of Flagstaff, Arizona.

TIMBERLINE-ALPINE TUNDRA

INDICATOR PLANTS

TREES: Subalpine Fir, Engelmann Spruce (often in *krummholz* growth form), Limber Pine, Whitebark Pine.

SHRUBS: *Arctic Willow* (looks like a wildflower), Barrenground Willow, Planeleaf Willow, Snow Willow, Mountain Alder, Sitka Alder.

HERBACEOUS SPECIES: Cushion plants include *Moss Campion (Catchfly)*, *Alpine Phlox*, Skymat (Alpine Forget-me-not), King's Crown, Lanceleaf Sedum, Alpine Nailwort, Alpine Sandwort, Thick Draba, White Draba, Alpine Clover, Dwarf Clover, Mountain Dryad. Also: *Elephant Head*, Alpine Sunflower, Goldflower, Alpine Avens (Dryad), Western Bistort, Snowball Saxifrage, Spotted Saxifrage, Nodding Saxifrage, Alpine Thistle, Alpine Poppy, Alpine Onion, Alpine Parsley, Alpine Anemone, White Marsh Marigold, Snowball Gilia, Jacob's Ladder, Wallflower, Alpine Paintbrush, Western Yellow Paintbrush, Snow Buttercup, Black-headed Daisy, Showy Daisy, Arctic Gentian, Star Swertia (Star Gentian), Moss Gentian, Alpine Ragwort, Rock Primrose, Arctic Sage, Elegant Camas, Dwarf Bitterroot, Mountain Candytuft, Snow-lover, Alpine Mouse-ears, Meadow Chickweed, Alpine Lousewort, Alpine Phacelia (Purple Fringe), Harebell (Bluebell), plus many grasses, rushes, and sedges including Black Sedge, Ebony Sedge, Alpine Fescue, Alpine Bluegrass, Tufted Hairgrass, Alpine Timothy, Spike Woodrush.

LICHENS: Yellow Reindeer Lichen, Map Lichen, Snow Lichen, finger lichens, Jewel Lichen, Rock Tripe.

INDICATOR ANIMALS

BIRDS: *White-tailed Ptarmigan, American Pipit, Brown Rosy Finch, Black-capped Rosy Finch,* Golden Eagle, Red-tailed Hawk, Peregrine Falcon, Prairie Falcon, American Kestrel, White-throated Swift, Broad-tailed Hummingbird, Rufous Hummingbird, Calliope Hummingbird, Common Raven, Clark's Nutcracker, Horned Lark, Rock Wren, Mountain Bluebird, American Robin, White-crowned Sparrow.

MAMMALS: *Yellowbelly Marmot, Pika,* Northern Pocket Gopher, Golden-mantled Ground Squirrel, Least Chipmunk, Mountain Vole, Heather Vole, Longtail Weasel, Shorttail Weasel, Badger, Bobcat, Grizzly Bear, Elk, Mule Deer, Mountain Goat, Bighorn Sheep.

Note to Hikers: Tundra vegetation is extremely vulnerable to damage, and recovery after disturbance takes many, many years. Trails and roads that have been abandoned for decades are still clearly visible, a clear indication that the process of ecological succession is extremely slow at these high-elevation, climatically severe areas. Please refrain from leaving the trail. Trampling on alpine tundra will permanently damage the vegetation.

Also remember that high elevation will affect your own physiology. Walking at 11,000 feet, when you are not used to it, can produce rapid heartbeat, hyperventilation, and even dizziness. Take it easy if you are not acclimated to the altitude.

DESCRIPTION

The climatic conditions that prevail at high elevations on western mountains prevent forests from reaching most of the summits. During the short summer growing season, the climate can be warm and pleasant, but for most of the year conditions are severe, with windswept slopes exposed to heat, rain, and numerous winter snowstorms. Winter winds can blow in excess of 100 m.p.h., summer lightning storms are often violent, and the mean annual temperature is below freezing. Annual precipitation totals about 40 inches, much of it as snow. The constant winds hasten evaporation, producing desertlike conditions in some alpine areas.

Beginning at about 11,000–11,500 feet in Colorado, and decreasing northward, tree line, or timberline, is the point at which trees yield to alpine tundra. Tree line is usually not sharp. Rather, the habitat consists of a patchwork of islands of small, densely clustered trees, as well as mountain slopes of short, scattered trees. Many of these trees have branches only on their leeward sides, their windward branches having been killed by severe exposure. These are called flag trees. On higher, more exposed sites, trees such as Engelmann Spruce and Subalpine Fir grow not as upright, conical trees but rather as clumps of prostrate, shrubby trees called *krummholz. Krummholz* means "twisted wood," a reference to the gnarled, twisted shapes of these prostrate tree mats. Among the *krummholz* are often dense thickets of alder or willow.

Tundra is the term for the treeless habitat of grasses, sedges, wildflowers, and lichen-covered rocks found beyond tree line. Tundra is also a patchwork; some areas are lush wet meadows, some are dry as deserts. Mixed among the grass and sedge-dominated areas are rocky fellfields, talus slopes, avalanche chutes, and slowly melting snowfields. Rocks appear to be coated with peeling paint, but these patches are actually thriving communities of various lichens, odd plants that are the result of an intimate association of an alga and a fungus. Lichens, which literally grow on bare rock, are able to survive where exposure is maximal and soil virtually nonexistent.

The diversity of tundra wildflowers is utterly dazzling. Dozens of species bloom during the short summer growing season. Some are close relatives of species living at lower elevations while others are circumpolar species found only beyond tree line, in high arctic as well as alpine areas. While numerous wildflowers of the alpine tundra are upright, many are *cushion plants,* named for their spreading, prostrate growth forms. Cushion plants are adapted to minimize exposure, thus reducing stresses caused by evaporation and wind. Many tundra plants have succulent leaves that retain moisture or leaves that are densely hairy or wax-coated, reducing evaporation from wind. Flowers tend to have a flattened shape so that they act like little solar collectors, concentrating the sun's rays on the reproductive parts of the plant and insuring the quickest possible development during the short growing season. Almost all of the plants are perennials, regrowing

Figure 23. Longtail Weasel

on the same roots year after year, and many are much older than they appear. In general, plants of the tundra are slow-growing. Some add only a leaf or two per year. Seeds germinate immediately after snowmelt, and much of the plant's early growth is below ground in a taproot or underground stem system. A small cushion plant may be as much as 100 years old. Annuals are rare in the tundra because the growing season is so short that plants do not have time to mature and set seed.

Animals, like the plants, have adapted to the exposed, windswept tundra. Myriads of insects, especially bees and butterflies, can be found throughout the growing season. While sedges and grasses are wind-pollinated, the vast majority of tundra wildflowers are pollinated by insects, as evidenced by their bright, showy, often upright flowers. Lepidopterists are particularly

Tree line at Rocky Mountain National Park, where spruce-fir intermingles with alpine tundra.

drawn to the tundra, as many butterfly species, including some uniquely alpine, thrive on the nectar-rich wildflowers. Two hummingbird species, the Broad-tailed and Rufous, also contribute to cross pollination in alpine meadows.

Relatively few birds frequent high elevations. American Pipits and Horned Larks may be seen walking among the grasses, and colorful Rosy Finches search the snowfields for seeds and insects. White-crowned Sparrows sing from the thickets of dwarf willows, while Clark's Nutcrackers fly past in their search for Limber Pine seeds. Mountain Bluebirds sing from flag trees and White-throated Swifts fly frantically overhead in their constant pursuit of insects. Fellfields and other rock-strewn areas are habitat for Rock Wrens and White-tailed Ptarmigans. The latter are well-camouflaged, chickenlike birds unique to the tundra.

Marmots, which look like alpine woodchucks, are conspicuous residents of rocky slopes and fellfields, their shrill, sharp whistles piercing the cool mountain air. While marmots recline leisurely on the big boulders, little rabbitlike Pikas spend their summer days collecting grasses and wildflower leaves to store for winter food. Pikas seem ever busy, bounding purposefully over the rocks, their mouths stuffed to overflowing with grass stalks to be added to their accumulating "haystacks." Pikas and marmots must be ever watchful for Golden Eagles, Prairie Falcons, Peregrine Falcons, and Longtail Weasels. Bighorn Sheep can be seen along the mountain crests, and Mountain Goats spend much of the hot summer day reclining on cool snowfields. In late afternoon, Elk and Mule Deer gather to feed in the lush meadows.

SIMILAR COMMUNITIES: See spruce-fir forest.

RANGE: From 11,200 feet elevation in the southern Rockies (northern

Snowfields and boulder fields amid stunted trees and alpine tundra, habitat for Rosy Finches, Ptarmigan, Pikas, and Marmots.

New Mexico and southern Colorado) to 8,000 feet in Montana, to 7,000 feet in the Canadian Rockies.

REMARKS

Tree line is a place of major ecological transition. The woody plants that have, in various forms and species combinations, dominated the landscape from the Lower Sonoran Zone upward give way to the grasses, sedges, wildflowers, and the most humble-looking of plants, the lichens. Slowly, almost painfully, the Hudsonian Zone spruces, firs, and pines are reduced in stature, twisted by the winds into odd shapes, sometimes becoming totally prostrate *krummholz*, the only growth form that permits their survival. Higher still, the trees are gone, having yielded entirely to the community of herbaceous species of the tundra, a word taken from Russian meaning "land of no trees."

As tree line is approached, trees show, in the most obvious of ways, the effects of increasingly harsh exposure. Flag trees all point to the direction from which the wind does not blow, as only the leeward side of the tree spire can survive. Trees are much shorter, reduced by the short growing season and severe climate. Somewhat higher in elevation, trees grow in prostrate, spreading mats called *krummholz*. The low form allows snow to protect the tree limbs under a blanket whose temperature is always 32°F.

This may seem cold, but consider that above the snow, wind chill could be equivalent to temperatures of -50, -75, or worse—a difference of more than 100 degrees! *Krummholz* is also affected by summer winds. Take a close look and you will see that a *krummholz* is essentially dead on its windward side. Like flag trees,

A "flag tree" shows the effects of windward pruning. The leeward side is to the right.

Tall snags have been killed by exposure to weather. Krummholz, forming on the left, is more durable.

krummholz mats act as weather vanes. The dead windward branches act as wind breaks to help protect the living branches on the leeward side. *Krummholz* is strictly a result of environment, not of genetics. Take seeds from the cones of *krummholz* trees, plant them at low, moist, protected elevations, and the resulting spruces and firs will be quite normal in shape.

Because of often subtle differences in slope, exposure, and other factors, alpine areas are variable. Some areas may accumulate enough moisture to result in wet meadows of sedge and wildflowers, while others are very dry and support meadows largely composed of grasses. Moist sites have more wildflower species than dry sites, and they are especially rich in species if afforded some protection against wind.

The branches of a tree in krummholz form are protected by winter snow cover.

Moist meadows are botanical rainbows of wildflowers. Brilliant yellow **ALPINE SUNFLOWERS** always face toward the sun, and **WESTERN YELLOW PAINTBRUSH, WALLFLOWER, GOLDFLOWER, SNOW BUTTERCUP,** and **ALPINE AVENS** add to the array of yellows. **WESTERN BISTORT,** with its conical white flower heads, often outnumbers all other species, and, along with **COMMON YARROW,** can indicate sites in which burrowing mammals such as voles or pocket gophers have stirred up the soil. More delicate and less abundant, **ALPINE MOUSE-EARS, ALP LILY,** and **WHITE MARSH MARIGOLD** add their white flowers to the meadow. **QUEEN'S CROWN,** one of several species of sedum, contributes red to the meadow, while **JACOB'S LADDER, HAREBELL,** and **PURPLE FRINGE** add the blues.

Among the most unusual looking of wildflowers is **ELEPHANT-HEAD.** This plant, a member of the figwort family, has fernlike leaves and a tall spike bearing 20 or more delicate dark pink flowers, each one of which looks like a tiny elephant's head, including ears and trunk. This plant, like so many other alpine species, is widely distributed, occurring on tundra from Greenland to Alaska.

Most wildflowers that inhabit rocky outcrops sink deep roots that firmly anchor them against the wind. Many of these species frequent disturbed sites—and disturbances, ranging from rock-slides to the activities of burrowing rodents, occur often. **LANCE-LEAF MERTENSIA,** a dense plant with deep blue, trumpet-shaped flowers, can be found here, as can clumps of yellow **ALPINE RAG-WORT.** This is also the habitat for the lovely **ARCTIC GENTIAN,** which unlike most gentians is not blue but white, with delicate lavender splashes. **ROCK PRIMROSE** is a tiny ground plant with an array of white flowers. Look closely to see it well. **MOUNTAIN SORREL** is a

Elephanthead.

larger plant that grows out from among the rocks. It has big, rounded, heart-shaped leaves and stalks with tiny pinkish flowers.

Fellfields present the most severe of challenges to plants. Consisting of jumbles of varying sized rocks and boulders, fellfields occupy the most exposed sites. Wind blows so hard that snow rarely accumulates. This means that the soil is dry—desert dry. The combination of arid, rocky soils plus extreme exposure to the vicissitudes of weather would seem to make occupation by plants problematical at best. Yet approximately 60 plant species grow on fellfields throughout the Rocky Mountains. Many of the most successful of these species are the cushion plants, prostrate, spreading plants that hug the ground. They put down vast root systems, usually with a deep taproot anchoring them securely against wind. Their compressed shape helps prevent wind from tearing them from their moorings. Shoots are densely packed, forming a flat cushion that insulates, helps trap soil particles, and retains old decomposing leaves and shoots, adding organic matter to the cushion. Cushion plants grow extremely slowly, each shoot adding but a leaf or two per growing season, the shoot lengthening only about 2 millimeters. The perennial cushion plants that you stop to admire and photograph are probably older than you are. Many routinely become centenarians.

The most common cushion plants are Moss Campion, Alpine Phlox, Alpine Nailwort, and Alpine Sandwort. They are generally similar, with sprays of bright flowers that grow directly on the cushion, not on stalks. **MOSS CAMPION** is circumarctic and grows not only on all western mountains, but on Mt. Washington in New Hampshire as well. Like most cushion plants it has tiny, dark green leaves, extremely densely packed like the pile of a rug.

Lichen-covered rocks and boulders are often overlooked amid the colorful tundra wildflowers.

Flowers are a delicate pink, 5-petaled, with a slight notch at the tip of each petal. **ALPINE PHLOX** has star-shaped, 5-petaled flowers, somewhat larger than Moss Campion's, ranging in color from lavender to white. **ALPINE NAILWORT** flowers are tiny, only about 0.10 inch across, with 5 greenish yellow petals and yellow anthers. **ALPINE SANDWORT** has bright white, 5-petaled flowers with yellow anthers. These species are from very different plant families. The cushion growth form is genetic (unlike *krummholz*), and cushion plants will grow as cushion plants no matter where they are planted. The diversity of plant families that have evolved cushion plants is an example of *convergent evolution*. In similar environments, different plants have evolved similar species.

Finally, there are the **LICHENS.** They grow where other plants

Alpine Sandwort.

A closer look reveals numerous interesting lichens, many of them quite old.

can't. They live for many decades on bare rock, their fungal strands holding tenaciously to the granite. The algal component of the lichen provides food through photosynthesis, while the fungus takes in minerals and gives the lichen a secure anchor. Lichens abound on alpine tundra, completely covering all rocks except those recently moved by avalanches or other disturbances. Lichens slowly erode rocks, adding tiny amounts of minerals to the soil, and they also help trap organic matter, sometimes facilitating invasion by other species, such as one of the stonecrops.

WHERE TO VISIT: In Colorado, Trail Ridge Road in Rocky Mountain National Park is an outstanding area for observing timberline-alpine tundra. Many trails along this continuous highway take the hiker among the various tree-line and tundra habitats. Also recommended is the road between Durango and Silverton. In Wyoming, Route 212 from Yellowstone National Park across Beartooth Pass will take you through alpine tundra and afford stunning views of the Rockies. Waterton-Glacier, Banff, and Jasper national parks offer extensive opportunities to see timberline-alpine tundra.

ANIMALS OF THE ALPINE TUNDRA   PLATE 16

MOUNTAIN GOAT *Oreamnos americanus*

For those of us who admit to some fear of heights, the Mountain Goat is an animal to be admired, if not envied. This shaggy white animal, its back hunched in a manner somewhat suggestive of a Bison, is a master at negotiating the steepest of precipices. Mountain Goats are truly alpine creatures. They commonly rest on high-elevation snowfields and find most of their food among the plants of alpine meadows. Their hooves are structured to permit balance and grip; the outer hoof is strongly reinforced and the bottom is lined with rubbery material, making the whole structure rather like a good hiking boot. These animals nonchalantly cross dizzying ledges, sometimes even at a trot. Though they rest for much of the summer day, you may see them foraging in a mountain meadow in late afternoon.

Males and females do not associate except during the fall mating season. In the summer, many females are accompanied by kids that were born in late spring. The kids can stand upright soon after delivery and walk with excellent balance soon thereafter. Kids are sometimes attacked by Golden Eagles, especially on exposed ledges. Males enter rutting season in late fall or early winter. They characteristically mark females with a scent from glands near the base of the horns. Though males threaten one another, they rarely fight, and they do not butt heads as Bighorn Sheep do.

Mountain Goats look different, especially with regard to body proportions, from other goats, and for good reason: Mountain Goats are not goats. They belong to a group called the goat-antelopes, and their nearest relative is the Chamois of the Eurasian alps. The differences between goat-antelopes and goats have to do with the structure of the horns and nature of the beard on the males, as well as with the overall body shape. Both male and female Mountain Goats have sharp horns that curve directly backward. A male Mountain Goat can weigh up to 300 pounds. Females are slightly smaller than males.

Mountain Goats are common in the national parks of the northern Rocky Mountains. They can be seen well at Waterton-Glacier, Banff, and Jasper. They have been introduced in the Black Hills of South Dakota. They can also be seen at Mt. Rainier National Park in the Washington Cascade Mountains, and, less reliably, at Olympic National Park on the Olympic Peninsula. Recently there has been an attempt to relocate all Mountain Goats out of Olympic National Park. The National Park Service claims that the goats were not native to the area but were introduced there. They further argue that the goats harm the delicate meadow vegetation. Other naturalists disagree, citing anthropological evidence that the goats were, indeed, longtime occupants of the Olympic Mountains.

PIKA *Ochotona princeps*
Hikers that traverse rocky alpine slopes often think they hear tiny goats under the rocks. They discover that the thin bleating sound

is coming from a cute little furry creature that looks like a kind of husky mouse. This is the Pika, certainly not a goat but also not a mouse. Pikas are lagomorphs, close relatives of rabbits and hares. Look at one closely and you will see it really does resemble a little 8-inch rabbit, but with very small ears.

It's not surprising that the Pika's external ears are small. The animal never hibernates but remains active even in the coldest weather. Heat can be lost through ears and other extremities, so small ears are adaptive for mammals living in cold climates. Arctic Foxes, Polar Bears, and Snowshoe Hares also have relatively small ears. On the other hand, many desert mammals, such as Kit Foxes and jackrabbits, have oversized ears that are ideal for losing heat.

Pikas spend the summer collecting wildflowers, grass, and sedge, constructing a pile of food that will largely sustain them during the winter months. The little haystacks are evident among the rocks along talus slopes. Pikas are territorial, each protecting its larder as the vegetation dries in the summer sun. In fall, the haystack is taken below the rocks to the Pika's den. Pikas mate in winter and give birth in late spring to litters of 2 to 6 babies. A female may have a second litter by the end of summer (they are, after all, related to rabbits).

There are two pika species, the Pika, found throughout western mountains wherever there are talus slopes, and the Collared Pika, found in northwestern Canada and southern Alaska. The Collared Pika looks very like the Pika but for a pale grayish collar around its neck.

Pikas are relatively easy to find at many national parks. Try Trail Ridge Road in Rocky Mountain National Park or Tioga Pass Road in Yosemite National Park. They are also at Waterton-Glacier, Crater Lake, Mt. Rainier, Kings Canyon, Yellowstone, and Grand Tetons. In winter, look for them near the lifts at ski resorts, such as Snowbird, near Salt Lake City, Utah.

ELLOWBELLY MARMOT *Marmota flaviventris*

Marmots are actually large ground squirrels that live in underground dens and are active by day. There are arguably six species in North America, and all but one is called a marmot. The other is the Woodchuck or Groundhog, a familiar eastern species.

The Yellowbelly Marmot, which is about the size of a Woodchuck and can weigh up to 1 o pounds, is common throughout the central and much of the southern portions of the Rocky Mountains, the Great Basin Mountains, and the Sierra Nevada. Yellowbellies have a rusty body and tail and a distinctly yellow-orange belly. The face is black, with white between the eyes. Yellowbellies live among alpine boulders, excavating a den under a large rock or boulder that serves as a sentinel post. Marmots, especially during midday, typically sprawl on boulders, seemingly as relaxed as a rodent could possibly be. However, should the marmot spot a Coyote or Golden Eagle, it will stand upright, emit a loud, shrill whistle, and scurry to the safety of its den. Marmot whistles are familiar sounds to alpine hikers. All marmots are vegetarians, foraging for food during the short growing season. Most people remark that marmots appear to be quite fat, especially in late summer. The fat is their winter food, since marmots hibernate, some entering their deep sleep as early as August. The added fat will be slowly metabolized during the winter months. The heartbeat and breathing rate of the hibernating marmot slow to a fraction of the summertime rates.

Yellowbelly Marmots are unafraid of humans in areas such as national parks, where they are protected. They often beg food and allow people to approach them closely. They are easy to observe at Rocky Mountain and Yosemite national parks, as well as many other places.

HOARY MARMOT *Marmota caligata*

The Hoary Marmot is named for its pale fur, which gives it a decidedly silvery look. Like the Yellowbelly, the Hoary has white on the face, accented by black extending from the forehead to behind the ears. The stubby, furry tail is darker than the body. Hoaries are marmots of the Pacific Northwest, found in suitable habitats from the northern Rockies, Cascades, and other mountains into far northern Alaska, where they are animals of the arctic tundra.

Hoary Marmots are considerably larger than Woodchucks and Yellowbelly Marmots, weighing in at as much as 20 pounds. Their added bulk is probably adaptive, a reflection of both their cold alpine habitat and more northern distribution. The colder the climate, the better it is for mammals to be husky, since larger body size means more volume in relation to surface area: Volume means body bulk, the part of the animal that produces heat, and heat is lost through exposed surface area.

Hoary Marmots are easily seen at Mt. Rainier National Park (Paradise and Sunrise), and at Waterton-Glacier, Banff, and Jasper national parks.

Most authorities recognize three other marmot species, the Olympic Marmot, found only on the Olympic Peninsula, the Vancouver Marmot, found only on Vancouver Island, British Columbia, and the Alaska Marmot, found in northern Alaska. Each of these animals looks distinct from the others. The Olympic Marmot is like a Hoary but browner. The Vancouver Marmot is like a dark Hoary. Some taxonomists believe it is more accurate to regard these populations not as full species but as subspecies of Hoary Marmot.

The variable and complex social organizations of marmots have been studied extensively (see essay below).

THE SOCIAL ORDERS OF MARMOTS

Marmots are large, diurnal ground squirrels that live in open areas where they can be observed relatively easily. Such characteristics make them ideal subjects for study, and studied they have been. Ecologists such as David P. Barash, Warren Holmes, and Douglas C. Andersen and his colleagues have devoted many hours to making detailed records of how marmots live, how they get along with one another, and how their rodent societies are actually structured.

Barash observed that marmot societies seem to change with severity of habitat. The familiar eastern Woodchuck (actually a marmot quite closely related to the western species), which maintains real estate in pastures and old fields throughout eastern North America, lives where the growing season normally exceeds 150 days. Woodchucks are strictly territorial. They are solitary and aggressive, repelling any other chucks from their turf. Even mating is a brief affair, with no pair bond formed between the sexes. They meet, quickly conceive some more Woodchucks, and go their separate ways.

In sharp contrast, the Olympic Marmot, a close relative of the husky Hoary Marmot, is a highly social beast. Olympic Marmots, which inhabit meadows high in the Olympic Mountains, live where the growing season is only 40 to 70 days. These marmots live in social groups, usually with one adult male, two adult females, some two-year-olds, some yearlings, and the young of the year. Unlike the Woodchuck, Olympic Marmots are playful and tolerant of each other, and they do not defend personal territories. They engage one another in greeting ceremonies (easily observed if you watch them for a bit), and they share an early morning visiting period, when the various members of the colony habitually enter each other's burrows and say "hi."

The Yellowbelly Marmot lives in elevations from sea level to high mountain meadows. It has been closely studied in Yellowstone, where the growing season is 70 to 100 days, intermediate between the long growing season where the Woodchuck lives and the short growing season where the Olympic Marmot lives. Its social order is also intermediate between the Woodchuck and Olympic Marmot. Yellowbellies live in colonies, but they are less tolerant of each other, and they do maintain their own personal territories within the colonies. They are much more aggressive with each other than Olympic Marmots are. Yellowbelly males are usually solitary, while females are colonial, with groups of mothers, young, and aunts living together. The pattern in marmot societies seems to be that the more severe the environment, the more friendly the marmots are to one another. But why?

Barash suggested that the harshness of the environment was the force most responsible for the range of marmot social patterns. Woodchucks are most reproductively successful by being highly solitary and territorial. Woodchucks born in a given summer mature and leave their mothers (biologists call this *dispersal*) during that long summer. Olympic Marmots, however, stay with their mothers until they are two years old and are not sexually mature until they are three years old. The difference between the two species is due to the differing amounts of time (growing season length) available for them to grow and mature. It is adaptive for a Woodchuck to force its young to disperse, because they are mature enough to do so with reasonable success. It is not adaptive for an Olympic Marmot to force its young to leave until they are much older. To do otherwise would doom them and would be an evolutionary failure on the part of the parent marmot—those young carry its genes. Therefore, it is adaptive for Olympic Marmots to be social and tolerant of one another.

One test of the idea that severity of climate is the strongest influence on marmot social structure would be to look at Yellowbelly Marmots living at different elevations, one medium and one high. The medium-elevation population would be predicted to behave more like Woodchucks, since growing season would be relatively long. The higher-elevation population would be more social. David Barash made such a comparison of two marmot populations in Rocky Mountain National Park. He found that members of the medium-elevation colony (8,700 feet) were relatively aggressive toward each other, each guarding its own home range, whereas those in the high-elevation colony (12,600 feet) were very tolerant of each other, behaving almost identically to Olympic and Hoary marmots.

The correlation between growing season length and marmot social order is strong and leads to the straightforward conclusion that the amount of food available to marmots, which is affected by growing season length, determines social order. However, in nature, simple explanations rarely suffice. In this case as in most of ecology, other causes also exert strong influences. Colonial behavior might be advantageous to marmots living at high elevations for reasons unrelated to the length of the growing season. For instance, the close groups of Yellowbelly Marmots may be better able to detect predators such as Golden Eagles and Coyotes. Even so, young, inexperienced marmots have been observed to spend far more time searching the skies and horizons for dangers than experienced adults. Young may take in less food, and thus grow more slowly, not just because of shorter growing season but because they spend so much time on guard.

Another factor in marmot survival is the availability of places to hibernate. High-elevation marmots need to be tucked in a secure burrow, under a blanket of snow. A sudden warm spell that melts snow and exposes marmot burrows, followed by severe cold weather, can be disastrous. Such conditions kill marmots. Suitable burrows may be in short supply, so it is to a marmot's advantage to share burrows, or *hibernacula,* with other marmots. That is exactly what most do.

WHITE-TAILED PTARMIGAN *Lagopus leucurus*

Ptarmigans are best thought of as alpine/arctic chickens. There are three species, and they look much alike. All change plumage with the seasons. In winter, ptarmigans become almost entirely white, while in summer they assume a mottled brown and white plumage. The seasonal transformation obviously provides cryptic coloration (camouflage), an important consideration for a bird that spends virtually all of its time in the open. Ptarmigans are adapted in other ways to their alpine and arctic habitats. Their claws lengthen considerably in winter, and their feet become densely feathered, helping them walk over soft snow. The feathering also holds in heat.

During courtship, male ptarmigans display the red combs above their eyes while strutting and vocalizing. They make a series of rapid notes ranging from dry growls to soft hoots and chucks. Ptarmigans nest among tundra vegetation, where they lay 6–8 eggs in a concealed, grassy nest. In winter they usually migrate to lower elevations, though they remain birds of the snow. Ptarmigans feed on vegetation, especially willow buds.

The White-tailed Ptarmigan is the southernmost ptarmigan species, found from central Alaska through British Columbia and Alberta, south to the central Rockies and Cascades. It has also been introduced and is now established in the Sierra Nevada. White-tails are the only ptarmigan with pure white tails. When they fly, they reveal not only the white tail but white wings as well. They frequent rocky areas such as talus slopes and avalanche chutes. Look for them along Trail Ridge Road at Rocky Mountain National Park. Other favorable locations include Mt. Rainier and Waterton-Glacier national parks.

Willow Ptarmigan and Rock Ptarmigan (not illustrated) are species of the far north, found across northern Canada and throughout Alaska. Both species also occur in Europe, where the Willow Ptarmigan is commonly called the Red Grouse. Willow Ptarmigan are slightly less northern and can be seen in summer at Churchill, Manitoba, and in winter at Waterton-Glacier. Rock and Willow ptarmigan can be seen at Denali and other Alaskan parks.

AMERICAN PIPIT *Anthus rubescens*

The 7-inch American Pipit, also known as the Water Pipit, is easily overlooked by visitors to the alpine tundra. This tawny-colored bird sings its loud, melodious song while soaring high overhead during courtship. You can hear the bird, but you may not see it, as it can fly to 200 feet or more. On the ground it is well camouflaged, and it walks, rather than hops, as it methodically searches the tundra for insect food. One useful behavioral field mark is that a pipit bobs its tail. Pipits often spring up unexpectedly before the alpine hiker, flashing their white outer tail feathers as they fly away.

American Pipits nest on alpine tundra throughout the Rocky Mountains as well as the mountains of the Pacific Northwest. They are abundant in far northern Canada and Alaska, nesting on arctic tundra. Long-distance migrants, they gather in large flocks and fly as far south as southern Central America. Pipit flocks frequent lowland agricultural areas during migration.

ROSY FINCHES *Leucosticte* spp.

Rosy Finches are elegant birds of the high snowfields. Larger and more husky than sparrows, they spend much time on the ground searching for seeds and insects revealed at the edges of melting snow. At first glance they look dark, usually brownish, but, when seen closely in good light, they become raspberry colored, especially on the sides and rump. Wings are a rich reddish pink, especially evident when the birds fly. Like pipits, Rosy Finches walk rather than hop, and they are usually in small flocks. They are relatively unwary and rather easy to approach at close range. Their song is a series of sparrow-like chirps. Rosy Finches build grassy nests under rock faces and in other sheltered areas. Nonetheless, their nests are frequently raided by Clark's Nutcrackers. One odd characteristic of Rosy Finch populations is that males outnumber females by about 6 to 1. Not surprisingly, males have been observed to fight during breeding season. In winter Rosy Finches flock together and migrate south and to lower elevations, often coming to bird feeders. They gather in large winter roosts, sometimes using old Cliff Swallow nests for shelter.

There are three Rosy Finch species, the Gray-crowned (*L. tephrocotis*), the Brown-capped (*L. australis*), and the Black (*L. atrata*). The Brown-capped has an all brown head. It is confined to the Rocky Mountains and is the most southern of the subspecies, occurring from southern Wyoming to New Mexico. Look for it along Trail Ridge Road at Rocky Mountain National Park, Pikes Peak, and Loveland Pass, all in Colorado. The Black Rosy Finch is much like the Gray-crowned but the head and upper body are black, not brown. Black Rosy Finches are in the central Rockies and mountains of the Great Basin, from southwestern Montana, through central Idaho, northeastern Nevada, and Utah. Look for it at Great Basin National Park. The Gray-crowned (not illustrated) is recognizable by its distinctly gray face and black forehead. It is found throughout Alaska and Canada as well as the northern Rockies and Cascades. Look for it at Mt. Rainier, Waterton-Glacier, Banff, and Jasper national parks.

PLATE 9

PINYON-JUNIPER FOREST

TWO-NEEDLE (COLORADO) PINYON *Pinus edulis*
To 45 ft. Rounded crown, short trunk. Long, stiff needles in bundles of 2. Cones 2 in., egg-shaped. Bark furrowed with scaly ridges.

UTAH JUNIPER *Juniperus osteosperma*
To 25 ft. Short, bushy shape. Leaves scalelike, overlapping. Female cones berrylike. Bark furrowed, peeling.

GAMBEL OAK *Quercus gambelii*
To 65 ft. Deciduous, leaves with 5–9 smoothly rounded lobes. Bark light, scaly.

BIG SAGEBRUSH *Artemisia tridentata*
To 6 ft. Aromatic shrub with long, pale blue-green leaves, 3 small lobes at tip.

ALDERLEAF CERCOCARPUS (MOUNTAIN-MAHOGANY) *Cercocarpus montanus*
To 15 feet but mostly shrubby. Leaves leathery, oval, deeply toothed. Seeds with long, feathery tails.

SEGO LILY *Calochortus nuttallii*
To 20 in. Broad, bowl-shaped flowers, mostly white, 3 petals, 3 sepals. Leaves long, edges often rolled up.

SCARLET GLOBEMALLOW *Sphaeralcea coccinea*
To 20 in. Bright orange-red, 5-petaled flowers in clusters, leaves rounded, 3 lobes.

BLUEBONNET (SILKY LUPINE) *Lupinus sericeus*
To 24 in. Blue-lavender flowers on spike, leaves compound with long leaflets in star-shaped pattern.

PINYON JAY *Gymnorhinus cyanocephalus*
9–12 in. Crow-shaped, uniformly deep blue, long bill. In flocks.

BUSHTIT *Psaltriparus minimus*
4 in. Slender gray bird, thin bill, very active, usually in flocks. Male has dark eyes, female has yellow eyes.

PLAIN T ITMOUSE *Parus inornatus*
5.5 in. Uniformly gray, with crest and black eye.

BLACK-CHINNED HUMMINGBIRD *Archilochus alexandri*
3.5 in. Male green with black "chin" and dark violet iridescent throat. Female green with white throat.

BLACKTAIL JACKRABBIT *Lepus californicus*
To 20 in. Long-legged rabbit with long (6–7 inches) black-tipped ears. Dark stripe on lower back, tail.

RINGTAIL *Bassariscus astutus*
Body 16 in., tail 15 in. Bushy tail with dark rings. Face doglike. Large dark eyes but no black mask.

COLLARED LIZARD *Crotaphytus collaris*
To 15 in. Body color variable, usually greenish with some blue. Prominent black and white neck stripes.

PLATE 9

PINYON JAY

UTAH JUNIPER

seed (wingless)

TWO-NEEDLE PINYON

GAMBEL OAK

BUSHTIT

PLAIN TITMOUSE

BIG SAGEBRUSH

seed x ½

ALDERLEAF CERCOCARPUS

BLACKTAIL JACKRABBIT

BLACK-CHINNED HUMMINGBIRD

BLUEBONNET

RINGTAIL

SCARLET GLOBEMALLOW

SEGO LILY

COLLARED LIZARD

PLATE 10

PONDEROSA PINE FOREST

PONDEROSA PINE *Pinus ponderosa*
To 200 ft., usually 125 ft. or less. Long needles (to 10 inches), usually 3 per bundle. Bark orangy, in large scales.

ROCKY MOUNTAIN JUNIPER *Juniperus scopulorum*
To 45 ft. Shrubby tree with scalelike leaves, bark reddish to gray with long, peeling ridges. Females have berrylike cones that smell like gin.

ANTELOPEBRUSH *Purshia tridentata*
To 3 ft. Shrub with long leaves, 3-lobed, like sagebrush but not aromatic. Flowers small, yellow, 5-petaled.

DESERT BUCKBRUSH *Ceanothus fendleri*
To 3 ft. Thorny shrub with small, oval-shaped, gray-green, smooth-margined leaves. Clusters of small white flowers.

CURLYCUP GUMPLANT (GUMWEED) *Grindelia squarrosa*
To 3 ft. Rounded flower head, bright yellow ray flowers. Leaves are slightly toothed.

HEPATIC TANAGER *Piranga flava*
7.5 in. Male is red below, brownish red above. Dark face patch. Female is dull yellow.

WESTERN BLUEBIRD *Sialia mexicana*
7 in. Male with blue throat, rusty on breast and above wings. Female is grayish and paler.

PYGMY NUTHATCH *Sitta pygmaea*
4 in. Slate blue back, brown head with white neck spot. Tail is short.

GRACE'S WARBLER *Dendroica graciae*
5 in. Bright yellow throat, streaks on side, yellow line through eye.

TASSEL-EARED SQUIRREL (ABERT SQUIRREL) *Sciurus aberti*
Body 12 in. Gray above, white below, with long rusty-tipped ear tufts.

COLORADO CHIPMUNK *Eutamias quadrivittatus*
Body 5 in. Mostly gray with pale rust on sides. Ears are black in front, white behind.

MOUNTAIN COTTONTAIL *Sylvilagus nuttallii*
14 in. Grayish brown with yellow cast. Tail and feet are white. Short ears.

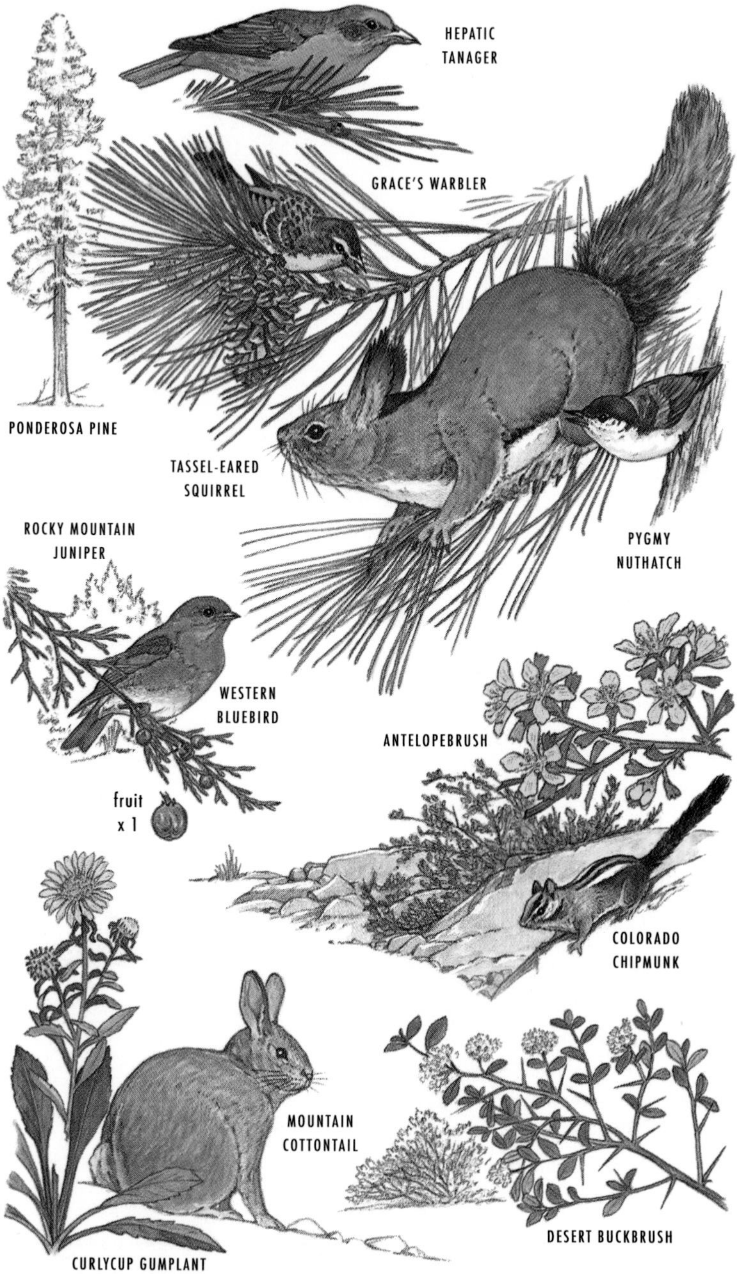

PLATE 10

HEPATIC TANAGER

GRACE'S WARBLER

PONDEROSA PINE

TASSEL-EARED SQUIRREL

PYGMY NUTHATCH

ROCKY MOUNTAIN JUNIPER

WESTERN BLUEBIRD

fruit x 1

ANTELOPEBRUSH

COLORADO CHIPMUNK

CURLYCUP GUMPLANT

MOUNTAIN COTTONTAIL

DESERT BUCKBRUSH

PLATE 11

ASPEN GROVE

QUAKING ASPEN *Populus tremuloides*
To 60 ft. Leaves heart-shaped, toothed, pale below, long petioles. Bark pale yellow-green, smooth.

ROCKY MOUNTAIN MAPLE *Acer glabrum*
To 30 ft. Deciduous, with opposite leaves, both finely and coarsely toothed. Bark smooth, reddish or gray.

ROUNDLEAF SNOWBERRY *Symphoricarpos rotundifolius*
To 2 ft. Shrub with thick, dull grayish, oval leaves, slightly toothed. Flowers pink, bell-shaped.

CHOKECHERRY *Prunus virginiana*
To 26 ft. Shrub or small tree. Leaves deciduous, alternate, with both fine and sharp teeth. Flowers white, in long clusters. Fruits dark red-black.

COLORADO COLUMBINE *Aquilegia caerulea*
To 3 ft. Flower with 5 sky blue sepals, 5 scooplike, white petals, long stamens. Leaves blue-green, compound.

SHOWY DAISY *Erigeron speciosus*
To 3 ft. Flower head diameter 2 in., with disk yellow, rays pink to white. Leaves lance-shaped.

SHOWY LOCO *Oxytropis splendens*
To 16 in. Plant densely covered with silver-white hairs. Flowers pink to lavender. Leaves in whorls around stem.

VIOLET-GREEN SWALLOW *Tachycineta thalassina*
5.5 in. Dark violet-green above, white below, with white feather puffs at base of tail.

MOUNTAIN BLUEBIRD *Sialia currucoides*
7 in. Male uniformly turquoise blue, female grayish brown with blue tail.

RED-NAPED SAPSUCKER *Sphyrapicus nuchalis*
9 in. Black and white bars with large white wing patch. Red on forehead, back of neck.

BROAD-TAILED HUMMINGBIRD *Selasphorus platycercus*
4 in. Male green above with bright red iridescent throat. Female with white throat, faintly streaked.

BEAVER *Castor canadensis*
Body to 30 in., tail 14 in. Flat, scaly, paddle-shaped tail.

PORCUPINE *Erethizon dorsatum*
Body to 25 in., tail to 14 in. Grizzled yellowish fur with spiny quills on back and tail.

PLATE 11

PORCUPINE

VIOLET-GREEN SWALLOW

QUAKING ASPEN

ROCKY MOUNTAIN MAPLE

RED-NAPED SAPSUCKER

CHOKECHERRY

MOUNTAIN BLUEBIRD

BROAD-TAILED HUMMINGBIRD

COLORADO COLUMBINE

ROUNDLEAF SNOWBERRY

SHOWY LOCO

SHOWY DAISY

BEAVER

PLATE 12

LODGEPOLE PINE FOREST

LODGEPOLE PINE *Pinus contorta*
To 100 ft. Slender tree, needles yellow-green, 2 per bundle. Small cones. Bark orange-brown to dark, finely scaled.

WHITEBARK PINE *Pinus albicaulis*
To 35 ft. Bushy tree with pale, furrowed bark, often in large scales. Needles in clusters of 5 are long, stiff, most dense near branch tips.

SNOWBRUSH (STICKY LAUREL) *Ceanothus velutinus*
To 8 ft., usually shorter. Rounded, thick, evergreen leaves, slightly toothed. Many clumps of small, white, 5-petaled flowers.

KINNIKINNICK *Arctostaphylos uva-ursi*
Prostrate, mat-forming shrub. Small, dark green, leathery, evergreen leaves. Bright red berries.

HEARTLEAF ARNICA *Arnica cordifolia*
To 2 ft. Flower heads 3.5 inches wide, bright yellow disk and rays. Leaves large, heart-shaped.

WYOMING PAINTBRUSH *Castilleja linariaefolia*
To 3 ft. Upright plant with bright red bracts around small, greenish flowers. Leaves lance-shaped, upper leaves with 3 slender lobes.

WHITE-BREASTED NUTHATCH *Sitta carolinensis*
6 in. Chunky. Blue and white with black upper head, no eye line. White below. Moves headfirst down tree trunks.

RED CROSSBILL *Loxia curvirostra*
6.5 in. Male is brick red with dark wings and tail. Female is yellowish. Crossed bill visible only at close range.

PINE GROSBEAK *Pinicola enucleator*
10 in. Large size, big black bill, long notched tail. Male rosy, female yellowish. Two wing bars.

MARTEN *Martes americana*
Body to 20 in., tail to 9 in. Color variable, light brown to dark, but always with buffy throat and chest.

RED SQUIRREL (PINE SQUIRREL) *Tamiasciurus hudsonicus*
Body to 8 in., bush tail to 7 in. Reddish above, white below, white eye ring.

PLATE 12

RED CROSSBILL

WHITEBARK PINE

LODGEPOLE PINE

RED SQUIRREL

WHITE-BREASTED NUTHATCH

MARTEN

PINE GROSBEAK

KINNIKINNICK

HEARTLEAF ARNICA

SNOWBRUSH

WYOMING PAINTBRUSH

PLATE 13

RIPARIAN FOREST

NARROWLEAF COTTONWOOD *Populus angustifolia*
To 60 ft. Leaves variable, oval to long, finely toothed. Bark pale, smooth on small trees, deeply furrowed on older trees.

NETLEAF HACKBERRY *Celtis reticulata*
To 50 ft. Oval, untoothed leaves with sharp tip, unsymmetrical base. Netlike leaf veins. Bark smooth with warty growths.

CHOKECHERRY *Prunus virginiana*
To 26 ft. Shrub or small tree. Leaves deciduous, alternate, with both fine and sharp teeth. Flowers white, in long clusters. Fruits dark red-black.

MOUNTAIN ALDER *Alnus tenuifolia*
To 30 ft. Leaves oval with large and small teeth. Netlike veins on underside of leaf. Small cones.

COMMON GOOSEBERRY (WHITESTEM GOOSEBERRY) *Ribes inerme*
To 3 ft. Thorny shrub with maplelike leaves. Greenish, bell-shaped flowers maturing to dark red to black berries.

WHITE CLEMATIS (VIRGIN'S BOWER) *Clematis ligusticifolia*
Climbing vine with opposite, slightly toothed leaves, small white flowers often quite dense.

COW PARSNIP *Heracleum lanatum*
To 8 ft. Very tall and hairy, with wide, platelike clusters of tiny, white flowers and compound leaves.

CORDILLERAN FLYCATCHER *Empidonax occidentalis*
5.75 in. Upright brown bird with two wing bars, eye ring. Must be identified by note, an abrupt *pit-wheet*.

AMERICAN DIPPER *Cinclus mexicanus*
8 in. Stocky, suggests a chunky wren. Slate gray. Rocky, fast streams.

MACGILLIVRAY'S WARBLER *Oporornis tolmiei*
5.75 in. Gray hood, yellow breast, olive-green above. Split eye ring.

YELLOW WARBLER *Dendroica petechia*
5 in. Uniformly bright yellow, male with red streaks on breast.

TIGER SALAMANDER *Ambystoma tigrinum*
13 in. Pale yellow-brown with sharp black stripes, often blotchy.

PLATE 13

CORDILLERAN FLYCATCHER

NETLEAF HACKBERRY

NARROWLEAF COTTONWOOD

CHOKECHERRY

AMERICAN DIPPER

MACGILLIVRAY'S WARBLER

COMMON GOOSEBERRY

MOUNTAIN ALDER

YELLOW WARBLER

COW PARSNIP

WHITE CLEMATIS

TIGER SALAMANDER

PLATE 14

SPRUCE-FIR FOREST

ENGELMANN SPRUCE *Picea engelmannii*
To 200 ft., usually 80 ft. or less. Needles dark bluish green, not highly prickly. Bark brown, scaly. Cones not prickly.

SUBALPINE FIR *Abies lasiocarpa*
To 100 ft., usually shorter. Needles flattened, thin white stripe on upper surface, bases curved. Bark pale and smooth, with resin blisters. Cones purple, upright.

BLUE SPRUCE *Picea pungens*
To 100 ft., rarely taller. Needles blue-green, cones rounded with ragged scales. Bark furrowed, dark.

GROUSE WHORTLEBERRY *Vaccinium scoparium*
To 5 ft. Greenish, spindly branches. Leaves small, oval, finely toothed. Berries red.

JACOB'S LADDER *Polemonium pulcherrimum*
To 2 ft. Large lavender flower with yellow anthers. Compound leaves, somewhat sticky.

EXPLORER'S GENTIAN *Gentiana calycosa*
To 12 in. Stem terminates in a single blue flower with small greenish spots inside. Leaves opposite, not toothed.

GRAY JAY *Perisoreus canadensis*
12 in. Gray above, paler below, dark on back of head. No crest. Often tame.

RUBY-CROWNED KINGLET *Regulus calendula*
4 in. Olive above with 2 wing bars, eye ring. Red rarely visible on male.

GOLDEN-CROWNED KINGLET *Regulus satrapa*
3.5 in. Like Ruby-crowned but with yellow head (orange in male), eye stripe rather than eye ring.

RED-BREASTED NUTHATCH *Sitta canadensis*
4.5 in. Rusty breast, blue back, black head with white eye stripe.

SNOWSHOE HARE *Lepus americanus*
18 in. Brown in summer (often with white feet), white in winter. Ears with black tips.

PLATE 14

SUBALPINE FIR

GRAY JAY

ENGELMANN SPRUCE

JACOB'S LADDER

RUBY-CROWNED KINGLET

GOLDEN-CROWNED KINGLET

RED-BREASTED NUTHATCH

BLUE SPRUCE

SNOWSHOE HARE (winter)

GROUSE WHORTLEBERRY

EXPLORER'S GENTIAN

SNOWSHOE HARE (summer)

PLATE 15

HIGH PINE FOREST

ROCKY MOUNTAIN BRISTLECONE PINE *Pinus aristata*
To 30 ft. Short (less than 2 inches), dark green needles in clusters of 5 tightly hug the branch. Cones 3 in., prickly. Bark pale brown, not deeply furrowed.

LIMBER PINE *Pinus flexilis*
To 50 ft. Trunk often wide (3 feet). Needles (2–2.5 inches) yellow-green, in clusters of 5. Cones 3–6 in. Trunk is dark and deeply furrowed.

SUBALPINE FIR *Abies lasiocarpa*
To 100 ft., usually shorter. Needles flat, thin white stripe on upper surface, bases curved. Bark is pale and smooth, with smooth, oval resin blisters. Cones are purple, upright.

SUBALPINE LARCH *Larix lyallii*
To 50 ft. Needles deciduous, in clumps, each needle 4-sided. Cones 2 in., scales with elongate bracts. Twigs are whitish and hairy.

COMMON JUNIPER *Juniperus communis*
Prostrate, shrubby growth, forms mats. Needles in whorls of 3. Seeds in juicy, dark blue, berrylike cones.

LANCELEAF SEDUM *Sedum lanceolatum*
To 2 ft. Basal rosettes of thick, fleshy, wax-coated leaves. Flowers are yellow.

ROCK CRESS *Arabis drummondii*
To 2 ft. Flowers white, 4-petaled. Seeds in upright pods. Leaves long.

CLARK'S NUTCRACKER *Nucifraga columbiana*
13 in. Gray with black wings and tail. White wing patches, white outer tail feathers. Often tame.

THREE-TOED WOODPECKER *Picoides tridactylus*
10 in. Barred black and white back. Streaked flanks. Male with yellow atop head.

LEAST CHIPMUNK *Eutamias minimis*
Body to 4.5 in., tail to 4.5 in. Color varies from rusty to grayish. Black side stripes go to base of tail.

BUSHYTAIL WOODRAT *Neotoma cinerea*
Body to 9 in., tail to 7 in. Light brown with bushy tail.

PLATE 15

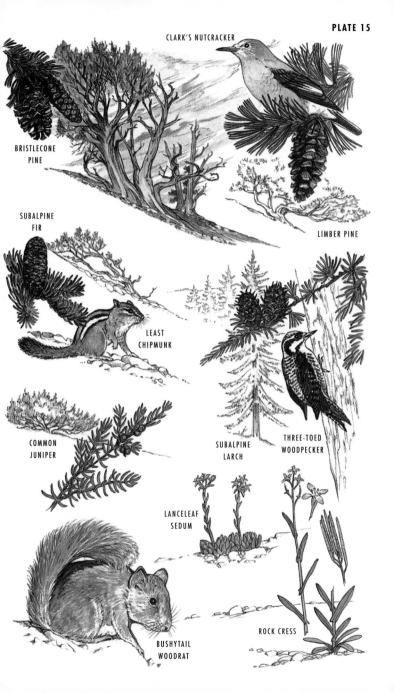

CLARK'S NUTCRACKER

BRISTLECONE PINE

LIMBER PINE

SUBALPINE FIR

LEAST CHIPMUNK

COMMON JUNIPER

SUBALPINE LARCH

THREE-TOED WOODPECKER

LANCELEAF SEDUM

BUSHYTAIL WOODRAT

ROCK CRESS

PLATE 16

ANIMALS OF TIMBERLINE-ALPINE TUNDRA

WHITE-TAILED PTARMIGAN *Lagopus leucurus*
13 in. Chicken-shaped. In summer, mottled brown with white tail, white wings. All white in winter.

AMERICAN PIPIT (WATER PIPIT) *Anthus rubescens*
7 in. Dark brown above, tawny below. Bobs its tail as it walks. White outer tail feathers.

ROSY FINCH *Leucosticte* ssp.
6.75 in. Raspberry wings, sides, rump. Walks, doesn't hop. Three species: Gray-crowned Rosy Finch (*L. tephrocotis,* not illustrated) with gray face, Brown-capped Rosy Finch (*L. australis*) with all-brown head, Black Rosy Finch (*L. atrata*) with mostly black head and breast.

YELLOWBELLY MARMOT *Marmota flaviventris*
Body to 20 in., tail to 9 in. Yellowish with black face with white spots. Short, thick tail.

HOARY MARMOT *Marmota caligata*
Body to 21 in., tail to 10 in. Grizzled silvery, with black on head extending to behind ears. Dark tail.

PIKA *Ochotona princeps*
8 in. Rabbitlike, brown, with small ears. Active, often seen with vegetation in its mouth. Bleating voice suggests a miniature goat.

MOUNTAIN GOAT *Oreamnos americanus*
To 3 ft. tall, 300 lbs. All white, somewhat shaggy, with thin horns curving directly backward. Back is slightly humped.

PLATE 16

MOUNTAIN GOAT

PIKA

HOARY MARMOT

YELLOWBELLY MARMOT

BROWN-CAPPED ROSY FINCH

WHITE-TAILED PTARMIGAN

(summer)

(winter)

BLACK ROSY FINCH

AMERICAN PIPIT

SOUTHWEST FORESTS

In the Southwest, the natural history of Mexico extensively mingles with that of the United States. In western Texas as well as parts of New Mexico and southern Arizona, the southernmost extensions of the Rocky Mountains come within close range of the Mexican cordilleras, the Sierra Madre Occidental and Sierra Madre Oriental. Ecologically, the result is a diverse mixture of species, many of which are typically Mexican in distribution, that make up what is called the Madrean forest (from Sierra Madre). Historically, much of the region was populated by the various Apache nations as well as Pueblos, Navajos, Paiutes, Yumas, Papagos, and Pimas. With such an abundance of human history, sights of interest abound.

The Southwest is primarily a rugged landscape of deserts and grasslands, their monotonous flatness broken up periodically by the foothill forests and various mountain ranges. Two major hot

Ancient Native American habitations at Mesa Verde National Park.

deserts, the Chihuahua and the Sonora, dominate the region. The Chihuahua Desert extends from Mexico into southwestern Texas, southern New Mexico, and extreme southeastern Arizona. It is a land of shrubs, especially Creosote Bush and the strange looking whip-plant, the Ocotillo. Mixed among them are an abundance of yuccas, odd members of the lily family with basal leaves that look like daggers and are almost as sharp. The Sonora Desert covers much of southern Arizona, extending west to Baja California (which is, of course, in Mexico, not California!), and, while Creosote Bush and Ocotillo are both abundant in many places, the Sonora is known mostly for its many cacti, including forests of tall, distinctively shaped Saguaros, the giant cactus that made its way into the background of most old Hollywood westerns.

Deserts, though dry most of the year, experience short periods of intense rainfall, both in spring and with the thunderstorms of late summer. These brief rains replenish the deserts, sometimes producing bursts of color as wildflowers bloom in response to the sudden availability of water. During heavy rains, desert washes (called arroyos) that are dry most of the time suddenly become raging torrents, as the water quickly runs off the hardened soils of the surrounding desert. Arroyos support dense gallery forests of mesquite and acacia, as well as other trees and shrubs that manage to grab sufficient moisture.

In Texas, where the Rio Grande makes a sharp bend northward before continuing east and then southeast to the Gulf of Mexico, there is a region called, appropriately, the Big Bend. This region is the site of Big Bend National Park, an 801,146-acre natural paradise where the Chisos Mountains jut up from the desert, among which are tall, inspiring canyons that embrace the Rio Grande.

Massai Point in the Chiricahua Mountains of southeastern Arizona, where Apaches once lived.

The Rio Grande cuts canyons through the Big Bend region in West Texas.

The Chisos are the southernmost part of the vast chain of Rocky Mountains, but unlike most of the Rockies, they are not greatly elevated. Emory Peak, the highest point in the Chisos, is a mere 7,835 feet, only a little over half the elevation of at least 50 peaks in Colorado alone. However, the Chisos are tall enough to support many life forms not found in the nearby desert, and they provide the best place to see the Mexican Madrean Foothill Forest. One Mexican warbler species, the Colima Warbler, nests near Boot Spring at Big Bend National Park, and nowhere else in the United States.

New Mexico is a land of contrasts. You can, for instance, explore the arid, alkali flatlands of White Sands National Monument near Alamogordo, close to the Trinity Site, where the first atomic bomb was tested. Not far from Alamogordo is Lincoln National Forest, where a singed bear cub named Little Smokey (see page 199) became a living symbol for prevention of carelessly set forest fires. In the nearby town of Lincoln is the old Lincoln County Courthouse, from which Billy the Kid escaped in a violent shoot-out with two deputies (you can still see the bullet holes in the wall). You can climb Wheeler Peak, elevation 13,160 feet, in Carson National Forest, a few miles from Taos, and experience the southernmost alpine tundra in the Rockies, hiking through meadows of wildflowers as you watch scurrying Pikas, and listen to the whistles of Yellowbelly Marmots. You can visit Carlsbad Caverns, in the southeastern part of the state and hike through Chihuahua Desert or descend 750 feet below ground to marvel at the natural art forms of stalactites and stalagmites that abound within the famous caverns. At dusk throughout the summer, Carlsbad Caverns features a nightly bat show, during which visi-

American Avocet at Bosque Del Apache National Wildlife Refuge.

tors watch close to a million Mexican Freetail Bats leave one of the caves. Near Socorro is Bosque del Apache National Wildlife Refuge, a 57,191-acre wetland that serves as wintering grounds for thousands of Lesser Snow Geese, Sandhill Cranes, and other waterfowl.

Arizona contains even more natural diversity than New Mexico. Most visitors, about 3.5 million annually, come to bear witness to what may be nature's most splendid feat of erosion, the Grand Canyon, a huge gorge cut one mile deep and up to 18 miles across by the unrelenting flow of the Colorado River. The Grand Canyon is located near Flagstaff, in the northern part of the state, near the San Francisco Peaks, where C. Hart Merriam first described western life zones (Chapter 3, "Life Zones"). A trip from

The Grand Canyon.

The Petrified Forest in northeastern Arizona consists of the fossilized remains of tall conifers.

the South Rim of the Grand Canyon down the narrow ledge trail to the Colorado River, a journey that can be accomplished on foot or on muleback (be warned, if you're afraid of heights it's a challenge), takes you past about 600 million years of frozen time, evidenced by the numerous fossils found within the strata of sedimentary rocks in the canyon walls.

Arizona's distant past is also revealed in a "forest" made entirely of rock, the Petrified Forest, east of Winslow in the northeastern part of the state. The tall conifer trees have been dead for nearly 200 million years, their fallen remains long since replaced by minerals, a replacement so precise that you can still see the fine details of the bark. Today Greater Roadrunners pursue snakes among big stumps changed by time into boulders. When those trees were alive, the small predatory dinosaur called *Coelophysis*, predecessor to the mighty *Tyrannosaurus rex,* stalked its prey in what was then a lush forest.

Traveling south from Flagstaff toward Phoenix along Interstate 17, you pass through part of Coconino National Forest as you descend along Oak Creek Canyon, a picturesque drive that takes you down the Mogollon Rim toward the Sonora Desert. Oak Creek Canyon is filled with broad-leaved cottonwoods, Ashleaf Maple (Box-elder), Arizona Sycamore, Arizona Walnut, and various willows. Forests of Ponderosa Pine and Common Douglas-fir carpet north-facing slopes, while south-facing slopes abound in Gambel Oak, Two-needle Pinyon, Rocky Mountain and Alligator junipers, and various mountain-mahoganies (cercocarpuses), manzanitas, and yuccas. Bordering Oak Creek Canyon are tall cliffs and buttes made of the reddest of sandstones, producing a vivid geological backdrop, especially when the early morning or late afternoon sun falls against the rock faces, transforming them to a brilliant orange-red. The Mogollon Rim is the great ecological divider in Arizona, separating the northern from the southern part of the state. In the north, on the Mogollon Rim, the ecology is like that of the southern Rocky Mountains. To the south, off the Rim, it is distinctly Madrean, with a strong representation of Mexican species.

From Phoenix to Tucson and continuing south to Mexico, you pass through much of the Sonora Desert. Its principal indicator species is the unmistakable and magnificent Saguaro cactus. In Tucson, known to locals as the Old Pueblo, are the Santa Catalina Mountains where you can drive from hot cactus desert up to cool evergreen forest in about an hour. Near the Mexican border is a series of unique, protected canyons—Ramsey, Madera, Carr, Guadalupe, and Cave Creek—where exotic species such as the Elegant Trogon and Sulphur-bellied Flycatcher live. In the mountains that surround these canyons, the Santa Ritas and Chiricahuas, Red-faced and Olive warblers feed in the cool Apache and Arizona Ponderosa pines, along with Painted Redstarts, Mexican Chickadees, and Yellow-eyed Juncos.

This chapter introduces the forests and many of the unique species that comprises the ecologically diverse Southwest.

Arroyo and Desert Scrub   Plate 17

Indicator Plants

Trees: *Honey Mesquite, Gregg Catclaw, French Tamarisk* (Salt-cedar), Screwbean Mesquite, Velvet Mesquite, Wright Catclaw (Texas only), Roemer Catclaw (Texas only), Blue Paloverde, Yellow Paloverde, Desert Ironwood, Allthorn, Crucifixion-thorn, Jerusalem-thorn, Desert-willow, Texas Kidneywood. In some wetter areas, Fremont Cottonwood, Narrowleaf Cottonwood, Canyon (Bigtooth) Maple.

Shrubs: *Texas Lignumvitae* (Guayacan), Seepwillow, *Texas Forestiera* (Desert-olive), Bursage, Tree Tobacco, Common Oleander, Burrobrush, Calliandra.

Herbaceous species: American Mistletoe, Desert Verbena, Texas (Desert) Milkweed, Sacred Datura (Jimsonweed), Crested Prickly Poppy, Devil's-Claws (Unicornplant), Common Reed, Camphor-weed, Desert Evening Primrose, Desertgold, Heronbill, Silverleaf Nightshade, New Mexico Thistle, Desert Beardtongue, Palmer's Penstemon, Scarlet Monkeyflower.

INDICATOR ANIMALS

BIRDS: *Crissal Thrasher, Phainopepla, Bell's Vireo, Black-tailed Gnat-catcher, Verdin, Lucy's Warbler, Pyrrhuloxia,* Gambel's Quail, Scaled Quail, Great Horned Owl, White-winged Dove, Inca Dove, Common Ground-Dove, Mourning Dove, Greater Road-runner, Common Nighthawk, Ladder-backed Woodpecker, Dusky Flycatcher, Black Phoebe, Vermilion Flycatcher, Western King-bird, Cassin's Kingbird, Brown-crested Flycatcher, Ash-throated Flycatcher, Cliff Swallow, Bewick's Wren, Blue-gray Gnatcatcher, Curve-billed Thrasher, Bendire's Thrasher, Loggerhead Shrike, Virginia's Warbler, Yellow Warbler, Common Yellowthroat, Yellow-breasted Chat, Summer Tanager, Blue Grosbeak, Northern Cardinal, Painted Bunting, Song Sparrow, Red-winged Blackbird, Orchard Oriole, Hooded Oriole, House Finch, American Goldfinch.

MAMMALS: Deer Mouse, Southern Plains Woodrat, Raccoon, Coati, Ringtail, Spotted Skunk, Hooded Skunk, Kit Fox, Collared Peccary, Mule Deer, Whitetail Deer.

REPTILES: Desert Spiny Lizard, Short-lined Skink, Greater Earless Lizard, Checkered Whiptail, Western Whiptail, Great Plains Rat Snake, Common Kingsnake, Coachwhip, Western Diamondback Rattlesnake, Mojave Rattlesnake.

AMPHIBIANS: Couch's Spadefoot Toad, Red-spotted Toad, Texas Toad, Woodhouse Toad.

DESCRIPTION

Even deserts get some water. In major rivers such as the Rio Grande, at least a trickle of water may be present throughout the year. More commonly, desert streams are bone dry for most of the year, the streambeds filling only during the brief but heavy rains of spring and often torrential downfalls of late summer. The surrounding desert soil is dry and often nearly impermeable to water, so rainwater flows over it more than into it. When the rains come, these *arroyos* can fill with frightening speed, flooding roads and surrounding areas. *Stay out of arroyos if it is raining hard.* Water does eventually drain into the sandy arroyo soil and become available to trees and other plants that can reach down deeply enough to get at it. As a result, arroyos are lined with unique *gallery forests,* mostly of leguminous trees with long taproots. These spiny trees, the acacias and mesquites, with their feathery compound leaves, look surprisingly delicate among the spine-covered cacti and rugged-looking, stiff-branched desert shrubs. Along with mesquites and acacias, the odd Allthorn, Crucifixion-thorn, and Yellow Paloverde trees form dense thickets in many places. These three species, all with long, sharp thorns and tiny leaves, do most of their photosynthesis in their green stems. The odd tamarisk,

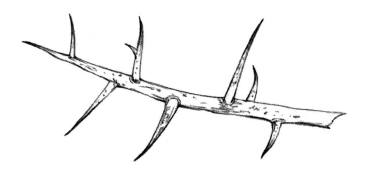

Figure 24. Allthorn

commonly known as salt-cedar, is native to Eurasia and was introduced as an ornamental and for erosion control. It has spread widely, occupying arroyos and gullies throughout the Southwest, pushing out native trees. The arroyo gallery forest provides important habitat for quite a few birds and other animals. Surrounding the arroyos are the deserts themselves, the Chihuahua to the east and the Sonora to the west.

The dense mesquite and acacia thickets that line the dry streambeds are nesting and feeding areas for many birds, including tiny Verdins, Black-tailed and Blue-gray gnatcatchers, and Lucy's Warblers. Nondescript Bell's Vireos, hiding in the shade of the mesquite, sing their monotonous question, an upslurred *chee-dle-cheedle-cheedle-dee?* answered with a downslurred *cheedle-cheedle-cheedle-do.* One of the more secretive birds of the arroyos, the slender Crissal Thrasher, like the vireo, is more often heard than seen. In early morning its melodious song is usually given from a perch atop a mesquite, but more often it skulks, out of sight. Easier to see, the colorful Pyrrhuloxia resembles a cardinal that has largely "gone gray." Many other species, including the colorful scarlet and black Vermilion Flycatcher and the more subtly colored Ash-throated Flycatcher, frequent the arroyos. Mistletoe abundantly parasitizes mesquite, and the nutritious mistletoe berries are heavily fed upon by the Phainopepla, a shiny black bird with bright red eyes and a ragged crest. Phainopeplas, which may be quite abundant at times, are important in dispersing mistletoe seeds. Husky White-winged Doves wail their mournful songs, sounding a bit like owls. Great Horned Owls do frequent the dense arroyo trees, but they hoot rather than wail. On the ground, coveys of Gambel's or Scaled quail scurry along the dry streambeds, searching for seeds.

Where desert streams are a bit more lush (particularly where there are some cottonwoods), species such as Yellow Warblers, Yellow-breasted Chats, Summer Tanagers, Painted Buntings, and Blue Grosbeaks are common.

Mammals also frequent arroyos and surrounding scrub deserts, including three members of the raccoon family: the Raccoon, Coati, and Ringtail. Kit Foxes stalk woodrats and other rodents beneath the spindly tree trunks.

While it is hardly a surprise that reptiles inhabit arroyos, it may seem odd to find amphibians in a land that is literally desert-dry. Some do live there, however. Couch's Spadefoot survives in a burrow below ground for the better part of the year, emerging (with the help of its spade, a nail-like digging device on its hind feet) only after the first heavy spring rains to mate and lay eggs.

SIMILAR FOREST COMMUNITIES: See Chihuahua Desert and giant Saguaro cactus forest; also Lower Rio Grande forest.

RANGE: From Texas west through the Chihuahua, Sonora, and Mojave deserts.

REMARKS

Mesquite and acacia (catclaw) species are the most common indicators of arroyo gallery forests. Both are members of the legume family, an immense collection of over 14,000 species that includes clovers, beans, and peas as well as many woody species such as the locusts. There are about 30 mesquite species in the world, and only three occur in the United States. Acacias, or cat-

An arroyo, or desert streambed.

claws, on the other hand, are much more diverse. There are over 1,000 species, all in the genus *Acacia*, and they occur abundantly in the tropics and subtropics, especially in Australia. There are 15 *Acacia* species native to North America, all shrubs or small trees.

HONEY MESQUITE is widely distributed throughout the Southwest and Mexico. It is often the most numerous tree of the arroyos and typically reaches a height of about 20 feet. Like all legumes it has compound leaves, usually with 10–20 pairs of narrow leaflets. The deciduous leaves tend to droop, making the tree look wilted. Mesquites are able to thrive along arroyos because their very long taproots can reach underground water. Don't grab carelessly at mesquite—the twigs have sharp paired thorns. The flowers are in pendulous, yellow clusters, and the seeds are in dry, brown pods. There are usually 10–12 seeds per pod. The bark is reddish brown, thin, and scaly. Another common mesquite, **SCREWBEAN MESQUITE,** is similar but has smaller, proportionately wider leaflets and pods that look tightly twisted. Screwbean has an odd distribution; it is common in the California Mojave Desert and along the Rio Grande in Texas, but sparse in between. The third mesquite, **VELVET MESQUITE,** is similar to Honey Mesquite, but its leaflets are hairy, not smooth. Some authorities regard it as merely a variety of Honey Mesquite. It occurs throughout much of Arizona and New Mexico.

The common desert *Acacias* are called catclaws for their numerous curved thorns. **GREGG CATCLAW,** which can grow as a shrub or as a tree up to 30 feet tall, is the most widely distributed species, occurring from south Texas and northern Mexico throughout the Southwest to southern California and Baja California. It often forms dense thickets that afford ideal cover for wildlife

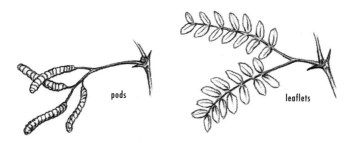

pods

leaflets

Figure 25. Leaflets and pods of Screwbean Mesquite

(shade is important when the daily summer temperature routinely exceeds 110° F). In spring, Gregg Catclaw produces an abundance of yellow flowers in pendulous clusters like those of Honey Mesquite. The trees are easily distinguished from each other, however, because the acacia's leaflets are smaller, and it has only 4–6 leaflet pairs per leaf. The pods are brown and flattened and twist in a helix shape. There are usually 4–5 seeds per pod. Two other *Acacia* species, the Roemer and Wright catclaws, are essentially confined to Texas.

FRENCH TAMARISK, commonly called Salt-cedar, is one of three tamarisk species, each from Eurasia, that have become naturalized in the United States. There are approximately 100 species in the tamarisk family, and none is native to North America. All of the three imported species, the French and Five-stamen tamarisks and Athel (Desert Tamarisk) thrive in the wild, outcompeting native vegetation, and they look similar. French Tamarisk, typical of the group, is a small, shrubby tree that rarely grows more than 30 feet tall. It grows abundantly in the Southwest, usually along watercourses but also on alkali flats and saline soils. It is often planted in rows as windbreak. Foliage consists of tiny, scale-like leaves on slender, drooping branches that give the tree its resemblance to a cedar. In spring, the tree is covered with long clusters of tiny pink flowers that mature into dry, brown fruit capsules. French Tamarisk has been widely used for erosion control, and it spreads quickly. Though it provides nesting area for a variety of bird species, it is not otherwise useful to wildlife.

TEXAS LIGNUMVITAE (Guayacan) and **TEXAS FORESTIERA** (Desert-olive) are common in the Chihuahua Desert in southwest Texas and neighboring Mexico. Lignumvitae is a stiffly branched, small (20 feet) evergreen tree. Leaves are compound, with tiny leaflets with sharply pointed tips. In spring the tree has deep violet, 5-petaled flowers with yellow stamens. The heart-shaped fruit is a dry capsule. Texas Forestiera is also a stiffly branched, evergreen desert species that shares a similar range with Texas Lignumvitae. It, too, is a small (to 15 feet), spreading tree or shrub. Leaves are small, long, and leathery, arranged opposite each other on the branch. Flowers are small, lack petals, and are in yellow-green clusters. Both Texas Lignumvitae and the two Desert-olive species have leaflets that tend to curl at the edges, an adaptation that reduces water loss in the hot desert.

The **CRISSAL THRASHER** is a robin-sized bird with a long tail that seems to hang loosely from its body. Overall rich brown, it is rusty under the tail. Its most obvious field mark is its long, decurved bill, suggesting a sickle. It is a permanent resident in mesquite thickets throughout the Southwest, from west Texas to extreme southeastern California. Many birders find it a challenge to see the Crissal well. It is a skulker, remaining in the shade of the mesquites and acacias and often flying deeper into the thicket before the birder gets a good binocular view. It often feeds on the ground, using its decurved bill to capture various invertebrates and small lizards hiding beneath the fallen mesquite leaves. When singing, usually around dawn, sometimes near dusk, the bird may be visible on an exposed song perch. Its song is a rich warbled whistle, *aura-lee, aura-lee, aura-lee.* Two other thrasher species, the **CURVE-BILLED THRASHER** and the **BENDIRE'S THRASHER,** frequent southwestern deserts. The gray Curve-billed Thrasher, despite its name, has a less decurved bill than the Crissal. It is common in upland desert areas as well as arroyos. Bendire's Thrasher is also grayish, with faint spotting on its breast and an even less decurved bill than the Curve-billed. Bendire's is local, much less common than the Curve-billed.

The **PHAINOPEPLA** is as obvious as the Crissal Thrasher is secretive. It is the most northern member of the silky flycatcher family, a subtropical group that specializes in feeding on mistletoe. This unique bird of the deserts is unforgettable. Phainopeplas are generally social, and loose colonies of them inhabit arroyos and surrounding areas. Males are sleek ebony and crested, like black cardinals with thin bills. Females are gray, and they too, have crests. Both sexes have deep red eyes, visible in good light at reasonably close range. Phainopeplas are devoted to mistletoe, a plant that parasitizes mesquite and other species. Phainopepla flocks actively defend their favored clumps of mistletoe, driving other birds away. They feed heavily on mistletoe berries and are important in disseminating the seeds. Because mistletoe is parasitic, growing literally into its host tree, its seeds must land on branches. By passing through the gut of a Phainopepla, which spends most of its time perched in the very trees that mistletoe parasitizes, seeds spread efficiently. Phainopepla courtship behavior is easy to see, as males fly upward several hundred feet and fly around in circles over their territories. Phainopeplas nest along arroyos from west Texas throughout the Southwest to southern California.

BELL'S VIREO is an active, nondescript inhabitant of mesquite and acacia thickets. In addition to the Southwest and southern California, where it lives along arroyos, it ranges throughout the Rocky Mountains, where it inhabits streamside willow thickets. Southwestern populations are much grayer than the yellowish olive birds of the Rockies. Both populations have dull wing bars and the merest suggestion of an eye ring. The questioning song of Bell's Vireo, described in the Description above, is among the easiest bird songs to remember.

LUCY'S WARBLER is a small, active warbler of the shady arroyo thickets. Both males and females are gray with rusty orange rumps. The male also has orange on the top of his head, though you must get a good look to see this field mark. Lucy's Warbler occurs throughout the Southwest as a summer resident, building its tiny nest beneath bark or in a tree cavity. In winter it migrates a relatively short distance to western Mexico. Lucy's Warbler has a rich, whistled, melodious warble, often given as it goes about its foraging activities. It tends to flick its tail and is sometimes mistaken for a gnatcatcher, which forages similarly.

Two gnatcatchers inhabit Southwestern deserts, the **BLUE-GRAY GNATCATCHER** and the **BLACK-TAILED GNATCATCHER,** and they look much alike. Both are blue-gray above and white below. These tiny, slender, insectivorous birds with long, flicking tails are active foragers. They flit among the mesquite branches, sounding their call note, a dry, buzzy *spee*. The Blue-gray Gnatcatcher (not illustrated), widely distributed in North America, is a common nester in eastern forests as well as throughout much of the West. In winter, it migrates to Central America and the Antilles and Bahamas. The Black-tailed Gnatcatcher is strictly a desert species, a permanent resident of southwestern arroyos. Southwestern populations of Blue-grays also nest along arroyos, however, so both species are present in the summer. The Black-tailed has a black cap, lacking on the Blue-gray, but the Blue-gray has a distinct eye ring, lacking on the Black-tailed. The black on the Black-tailed refers only to the *underside* of the tail, as both gnatcatcher species have black on the upper part of the tail. The underside of a Blue-gray's tail is mostly white, but with a little black in the middle.

Confused? Wait, there's more. A third species, the **BLACK-CAPPED GNATCATCHER,** has just a bit more of a black cap than the Black-tailed, and a white tail underside like a Blue-gray. Essentially confined to Mexico, the Black-capped is rare and localized compared with the Blue-gray and Black-tailed, though it is sometimes seen in southern Arizona and has even bred there. Recently, a fourth species appeared on the scene, in a manner of speaking. In coastal southern California, a race of Black-tailed Gnatcatcher was recognized to be, in fact, a separate species, and is now known as the California Gnatcatcher.

Though gnatcatchers may be confusing, the **VERDIN** isn't. There is only one species, and it is easy to see and easy to identify. It's a small bird, very much like the Bushtit, to which it is closely related, and is an active little forager on the outer branches. Both sexes are gray, with a bright yellow head and a tiny rusty shoulder patch. Verdins occur as permanent residents from southeastern Texas through southern California, and they are widely distributed in Mexico. Verdins build a distinctive large woven nest with a side entrance, situated among cactus branches or deep among mesquite branches. Their call note, given while foraging, is a robust *zeep!*

Birders sometimes confuse the **PYRRHULOXIA** with the Cardinal, as the two species are the same size and shape, both are crested, and both have a lot of red. However, the Pyrrhuloxia has a yellow bill, whereas the Cardinal's bill is orange-red. The shape of the bill is also different between the two species. The Pyrrhuloxia's bill has been compared with that of a parrot, rounded, with the upper mandible overhanging the lower. The Cardinal's is a grosbeak's bill, not rounded and not overhanging. Pyrrhuloxias are permanent residents in deserts throughout the Southwest, and they range widely through Mexico. Male and female forage together and are usually relatively easy to see, as they tend to perch in the open.

WHERE TO VISIT: Arroyos are found throughout the deserts of the Southwest. In Big Bend National Park, Santa Elena and Bouquillas canyons offer ideal examples. In southern Arizona, Florida Wash, near Madera Canyon, and Sonoita Creek, near Patagonia, are recommended. There are many arroyos in the Tucson area, including at Sabino Canyon near the main road to Mt. Lemmon in the Santa Catalina Mountains. Saguaro National Monument (western section) has excellent arroyos. Also recommended are the roads through the desert leading to Portal, in southeastern Arizona.

ESSAY

SONOITA CREEK, OASIS IN THE DESERT

To many people the name Patagonia refers to the southernmost part of the continent of South America, where gauchos and guanacos roam windswept open pampas in proud but perhaps lonely desolation. To birders, however, the name Patagonia means southern Arizona, and a place called Sonoita Creek. Located approximately 50 miles south of Tucson, the diminutive town of Patagonia and neighboring Sonoita Creek is anything but lonely. It annually attracts thousands of birders in search not only of various rarities but also of everyday species, for Sonoita Creek knows few rivals when it comes to great birds and lots of them. The heart of Sonoita Creek is the 312-acre Patagonia-Sonoita Creek Sanctuary, owned and operated by The Nature Conservancy. This land, which abuts a 1.5-mile section of Sonoita Creek, is laced with trails that take you along the floodplain and adjoining area. In addition, there is a famous roadside rest, on the eastern side of the highway, just south of The Nature Conservancy sanctuary, that is famous as a host of rare birds, including the Thick-billed Kingbird.

The hilly area around Sonoita Creek is essentially desert, with an abundance of mesquite, acacia, Ocotillo, and Creosote Bush, interspersed with grassland and large ranches where cattle graze. The creek itself is bordered by a wide expanse of huge, shady Fremont Cottonwoods, including a fair number of individuals over 100 feet tall. In addition to the cottonwoods, the floodplain supports an abundance of Velvet Ash, Arizona Walnut, Texas Mulberry, and a diversity of willows, many of them clumped in dense thickets affording ideal cover for birds and other animals.

The juxtaposition of desert and wide, broad-leaved deciduous floodplain explains the amazing variety of birds concentrated in the areas along Sonoita Creek. Because the Mexican border is only 20 miles from Patagonia, regularly occurring species are occasionally augmented by rare Mexican species. In the thorny woodlands of acacias and mesquites, Inca, White-winged, and Mourning doves, Bell's Vireos, Black-chinned and Broad-billed hummingbirds, Lucy's Warblers, Pyrrhuloxias, Brown-crested and Ash-throated flycatchers, Cassin's Kingbirds, Black-tailed Gnatcatchers, Phainopeplas, Canyon Towhees, and Rufous-crowned Sparrows are all common. This is a splendid habitat in which to search for the less common, brilliant Varied Bunting. Rare Mexican species, like Thick-billed Kingbird, Northern Beardless-Tyrannulet, Gray Hawk, and Black-capped Gnatcatcher are occasionally seen as well. In the canopy of the cottonwoods that line the creek you can find Summer Tanagers, Hooded and Northern orioles, Blue Grosbeaks, Bridled Titmice, Yellow-billed Cuckoos, and Gila, Acorn, and Ladder-backed woodpeckers. With great luck, you may see the Common Black-Hawk, another species from south of the border. Both Great Horned and Western Screech-Owls nest in the tall trees, and you may be fortunate enough to find the huge rounded nest of the Rose-throated Becard, the only representative of its tropical family to reach the United States. Along the creek itself, the small Green Kingfisher occasionally lurks, and you are essentially guaranteed of seeing Black Phoebe. A Willow Flycatcher or Say's Phoebe may be snatching airborne insects as well. Along the roads that border various portions of the creek, Greater Roadrunners and Gambel's and Montezuma quails scurry along, and a Zone-tailed Hawk may circle overhead with the usual Turkey Vultures. Small ponds provide habitat for Black-bellied Whistling-Ducks.

Mammals are also abundant at the Sonoita oasis. Herds of Collared Peccaries and Whitetail Deer are often seen. Rock Squirrels

Herds of Collared Peccaries roam the arroyos and desert scrub.

and Yuma Antelope Squirrels join Blacktail Jackrabbits and Desert Cottontails in the (relatively) cool shade beneath the thorny desert trees, while Arizona Gray Squirrels scurry about in the cottonwoods. Coatis and Ringtails are less frequently seen, but they are there. At night, four skunk species—Hognose, Striped, Hooded, and Spotted—join Raccoons for a cool drink from the creek.

Several rare reptile and amphibian species, including the Colorado River Toad and Desert Tortoise, can also be found. The creek contains a population of Gila Topminnow, reputed to be the most endangered fish species in the Southwest.

Once much more widespread, the rich cottonwood floodplain forest is a rare sight in most of the Southwest today. Sonoita Creek, especially within the Patagonia-Sonoita Creek Sanctuary, represents a remnant ecosystem, a kind of natural trust dedicated to the preservation of the region's finest biodiversity.

Mexican Madrean Foothill Forest   Plate 18

Indicator Plants

Trees: *Mexican Pinyon, Weeping Juniper, Gray Oak, Texas Madrone,* Alligator Juniper, Oneseed Juniper, Pinchot Juniper, Mohr Oak, Emory Oak, Chisos Oak, Netleaf Oak, Graves Oak, Arizona Oak, Gambel Oak, Goldenball Leadtree, Gregg Ash, Fragrant Ash, Chihuahua Ash, Velvet Ash. In protected canyons: Ponderosa Pine, Arizona Cypress, Common Douglas-fir, Quaking Aspen.

Shrubs: *Apache-plume, Scarlet Bouvardia,* Lechuguilla, Century Plant,

Spanish Dagger, Carneros Yucca (Giant Dagger), Sotol, Beaked Yucca, Soaptree Yucca, Nolina Beargrass, Spiny Hackberry, Agarito, Pink Mimosa, Desert Buckbrush, Creosote Bush, Four-wing Saltbush, Mormon-tea, Ocotillo.

HERBACEOUS SPECIES: *Big Bend Penstemon,* Fendler's Penstemon, Cooper's Paperflower, Woolly Locoweed, Texas Milkweed, Wright's Mustard, Longspur Columbine, Desert Evening Primrose, Cardinal Flower, Fingerleaf Gourd, Bracted Paintbrush, Imperial Morning Glory, American Mistletoe, various cacti, and vines such as White Clematis and grape.

INDICATOR ANIMALS

BIRDS: *Gray-breasted Jay, Gray Vireo, Spotted Towhee, Lucifer Hummingbird,* Turkey Vulture, Zone-tailed Hawk, Red-tailed Hawk, Ferruginous Hawk, American Kestrel, Prairie Falcon, Elf Owl, Great Horned Owl, Scaled Quail, Mourning Dove, Greater Roadrunner, Common Nighthawk, Common Poorwill, White-throated Swift, Black-chinned Hummingbird, Acorn Woodpecker, Ladderbacked Woodpecker, Northern Flicker, Say's Phoebe, Western Kingbird, Cassin's Kingbird, Ash-throated Flycatcher, Browncrested Flycatcher, Horned Lark, Cliff Swallow, Scrub Jay, Chihuahuan Raven, Common Raven, Juniper Titmouse, Verdin, Bushtit, Rock Wren, Canyon Wren, Blue-gray Gnatcatcher, Mountain Bluebird, Loggerhead Shrike, Plumbeous Vireo, Blackcapped Vireo, Virginia's Warbler, Colima Warbler (Big Bend only), Lucy's Warbler, Black-throated Gray Warbler, Northern Cardinal, Varied Bunting, Green-tailed Towhee, Canyon Towhee, Rufous-crowned Sparrow, Black-chinned Sparrow, Brewer's Blackbird, Scott's Oriole, House Finch, Lesser Goldfinch, American Goldfinch.

MAMMALS: *Western Pipistrel,* Pinyon Mouse, *Rock Squirrel,* Whitetail Antelope Squirrel, Spotted Ground Squirrel, Whitethroat Woodrat, Desert Cottontail, Blacktail Jackrabbit, Bobcat, Mountain Lion, Longtail Weasel, Ringtail, Coyote, Hognose Skunk, Spotted Skunk, Striped Skunk, Gray Fox, Collared Peccary, Mule Deer, Whitetail Deer.

REPTILES: *Black-tailed Rattlesnake,* Rock Rattlesnake, Western Diamondback Rattlesnake, Black-necked Garter Snake, Common Kingsnake, Long-nosed Snake, Striped Whipsnake, Gopher Snake, Western Coachwhip, Trans-Pecos Rat Snake, Common Chuckwalla, Short-horned Lizard, Western Whiptail, Many-lined Skink, Western Collared Lizard, Texas Banded Gecko, Reticulated (Big Bend) Gecko, Crevice Spiny Lizard, Canyon Lizard.

AMPHIBIANS: Great Basin Spadefoot, Red-spotted Toad, Canyon Treefrog.

DESCRIPTION

The number of species that occur in upper Sonoran zone foothill woodlands increases as you move south. In west Texas, much of Mexico, and parts of southern New Mexico and Arizona, pinyons and junipers are joined by many oak species, most of which have small, evergreen, leathery leaves. Oak diversity is high, with approximately 112 oak species ranging within the Mexican Plateau. The woodland is generally open, with widely spaced, shrubby trees. Species composition varies considerably between Texas-Mexico and southern Arizona, thus we recognize both a Mexican and an Arizona Madrean foothill forest. Though the forest itself is widespread along the slopes of the Mexican cordilleras, the only ideal location for seeing the Mexican Madrean forest community in the United States is the Chisos Mountains in Big Bend National Park in west Texas.

Climate in this forest is characterized by mild winters and relatively hot, wet summers, with most precipitation falling between May and August.

Two species, Weeping Juniper and Texas Madrone, are principal indicator species, along with an abundance of Mexican Pinyon. However, other species, especially Oneseed Juniper, along with a high diversity of scrubby oaks, add a unique character to this woodland. Weeping Juniper is quite unmistakable, as its drooping foliage gives it the look of a plant permanently wilted. Texas Madrone is also an easy identification because of its smooth, reddish bark and bright red berry clusters. Several ash species, especially Gregg, Fragrant, and Chihuahua ashes, grow among the oaks on exposed, rocky slopes.

The land is arid, and exposed hillsides and south-facing slopes have a real desertlike quality, with scattered yuccas, especially Spanish Dagger and Sotol. Similar in appearance, but members of the amaryllis, rather than the lily family, Lechuguilla and Century Plant stand tall among the shrubby pinyons and junipers. When Century Plants are in full bloom (every 25 to 50 years, not every 100 years as the name implies), each tall stalk will contain up to a dozen or more wide, dish-shaped, yellow flower heads, held horizontally. The rich nectar of the flowers is sought by many bird species, including several hummingbirds, and the Scott's Oriole. Several senna species, members of the legume family, add a bright yellow wash of color to the arid landscape when they produce their abundant five-petaled flowers.

Locos such as Woolly Locoweed, also members of the legume family, are often abundant. They have clusters of violet flowers and fine, fernlike, compound leaves. Locos are named for their poisonous quality. Cattle that eat locoweed may act erratically

Lechuguilla, Madrone, and Juniper are among the plant species found in Big Bend National Park.

and even die. The soil affects the toxicity of locos. Locos growing in soils high in calcium may be extremely toxic, but the same species in noncalcareous, sandy soil may be quite palatable for livestock.

Many grasses are common among the other foothill vegetation, and wildflowers display an array of colors from spring through summer. Several penstemons can be found, the most noticeable of which is Big Bend Penstemon, with its bright red, tubular flower.

A few tree species characteristic of cooler, moister climates manage to survive along north-facing slopes. Ponderosa Pine, Common Douglas-fir, Quaking Aspen, and Arizona Cypress reach the limits of their ranges in the cool, protected shadows of the Chisos Mountains.

Many bird species live here, especially during the breeding season. Some, like the Greater Roadrunner and Elf Owl, are typical desert species, whereas others, like the Gray-breasted Jay and Gray Vireo, are highly indicative of pinyon-juniper habitat. One species, the Colima Warbler, looks like a large hybrid between the more widespread Virginia's and Lucy's warblers. The Colima, gray with a rusty crown and yellow rump, breeds along the trail to Boot Spring in Big Bend National Park, its only breeding place in the United States.

Mammals are common in the Madrean foothill forest. The relatively open habitat is suitable for small herds of Peccaries (locally called javelinas), as well as both Mule and Whitetail Deer. Rock Squirrels are particularly common, and some desert species such as Ringtail regularly venture up into the pygmy forest of the foothills.

The hot temperatures and rocky terrain are ideal for reptiles,

The moon rises above the Chisos Mountains of the Big Bend.

and many species, including several rattlesnakes, can be found. More commonly sighted are various lizards, especially the Western Whiptail, Short-horned Lizard, and Collared Lizard.

SIMILAR FOREST COMMUNITIES: See Arizona Madrean foothill forest; Rocky Mountain pinyon-juniper forest.

RANGE: Chisos Mountains in the Big Bend area of Texas and south into Mexico, usually at elevations of 4,400–8,700 ft.

REMARKS

Rising in elevation from the hot desert floor, a land of scorched shrubs and cacti begins to change into one of grassland, yuccas, Lechuguilla, and small, leathery oaks. Eventually the rounded, dark green forms of scattered Mexican Pinyons appear, standing out boldly among the more desert-type species. Higher still, Mexican Pinyons become abundant, joined by Texas Madrone and Weeping and Oneseed junipers, making a dense, canopied woodland. Oaks remain abundant, some growing as trees, some as shrubby thickets.

MEXICAN PINYON is as widely distributed in Mexico as Two-needle Pinyon is in the United States, but Mexican Pinyon crosses the border only at the Big Bend area of Texas and extreme southeastern Arizona. Unlike its northern cousin, Mexican Pinyon has needles in bundles of three. Otherwise, the two species are similar in size, shape, needle color, cones, and bark characteristics. Mexican Pinyon rarely exceeds 20 feet in height, though it can reach 30 feet. Like Two-needle Pinyon, it produces large, energy-rich seeds sought by many bird and rodent species, including the Gray-breasted Jay shown in the plate.

WEEPING JUNIPER, sometimes called Drooping Juniper, is unmistakable. Its scaly, spreading branches hang pendantlike, making the small tree resemble an evergreen version of Weeping Willow. The bark, as distinctive as the foliage, is reddish brown and peels in long strips. As with all junipers, the cones are berrylike. In this species, they are bright reddish brown and hang in small clusters from the drooping branches. Like Mexican Pinyon, Weeping Juniper ranges widely along the foothills of the Mexican Cordilleras but reaches the United States only in west Texas.

The closely related **PINCHOT JUNIPER** is essentially confined to Texas, from west Texas through the Panhandle. Like Weeping Juniper, it is a small tree, rarely exceeding 20 feet in height, but its branches do not droop, though they often are so dense that they touch the ground. Its bark is similar to that of Weeping Juniper but its foliage is yellow-green, and the berrylike cones are quite red, not reddish brown.

TEXAS MADRONE, like its coniferous companions of the foothills, rarely exceeds 20 feet in height. It is a broad-leaved evergreen and a member of the heath family, a kinship evidenced by its delicate white or pink flowers. Like blueberries, whortleberries, manzanitas, and other heaths, madrone flowers are bell- or urn-shaped, dangling in small clusters at branch tips. The fruits are dark red berries with rough surfaces. Texas Madrone is indeed striking, its bright reddish, peeling bark revealing a smooth undersurface and its branches covered with clusters of bright red fruits. It is heavily fed upon by many bird species, some of which are important in distributing seeds. Texas Madrone is found mostly in Texas, though it ranges into southeastern New Mexico and south into Mexico. In Texas, it is found from the Edwards Plateau (see Chapter 6) to parts of the Panhandle and west Texas.

GRAY OAK is one of many common small oaks that thrive in the soils of the hot southwestern foothills. Most grow as either shrubs or small, spreading trees. Gray Oak is evergreen, with small, oval leaves that feel very leathery. It gets its name from its leaves, which are distinctly gray-green and have tiny hairs on both the upper and lower surfaces, a good field mark that separates this species from other oaks. Acorns range in size from about .5 inches to .8 inches.

MOHR OAK is very similar to Gray, but its leaves are shiny, dark green above and gray below. Mohr Oak leaves are hairy only on their undersides. Mohr and Gray oaks separate somewhat by soil type, with Mohr Oak essentially confined to soils high in calcium. Chisos Oak is a rare species found only in the Chisos Mountains. Its evergreen leaves are distinctly lobed, with pointed tips. Leaves are shiny green above, dull below. Acorns from all oaks are widely fed upon by peccaries, deer, squirrels, and birds such as jays.

APACHE-PLUME is a spreading shrub that grows to about 4–6 feet in height. The name derives from the slight resemblance of the fruit to an Indian's feathered war bonnet. It is easily recognized by its large, 5-petaled, white flowers that look much like roses. Indeed, this common shrub is a member of the rose family, and its other common name is feather-rose, for the feathery fruits that replace the flowers. The flowers bloom from June to August. The fruits are initially green, then turn reddish. The fruits remain on the plant for a considerable time, making it easy to identify most of the year. Leaves are tiny, with minute hairs. Apache-plume is wide-ranging, occurring from southeastern California, throughout the southern Rockies, west Texas, and northern Mexico.

A **SCARLET BOUVARDIA** in full bloom is a sight not easily forgotten. This densely branched shrub, also called Trumpetilla, grows to a height of about 3 feet. It can be covered with brilliant red, trumpet-shaped blossoms that attract numerous hummingbirds, among them the rare Lucifer. The plant, a member of the madder family, blooms from July through October and is a valuable nectar source not only for resident hummingbirds but for migrants as well. Leaves are in whorls, usually 4 per whorl.

BIG BEND PENSTEMON has one of the most restricted ranges of the 31 penstemon species found in the Southwest. Its common name reflects the fact that it is only found in the Big Bend region of Texas. Big Bend Penstemon is most easily identified by its wide, oval leaves. All penstemons have opposite leaves, but many of the red penstemons have lance-shaped or elongated leaves. Red penstemons are pollinated by hummingbirds as they feed on the flowers' nectar.

The male **LUCIFER HUMMINGBIRD** is identified by its iridescent violet throat, forked tail, and long, somewhat decurved bill. It, like most of its food plants, is essentially a Madrean species largely confined to Mexico. In the United States, it regularly nests only in the Big Bend region of west Texas, though it is occasionally found in southern New Mexico and southeastern Arizona. In addition to bouvardia and penstemons, Lucifers frequently feed on Century Plants, hovering around the huge yellow flowerheads. The male sometimes utters a loud, abrupt *squeek.*

GRAY-BREASTED JAYS, formerly called Mexican Jays, closely resemble dull versions of widespread Scrub Jays. Like the Scrub Jay, the Gray-breasted Jay lacks a crest and is dull brown on its otherwise slaty-blue back. The breast, true to the name, is dull gray. The species is common throughout the foothills of the Mexican Cordilleras, reaching the United States in southern Arizona and the Big Bend region of Texas. Gray-breasted Jays are year-round residents, living in permanent flocks of 6–24 individuals. Not every bird breeds in a given year. Like a few other species, including the Florida Scrub Jay, Gray-breasted Jays have nest helpers, non-breeding individuals that aid a nesting pair in activities such as nest building and bringing food to the young. Gray-breasted Jays feed most heavily on acorns, not surprising considering the diversity and abundance of oaks. Like Pinyon Jays (Plate 9) and Clark's Nutcrackers (Plate 15), they cache seeds (in this case acorns, not pine seeds), and by doing so they help spread the trees.

The nondescript, 5.5-inch **GRAY VIREO** is a "voice in the scrub." This species is found in most southwestern pinyon-juniper and oak woodlands. Its song is a warbling whistle, suggestive of a robin or Solitary Vireo. It is uniformly gray, without wing bars, but with a thin eye ring. Trying to see the bird well can be difficult, as it is normally active, usually within thick foliage. Its behavior is similar to that of a gnatcatcher (also common in the same habitat), with much tail flicking.

The **SPOTTED TOWHEE** inhabits all forms of scrubby undergrowth throughout the West, usually as a permanent resident. Once considered a subspecies, lumped with the Eastern Towhee, the western species is black above with large white spots on the shoulder and back. Eastern birds lack the spots. In addition, both male and female are black above in western birds (though the female is duller, less ebony than the male), but females are rusty brown in the eastern subspecies. Nonetheless, where the ranges of the two subspecies overlap, they hybridize successfully, so they are considered to be one species. Towhees are really large sparrows, ground foragers that kick leaf litter with both legs simultaneously, exposing anything from seeds to small invertebrates. You can often locate a towhee by listening for its scratching. Males will sing from perches in shrubs and small trees.

Many species of bats occur in the Madrean foothill forests, but most are nocturnal and difficult to identify unless seen perched or in the hand. Not so with the **WESTERN PIPISTREL.** This dainty 3-inch bat is so small that it stands out for that reason alone. The Western Pipistrel is the hummingbird of the bat world, the smallest species found in the United States. It is common throughout the Southwest, ranging as far north as Oregon and Washington. Unlike most other bats, it becomes active well before the sun sets, and it is not unusual for it to fly in total daylight. Its flight is rather like that of a butterfly, delicate and light. It is common not only in the foothills but along streams and rivers, where it dips down to take a drink on the wing.

The husky, all-gray, 19-inch **ROCK SQUIRREL** is a ground squirrel, though it has a 9-inch bushy tail like a tree squirrel's. It is found throughout the Southwest, always within the pinyon-juniper woodlands. It frequents rocky slopes, and like a marmot, reclines for much of the day on a favorite large rock. Rock Squirrels make burrows beneath rocks. They are active year-round throughout the southern part of their range, but those nearer the Great Basin desert, in Utah and Colorado, hibernate during the winter months. The Rock Squirrel readily climbs into pinyons and oaks, feeding on pine seeds and acorns.

The **BLACK-TAILED RATTLESNAKE** is easy to identify because it is the only rattlesnake with an all-black tail. Otherwise, it is similar to other rattlers, brown with black diamonds on its back. It is confined to the extreme Southwest and Mexico. It is generally less aggressive than other rattlesnake species, but give it a wide berth nonetheless. All poisonous snakes are best enjoyed from a respectful distance. Like other rattlers, it feeds on mammals, including Rock Squirrels. It can reach a length of nearly 5 feet.

WHERE TO VISIT: The magnificent Big Bend National Park is by far the best place to see this habitat. Drive to the Basin (from Basin Junction, three miles west of the Panther Junction Visitor Station) and you will be well within the Chisos Mountains and the Madrean foothill woodland. Trails go to Boot Spring, Window View, and other scenic areas.

ARIZONA MADREAN FOOTHILL FOREST   PLATE 19

INDICATOR PLANTS

TREES: *Mexican Pinyon, Alligator Juniper, Silverleaf Oak, Arizona Oak,* Chihuahua Pine, Rocky Mountain Juniper, Mexican Blue Oak, Netleaf Oak, Toumey Oak, Emory Oak, Gray Oak, Turbinella Oak, Dunn Oak, Gambel Oak. In moist canyons and north-facing slopes, Ponderosa Pine, Apache Pine, Common Douglas-fir, Arizona Cypress.

SHRUBS: *Pointleaf Manzanita, Schott Yucca, Nolina Beargrass,* Sotol, Soaptree Yucca, Navajo Yucca, Cliffrose, Birchleaf Cercocarpus, Alderleaf Cercocarpus, Curlleaf Cercocarpus, Wavyleaf Silktassel, Squawbush, California Buckthorn, Mogollon Ceanothus, Roundleaf Snowberry, Apache-plume, Utah Juneberry, Antelopebrush, Little Fendlerbush.

HERBACEOUS SPECIES: Crested Prickly Poppy, Texas Milkweed, Esteve's Pincushion, Sacred Datura (Jimsonweed), Southwestern Penstemon, Bridges's Penstemon, Southwestern Paintbrush, Common Alumroot, Western Valerian, Golden Columbine, Hooker's Evening Primrose, Scarlet Monkeyflower, Woolly Mullein, Indian Pink, Cutleaf Coneflower, Western Larkspur, Blumer's Lupine, Bowl Flax, Spreading Fleabane, Mountain Pussytoes, Common Yarrow; various cacti including Rainbow Cactus, Barrel Cactus, Chain Cholla, Engelmann's Prickly-pear, several hedgehogs.

INDICATOR ANIMALS

BIRDS: *Black-throated Gray Warbler, Plumbeous Vireo, Hutton's Vireo, Montezuma Quail,* Red-tailed Hawk, Cooper's Hawk, Great Horned Owl, Northern Pygmy-Owl, Western Screech-Owl, Band-tailed Pigeon, White-winged Dove, Black-chinned Hummingbird, Magnificent Hummingbird, Blue-throated Hummingbird, Elegant Trogon, Ladder-backed Woodpecker, Downy Woodpecker, Strickland's Woodpecker, Acorn Woodpecker, Lewis's Woodpecker, Northern Flicker, Western Kingbird, Say's Phoebe, Dusky-capped Flycatcher, Gray Flycatcher, Greater Pewee, Western Wood-Pewee, Pinyon Jay, Gray-breasted Jay, Scrub Jay, Juniper Titmouse, Bushtit, White-breasted Nuthatch, House Wren, Bewick's Wren, Rock Wren, Canyon Wren, Western Bluebird, Mountain Bluebird, Blue-gray Gnatcatcher, Virginia's Warbler, Brewer's Blackbird, Scott's Oriole, Hepatic Tanager, Northern Oriole, Black-headed Grosbeak, Lesser Goldfinch, House Finch, Spotted Towhee, Canyon Towhee, Rufous-crowned Sparrow.

MAMMALS: Blacktail Jackrabbit, Apache Fox Squirrel, Rock Squirrel, Whitetail Antelope Squirrel, Cliff Chipmunk, Deer Mouse, Ringtail, Raccoon, Longtail Weasel, Striped Skunk, Coyote, Gray Fox, Bobcat, Collared Peccary, Mule Deer, Whitetail Deer.

REPTILES: Tree Lizard, Side-blotched Lizard, Eastern Fence Lizard, Western Whiptail, Chihuahuan Spotted Whiptail, Madrean (Arizona) Alligator Lizard, Ringneck Snake, Mountain Patch-nosed Snake, Long-nosed Snake, Common Kingsnake, Western Diamondback Rattlesnake, Western Rattlesnake, Black-tailed Rattlesnake.

AMPHIBIANS: Tiger Salamander, Red-spotted Toad, Western Spadefoot Toad, Canyon Treefrog.

DESCRIPTION

This forest is structurally similar to the Mexican Madrean foothill forest, but it does not share all of the same species. Though Mexican Pinyon remains, it is often joined by Chihuahua Pine. Alligator Juniper replaces Weeping Juniper, and various evergreen oaks not present in west Texas and adjacent Mexico are common in this woodland. Several yucca species are usually common, especially Schott Yucca and the odd-looking Nolina Beargrass. The foothill habitat is a mosaic of scattered pinyons and junipers, with dense oak groves and thickets intervening. Exposed ridges and rock faces with dry soils are colonized mostly by yuccas, manzanitas, and various cacti. More sheltered areas, especially those highest in elevation, often have stands of Ponderosa and Apache pines, Common Douglas-fir, and Arizona Cypress. Many shrub species may be found, with much variability from one site to another. Pointleaf Manzanita and Cliffrose are particularly common, along with various mountain-mahoganies. Many grasses and wildflowers are usually present in abundance, including some, such as prickly poppies, that also occur commonly on the desert.

The dense oak thickets and open pinyon-juniper forest are ideal habitats for many bird species, including two vireos, the Plumbeous and the kingletlike Hutton's Vireo. Roving flocks of Juniper Titmouse and Bushtits search for insects among the foliage, often joined by Virginia's Warbler. The distinctive Black-throated Gray Warbler gleans insects from the branches of pinyons and junipers, and occasionally, nomadic flocks of Pinyon Jays come in search of pine seeds. Two other jays, the Gray-breasted and Scrub, along with flocks of Band-tailed Pigeons, are mostly attracted to the periodic abundance of acorns. Many flycatchers live here, including the diminutive, nondescript Gray Flycatcher. Rocky outcrops are ideal habitat for the Rock Wren and for the Canyon Wren, whose haunting, descending song echoes from canyon walls. A quiet walk along a grassy hillside may disturb a covey of outrageously patterned Montezuma Quail. These quail rarely fly, preferring to scurry away in the underbrush.

Mammals are also abundant, especially rodents. Apache Fox Squirrels perambulate through the trees, while Rock Squirrels and Cliff Chipmunks stay mostly on the ground. Blacktail Jackrabbits and small herds of Peccaries are common. Deer browse the many shrub and herb species, taking care to avoid poisonous ones, like Jimsonweed.

Figure 26. Canyon Wren

Oak thickets, yuccas, and junipers characterize this foothill forest near Tucson, Arizona, on the drive to Mt. Lemmon.

Lizards and snakes frequently sun on rocks or take shelter under them.

SIMILAR FOREST COMMUNITIES: See Mexican Madrean foothill forest; also Rocky Mountain pinyon-juniper forest.

RANGE: Southern Arizona south of the Mogollon Rim, including the Santa Catalina Mountains, Rincon Mountains, Santa Rita Mountains, and Chiricahua Mountains, usually at elevations of 4,500–8,000 ft.

REMARKS

Southern Arizona, like southern Texas and the Big Bend region, is ecologically part of Mexico. Species of plants and animals that range widely along the Mexican cordilleras reach the northern limits of their ranges in Arizona. Arizona, in fact, can be thought of as two broad ecological regions, the high-elevation north and the low-elevation south, divided by the vast Mogollon Rim. A drive through Oak Creek Canyon is a drive either down or up the Mogollon Rim. The northern part of the state, up on the Rim and including such places as the Grand Canyon and the San Francisco Peaks, is typical of the southern Rocky Mountains. No Mexican species occur there. But the southern part, from Phoenix south to Tucson and continuing south to the Mexican border, is low-elevation desert, interrupted by scattered mountain ranges, all of which have a strong Madrean or Mexican flavor. For this reason, birders and botanists alike covet a visit to southern Arizona, where they can find species seen nowhere else in the United States.

MEXICAN PINYON continues as the resident pinyon along the southern Arizona foothills. It is joined at scattered locations by **CHIHUAHUA PINE** (Plate 21), a species that ranges widely in Mexico along the cordilleras but barely makes it into the United States.

ALLIGATOR JUNIPER is named for the unique checkered pattern of square scales on its grayish black bark that really does resemble the hide of an alligator. It is abundant throughout the foothills and sometimes shares the upper elevation forests with Ponderosa Pine. The tree is usually between 20 and 50 feet tall, and real giants reach only 65 feet. As with all junipers, the bluish green leaves are scalelike and overlap. Cones are leathery "berries," distinctly reddish but with a filmy white cast. Many birds and mammals, including Black Bear and Gray Fox, consume the cones, which are produced somewhat cyclically (it takes two years for a cone to mature). Alligator Juniper is restricted to extreme northern Mexico, and most of its range is in central and southern Arizona and New Mexico.

Ten species of oaks are found in the Madrean foothills of southern Arizona. Most have small, leathery, evergreen or nearly evergreen leaves. They often hybridize, and identifications can sometimes be difficult. Most produce acorn crops in cycles, but because there are so many species, acorns are usually readily available for wildlife at any time.

ARIZONA OAK, sometimes called Arizona White Oak, is recognized by its broad, oval, gray-green leaves, which tend to be hairy below. Some teeth are usually present along the margin. Leaves are usually evergreen, though they may drop in late winter. Arizona Oak, which ranges in elevation from 4,900 to 11,000 feet, is considered the most abundant oak species in the region. It can grow up to 65 feet in height, or it may grow as a spreading shrub at higher, more exposed elevations. Bark is grayish and scaly, developing deep furrows in old trees. Arizona Oak is scattered in locations south of the Mogollon Rim and into northern Mexico.

SILVERLEAF OAK has the narrowest leaves of any of the foothill oaks. The slender, lance-shaped leaves make the tree look more like a willow than an oak. The underside of the leathery leaves is quite silvery. Above, the leaf is dark green. The leaves are toothless and tend to roll at the edges, another useful field mark. Silverleaf Oak can reach heights of 60 feet, though it is usually considerably shorter. Acorns have pointed tips, less rounded than in most other species. Silverleaf Oak occurs at scattered locations from west Texas to Arizona and Mexico.

MEXICAN BLUE OAK is a small, shrubby, deciduous oak, usually found at lower elevations along the foothills. Rarely exceeding 30 ft. in height, its long, toothless leaves have a distinctly blue-green cast.

TURBINELLA OAK and **DUNN OAK** both occur at lower elevations. These evergreen oaks usually grow in shrubby thickets. Turbinella Oak has gray-green, sharply toothed leaves that resemble holly leaves. Dunn Oak is almost identical but has a long, sharply pointed acorn with a flared cup.

POINTLEAF MANZANITA is a common evergreen shrub, identified by its smooth reddish bark and hard, brittle wood. Leathery leaves are oval, with sharp points. Their bluish green color is due to a covering of minute hairs. Pointleaf Manzanita can spread into dense, impenetrable thickets because when a branch of the widely spreading shrub touches the ground, it can form roots at

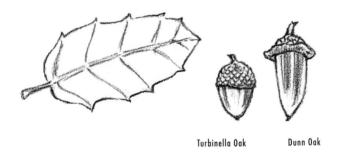

Turbinella Oak   Dunn Oak

Figure 27. Turbinella and Dunn oaks

that point. There are 36 species of manzanitas in the United States, and most are part of the California coastal chaparral (see our companion volume, *California and Pacific Northwest Forests*). Including those in Mexico, there are nearly 50 species. Manzanita means "little apple," a reference to the brownish, applelike fruit that can be made into a tasty jelly. Manzanitas are members of the heath family.

CLIFFROSE is a common shrub (sometimes a small tree) that occurs not only in Mexico and the Southwest but through parts of the Rockies and Great Basin as well. It is similar to **APACHE-PLUME,** with tiny, smoothly lobed leaves, small, pale yellow, 5-petaled flowers, and fruits on feathery stalks. Leaf edges roll under, a good field characteristic for this species.

Yuccas, also known as Spanish bayonets or Spanish daggers, are unmistakable. Leaves are large, stiff, sharply pointed, and often lined with spines, forming a dense rosette from which a flowering stalk emerges at the center. Some yuccas have only basal rosettes whereas others, like the famous Joshuatree of the Mojave Desert, or the **SOAPTREE YUCCA** of the Southwest, have distinct trunks covered by dead leaves. Yucca fruits are podlike, leathery, and form clusters on the plant, eventually falling to the ground. Upon seeing yuccas for the first time, many people think them to be some kind of odd cactus, but they are actually members of the lily family. All have large, white flower clusters, and all are pollinated exclusively by small, white, highly nocturnal moths in the genus *Pronuba,* the yucca moths. Yucca moths lay their eggs within the ovaries of the yuccas, and the caterpillars feed on yucca seeds after hatching. This parasitic act is not detrimental to the yucca because the female moth, while laying her eggs in the flower, pollinates the flower with pollen she has taken from another yucca. Thus the moth and the yucca facilitate each other's reproduction, an example of mutualism and coevolution.

SCHOTT YUCCA is common throughout the Madrean foothills. The daggerlike leaves can be up to a yard long, and the plant can reach 15–20 feet, with a trunk diameter of 12 inches. The hairy stalk is about a yard long.

NOLINA BEARGRASS, or Sacahuista, is another member of the lily family. Its basal leaf rosette looks quite grasslike, and the plant is often mistaken for a grass. Unlike yucca leaves, Nolina leaves lack spines along the margins. Flowers are creamy white on a long, drooping, plumelike stalk. Unlike yuccas, Nolinas are never found on the flat, lower deserts, but always inhabit the foothills, usually from 3,000 feet upward.

Flitting among the pinyons and junipers in search of caterpillars and other insects, the **BLACK-THROATED GRAY WARBLER** sings its buzzy song, a dry *veer, veer, veer, vree*. This warbler is a close relative of the eastern Black-throated Green Warbler, as well as the western Hermit and Townsend's warblers and the Golden-cheeked Warbler of Texas's Edwards Plateau. During glaciation, a southern population was probably isolated long enough to evolve into the Black-throated Gray, which is now closely tied to pinyon-juniper and dry oak habitat. Males and females look alike, with gray backs and black and white stripes that are especially pronounced on the face. At very close range you can see a tiny yellow spot in front of each eye. Black-throated Gray Warblers can be found in foothill habitat throughout the West. They winter in Central America.

Two vireos are common in the foothill forest. The **PLUMBEOUS VIREO,** until recently considered a Rocky Mountain subspecies of Solitary Vireo, is much duller than the eastern species. The Plumbeous ("lead-colored") is dull gray with two wing bars and a complete eye ring. The smaller **HUTTON'S VIREO** is easily mistaken for a Ruby-crowned Kinglet. Hutton's is greenish gray, with two wing bars and an incomplete eye ring, much like the Ruby-crowned. Hutton's is a bit larger than the kinglet, with a thicker bill. Plumbeous Vireos are skulkers, methodically patrolling the inner and outer limbs in search of prey, whereas Hutton's Vireos, again like kinglets, are flitty, often briefly hovering around the outer foliage as they glean insects. The Plumbeous Vireo is a summer resident throughout most of the West, wintering in Central America. Hutton's Vireo is confined to the Southwest and Pacific coast and is a permanent resident. All vireos build cuplike nests that hang between the forks of a branch.

If you are lucky enough to see **MONTEZUMA QUAIL,** you will not find the identification difficult. Nothing looks like a Montezuma Quail but another Montezuma Quail. They resemble chunky, dramatically patterned little chickens. Montezuma Quail, once named Harlequin Quail, are found only in the grassy foothills of the Southwest and Mexico. They will squat low to the ground, and you sometimes almost have to step on them to know they are there. They will often walk hastily away rather than fly.

WHERE TO VISIT: The road to Mt. Lemmon (Santa Catalina Mountains) from Tucson, through the Coronado National Forest, is an ideal way to visit this habitat. Another fine location is Chiricahua National Monument near Willcox in southeastern Arizona. Also recommended is a visit to the Huachuca Mountains, part of Coronado National Forest, accessed through Fort Huachuca at Sierra Vista, Arizona. Roads to nearby Ramsey and Carr canyons (off I-92) also pass through foothill habitat. Madera Canyon, off I-19 in the Santa Rita Mountains, is also recommended.

INDICATOR PLANTS

TREES: *Arizona Sycamore, Arizona Walnut, Arizona Cypress,* Fremont Cottonwood, Narrowleaf Cottonwood, Apache Pine, Arizona Alder, Velvet Ash, Canyon (Bigtooth) Maple, Bonpland Willow, Water Birch, Mountain Alder, Emory Oak, Arizona Oak, Mexican Blue Oak, Honey Mesquite.

SHRUBS: *Birchleaf Cercocarpus,* Netleaf Hackberry, River Hawthorn, Cerro Hawthorn, Western Hophornbeam, Blue Elderberry, New Mexico Blue Elderberry, Red Elderberry, New Mexico Raspberry, Red-osier Dogwood, Texas Mulberry, Common Buttonbush, Russian-olive, Seepwillow, Western Soapberry, Birchleaf Buckthorn, Trumpet Creeper, Virginia Creeper, Poison-ivy.

HERBACEOUS SPECIES: Western Wallflower, Redstem Storksbill, Western Shooting Star, Desert Gilia, Parry's Penstemon, Sacred Datura, Scarlet Monkeyflower, Yellow Monkeyflower, London Rocket, Smooth Milkvine, Golden Columbine, Orange Flame Flower, Coral Bells, Orange Milkweed (Butterflyweed), Betony, Southwestern Paintbrush, Southwestern Penstemon, Arizona Thistle, Fingerleaf Gourd, Birdbill Dayflower, Palmer's Lupine, Common Reed, Bracken Fern.

INDICATOR ANIMALS

BIRDS: *Elegant Trogon, Bridled Titmouse, Sulphur-bellied Flycatcher, Painted Redstart, Strickland's Woodpecker,* Cooper's Hawk, Great Horned Owl, Western Screech-Owl, Whiskered Screech-Owl, Spotted Owl, Flammulated Owl, Elf Owl, Green Kingfisher, Black-chinned Hummingbird, Blue-throated Hummingbird, Magnificent Hummingbird, Broad-billed Hummingbird, White-throated Swift, Acorn Woodpecker, Downy Woodpecker, Cassin's Kingbird, Western Kingbird, Western Wood-Pewee, Brown-crested Flycatcher, Dusky-capped Flycatcher, Northern Beardless-Tyrannulet, Black Phoebe, Rose-throated Becard, Gray-breasted Jay, Bushtit, Bewick's Wren, Canyon Wren, Rock Wren, Hermit Thrush, American Robin, Yellow Warbler, Black-throated Gray Warbler, Northern Oriole, Hooded Oriole, Summer Tanager, Hepatic Tanager, Black-headed Grosbeak.

MAMMALS: *Coati,* Raccoon, Striped Skunk, Hooded Skunk, Hognose Skunk, Cliff Chipmunk, Rock Squirrel, Arizona Gray Squirrel, Apache Fox Squirrel, Eastern Cottontail, Gray Fox, Coyote, Collared Peccary, Whitetail Deer.

REPTILES: Great Plains Skink, Desert Spiny Lizard, Greater Earless Lizard, Madrean (Arizona) Alligator Lizard, Giant Spotted Whiptail, Gopher Snake, Mexican Vine Snake.

AMPHIBIANS: Canyon Treefrog, Woodhouse Toad, Southwestern Woodhouse Toad.

DESCRIPTION

The mountains of southeastern Arizona serve as a backdrop for some of the most splendid riparian forests in the West. Once the home of the Apache tribe, including such well-known figures as Cochise and Geronimo, the Chiricahua and Santa Rita Mountains rise as steep, splendid escarpments providing protection for riverine canyon forests. The beautiful Arizona Sycamore is joined here by Arizona Walnut and Arizona Cypress. Sycamores are usually most abundant, unmistakable with their white bark and peeling brown flakes. They line stream and riverbeds and are replaced by oaks and pines away from water. Other riverine species such as Fremont and Narrowleaf cottonwoods, various willows, and Honey Mesquite often are part of this community.

There is usually an understory of shrubs, especially the various mountain-mahoganies, elderberries, currants, and Poison-ivy. Wildflowers are also abundant, including such colorful species as Wallflower and Butterflyweed.

Along the floodplains oak species such as Arizona Oak, Emory Oak, and Mexican Blue Oak predominate, along with Apache Pine and Arizona Cypress.

These protected riverine habitats are oases in the desert. As such, they provide habitat for wandering flocks of Gray-breasted Jays, Bridled Titmice, and Bushtits as well as many other bird species. Birders come from all over the world to walk for a few days along the sycamore-lined streambeds in search of species found nowhere else north of Mexico. The magnificent descending trills of Canyon Wrens seem to fall from the red sandstone walls as

Figure 28. Hognose (left) and Hooded skunks

The tall escarpments protect canyons, creating habitat for numerous specialty species. This is the entrance to Cave Creek Canyon.

birders search for the brilliant Elegant Trogon, the equally striking Painted Redstart, the noisy and conspicuous Sulphur-bellied
Flycatcher, and the quiet, unobtrusive Strickland's Woodpecker.
The trogon and the flycatcher are found only in sycamore canyons.

Unusual hummingbirds, all eagerly sought by birders, frequent
the Skyrocket, Betony, and Scarlet Penstemon that grow on the
flood plain. Two large hummingbirds, the Magnificent and Blue-
throated, join the more widespread and smaller Black-chinned.
These large hummers (each is 5–5.5 inches) are unmistakable.
The Blue-throated is green with a gray breast and brilliant blue
iridescent throat. It is easily identified by its white outer tail
feathers, obvious as it zooms by. The Magnificent Hummingbird
is very dark below, shiny green above, with an emerald green
throat and violet forehead, both of which glitter in full sunlight. It
lacks the white outer tail feathers of the Blue-throated. Less common but equally colorful, the Broad-billed Hummingbird is brilliant green with a bright red bill and deep blue chin. The Broad-
billed, like the Elegant Trogon and Sulphur-bellied Flycatcher, is
basically a Mexican species that crosses the U.S. border only
along these lush southern Arizona riparian forests. Even rarer
Mexican species, such as the White-eared and Violet-crowned
hummingbirds, are regularly seen in southern Arizona.

Owls thrive in the sycamore canyons. On a quiet evening when
the wind is still, you may hear any of six owl species, the Great
Horned, the Spotted, the Flammulated, the Elf, the Whiskered
Screech-Owl, or the Western Screech-Owl, an amazing diversity
found in few places in North America.

Mammals such as Gray Fox and Whitetail Deer are common. The rich orangy Apache Fox Squirrel is as common in the trees as Rock Squirrels and Cliff Chipmunks are on the ground. Three skunks, the Hooded, Hognose, and Striped, all snuffle along after dark, along with small herds of Peccaries. Much less common is another visitor from south of the border, the raccoonlike Coati.

SIMILAR FOREST COMMUNITIES: Other lowland riverine forests dominated by cottonwoods and ash have species in common, but only in southeastern Arizona canyons will you find the unique combination of abundant Arizona Sycamore, Arizona Walnut, Arizona Cypress, and Apache Pine. For comparison, see prairie riparian forest.

RANGE: Southeastern Arizona among the Chiricahua, Huachuca, and Santa Rita Mountains including Cave Creek Canyon, Guadalupe Canyon, Ramsey Canyon, Carr Canyon, and Madera Canyon.

REMARKS

The distinctive **ARIZONA SYCAMORE,** with its deeply lobed, star-shaped leaves and mottled, white-and-brown bark, dominates one of the most picturesque series of oases among the American deserts. Steep rocky canyon walls and spires colored boldly in reddish and rosy hues jut abruptly from the desert floor. The clear flowing creeks that traverse these canyons are lined with sycamores, which are joined by Black Walnut, cottonwoods, evergreen oaks, and pines, forming habitat for many birds and mammals. This habitat is, in many ways, a *relict forest,* a kind of living fossil community representative of what was once a much more widespread forest of broad-leaved trees. As the climate has changed, become drier and more temperate, deserts and grasslands have expanded, forcing the once vast, broad-leaved forests of the Southwest to retreat within the protection of canyon walls.

Arizona Sycamore, the largest deciduous tree in Arizona, often reaches heights of 100 feet. Its thick trunk, which can measure as much as 9 feet across, is usually divided into two or more major boles that give the tree a widely spreading appearance. The tree's leaves may seem limp, drooping rather hopelessly during the hottest summer months, but the tree is highly drought resistant and manages to survive. In early spring, sycamore leaves unfold quite slowly. When mature, these deeply cleft, hairy, star-shaped leaves are the largest of any of this region's desert plants. Sycamore bark peels readily, the outer brown bark flaking away in pieces resembling a jigsaw puzzle, revealing white, smooth inner bark below. Sycamore flowers are small, occurring in spherical clusters. Separate clusters of male and female flowers are present on the same tree. Fruits, sometimes called buttonballs, occur in clusters numbering 3–5 per stalk (see plate). Fruits have essentially no value to wildlife, but the tree itself is immensely valuable. Numerous bird and mammal species nest in the Arizona Sycamore. Four of the five bird species shown on the plate (Strickland's Woodpecker, Elegant Trogon, Bridled Titmouse, and Sulphur-bellied Flycatcher) nest in cavities, usually in a sycamore. Many other bird species build open nests among the boughs of sycamore. The Arizona Sycamore and the California Sycamore are similar, and some botanists believe they should be lumped into a single species.

ARIZONA WALNUT, sometimes called Arizona Black Walnut, is identified by its large compound leaves with 9–15 toothed leaflets and its hairy twigs. Grayish brown bark has deep furrows, especially pronounced on old trees. The fruit of Arizona Walnut, like all walnuts, is a large, green ball that contains the hard-shelled nut. Local residents eat the walnuts, called *nogales* in Spanish. Arizona Walnut normally grows 30–50 feet tall. It probably should be called Mexican Walnut, since its range is essentially Mexico, with scattered populations in Arizona, New Mexico, and Texas. It is often planted as a shade tree and is not confined to valleys, occurring at elevations of 3,500–7,000 feet.

ARIZONA CYPRESS can grow as tall as 70 feet, but heights of

Within the protected confines of the canyon, lush Arizona Sycamores thrive.

about 30–40 feet are more common. It is easy to identify because of its conical or rounded crown and scalelike, blue-green leaves. Bark tends to shed in thin scales, revealing reddish inner bark underneath. The spherical cones are about 1 inch in diameter, with large, flat scales. Arizona Cypress occurs not only in canyons but also among evergreen oaks and junipers in foothill forests, at elevations of 3,500–7,200 feet. Arizona Cypress, like Arizona Walnut, ranges mostly in Mexico, coming north into southern New Mexico and southeastern Arizona. There is also an isolated population in the Chisos Mountains in west Texas. Some botanists argue that the central Arizona population should be considered a separate species called Smooth Cypress because of its smooth outer bark. Smooth Cypress is cultivated and used as a Christmas tree.

BIRCHLEAF CERCOCARPUS (MOUNTAIN-MAHOGANY) is one of several evergreen shrubs that are common from canyons to mountain forests in the Southwest, ranging up to 10,000 feet. A similar species, **HAIRY CERCOCARPUS,** is also found in scattered locations throughout the Southwest. Birchleaf Cercocarpus ranges from Arizona and Baja California north through California and into southern Oregon. All of the cercocarpus species have seeds attached to long (up to 4 inches), feathery plumes, an easy way to recognize them. Leaves of the Birchleaf species are oval toothed, similar to those of a birch. Hairy Cercocarpus leaves are smaller with almost no teeth. Flowers of both species are small and yellowish. Though normally a spreading shrub, Birchleaf Cercocarpus can grow as tall as 25 feet.

Of the many bird species living along the sycamore-lined creeks, probably none is more sought by birders than the **ELEGANT TROGON.** The bird's looks bespeak its tropical ancestry. There are 39 trogon species, and all but a few occur in the western hemisphere. The group includes such glamorous species as the Resplendent Quetzal, considered by many to be one of the world's most beautiful birds. Until recently, the Elegant Trogon, formerly called the Coppery-tailed Trogon, was the only member of its pantropical family to breed in the United States. The male Elegant Trogon is, at first glance, rather parrotlike. It is colorful— gorgeous in fact—with a short, rounded, yellow bill. Most of the bird is deep iridescent green, with a bright red breast, a white band across the breast, and orangy upper tail. Females are brown, with a pink breast and white "ear" mark. A second, somewhat larger species, the Eared Trogon, has recently colonized some southern Arizona canyons. Male Eared Trogons are similar to Elegants, but their bills are black, not yellow, they are all white under their tails (Elegants have finely barred tails), and they lack a white breast band. Trogons sit upright, often remaining quite still. When they fly, they undulate, swooping from tree to tree. The Elegant Trogon's song, a soft, repeated *co-ah*, has been compared to that of a frog. Trogons nest in tree cavities, usually in a sycamore along a creek. They feed on large insects, especially dragonflies, and on fruits, which they take by briefly hovering. Elegant Trogons breed as far south as Costa Rica. U.S. birds migrate in fall and spend the winter in Mexico.

Even during the hottest part of a summer's day, the quiet of the sycamore canyons can be shattered by an emphatic *kee-zee-eek!* coming from somewhere in the leafy canopy. This nonmusical exclamation belongs to the **SULPHUR-BELLIED FLYCATCHER,** yet another Mexican species that finds the sheltered canyon streams to its liking. Approximately the size of a kingbird, the Sulphur-belly is boldly streaked on its breast. It is a summer resident that winters as far south as Peru and Bolivia. The most distinct field mark is the bright reddish tail, visible as the bird chases after insect prey. The species nests in tree cavities, nesting a bit later than most other canyon birds. It begins its southward migration by mid-September.

The less conspicuous **NORTHERN BEARDLESS-TYRANNULET** (not illustrated) is a Central American and Mexican flycatcher that just makes it into the United States in southeastern Arizona. This little (4.5 inches) greenish gray flycatcher is often quite active, behaving somewhat like a kinglet or warbler as it chases after insects. It is identified by its brown wing bars and the slight suggestion of a crest on its head.

A quiet tapping in a pine or oak could be a **HAIRY WOODPECKER** at work, but to the excitement of birders, it could also mean that a **STRICKLAND'S WOODPECKER** is around. Strickland's, formerly called the Arizona Woodpecker, is found only in the mountains and canyons of southeastern and central Arizona and a small part of New Mexico. Like so many other birds of the region, it is primarily a Mexican species, ranging well into central Mexico. Strickland's is similar in size and habits to the Hairy Woodpecker, but is uniformly brown on back and wings, with spots along its sides. Both sexes have a large black patch on the face, and males are red on the neck. The call note is a sharp *pik,* much like that of a Hairy.

The **BRIDLED TITMOUSE** is yet another unmistakable and unique species of the sycamore canyons and surrounding mountains. It is most common in the oaks of southeastern Arizona, though it ranges as far north as Oak Creek Canyon in the central part of the state. Overall the size and shape of a Juniper Titmouse, the Bridled is far fancier. It has a sharp crest and its face is outlined in black, somewhat like a bridle. It ranges well into southern Mexico. Populations in Arizona are permanent residents, foraging in flocks that are often joined by other species such as kinglets, nuthatches, warblers, and vireos. The call note is a dry scolding chatter, quite similar to other titmice.

No one misidentifies a **PAINTED REDSTART,** a splendid, colorful warbler that can be found from the canyons well up into the oaks and junipers of the mountain slopes. Sometimes called *mariposa* (Spanish for "butterfly"), the Painted Redstart forages with its wings and tail spread, flitting erratically and almost bouncing from tree trunk to branch, much like a feathered butterfly. Adults are black with a red and white breast, white wing patches, and white outer tail feathers, easily visible when the tail is spread. Juvenile birds lack the red. Painted Redstarts range from Nicaragua north through Mexico and into central Arizona and western New Mexico. They are resident throughout most of their range, but the Arizona birds migrate to Mexico in fall. Painted Redstarts spend much of their time foraging near the ground, making them delightfully easy to observe. They also nest on the ground, sometimes in a small depression along an embankment. Males are frequently polygynous, mating with several females, each of which is then exclusively responsible for brooding her eggs.

Many other Mexican birds show up unpredictably from time to time in southern Arizona, adding more potential for excitement to birding the region. Birders rarely stop at the resident exotic species, but diligently search the canyons in hopes of discovering a Flame-colored Tanager, Yellow Grosbeak, Rufous-capped Warbler, Nutting's Flycatcher, or Gray Silky-Flycatcher.

The **COATI,** sometimes called Coatimundi, is a sleek, tropical member of the raccoon family. Coatis rarely forage alone; bands of up to two dozen Coatis roam the woods, usually at night, in search of food that may be anything from insects and lizards to prickly-pears and manzanita fruits. Coatis are far more social and are noisier than their North American Raccoon cousins. They are usually found on the ground, but they are good tree climbers, as their slender, barred tail is partly prehensile (able to grasp objects such as branches). Like Raccoons, Coatis look cute, but they are wild, strong, potentially dangerous animals. They range throughout Central and South America, reaching the United States in southern Texas, New Mexico, and Arizona. The most abundant U.S. population by far is that of southeastern Arizona, especially in the Huachuca Mountains, where they are quite common.

WHERE TO VISIT: Several ideal locations for seeing sycamore canyon forest can be found in the Chiricahua Mountains near the town of Portal, a few miles from the New Mexico border. From Portal, visit Chiricahua National Monument and Cave Creek Canyon, part of the Coronado National Forest. At Cave Creek Canyon, the South

Fork campgrounds and trail are excellent places to search for trogons and other species, and the sycamores are splendid. Farther west, Sierra Vista affords access to Fort Huachuca and the Huachuca Mountains, including Sawmill and Scheelite Canyons, as well as nearby Ramsey Canyon, Carr Canyon, and Miller Canyon. The Nature Conservancy maintains a sanctuary at Ramsey Canyon, where hummingbird feeders attract virtually every species in the area. The nearby San Pedro River is an excellent location for riverine species. Madera Canyon, located in the Santa Rita Mountains near the town of Continental, is also recommended.

SOUTHWEST MOUNTAIN FOREST   PLATE 21

INDICATOR PLANTS

TREES: Middle elevations: *Apache Pine, Chihuahua Pine, Ponderosa Pine* (Arizona variety), New Mexico Locust, *Canyon (Bigtooth) Maple,* Rocky Mountain Maple, Arizona Cypress, Gambel Oak, Mountain (Thinleaf) Alder, Water Birch. Higher elevations: Common Douglas-fir, White (Corkbark) Fir, Engelmann Spruce, Blue Spruce, Subalpine Fir, Limber Pine, Southwestern White Pine, Lodgepole Pine, Quaking Aspen.

SHRUBS: Middle elevations: *New Mexico Locust, Arizona Rose,* Antelope-brush, Shrubby Cinquefoil, Bitter Cherry, Common Chokecherry, Cliffrose, California Buckthorn, Birchleaf Buckthorn, Blue Elderberry, Greenleaf Manzanita, Curlleaf Cercocarpus, Mountain Snowberry, Arizona Honeysuckle, Rocky Mountain Maple, various gooseberries. Higher elevations: Common Juniper, Utah Honeysuckle, Red Elderberry, Mountain Ninebark, Mountain-lover, Kinnikinnick, Utah Juneberry, Arizona Mountain-ash, Scouler Willow.

HERBACEOUS SPECIES: Wandbloom Penstemon, Western Shooting Star, Parry's Primrose, Red Fireweed, Rocky Mountain Clematis, Many-flowered Gilia, Parry Gentian, Common (Silvery) Lupine, Rocky Mountain Iris, Monkshood, Hoary Ragwort, Heartleaf Arnica, Orange Sneezeweed, Mountain Goldenrod, Primrose Monkeyflower, Golden Draba, Spreading Dogbane, Common Alumroot, stonecrop, Rocky Mountain Pussytoes, Sidebells Pyrola, Shortleaf Wintergreen, Cow Parsnip, Canada Violet, Richardson's Geranium, Thimbleberry, Star Solomon's-seal, Pinedrops, Death-camas, False-hellebore.

INDICATOR ANIMALS

BIRDS: *Northern Pygmy-Owl, Greater Pewee, Mexican Chickadee, Olive Warbler, Red-faced Warbler, Yellow-eyed Junco,* Turkey Vulture, Zone-tailed Hawk, Red-tailed Hawk, Cooper's Hawk, Band-tailed

Tall conifer and mixed forests can be found at higher elevations in southeastern Arizona.

Pigeon, Great Horned Owl, Spotted Owl, Whip-poor-will, Broad-tailed Hummingbird, Hairy Woodpecker, Northern Flicker, Cordilleran Flycatcher, Buff-breasted Flycatcher, Western Wood-Pewee, Steller's Jay, Common Raven, Mountain Chickadee, Red-breasted Nuthatch, Pygmy Nuthatch, Brown Creeper, House Wren, Ruby-crowned Kinglet, Violet-green Swallow, Hermit Thrush, Eastern Bluebird, Western Bluebird, American Robin, Yellow-rumped Warbler, Grace's Warbler, Painted Redstart, Western Tanager, Hepatic Tanager, Evening Grosbeak, Red Crossbill, Pine Siskin, Chipping Sparrow.

MAMMALS: Long-eared Myotis, Long-legged Myotis, Big Brown Bat, Western Big-eared Bat, Cliff Chipmunk, Apache Fox Squirrel, Porcupine, Mexican Woodrat, Bushytail Woodrat, Eastern Cottontail, Coyote, Black Bear, Mountain Lion, Bobcat, Whitetail Deer.

REPTILES: Mountain (Yarrow) Spiny Lizard, Tree Lizard, Short-horned Lizard, Mountain Skink, Gopher Snake, Western Rattlesnake, Twin-spotted Rattlesnake, Ridge-nosed Rattlesnake.

AMPHIBIANS: Canyon Treefrog.

DESCRIPTION

Southwestern mountains, though not high enough or far enough north to support alpine tundra, do have a well-defined Transition Zone at 6,500–8,000 feet, where a cooler, moister climate supports pine forests (with some oak) rather than dry Upper Sonoran pinyon-juniper-oak woodlands. At higher elevations (8,000–11,500 feet), the Transition Zone is gradually replaced by a Canadian Zone of mixed conifers. Annual precipitation is 20–25 inches in the Transition Zone, increasing to 25–30 inches in the Canadian Zone.

The Transition Zone, often called the pine belt, comprises a strong element of Mexican species, including Chihuahua and Apache pines, as well as a unique variety of Ponderosa Pine (see Remarks). The forest is often open and parklike, with a soft litter layer of fallen pine needles. The fragrance of pine resin permeates the air. Shrubs are present where there is ample sunlight, most commonly manzanitas, buckthorns, gooseberries, Arizona Rose, and Antelopebrush. Clumps of Gambel Oak are not uncommon, especially on sunny sites at lower elevations. Along streamsides and other moist areas, Mountain Alder, Water Birch, and Rocky Mountain and Canyon maples are common. Herbaceous species including Wandbloom Penstemon, Rocky Mountain Iris, Silvery Lupine, and Orange Sneezeweed each add a splash of color to the dark green forest.

Like the trees, some of the bird species that inhabit the Transition Zone pines are also basically Mexican and can be seen nowhere else in the United States except in these forests. These species include the colorful Red-faced Warbler, Olive Warbler, Mexican Chickadee, Yellow-eyed Junco, Greater Pewee, and Buff-breasted Flycatcher (local in Huachuca Mountains). Mexican Chickadees forage in flocks that are sometimes joined by Red-breasted and Pygmy nuthatches, Brown Creepers, Painted Red-starts, and Yellow-rumped Warblers. Steller's Jays and American Robins are common, especially around picnic areas. Both Western and Hepatic tanagers frequent the pines, along with Grace's Warblers, and the nondescript Greater Pewee often perches atop a pine or tree snag. The oft-repeated song of the Whip-poor-will punctuates the night. Apache Fox Squirrel and Cliff Chipmunk are the two most frequently sighted mammals.

The Canadian Zone hosts mostly Rocky Mountain species, including Common Douglas-fir, Engelmann Spruce, Subalpine Fir, the Corkbark variety of White Fir, and on exposed sites, Limber Pine (New Mexico) or Southwestern White Pine (Arizona), which some authorities consider a variety of Limber Pine. Stands of Lodgepole Pine or Quaking Aspen occur on disturbed sites, especially on north-facing slopes. Canadian Zone forests of the Southwest are referred to as mixed conifer forests because species composition varies substantially from site to site, depending on elevation and exposure, and there is a lot of intergradation between life zones. North-facing slopes, which often retain patches of snow on the ground until early May, support a mixed conifer forest of spruces and firs, while south-facing slopes tend to be dominated by a mixture of Ponderosa Pine and Common Douglas-fir. Mixed conifer forests are shady because the trees grow close together. Litter consists of dense accumulations of needles and decomposing tree trunks and branches. Shortleaf Wintergreen, Pinedrops, and Canada Violet are common wildflowers, and Fireweed is abundant on disturbed sites. Shrubs are best represented on exposed or disturbed sites and often include Common Juniper, Mountain-lover, Arizona Mountain-ash, and Kinnikinnick.

The most common birds are Steller's Jay, Red-breasted Nuthatch, Ruby-crowned Kinglet, Hermit Thrush, Red Crossbill, Pine Siskin, Evening Grosbeak, and Chipping Sparrow. Porcupines are about but are infrequently sighted.

SIMILAR FOREST COMMUNITIES: See Rocky Mountain Ponderosa Pine forest and Rocky Mountain spruce-fir forest.

RANGE: Southern New Mexico (Guadalupe Mountains) and southern Arizona (south of the Mogollon Rim), including the Santa Catalina, Galiura, Pinaleno, Rincon, Santa Rita, Huachuca, and Chiricahua mountains.

Remarks

PONDEROSA PINE is one of the most abundant trees of the American West, and it is certainly well represented in the Southwest. Here, though, Ponderosa Pine is sometimes present as a unique variety, one with needles in bundles of 5 rather than the normal bundles of 3. In addition to the distinction between needle bundles, this variety, commonly called Arizona Pine, has cones that are more egg-shaped and only half the length (3 inches) of normal Ponderosa Pine cones. Arizona Pine is most abundant in southeastern Arizona, southwestern New Mexico, and northern Mexico. To the north, normal Ponderosa Pine prevails, especially on the Mogollon Rim.

APACHE PINE is sometimes called Arizona Longleaf Pine, and with good reason. The needles average about 10 inches long and may be up to 15 inches long. Ponderosa Pine needles rarely exceed 10 inches and are usually 4–8 inches. Apache Pine needles are not as dark green as those of Ponderosa. Like the 5-needle form of Ponderosa Pine, Apache Pine occurs only in southeastern Arizona, southwest Mexico, and northern Mexico. Some botanists argue that Apache Pine is yet another variety of Ponderosa Pine, suggesting a very active evolution indeed, but not out of the question. During glaciation in the north, the climate became colder and drier, and it is likely that isolated populations of Ponderosa Pine diverged genetically, evolving into both Arizona Pine and Apache Pine. At any rate, Apache Pine is without question similar to Ponderosa. It has long (5–7 inches) needles in bundles of 3, prickly cones (Ponderosa cones are just a bit shorter), and yellowish bark in plates. One major difference between Ponderosa and Apache pines is that Apache Pine is a much

Typical southwestern Transition Zone, with some broad-leaved aspens among mixed conifers.

shorter tree that rarely grows beyond 60 feet tall, whereas Ponderosa Pine frequently reaches more than double that height.

CHIHUAHUA PINE is a small, rugged-looking tree that can be found from the Upper Sonoran Zone (5,000 feet) to as high as 8,000 ft. It is particularly abundant at Chiricahua National Monument in southeastern Arizona. It has blue-green needles, 2–4 inches long, in bundles of 3. The sheath that surrounds the needle bundle is deciduous in this species, falling away easily (an unusual characteristic for a pine). The 2–3-inch cones, which must remain on the tree for three years to reach full maturity, are sometimes but not always prickly, and bark is very dark. Chihuahua Pine is a member of a group called the white pines, a group with soft wood and needles in bundles of 5. The Arizona population is considered to represent a distinct variety or subspecies, since it has needles in bundles of 3. Throughout most of Mexico, this species, like other white pines, has needles in bundles of 5.

SOUTHWESTERN WHITE PINE is a 5-needle pine that replaces Limber Pine in Mexico and scattered mountains in Arizona and New Mexico (between 5,000 – 10,000 feet in elevation). It has long (5–9 inches) cones with blunt, turned-back scale tips. It is common at Mt. Lemmon in the Santa Catalina Mountains near Tucson, where it is locally called Mexican White Pine.

CANYON, or **BIGTOOTH, MAPLE** is a close relative of the eastern Sugar Maple, though it is considerably smaller. Growing as either a shrub or small tree, it rarely exceeds 35 feet. Leaves are deciduous and turn brilliant gold or orange in fall, adding some color to the green landscape. The name Bigtooth refers to the leaves, which are deeply lobed and have a few large, blunt teeth along the margins. As with all maples, leaves are opposite. Bark is light brown or gray, with ridges and shallow furrows. Canyon Maple is widely browsed by deer for its nutritious foliage and twigs. Canyon Maple has an odd distribution, occurring from the Idaho-Wyoming border south to Arizona, New Mexico, Texas, and northern Mexico. It is most abundant in the Wasatch Mountains of Utah, and the easternmost population is restricted to the Edwards Plateau in central Texas, a probable remnant from an isolation caused during glaciation.

NEW MEXICO LOCUST is a spreading shrub (6−10 feet) or little tree (up to 25 feet) with delicate compound leaves, usually with 9−21 smooth-margined, oval leaflets. Each leaflet is tipped with a tiny spine. Stems have very sharp (not tiny) spines at the base of each leaf. The showy lavender-pink flowers hang in clusters near the tips of the branches. Pods, shaped like pea pods, are brown and hairy. Though most common in southeastern Arizona, New Mexico Locust occurs in scattered locations throughout the Southwest. Like Canyon Maple, the leaves and twigs of locust are valuable food for browsing animals.

ARIZONA ROSE occurs only in Arizona and New Mexico, always growing as a shrub 1−3 feet tall. Leaves are compound, and leaflets are toothed and hairy. Stems have flaky bark and sharply curved thorns. Flowers are rosy pink. This species closely resembles the much more widespread **FENDLER ROSE,** which grows taller (to 8 feet) and has reddish stems. Many animals browse the nutritious fruits of roses, called rose hips.

The **NORTHERN PYGMY-OWL** is a common though infrequently observed small owl of all western forests. It is a permanent resident from coastal British Columbia south through Mexico. It is common in Transition Zone pine forests but is equally at home in the spruces and firs of the Canadian Zone. It is a mere 7 inches in length, hence its scientific name *gnoma,* meaning gnome. It is at least partly diurnal and can be both heard and seen in daytime. Field marks are its long tail, longer than that of other small owls, its rounded head that lacks ear tufts, strong streaking on the flanks, and two black slashes, one on each side of its neck. The call notes consist of repeated, easily imitated whistles, given in a monotone.

As Plate 21 shows, a Northern Pygmy-Owl can easily attract a crowd. Small birds are apt to mob a predator discovered in their midst. Though pygmy-owls hunt mostly rodents, small birds such as warblers and chickadees nonetheless seem to regard them as a potential danger. As a birder, you can use this behavior to your advantage by imitating the whistle of a Northern Pygmy-Owl, which will often attract many small birds. Since mobbing involves approaching a potential predator, it may seem to be a risky behavior.

The risk is probably quite minimal, though, since the predator is clearly under observation at all times. There is no way it can make a surprise attack, which is how virtually all avian predators capture prey. Also, mobbing may drive the predator from that particular section of forest, making life more secure for the passerines (perching birds). Birds of several species may seem to cooperate as they mob a predator, but each is really acting in its own self-interest, since its nest and young are also in the forest.

In the U.S., the **MEXICAN CHICKADEE** is found only in the pine forests of extreme southeastern Arizona. It is very much a Mexican species, common all along the Mexican mountains, but it just barely reaches the United States, where it occupies the same types of habitats as the **MOUNTAIN CHICKADEE,** which is absent from southeastern Arizona. Its field marks are its very gray sides and large black bib, covering not only the throat but extending to the breast, unlike the bibs of other chickadee species. Its dry, buzzy call notes are recognizable as a chickadee's, and it normally forages in small flocks, often joined by other species. It is most common in pines and Douglas-firs but can also be found in the spruce-fir forests. It is a permanent resident throughout its range.

Two stunning warblers, the **RED-FACED WARBLER** and the **OLIVE WARBLER,** are much sought by birders in the Southwest. Both inhabit pine forests in southern and central Arizona and western New Mexico, but the Red-faced is a summer resident and the Olive is essentially a permanent resident. Both species are much more widely distributed in Mexico.

The Red-faced Warbler, which lives in oaks as well as pines, is unique. Both sexes look alike, gray birds with white rumps, black heads, and brilliant, vivid red faces. They forage at all heights but generally stay close to the ground, sometimes affording outstanding views for birders. They usually nest on the ground. Red-faced Warblers winter in Central America.

The Olive Warbler is a bird of the pine forests, a treetop species that forages among the long needles of Ponderosa and Apache pines. Males are gray with two white wing bars and an orange head punctuated by a black mark behind the eye. Females are similar but the orange color is replaced by pale yellow. The inapt name Olive Warbler probably comes from the upper parts of females, which are rather olive. This is one of the few cases where a bird's common name is based on the female rather than the male plumage. Olive Warblers have been a curiosity to ornithologists for some time. Some believe the species is what it looks like, a wood warbler, a member of the family Parulidae. Others believe it is evolutionarily most closely related to Old World warblers in the family Sylviinae, in part because its young do not produce waste in fecal sacs. The sacs are easily removed by the parents, which helps keep the nest clean. Old World warblers do not make fecal sacs, but New World warblers do. The most unusual suggestion is that the Olive Warbler is neither a New World nor Old World warbler but a finch, a member of the huge and evolutionarily active family Fringillidae, the same group to which cardinals belong. This assertion is based on study of the DNA of the Olive Warbler, which is more like finch DNA than warbler DNA. If this is true, the Olive Warbler represents an impressive evolutionary convergence, since it doesn't look or act at all like a finch.

The **YELLOW-EYED JUNCO** is perhaps not quite as much of an evolutionary curiosity as the Olive Warbler, but it, too, has its idiosyncrasies. A few years ago all the junco species in the United States save one were lumped into one species named the Dark-eyed Junco. The American Ornithologists Union, final authority in such matters, wiped out the Slate-colored, Oregon, Pink-sided, Gray-headed, and White-winged juncos, relegating each to the rank of subspecies rather than full species. But the Yellow-eyed Junco remained a full species. This may seem surprising since the Yellow-eyed Junco looks quite a bit like the gray-headed form of Dark-eyed Junco, but the similarity is not meaningful. The Yellow-eyed Junco is a Mexican and Central American species (its former name was Mexican Junco), reaching the northern limit of its range in southeastern Arizona. There is no evidence to suggest that Yellow-eyed Juncos can successfully hybridize with any race of Dark-eyed Junco. Yellow-eyed Juncos do, indeed, have bright yellow eyes, an important field mark. They also behave differently from Dark-eyed Juncos. They move by walking rather than hopping, shuffling along in a gait quite distinct from the typical sparrowlike hopping of Dark-eyed Juncos. Breeding behavior also is distinct, as male Yellow-eyes can be much more aggressive toward one another than Dark-eyed Juncos. Yellow-eyed Juncos are birds of the understory and ground, often visiting picnic areas. In winter they gather in flocks and migrate to lower elevations.

Two more Mexican birds, the **GREATER PEWEE** and the **BUFF-BREASTED FLYCATCHER,** reach the northern limits of their ranges in southern Arizona. Greater Pewee, formerly called Coues' Flycatcher, is a husky brown flycatcher without wing bars and with a gray breast. This big-headed bird, which is about the size and shape of the North American Olive-sided Flycatcher, is prone to sit in the open, atop a dead branch, periodically flying out in pursuit of aerial insect prey. The bird's song is easy to learn and has earned it the nickname José Maria. It is a slurred *ho-say-haree-ah,* or *ho-say-re-ah.* The Greater Pewee breeds as far south as Nicaragua. The Buff-breasted Flycatcher (not illustrated) is the smallest member of the genus *Empidonax,* a group of little fly-catchers that are notoriously difficult to distinguish unless you hear them. Like any *Empidonax,* the Buff-breasted Flycatcher has a white eye ring and two wing bars. However, this bird, which ranges throughout Mexico and Central America as far south as Honduras, has a distinctly buffy breast, setting it apart from other small flycatchers. It is fond of pine forests, often forages in the understory, and is common in summer at Sawmill Canyon in the Arizona Huachuca Mountains. None of the Empidonax group is musical, and the Buff-breasted is no exception. Its song is a brief, two-note *slee-eek!*

WHERE TO VISIT: The Coronado National Forest in the Chiricahua Mountains has some ideal places to visit southwestern mountain forests. Recommended are Rustler Park, Barfoot Park, the Onion Saddle, and Pinery Canyon Campground near Portal, Cave Creek Canyon, and Chiricahua National Monument. Another good location is the Huachuca Mountains, accessed through Ft. Huachuca at Sierra Vista. This area is also part of the Coronado National Forest. Nearby Miller Peak Trail in Miller Canyon takes you from desert through oaks and Ponderosa Pine to a forest of Common Douglas-fir and Engelmann Spruce.

ESSAY

ARIZONA'S OCCASIONAL PARROT

Only one of the world's more than 300 parrot species, the Carolina Parakeet, was a native breeding bird in the United States. The last Carolina Parakeet died in captivity in 1914. The species, once common and widespread in the Southeast, was literally trapped and shot to death by so-called hunters, many of whom simply liked watching the colorful birds fall to the ground. One excuse given for the slaughter was that the parakeets ate fruit and were a threat to orchards. Now the species is gone forever.

Parrots inhabit the tropics and subtropics, but some, including the Monk Parakeet of Argentina, can tolerate cool temperatures. The Monk Parakeet, a common cage bird in the United States, has established feral breeding populations in such chilly areas as downtown Chicago and the outskirts of Providence, Rhode Island. It survives, but is not a native North American species.

The Thick-billed Parrot is another species that can tolerate the cold, and it is native to North America, though it has never bred in the United States. This 15-inch green parrot, with red forehead, red shoulders, and a thick black bill, is an inhabitant of the Sierra Madre Oriental mountains of Mexico, living at 4,000 –

Figure 29. Thick-billed Parrot

10,000 feet in the mountain pine forests. Because these mountains are, at the northernmost range, close to the mountains of southeastern Arizona, Thick-billed Parrots have occasionally crossed the border. The last major invasion occurred in July of 1917, when as many as 1,500 birds spent the fall and winter in several locations in the Chiricahua Mountains. The birds fed on the seeds of Chihuahua Pines, and they reportedly consumed virtually the entire year's crop. They then devoured seeds of Ponderosa Pine as well as acorns from various oaks. By March of 1918 the birds had left the area, presumably returning to breed in Mexico. Prior to the 1917 invasion, a huge flock estimated at between 700 and 1,000 birds was seen in 1904. Earlier still, Thick-billed Parrots were reported to have wandered as far as northern Arizona. After 1918, reports of Thick-billed Parrots continued sporadically throughout the 1930s and 1940s. Then the reports stopped. Why?

The reason is loss of habitat. Extensive deforestation along the Sierra Madre Occidental has resulted in a significant reduction in the population of the Thick-billed Parrot. The pine forests that cover most of the slopes of western Mexico's mountains are occupied by a rich diversity of bird species, including the brilliant Red Warbler, the melodious Brown-backed Solitaire, and the spectacular Tufted Jay. Now much of this habitat has been logged, and species such as the Thick-billed Parrot have suffered serious population declines. The huge Imperial Woodpecker, which once ranged widely throughout these mountains, is probably now extinct. There are so few Thick-billed Parrots, there are virtually none that fly north into Arizona.

During the 1980s an attempt was made to reintroduce Thick-billed Parrots to the Chiricahua Mountains. Reintroductions are sometimes successful, but this attempt was a failure. The species remains in Mexico, now separated from the United States by too much deforested area to assume that it will return any time soon.

CHIHUAHUA DESERT

INDICATOR PLANTS

TREES: *Honey Mesquite, Gregg, Roemer,* and *Wright catclaws,* Screwbean Mesquite, Texas Paloverde.

SHRUBS: *Lechuguilla, Creosote Bush, Texas Lignumvitae, Ocotillo,* Four-wing Saltbush, Mormon-tea, Ceniza, Guajillo, *Spanish Bayonet,* Torrey Yucca, Beaked Yucca, Soaptree Yucca, Agarito, Allthorn, Apache-plume, Sotol, Century Plant, Havard Agave.

HERBACEOUS SPECIES: *Candelilla,* Desert Verbena, *Woolly Locoweed,* Fendler's Bladderpod, California Poppy, Texas Prickly Poppy, Warnock's Rock Nettle, Twoleaf Senna, Desert Tobacco, Wright's Vervain, Bearded Dalea, Shy Bluebonnet, Bracted Paintbrush, Narrowleaf Gromwell, Spider Antelope Horns, many grasses.

CACTI: Beehive Nipple Cactus, Tangled Fishhook, Big Needle Cactus, Horse Crippler, Purple Prickly-pear, Rainbow Cactus, Claret Cup, Peyote, Chain Cholla, Engelmann's Prickly-pear.

INDICATOR ANIMALS

BIRDS: *Scaled Quail, Greater Roadrunner, Chihuahuan Raven, Curve-billed Thrasher, Pyrrhuloxia, Black-throated Sparrow,* Turkey Vulture, Black Vulture, Red-tailed Hawk, Zone-tailed Hawk, Crested Caracara, Prairie Falcon, American Kestrel, White-winged Dove, Mourning Dove, Inca Dove, Common Ground-Dove, Great Horned Owl, Elf Owl, Common Poorwill, Lesser Nighthawk, Black-chinned Hummingbird, Western Kingbird, Cliff Swallow, Common Raven, Verdin, Cactus Wren, Rock Wren, Canyon Wren, Blue-gray Gnatcatcher, Black-tailed Gnatcatcher, Loggerhead Shrike, Varied Bunting, Scott's Oriole.

MAMMALS: *Texas Antelope Squirrel, Collared Peccary,* Mexican Freetail Bat, many other bats, Blacktail Jackrabbit, Desert Cottontail, Spotted Ground Squirrel, Merriam Pocket Mouse, Ord Kangaroo Rat, Merriam Kangaroo Rat, Cactus Mouse, Southern Plains Woodrat, Ringtail, Badger, Coyote, Kit Fox, Bobcat, Mule Deer, Pronghorn.

REPTILES: *Common Chuckwalla, Texas Horned Lizard, Desert Spiny*

Lizard, Texas Banded Gecko, Greater Earless Lizard, Collared Lizard, Leopard Lizard, Side-blotched Lizard, Western Whiptail, Glossy Snake, Night Snake, Common Kingsnake, Coachwhip, Bullsnake, Mexican Blackhead Snake, Western Diamondback Rattlesnake, Mojave Rattlesnake, Desert Tortoise.

AMPHIBIANS: Couch's Spadefoot Toad, Texas Toad.

DESCRIPTION

The Chihuahua is a hot desert comprising mostly shrubs, yuccas, and agaves, with mesquite and catclaw abundant along arroyos and river banks. Cacti are also abundant, but they are smaller in size and there are fewer species here than in the Sonora Desert. The most common cacti are prickly-pears, all in the genus *Opuntia.* The most abundant shrub is Creosote Bush (Plate 22), which can occupy thousands of acres of flat desert. Much of the soil is derived from limestone and gypsum. Annual rainfall is low, from 3 to 20 inches, the vast majority of it falling from mid-June through mid-September. Summer temperatures approach and frequently exceed 100°F. Elevation throughout the Chihuahua Desert varies from about 3,000 feet to 6,000 feet.

Much of the Chihuahua Desert is a flat, parched-looking landscape of scattered Creosote Bush and other small shrubs, the monotony interrupted by occasional yuccas and clumps of mesquite. As with all deserts, there is much bare ground between plants, though in some areas, bunch grasses can form an almost complete cover. Though Creosote Bush is the most abundant plant of the Chihuahua Desert, other species, like Lechuguilla, are also abundant, often forming large stands. In fact, the desert flora are rather like a mosaic, with scattered stands not only of

Chihuahua Desert at Big Bend National Park. The conspicuous yuccas are Lechuguillas, indicator species of this ecosystem.

Lechuguilla, but also of Ocotillo (Plate 22), Soaptree Yucca, or Beaked Yucca, depending upon site history, elevation, exposure, and soil characteristics. Lechuguilla is perhaps the best indicator species for the Chihuahua Desert, since it occurs nowhere else.

The handsome Black-throated Sparrow, often seen perched on a Creosote Bush or Tarbush, is one of the most abundant birds of the Chihuahua Desert. Inca Doves, Common Ground-Doves, Greater Roadrunners, Scaled Quail, and Curve-billed Thrashers are also common roadside species. Overhead, vultures circle, as do various raptors such as Red-tailed Hawks and the rare Zone-tailed Hawk. Western Kingbirds, Loggerhead Shrikes, and American Kestrels perch on telephone wires. The Chihuahuan Raven, a smaller relative of the widespread Common Raven, is identified by its more high-pitched voice and a ruff of white feathers on the back of its neck, the reason it was formerly called White-necked Raven. The ruff is visible only at close range.

Many mammal species live in the Chihuahua Desert, especially rodents, including the long-tailed, hopping kangaroo rats. These mammals are so well adapted to the desert that they never have to drink water. All their water needs are served by water produced during digestion of their plant food (mostly seeds). Rodents are prey for Badgers, Coyotes, Kit Foxes, and hawks and owls. Mexican Freetail Bats (see page 132) hunt for insects during the cool of the night.

The many lizard and snake species present make the Chihuahua Desert an ideal place to search for reptiles.

MILAR COMMUNITIES: See arroyo and desert scrub and giant Saguaro cactus forest.

ANGE: From the Big Bend region of west Texas west through southern

Figure 30. Black-throated Sparrow

Creosote Bush covers thousands of acres of flatlands in the Chihuahua Desert.

New Mexico and into extreme southeastern Arizona, where it is replaced by the Sonora Desert. Extensive throughout northwestern Mexico, between the Sierra Madre Occidental and Sierra Madre Oriental mountain ranges.

REMARKS

The four North American deserts rank in size as follows: Great Basin, Chihuahua, Sonora, Mojave. Though it is the second largest of North American deserts, very little of the Chihuahua crosses the United States's border. To see the Chihuahua from the U.S., you must visit west Texas or south-central New Mexico.

The Chihuahua Desert is a desert because mountains surround it on three sides. To the east, the Sierra Madre Oriental range blocks moisture from the Gulf of Mexico. To the north, the southernmost Rockies block what little moisture would otherwise come from the United States, and to the west, the Sierra Madre Occidental range blocks westerlies and storm systems originating in the Pacific.

There is a gradual transition from the Chihuahua to the Sonora Desert, and it is difficult to draw a sharp line of separation. The Sonora (see Giant Cactus Forest) and Chihuahua share many species in common, particularly **CREOSOTE BUSH** and **OCOTILLO**. The most obvious difference between the two deserts is the presence of giant cacti as well as more species of cacti in the Sonora, and the greater abundance of yuccas and agaves in the Chihuahua.

Like Century Plant, **LECHUGUILLA** is an agave, a member of the amaryllis family. Agaves resemble yuccas, as both plant groups have large, spikelike leaves arranged in basal rosettes. This resemblance is an example of evolutionary convergence, not close genetic relationship.

Another distinctive plant of the Chihuahua Desert is **CANDELILLA**, or Wax Plant. This odd species is a member of the spurge family, but it looks, at first glance, more like a small cactus. Candelilla grows as a cluster of blue-green stems up to 3 feet tall. There are virtually no leaves or thorns. Photosynthesis is done through the stems. The tiny, pink-white flowers are clustered mostly at the stem tips. Candelilla is much reduced in abundance because it has been illegally harvested for the wax in its stems.

Heat rising from the desert floor creates an abundance of thermal currents, ideal for soaring vultures and hawks, including the rare **ZONE-TAILED HAWK**. A Zone-tailed Hawk is a slender soaring hawk, almost all black but with gray under the wings and several white bands on the tail. This most interesting raptor, which tends to be rare, is sometimes mistaken for the abundant **TURKEY VULTURE**. Indeed, the Zone-tailed Hawk resembles a Turkey Vulture, soars like it with wings held slightly upward in a dihedral, and tends to stay near kettles of soaring vultures. Many ornithologists believe the similarity between hawk and vulture to be a case of *mimicry,* in which the hawk appears to behave like a vulture. This adaptation may benefit the hawk because vultures eat only dead animals. Live mice, ground squirrels, and other hawk food have nothing to fear from vultures, and consequently these potential prey species do not react to the presence of vultures. Because the Zone-tailed Hawk looks and acts rather like a vulture, it may be able to get much closer to its prey.

Figure 31. Candelilla

WHERE TO VISIT: Without question, the best place in the United States to experience the Chihuahua Desert is Big Bend National Park, near Marathon, Texas. The nearest major city is San Antonio. As in all national parks, there are interpretive displays, lectures, and hikes.

ESSAY

HOW A GRASSLAND BECOMES A DESERT

When you travel through the Southwest observing the Chihuahua and Sonora deserts, it is natural to assume that the species you see are normal for the climate and soils of the region. In other words, you see deserts dominated by mesquite, shrub, yucca, and cactus because conditions are too hot and dry for other kinds of habitats. In many cases you would be right to assume such a thing, but not in all cases. You may well be driving past an area that, had you passed it a hundred or two hundred years earlier, would have been dominated by at least 20 species of grasses, perhaps with a few scattered yuccas and shrubs mixed among them. Historical records from the 19th century based on notes kept by explorers, gold miners, and surveyors suggest strongly that grassland was at least twice as expansive as it now is. Since that time, mesquite alone has been estimated to have doubled its range of abundance, now covering at least 70 million acres where once it covered but 35 million or so. Other woody species, especially Creosote Bush, have also increased dramatically. Why? Has the climate changed over this period? Has rainfall decreased, forcing out the grasses? Perhaps some change has occurred, but not much. The reasons for the expansion of deserts and contraction of grassland lie elsewhere.

One key element is cattle. When Coronado traversed the Southwest from 1540–1542 in search of the seven cities of Cibola, he brought with him 1,000 horses, 500 cattle, and 5,000 sheep. Some of these animals strayed from domestication and established their own herds that remained long after Coronado. Following Coronado, pioneers recognized that ranching could provide a very ample living. Cattle and sheep, but especially cattle, became the industry of the Southwest. In 1891, when cattle grazing in Arizona was at its peak, there were approximately 1.5 million head of cattle on Arizona rangeland. Such a huge number resulted in overgrazing. Grasses, most of which are adapted to sustain a certain level of grazing, could not grow back quickly enough. There were just too many bovine mouths waiting for the tender grass shoots.

Scottish farmers have long known that thistle rapidly invades pastures, sometimes so densely as to choke out other species. The reason for thistle's success is that the spiny leaves are largely avoided by grazing animals, giving thistle an advantage over other plants in fields populated by hungry cattle. Likewise, cattle in the Southwest apparently did not care for thorny mesquite, spiny cacti, dagger-sharp yuccas, or the chemically powerful Creosote Bush. But they loved the grasses. As cattle put increasing pressure on natural grasses, seeds from these other species germinated, seedlings grew to maturity, and more woody species invaded. The cattle tipped the delicate balance between grasses and woody desert species. Overgrazing changed a diverse grassland into shrub desert. Prairie dogs disappeared, replaced by kangaroo rats.

In ecology, few questions have simple answers. Although overgrazing is widely acknowledged as the major cause of grassland loss in the Southwest, other factors have also had various degrees of influence. Kangaroo rats, pocket mice, and rabbits stash mesquite and cactus seeds but do not subsequently retrieve all of them, often resulting in germination. These little mammals have probably contributed, at least to some degree, to the spread of desert vegetation at the expense of grassland.

Fire—and the lack of it—also has a role in the spread of desert. Grasslands are flammable, especially during hot, dry summers, when lightning is frequent. Historical records, though somewhat anecdotal, provide a consistent account of frequent, sometimes extensive fires throughout the Southwest. Frequent fires helped offset any encroachment of deserts into grassland, by starting over the game of competition between grasses and woody desert species. A quote from a U.S. Department of Agriculture researcher (Cook, 1908) tells the tale:

"Before the prairies were grazed by cattle the luxuriant growths of grass could accumulate for several years until conditions were favorable for accidental fires to spread. With these large supplies of fuel, the fires that swept over these prairies were very besoms of destruction not only for man and animals, but for all shrubs and trees which might have ventured out among the grass, and even for any trees or forests against which the burning wind might blow. That such fires were evidently the cause of the former treeless condition of the southwestern prairies is also shown by the fact that trees are also found in all situations which afford protection against fires."

By the end of the 19th century, fires were relatively well controlled and much reduced in frequency. This change, plus the presence of cattle, proved too much for the grasses. Woody desert species invaded, and what was once grassland was converted to desert. As deserts increased, cattle continued to graze on what grasses remained.

Grazing was hard on the woody desert plants, too. Saguaro especially suffered, as their seedlings were both eaten and trampled by cattle. Grazing in the Rincon Mountain section of Saguaro National Monument was terminated in 1958, and since then, the Saguaros have dramatically rebounded. All grazing in Saguaro National Monument was stopped in 1984. But by then the woody desert species were so well established that grasses could not regain a foothold.

GIANT SAGUARO CACTUS FOREST (SONORA DESERT)
PLATE 22

INDICATOR PLANTS
TREES: *Saguaro, Blue Paloverde,* Yellow Paloverde, Desert Ironwood, Velvet Mesquite, Desert-willow, Soaptree Yucca, Joshuatree, Boojum (Baja only), California Washingtonia (local in California).

SHRUBS: *Creosote Bush, Ocotillo,* Brittlebush, Bursage, Calliandra, Jojoba, Desert Elderberry, Century Plant, American Mistletoe (parasitic).

HERBACEOUS SPECIES: *Mexican Goldpoppy,* Southwestern Vervain, Desert Evening Primrose, Desert-marigold, Ajo-lily, Blanketflower, Scarlet Globemallow, Prairie Delphinium, Desertgold, Desert-sunflower, Scorpionweed, Coulter's Lupine, Sego Lily, Goldfields, Coyote Gourd, Blazingstar, Owl-clover, Desert-chicory, Sacred Datura, Desert Rosemallow, Wild Zinnia, Devil's-claws, Sand-verbena.

CACTI (in addition to Saguaro): *Chain (Jumping) Cholla,* Engelmann's Prickly-pear, Organpipe Cactus (extreme south), Night-blooming Cereus, Esteve's Pincushion, Buckhorn Cholla, Staghorn Cholla, Sagebrush Cholla, *Barrel Cactus,* Purple Prickly-pear, Common Beavertail, Porcupine Prickly-pear, Strawberry Hedgehog, Engelmann's Hedgehog, Claret Cup, Tangled Fishhook.

INDICATOR ANIMALS
BIRDS: *Elf Owl, Greater Roadrunner, Gila Woodpecker, Cactus Wren, White-winged Dove, Northern (Gilded) Flicker,* Turkey Vulture, Red-tailed Hawk, Swainson's Hawk, Harris's Hawk, Common Black-Hawk, Gray Hawk, American Kestrel, Scaled Quail, Gambel's Quail, Great Horned Owl, Inca Dove, Mourning Dove, Common Ground-Dove, Lesser Nighthawk, Black-chinned Hummingbird, Costa's Hummingbird, Ladder-backed Woodpecker, Western Kingbird, Cassin's Kingbird, Brown-crested Flycatcher,

Ash-throated Flycatcher, Vermilion Flycatcher, Horned Lark, Purple Martin, Common Raven, Chihuahuan Raven, Verdin, Bushtit, Rock Wren, Canyon Wren, Bewick's Wren, Northern Mockingbird, Curve-billed Thrasher, Blue-gray Gnatcatcher, Black-tailed Gnatcatcher, Phainopepla, Loggerhead Shrike, Bell's Vireo, Lucy's Warbler, Yellow-breasted Chat, House Sparrow, Hooded Oriole, Scott's Oriole, Northern Cardinal, Pyrrhuloxia, House Finch, Canyon Towhee, Abert's Towhee, Lark Sparrow, Black-throated Sparrow.

MAMMALS: *Yuma (Harris's) Antelope Squirrel, Roundtail Ground Squirrel, Desert Cottontail,* Western Pipistrel, many other bat species, Rock Squirrel, Arizona Pocket Mouse, Desert Pocket Mouse, Cactus Mouse, Whitethroat Woodrat, Mexican Woodrat, Blacktail Jackrabbit, Ringtail, Hooded Skunk, Hognose Skunk, Kit Fox, Gray Fox, Coyote, Bobcat, Collared Peccary, Mule Deer, Whitetail Deer.

REPTILES: *Gila Monster, Desert Iguana, Desert Tortoise,* Common Chuckwalla, Banded Gecko, Zebra-tailed Lizard, Collared Lizard, Regal Horned Lizard, Tree Lizard, Desert Spiny Lizard, Side-blotched Lizard, Western Whiptail, Great Plains Skink, Coachwhip, Western Patch-nosed Snake, Gopher Snake, Common Kingsnake, Banded Sand Snake, Western Hognose Snake, Western Diamondback Rattlesnake, Tiger Rattlesnake, Western Rattlesnake.

AMPHIBIANS: Couch's Spadefoot Toad, Western Spadefoot Toad, Woodhouse Toad, Red-spotted Toad, Great Plains Toad, Northern Leopard Frog.

DESCRIPTION

The Saguaro cactus forest is without question the most unusual forest community in North America. Nothing else remotely resembles it. The Saguaro (pronounced sah WAH roh) is by far the largest North American cactus, and it is an important indicator species of the Sonora Desert. This tree-sized cactus dominates gentle slopes, called *bajadas,* throughout much of the Sonora Desert. Saguaros grow up to 50 feet and occasionally taller, with accordion-like pleated stems lined with spines. Large specimens have multiple arms, sometimes as many as 50 but usually far fewer. Because Saguaros vary dramatically in size and in number, and position of arms (upright, downturned, outward, inward), they are readily recognizable as individuals, and some even seem to take on personalities. Saguaros with drooping arms may appear to be hugging themselves, looking sad. Those with arms pointing straight upward appear to be rigidly at attention, saluting the desert sun. A drive through the Saguaro forest in the warm reddish light of early morning or late afternoon can seem like a visit to another planet, where the odd life forms stand tall, never moving, at peace with themselves and their environment.

Besides Saguaros, the desert abounds with small paloverde trees, recognizable by their green bark, as well as many shrubs, including Creosote Bush and the unmistakable Ocotillo, the whip-plant. Washes and arroyos are lined with Velvet Mesquite, paloverdes, Desert Ironwood, and Desert-willow. In spring, many wildflowers are evident including desert annuals, which briefly bloom and set seed after the spring rains. These include Blanket-flower, lupines, and, most spectacular of all, Mexican Poppy, which sometimes carpets the desert in brilliant orange.

Many cacti other than Saguaro are present, and some are incredibly spiny, so walk carefully through the desert. Chollas (pronounced CHOY ah), various prickly-pears, barrels, beavertails, fishhooks, and hedgehogs are among the abundant cacti.

Most desert plants, including the annual and perennial wildflowers as well as the cacti, are pollinated by insects, bats, or hummingbirds. These plants produce large, showy blossoms, making the Sonora Desert spectacularly beautiful during much of spring and summer.

Many bird species live among the Saguaros. Indeed, many birds and other animals, are utterly dependent on the giant cacti (see essay, page 328). American Kestrels, Brown-crested Flycatchers, Elf Owls, and 13 other bird species routinely use old woodpecker holes, made by Gila Woodpeckers and the Gilded subspecies of Northern Flicker, as nest sites. White-winged Doves, Hooded Orioles, and Scott's Orioles sip nectar from big, white Saguaro flowers. Spine-covered chollas provide nest sites for Curve-billed Thrashers and Cactus Wrens, both abundant residents of the desert. Greater Roadrunners chase after lizards and snakes, pausing in the shade of a dense paloverde clump with a covey of Gambel's Quail seeking protection from the midday sun.

The most frequently seen desert mammals are ground squirrels, Desert Cottontails, and jackrabbits, but many other species can be found, especially at night around waterholes. These include Hooded and Hognose skunks, herds of Peccaries and deer, and predators such as Bobcat, Kit Fox, and Coyote. Indeed, at sunset, no matter where you might be in the desert, you can usually hear several choruses of Coyotes serenading the end of another day. At least 18 bat species fly around on any given night. While most are in vigorous pursuit of insects, some seek nectar and are important pollinators of Saguaro. Woodrats, though infrequently seen, are evident by their large middens, obvious beneath clumps of paloverdes and other shrubs.

The Saguaro community enjoys an abundance of reptiles, including the Gila Monster, the only poisonous lizard in the United States. Many nonpoisonous lizards also reside in the desert, and snakes are numerous as well. Though lizards are commonly seen in daytime, snakes are far more likely to be most active after dark, when the desert cools. The sedate Desert Tortoise, sadly reduced in numbers in recent years, is active both by day and night, emerging from its burrow to take a bite of prickly-pear.

Many invertebrates are common on the desert, and some can be a bit intimidating. Scorpions are often abundant in the litter, especially in decomposing cactus stems. Giant, hairy tarantulas are often encountered crossing roads at night.

SIMILAR COMMUNITIES: Many species characteristic of the Sonora Desert also occur in the Chihuahua Desert.

RANGE: Southwestern and south-central Arizona, extreme southeastern California, the western half of Sonora, Mexico, and much of Baja California.

REMARKS

The Saguaro forest is part of the Sonora Desert, a diverse, hot desert occupying about 120,000 square miles of the Southwest. Though the Saguaro is restricted to the Sonora Desert, it does not occur uniformly throughout the Sonora. It is largely absent from flat plains, which tend to be dominated by shrubs, especially Creosote Bush. Other species are dominant south of the border, in Sonora and Baja California. Saguaros occur in abundance only on lands of gentle slopes, called *bajadas*. They are particularly abundant in the Tucson area.

The Sonora Desert climate is one of biseasonal rainfall, sparse total precipitation, and seemingly endless hot days. Annual precipitation ranges from 3 inches in Yuma (southwestern Arizona) to about 11 inches in Tucson. Winters are mild, and rains come in both spring and late summer, the latter accompanied by frequent late afternoon thunderstorms. Spring rains bring about the blooming of annuals, ephemeral plants that can suddenly blanket the desert with waves of color. From late spring through summer, it is not unusual for the Sonora Desert to experience 90 consecutive days with temperatures in excess of 100°F. Humidity is extremely low, resulting in a dry heat, similar to what it must feel like inside an oven.

Be careful not to overexert yourself during the heat of the day — sunstroke is not uncommon and is quite potentially dangerous. Worry more about sunstroke than snakes.

The **SAGUARO** cactus, like the many other species with which it shares the desert, is a kind of plant called a *succulent*, a growth form specifically adapted for accumulating and storing water.

A *typical* bajada, *the landscape of gentle slopes where saguaros thrive.*

Cacti are not the only succulents. Yuccas, agaves, and many other plants, including the California Yellow Ice Plant that grows on coastal sand dunes, are all succulents. Cacti, which are distantly related to roses, are endemic to the Western Hemisphere and are thought to have evolved as recently as 20,000 years ago, probably in the West Indies. All cacti share an array of adaptations: they are perennial, requiring more than one season to reach maturity; they have no leaves, so all photosynthesis is accomplished through chlorophyll in the stem; the stem is thick and stores water; stems have structures called areoles from which grow sharp spines or flower buds; and root systems are wide-spreading and shallow, able to soak up water rapidly.

Upon seeing a fully mature Saguaro, perhaps topping 50 feet tall, it is natural to wonder how old it is and how long it took it to grow. Saguaros lack growth rings, so aging them is difficult, but research indicates that they can live from 175 to 250 years. Once mature, the most common cause of mortality is lightning or a wound that is invaded by necrotic bacteria. In the northern limits of their range, Saguaros also suffer the effects of winter freezing. Saguaros are surprisingly slow growing. After two years, a seedling Saguaro is only about a quarter of an inch tall. By five years of age, the future giant cactus is barely 6 inches high. By age 20 it will be 10 inches high and by age 30, it will still be only a mere 3 feet high. If it survives to be between 70 and 80 years old, it will be 6–8 feet tall, and it will then develop its first blossoms and arms. At full maturity, it should be between 35–40 feet tall or more.

Saguaros are adapted to soak up water and store it. Their root systems are shallow, only 8–20 inches below ground, but exten-

Mature Saguaro.

sive, radiating out from the 2-foot-thick stem at least 45 feet, making a total root diameter of 90 feet. Any rain is quickly taken up by the roots and transferred to the stem for storage. The accordion-pleated stem can enlarge and contract, depending upon how much water is stored within. A mature Saguaro is normally up to 95 percent water, weighing between 3.5 and 7 tons. Because it cannot control its water intake, it is possible for a Saguaro to absorb too much water and actually rupture its stem, obviously a rare occurrence in the dry desert.

Saguaros are not covered by woody bark, nor do they have extensive wood inside. What holds them up? Saguaros manage to stand tall by virtue of an interior design much like the steel rod reinforcements that are buried within concrete buildings and bridges. A support structure consisting of rings of parallel woody rods is contained within the pulpy stem, holding the cactus up even against strong desert winds. After the plant dies and the pulp rots away, the odd, woody skeleton of the cactus often remains standing like a ghost in the desert.

Though it takes a very long time for a Saguaro to grow to maturity, a single mature plant can produce a staggering number of seeds each year. Saguaro flowers grow on the stem and arm tips, clusters of huge white blossoms with dense, brushlike yellow anthers at the center. Each flower is 2–3 inches wide, with about 3,000 pollen-containing anthers and nearly 200 ovules in the ovary. Flowers, which bloom from May through July, are cross-pollinated by bees and bats. (Bees are not native to the desert—all were introduced by bee keepers. Longnose Bats, the normal pollinators of Saguaro, have been reduced by the unfortunate effects of pesticide poisoning and loss of roosting sites, so bees now do most of the pollination.) Each adult Saguaro makes about 300 flowers per season and is capable of producing about 40 million seeds in its lifetime. It takes two plants to make one seed, even though each plant has both sets of sex organs—they must cross-pollinate.

Approximately one month after flowering, the Saguaro's egglike green fruits split open, revealing a bright red pulp and tiny black seeds. The fruits, called *pitahayas* in Spanish, are eaten by many animals as well as Native Americans. Both the Papagos and Pimas tribes celebrate the Saguaro harvest in July, when the people dislodge the fruits using traditional long poles made of woody rods from the insides of Saguaros. Fruits are made into jams, syrup, preserves, or fermented beverage. Seeds, which are quite oily, are made into a kind of butter.

The normal population of adult Saguaros on the *bajada* is about 15–20 per acre. However, in late summer, when the Saguaro fruits have dropped and seeds have scattered, there are about 2 million Saguaro seeds per acre. Obviously, the vast majority don't make it. In one experiment, a researcher disseminated 64,000 Saguaro seeds; only 185 (.29 percent) became established. However, to maintain an adult population of 15–20 per acre, only one seedling need be established every 5 years! Seeds

are consumed by many birds, from Gambel's Quail to House Finches; they are devoured by ground squirrels, woodrats, and other mammals; and they are removed en masse by harvester ants, which make little pyramid-shaped nests. One researcher noted that harvester ants carried off about 1,000 Saguaro seeds per hour. If a seed survives all of the seed predators and actually germi-

Saguaro sapling protected beneath the shade of a "nurse" Paloverde.

nates, it will in all likelihood be eaten by a herbivore, perhaps a Desert Cottontail, Mule Deer, Collared Peccary, or domestic cattle.

Even if the seedling escapes herbivores, it may not survive. The desert is a hot place, too hot for baby Saguaros. One probable reason the giant cacti do not grow on the flatlands is that they cannot stand the heat created by the unrelenting sunshine. Seedlings need shade in order to survive. Usually, the shade is supplied by a neighboring paloverde, Jojoba, or other desert shrub. These shrubs and small trees, called *nurse plants,* provide just enough shade to prevent the small cactus from overheating. As you look at young Saguaros, notice how many are poking up through a clump of paloverde or some other shrub. One researcher kept track of 1,200 seedlings placed in direct sunlight. All died within a year. However, of 1,200 seedlings placed in shade, 45 percent survived the year, a very important difference.

Saguaros are protected wherever they occur in Arizona, a protection they very much need. Saguaro populations have been seriously reduced by the grazing of cattle, home building, and vandalism. A small pickup truck can bump a mature Saguaro and knock it down, instantly killing a plant that took over 50 years to grow. Gunshot wounds on Saguaros used for target practice invite bacterial invasion, killing the cactus.

Mesquite and Paloverde are among the most successful trees that inhabit the *bajada.* Paloverde is known for its colorful blossoms, signaling that spring has come to the desert.

Ocotillo also occupies the giant cactus forest. Commonly called whip-plant, the Ocotillo resembles a cluster of gray-green buggy whips stuck together at a common base. Ocotillo is in a family of its own, a

A mature Saguaro now overtops its nurse plant, a Mesquite.

thorny shrub that grows tiny leaves only after it rains. For most of the year it is leafless. It is abundant both in the Chihuahua and Sonora deserts, usually along rocky slopes such as *bajadas*. Flowers, which bloom from March through May, are red and tubular, growing in brilliant clusters at the branch tips. Spring flowering coincides with hummingbird migration. Six hummingbird species, Black-chinned, Costa's, Anna's, Broad-billed, Broad-tailed, and Rufous, all feed on and aid in cross-pollinating Ocotillo. Hummingbird-pollinated flowers are usually red, orange, or purple and are rich in sucrose, the same substance as table sugar. Bat-pollinated flowers, like those of Saguaro, have nectars composed mostly of glucose and fructose, simpler sugars.

CREOSOTE BUSH, sometimes called Greasewood, is, like Ocotillo, abundant both in the Chihuahua and Sonora deserts. Creosote Bush is a spreading, multi-stemmed shrub, easily identified by its strong odor and tiny paired leaves, pointed at the ends. The small size and leathery texture of the leaves help retard water loss through evaporation. Under ideal conditions, Creosote Bush can grow to 12 feet high. Flowers are small, 5-petaled, and yellow, pollinated by bees, wasps, and flies. Blooming is normally March to April and again from November through December. Seeds are in pale, hairy capsules. Creosote Bush lives where Saguaros cannot, in the most scorching heat on the flat alluvial plains. Individual plants are widely separated, their shallow root systems in severe competition for available moisture.

The words *palo verde* mean green stem or green bark, a characteristic that helps identify **BLUE PALOVERDE**. This common plant of the Sonora Desert grows as a shrub or small, spreading tree. Paloverdes, like mesquite and acacia, are legumes, with feathery

Blue Paloverde in full blossom.

Chollas and Ocotillos abound on the bajada.

compound leaves. However, paloverdes are easily distinguished by their smooth, bright green branches. Blue Paloverdes are covered with bright yellow blossoms during their brief flowering period in April and early May.

CHAIN CHOLLA, also called Jumping Cholla, is a plant to be appreciated from a respectful distance. This densely branched, shrublike cactus grows 6–10 feet tall. Like all chollas, it bears immense numbers of long, barbed spines. The drooping branches are tipped with joints, modified branches connected together in a hanging chain. These joints are very easy to dislodge. In fact, the cholla is disseminated by the spreading of its joints, each of which can root and grow into a new plant. Cholla joints detach so easily that some victims have insisted they "jump" onto skin. Not so. Should you become attached to a cholla joint, either from this or any other cholla species (there are several), use a comb to gently lift the sticky object off your skin or clothing. Cholla flowers, which are deep pink-red, are also contained on drooping branches. Bees pollinate the flowers. Chollas are abundant throughout the Sonora Desert. Another common species is Teddy Bear Cholla.

Just as there are a number of cholla species, so there are a number of prickly-pears and other cacti, such as the closely related Barrel and Fishhook cacti. Chollas and prickly-pears are closely related; both are in the genus *Opuntia*. **ENGELMANN'S PRICKLY-PEAR,** a very common species, is representative of the group. It is a variable species that ranges in color from white to brown, with spines that may be straight or curved. Its pads may stand upright or lie prostrate along the ground. The flowers may be golden-yellow or deep orange-red. The flowers bloom from mid-April through early June, and they are pollinated by bees.

Barrel cactus in full bloom.

Peccaries, Desert Cottontails, and Desert Tortoises all enjoy feasting on the round fruits.

The **GREATER ROADRUNNER** runs along desert roads from southeastern Texas throughout the Southwest and into central California. This large member of the cuckoo family pursues, captures, and eats all manner of large arthropods as well as an array of lizards, mice, and birds (usually nestlings). It also takes some fruits, including Saguaro. Pairs of roadrunners remain together throughout the year. Despite their cartoon image, roadrunners do not cry *beep beep!*, nor do they move at warp speeds. They do trot briskly along at about 15 m.p.h.—not bad, especially when the temperature is 115° F.

The **ELF OWL** is the smallest owl in the world, a sparrow-sized bird that nests in Saguaros. This 5–6-inch owl is nocturnal but is often seen at dusk, when it becomes active. Highly vocal and loud, the bird emits a high-pitched, repeated yip, easy to remember once you hear it. It occurs from southern Texas and Mexico through central Arizona. It is not confined to desert, living in canyons as well. Little owls eat little prey, mostly insects.

The Elf Owl usually owes its desert real estate to the work of a **GILA WOODPECKER**. This abundant bird of the Saguaro forest excavates cavities in the giant cacti, and these cavities are widely used by other species (see page 328). Gila Woodpeckers are indicators of Sonora Desert, as their range correlates almost exactly with the Sonora. They occur in the desert, along arroyos, and in towns. Both sexes are tawny brown with black and white zebra-striped backs, wings, and tail. Males have red atop their heads. Gilas communicate with a loud, rattling call, often given as they swoop onto a Saguaro.

Though chollas intimidate people, they seem to pose utterly no problem for **CACTUS WRENS.** These birds, the largest North American wrens, choose chollas more than any other plants as nest sites. The nest is a large structure reached by a narrow tunnel-like passage. It is usually located on the northern side of the plant, where sunlight is less intense, thus receiving large measures of shade, allowing the eggs and young to enjoy some protection from the worst of the desert heat. Cactus Wrens live in noisy family groups that often move together as they forage. Pairs are territorial all year. The species is easy to identify by its large size, distinctive pattern, and zebra-striped outer tail feathers. Cactus Wrens are common desert residents from south Texas throughout the Southwest to southern California and parts of Nevada. They feed on a variety of insect and plant foods, including Saguaro.

The **GILA MONSTER** is a stubby, slow, colorful lizard that tends to be active only at night. During the day, it lounges beneath a rock or in a burrow. Scales are beaded rather than overlapping, one of two characteristics that distinguish it and its nearest relative, the Mexican Beaded Lizard. The other characteristic is that both are poisonous, in fact they are the only poisonous lizards. Gila Monsters, which can grow to about 24 inches including tail, hunt small prey such as mice, birds, and other lizards. They have powerful jaws and hold their prey firmly. Often, but not always, they inject poison from glands in the lower jaws. The tail of a Gila Monster indicates its overall state of nutrition, as excess fat is stored in the tail. A thick tail indicates good pickings. Gila Monsters are aggressive only if intimidated. If they bite, they don't let go. Their poison is very painful to humans, but it is not reported to be fatal. Gila Monsters range from central Mexico through the Arizona deserts into southern Nevada.

The **DESERT TORTOISE** is becoming increasingly rare and is pro-

The sparrow-sized Elf Owl nests in the Saguaros.

Figure 32. Desert Tortoise

tected everywhere it occurs. This burrowing animal of the desert ranges throughout the Southwest. It is often found around arroyos or oases but can be encountered virtually anywhere on the desert. Tortoises are vegetarians, feeding on cacti and grasses. During the heat of the day they usually retreat to their cool, dark burrows. In winter they tend to congregate and hibernate in burrows.

WHERE TO VISIT: Start with Saguaro National Monument near Tucson. There are two parts to the monument, one east of the city near the Rincon Mountains and one west of the city near the Tucson Mountains. Both have nature trails, driving tours, and interpretive displays, and both are strongly recommended. The western part of the monument is close to the Arizona-Sonora Desert Museum, one of the nation's best interpretive zoos. *Don't miss it.* Also recommended is Organ Pipe Cactus National Monument, adjacent to the Papago Indian Reservation in extreme southern Arizona, the only place where you can see mature Organpipe Cactus.

ESSAY

THE SAGUARO: KEYSTONE SPECIES OF THE BAJADA

In 1877, the European biologist Karl Mobius published an essay about an oyster bed community in which he detailed the subtle interdependencies that existed among the many creatures that shared the habitat. He termed the entire community of living beings a *bioconosis,* a term which we no longer use, instead substituting the simple word *community.* Bioconosis comes from the

Greek, roughly translated to "life forms that have something in common." In this case, all the life forms that shared the oyster bed were in some way dependent on oysters. Oysters provided substrate for colonization and served as important food for other organisms both as larvae and as adults. The entire ecological community would not have existed were it not for one species, the oyster. When a single species is dominant in a community, not only in numbers but also in its importance to the continuing welfare of other species, it is a keystone species in that community.

The Saguaro cactus is in every way a keystone species on the Sonora Desert *bajadas*. Without it, much of the richness of species would soon be dramatically reduced. For instance, many of the birds of the *bajada* either feed or nest (or both) on Saguaros. Gila Woodpeckers, Ladder-backed Woodpeckers, and Northern (Gilded) Flickers hollow out nest cavities that are later used by American Kestrels, Elf Owls, Western Screech-Owls, Purple Martins, and Brown-crested and Ash-throated flycatchers, as well as various species of bats. Approximately 30 bird species, most recently the European Starling, have been documented to nest in woodpecker-carved Saguaro cavities. House Finches, Chihuahuan Ravens, Harris's and Red-tailed hawks, and Great Horned Owls use the tall cactus arms as nest sites. Saguaro blossoms are fed upon by White-winged, Mourning, and Inca doves, Scott's and Hooded orioles, House Finches, Cactus Wrens, and Curve-billed Thrashers. Sparrows and finches consume the seeds.

Other animals are equally dependent on the giant cacti. Saguaro seeds are eaten by essentially all of the Sonora Desert rodents as well as numerous insects, especially harvester ants. The fruits are delicacies to Mule Deer, Peccaries, and skunks. Seedlings are readily consumed by rabbits, rodents, deer, and Peccaries. Decaying arms that have fallen to the desert floor shelter hordes of invertebrates including scorpions, whip-scorpions, and tarantulas, plus a wide range of insects, as well as various snakes and lizards.

Saguaros, however, do not stand alone. Without other species, Saguaros themselves could not persist. The giant cactus is dependent on pollinators, now mostly bees but traditionally bats. Saguaros also need "nurse trees" such as paloverdes to provide shade during the early years of slow growth.

More subtle interactions also occur. A Saguaro whose stem is injured is subject to rapid and fatal necrosis from bacterial invasion. However, the site of the injury is an ideal place for a Gila Woodpecker to begin excavating a nest cavity. In doing so, the woodpecker may remove all of the diseased tissue, essentially curing the cactus of what might have been a fatal bacterial infection.

PLATE 17

ARROYO AND DESERT SCRUB

HONEY MESQUITE *Prosopis glandulosa*
> To 20 ft. Drooping compound leaves, yellowish pendulous blossoms, seeds in long brown pods. Deciduous.

GREGG CATCLAW *Acacia greggii*
> To 30 ft. Small compound leaves, sharply hooked thorns on branches. Brown pods are flat and twisted.

FRENCH TAMARISK *Tamarix gallica*
> To 20 ft. Leaves scaly, resembling cedar. Stems droop. Tiny pink flowers in long, dense clusters. Eurasian.

TEXAS LIGNUMVITAE (GUAYACAN) *Guaiacum angustifolium*
> To 20 ft. Shrubby; compound leaves with small leaflets. Violet, 5-petaled flowers. Fruits are heart-shaped.

TEXAS FORESTIERA (DESERT-OLIVE) *Forestiera angustifolia*
> To 15 ft. Leaves are compound, small leaflets roll at edges. Small, greenish yellow flowers.

CRISSAL THRASHER *Toxostoma crissale*
> 12 in. Brown with strongly decurved bill, rusty under tail.

PHAINOPEPLA *Phainopepla nitens*
> 7.5 in. Male is shiny black with a crest and a thin bill. Female is gray.

BELL'S VIREO *Vireo bellii*
> 5 in. Gray with faint wing bars, no clear eye ring. Voice distinctive (*cheedle-cheedle-cheedle-dee?*).

BLACK-TAILED GNATCATCHER *Polioptila melanura*
> 4.5 in. Slender, blue-gray with black cap and black tail.

VERDIN *Auriparus flaviceps*
> 4 in. Small, gray with yellow head. Rusty patch on shoulder.

LUCY'S WARBLER *Vermivora luciae*
> 4 in. Gray with rusty rump patch, small rusty patch on top of head. Thin bill.

PYRRHULOXIA *Cardinalis sinuatus*
> 8 in. Male gray with red crest, red on breast and face. Female lacks red on breast. Yellow bill.

PLATE 17

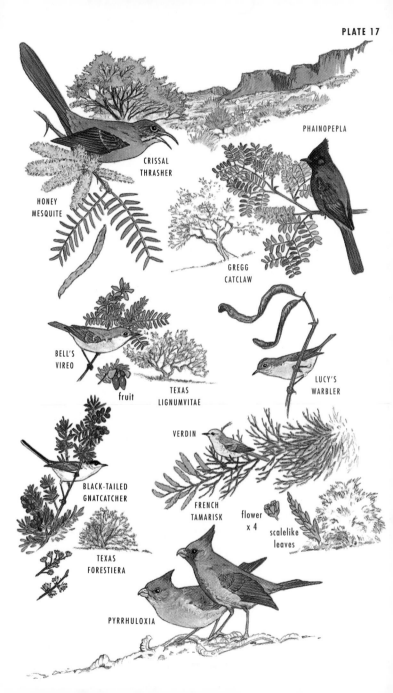

CRISSAL THRASHER

PHAINOPEPLA

HONEY MESQUITE

GREGG CATCLAW

BELL'S VIREO

fruit

TEXAS LIGNUMVITAE

LUCY'S WARBLER

VERDIN

BLACK-TAILED GNATCATCHER

FRENCH TAMARISK

flower x 4

scalelike leaves

TEXAS FORESTIERA

PYRRHULOXIA

PLATE 18

MEXICAN MADREAN FOOTHILL FOREST

MEXICAN PINYON *Pinus cembrioides*
To 30 ft. Dark, stiff, 1–2.5-inch needles, in clusters of 3.

WEEPING JUNIPER *Juniperus flaccida*
To 30 ft. Yellow-green, scaly foliage that droops. Cones berrylike, reddish brown. Bark peels in reddish brown strips.

TEXAS MADRONE *Arbutus texana*
To 25 ft. Evergreen, oval leaves. Reddish bark peels as scaly plates. Bright red fruit clusters.

GRAY OAK *Quercus grisea*
To 65 ft. Evergreen, leaves unlobed, grayish, usually without teeth.

APACHE-PLUME *Fallugia paradoxa*
Shrub, 4–6 ft. Flowers bright white, roselike. Fruits attached to feathery tufts. Leaves tiny.

SCARLET BOUVARDIA *Bouvardia ternifolia*
Shrub, 3 ft. Many bright red, trumpet-shaped flowers. Leaves long, in whorls.

BIG BEND PENSTEMON (HAVARD PENSTEMON) *Penstemon havardii*
To 3 ft. Bright red, tubular flower with yellow upper lips. Leaves blue-green, widely oval.

GRAY-BREASTED JAY *Aphelocoma ultramarina*
13 in. Dull blue above with faint brown on back. Gray below. Lacks crest.

GRAY VIREO *Vireo vicinior*
5.5 in. Dull gray above, no wing bars, thin eye ring. Flicks its tail.

SPOTTED TOWHEE *Pipilo erythrophthalmus*
8 in. Black above with white spots, rusty sides, and white outer tail feathers.

LUCIFER HUMMINGBIRD *Calothorax lucifer*
3.5 in. Male with violet throat, forked tail, decurved bill. Female with rusty sides, dark cheek patch.

WESTERN PIPISTREL *Pipistrellus hesperus*
3 in. Small size, buffy, butterflylike flight. Often diurnal.

ROCK SQUIRREL *Citellus variegatus*
Body 11 in. Grizzled gray, darker on bushy, 9-inch tail.

BLACK-TAILED RATTLESNAKE *Crotalus molossus*
To 5 ft. Black tail. Body brown with black diamond pattern.

PLATE 18

GRAY-BREASTED JAY

WESTERN PIPISTREL

MEXICAN PINYON

GRAY VIREO

TEXAS MADRONE

WEEPING JUNIPER

GRAY OAK

APACHE-PLUME

RUFOUS-SIDED TOWHEE

BLACK-TAILED RATTLESNAKE

SCARLET BOUVARDIA

LUCIFER HUMMINGBIRD

HAVARD PENSTEMON

ROCK SQUIRREL

PLATE 19

ARIZONA MADREAN FOOTHILL FOREST

ALLIGATOR JUNIPER *Juniperus deppeana*
To 50 ft. Scaly, blue-green foliage. Bark in square scales, resembling alligator skin. Cones are fruitlike, reddish.

SILVERLEAF OAK *Quercus hypoleucoides*
To 60 ft. Leaves are long, dark, shiny green above and silvery below.

ARIZONA OAK *Quercus arizonica*
To 65 ft. Leaves wide, oval-shaped, dull green above, usually hairy below.

POINTLEAF MANZANITA *Arctostaphylos pungens*
Shrub, 3–6 feet tall. Blue-green, leathery leaves with fine hairs. Bark is reddish, twigs are hairy. Berries are brown.

SCHOTT YUCCA *Yucca schottii*
To 15 ft. Sharp, daggerlike leaves. Large, white flowers grow in clusters on the central stalk.

NOLINA BEARGRASS *Nolina microcarpa*
To 8 ft. Grasslike base, many small, white flowers on drooping stalk.

BLACK-THROATED GRAY WARBLER *Dendroica nigrescens*
5 in. Gray above with bold black and white head pattern. Two wing bars, streaks on sides.

SOLITARY VIREO *Vireo solitarius*
5–6 in. Dull gray with wide eye ring. Two wing bars.

HUTTON'S VIREO *Vireo huttoni*
4.5 in. Gray with 2 wing bars, broken eye ring. Closely resembles female Ruby-crowned Kinglet.

MONTEZUMA QUAIL *Cyrtonyx montezumae*
9 in. Chunky, spotted on sides, distinct black and white face pattern. Often tame.

BLACK-THROATED
GRAY WARBLER

ALLIGATOR
JUNIPER

HUTTON'S
VIREO

SOLITARY
VIREO

SILVERLEAF
OAK

ARIZONA
OAK

POINTLEAF
MANZANITA

fruit
x ½

leaf blade
x 1/12

SCHOTT
YUCCA

fruit
x 1/7

flower
x 1/7

NOLINA
BEARGRASS

flower
x 2

female

male

MONTEZUMA QUAIL

PLATE 20

ARIZONA CANYON RIPARIAN FOREST

ARIZONA SYCAMORE *Platanus wrightii*
> To 60 ft. Deeply lobed, untoothed leaves. Scaly, pale bark. Fruits are hanging balls.

ARIZONA WALNUT *Juglans major*
> To 50 ft. Large (12 inches) compound leaves with pointed, toothed leaflets. Round fruits.

ARIZONA CYPRESS *Cupressus arizonica*
> To 70 ft. Needles scalelike, blue-green. Bark grayish, often dark. Cones are rounded.

BIRCHLEAF CERCOCARPUS (MOUNTAIN-MAHOGANY) *Cercocarpus betuloides*
> A spreading shrub with evergreen, oval, toothed leaves. Fruits with long plumes.

ELEGANT TROGON *Trogon elegans*
> 12 in. Sits upright. Male has red breast, white breast band, shiny green head and back. Female is brown with white ear spot and pink breast.

SULPHUR-BELLIED FLYCATCHER *Myiodynastes luteiventris*
> 8 in. Brown with pale yellow breast, heavily streaked on face and body. Rusty tail.

STRICKLAND'S WOODPECKER *Picoides stricklandii*
> 8 in. Brown on back and wings, spots on sides. Large black cheek patch.

BRIDLED TITMOUSE *Parus wollweberi*
> 5 in. Gray with crest, distinctive black pattern on face.

PAINTED REDSTART *Myioborus picta*
> 5.5 in. Unmistakable. Black with white outer tail feathers, white on wing, red below. Juveniles lack red.

COATI *Nasua narica*
> Body to 50 in., tail to 25 in. Suggests a slender raccoon. Pointed snout and long, banded tail.

PLATE 20

STRICKLAND'S WOODPECKER

ELEGANT TROGON

ARIZONA SYCAMORE

ARIZONA WALNUT

SULPHUR-BELLIED FLYCATCHER

BRIDLED TITMOUSE

ARIZONA CYPRESS

PAINTED REDSTART

BIRCHLEAF CERCOCARPUS

fruit

flower

COATI

PLATE 21

SOUTHWEST MOUNTAIN FOREST

APACHE PINE *Pinus engelmannii*
To 70 ft. Needles dark green, very long (to 15 inches), in bundles of 3. Cones to 6 in., sometimes prickly. Bark deeply furrowed, dark brown.

CHIHUAHUA PINE *Pinus leiophylla*
To 80 ft. Needles blue-green, to 4.5 in., in bundles of 3. Cones wide, mildly prickly. Bark thick, furrowed, almost black.

PONDEROSA PINE (ARIZONA VARIETY) *Pinus ponderosa arizonica*
To 125 ft. Long (to 7 inches) needles in bundles of 5. Cones to 5 in., prickly. Bark yellow-brown with scaly plates.

CANYON MAPLE (BIGTOOTH MAPLE) *Acer grandidentatum*
To 35 ft. or shrubby. Leaves deciduous, opposite, with 5 untoothed lobes. Bark brown-gray, with shallow furrows.

NEW MEXICO LOCUST *Robinia neomexicana*
To 25 ft. Deciduous, compound leaves with 9–21 oval leaflets, each with a bristled tip. Flowers pink, pods brown. Twigs thorny.

ARIZONA ROSE *Rosa arizonica*
Many-branched shrub up to 3 feet high. Leaves hairy, thorns curved. Bark flakes. Similar to Fendler Rose (not shown).

NORTHERN PYGMY-OWL *Glaucidium gnoma*
7 in. Small, diurnal owl with a long tail and streaked breast. Large black patches behind neck.

GREATER PEWEE *Contopus pertinax*
7.5 in. Dark gray back and wings, gray breast, no wing bars. Song distinctive (*ho-say-haree-ah* or *ho-say-re-ah*).

MEXICAN CHICKADEE *Parus sclateri*
5 in. All-gray sides, large black bib.

RED-FACED WARBLER *Cardellina rubrifrons*
5 in. Gray with black head, brilliant red face. Rump is white.

OLIVE WARBLER *Peucedramus taeniatus*
5 in. Mostly gray, two white wing bars. Male with orange head and throat; yellow in female. Black patch behind eye.

YELLOW-EYED JUNCO *Junco phaeonotus*
6.5 in. White outer tail feathers, rusty back, yellow eyes. Walks rather than hops.

PLATE 21

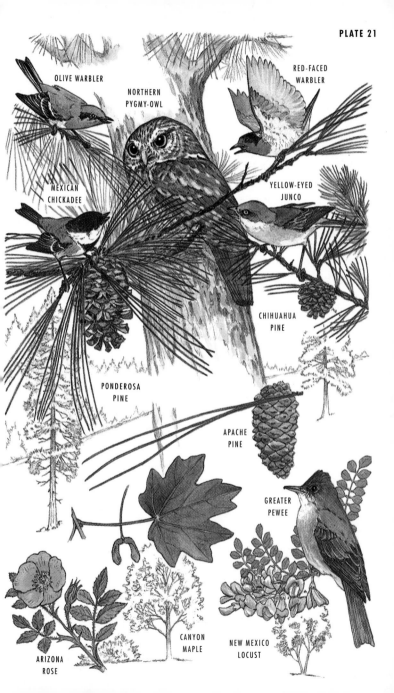

OLIVE WARBLER

NORTHERN
PYGMY-OWL

RED-FACED
WARBLER

MEXICAN
CHICKADEE

YELLOW-EYED
JUNCO

CHIHUAHUA
PINE

PONDEROSA
PINE

APACHE
PINE

GREATER
PEWEE

ARIZONA
ROSE

CANYON
MAPLE

NEW MEXICO
LOCUST

PLATE 22

GIANT SAGUARO CACTUS FOREST

SAGUARO *Cereus giganteus*
> To 50 ft. Unmistakable tree-sized cactus with pleated sides. Branches present in older individuals. Large white flowers at branch tips.

CREOSOTE BUSH *Larrea tridentata*
> To 8 ft. Shrub with tiny, paired, pointed leaves. Flowers are small and yellow.

OCOTILLO *Fouquieria splendens*
> To 15 ft. Whiplike branch clusters, tiny leaves (often absent), red flower clusters at branch tips.

CHAIN CHOLLA (JUMPING CHOLLA) *Opuntia fulgida*
> To 8 ft. Shrublike, with draping branches covered by dense spines. Flowers are pink-red.

ENGELMANN'S PRICKLY-PEAR *Opuntia phaeacantha*
> To 3 ft. Stems as broad pads with long spines. Flowers range from bright yellow to orange-red.

ELF OWL *Micrathene whitneyi*
> 6 in. Tiny owl with short tail, white blazes on wings.

GREATER ROADRUNNER *Geococcyx californianus*
> 24 in. Large, streaked, slender ground bird. Long tail, ragged crest.

YUMA ANTELOPE SQUIRREL (HARRIS'S ANTELOPE SQUIRREL)
Ammospermophilus harrisi
10 in. Pale ground squirrel with gray underside of tail.

GILA WOODPECKER *Melanerpes uropygialis*
> 9 in. Has zebra stripes on back, tawny head and breast, and red cap.

CACTUS WREN *Campylorhynchus brunneicapillus*
> 8.5 in. Large, streaked wren with white eye line and black and white outer tail feathers.

GILA MONSTER *Heloderma suspectum*
> 24 in. Thick-bodied lizard with beadlike scales, mottled pinkish orange and black.

PLATE 22

OCOTILLO

ELF OWL

flower
x 1

leaves
x 3

CREOSOTE
BUSH

SAGUARO

GILA
WOOD-
PECKER

ENGELMANN'S
PRICKLY-PEAR

YUMA
ANTELOPE
SQUIRREL

CACTUS
WREN

CHAIN
CHOLLA

GILA
MONSTER

GREATER
ROADRUNNER

REFERENCES

INDEX

REFERENCES

For readers interested in obtaining more information, I include the following very selective list of additional references, many of which are local regional guides.

FIELD GUIDES

Burt, William Henry. 1980. *A Field Guide to Mammals.* Boston: Houghton Mifflin Company.

Craighead, John, Frank Craighead, and Ray Davis. 1963. *A Field Guide to Rocky Mountain Wildflowers.* Boston: Houghton Mifflin Company.

Niehaus, Theodore F. 1984. *A Field Guide to Southwestern and Texas Wildflowers.* Boston: Houghton Mifflin Company.

Peterson, Roger Tory. 1990. *A Field Guide to Western Birds.* Boston: Houghton Mifflin Company.

Petrides, George A. 1992, 1998. *A Field Guide to Western Trees.* 1st ed., expanded. Boston: Houghton Mifflin Company.

Stebbins, Robert C. 1985. *A Field Guide to Western Reptiles and Amphibians.* Boston: Houghton Mifflin Company.

GENERAL REFERENCES

Arno, Stephen F., and Ramona P. Hammerly. 1984. *Timberline: Mountain and Arctic Forest Frontiers.* Seattle: The Mountaineers.

Barbour, Michael G., and Wm. D. Billings. 1988. *North American Terrestrial Vegetation.* New York: Cambridge University Press.

Brock, Mohlen. 1984. *A Field Guide to U.S. National Forests.* New York: Congdon and Weed, Inc.

Cahalane, Victor H. 1947. *Mammals of North America.* New York: The Macmillan Company.

Ehrlich, Paul R., David S. Dobkin, and Darryl Wheye. 1988. *The Birder's Handbook.* New York: Simon and Schuster, Inc.

Elias, Thomas S. 1980. *The Complete Trees of North America*. New York: Van Nostrand Reinhold.

National Geographic Society. 1989. *National Parks of the United States*. Washington, D.C.: National Geographic Society.

Peattie, Donald C. 1991. *A Natural History of Western Trees*. Boston: Houghton Mifflin Company.

Rapkin, Richard, and Jacob Rapkin. 1981. *Nature in the West*. New York: Holt, Rinehart and Winston.

Shelford, Victor E. 1963. *The Ecology of North America*. Urbana: University of Illinois Press.

Spurr, Stephen H., and Burton V. Barnes. 1964, 1973, 1980. *Forest Ecology*. New York: John Wiley and Sons, Inc.

West, Darrell C., Herman H. Shugart, and Daniel B. Botkin. 1981. *Forest Succession, Concepts and Application*. New York: Springer-Verlag.

BLACK HILLS

Froiland, Sven G. 1978. *Natural History of the Black Hills*. South Dakota: The Center For Western Studies.

Pettingill, Olin S. Jr., and Nathaniel R. Whitney Jr., 1965. *Birds of the Black Hills*. New York: Laboratory of Ornithology at Cornell University.

ROCKY MOUNTAINS

Benedict, Audrey DeLella. 1991. *A Sierra Club Naturalist's Guide, the Southern Rockies*. San Francisco: Sierra Club Books.

Emerick, John C. 1984. *From Grassland to Glacier*. Colorado: Johnson Books.

Moenke, Helen. 1971. *Ecology of Colorado Mountains to Arizona Deserts*. Colorado: Denver Museum of Natural History.

Whitney, Stephen. 1982. *A Field Guide to the Grand Canyon*. New York: Quill.

TEXAS

McAlister, Wayne H., and Martha K. McAlister. 1987. *Guidebook to the Aransas National Wildlife Refuge*. Texas: Mince Country Press.

Schmidly, David J. 1977. *The Mammals of Trans-Pecos Texas*. Texas: Texas A&M University Press.

Wauer, Roland H. 1985. *A Field Guide to Birds of the Big Bend*. Texas: Texas Monthly Press.

Wauer, Roland H. 1973, 1980. *Naturalist's Big Bend*. Texas: Texas A&M University Press.

Alcock, John. 1985. *Sonoran Desert Spring*. Chicago: Univ. Chicago Press.

Brown, David E. 1982. "Biotic Communities of the American Southwest — United States and Mexico." *Desert Plants,* Vol. 4, Nos. 1–4. Arizona: Univ. Arizona Press.

Humphrey, Robert R. 1958. *The Desert Grassland*. Arizona: Univ. Arizona Press.

Jaeger, Edmund C. 1940. *Desert Wild Flowers*. Stanford Univ. Press.

Larson, Peggy. 1977. *The Deserts of the Southwest, A Sierra Club Naturalist's Guide*. San Francisco: Sierra Club Books.

Lowe, Charles H. 1964. *Arizona's Natural Environment*. Arizona: Univ. Arizona Press.

Lowe, Charles H. 1964. *The Vertebrates of Arizona*. Arizona: Univ. Arizona Press.

McGinnies, William G. 1981. *Discovering the Desert*. Arizona: Univ. Arizona Press.

Olin, George. 1977. *House in the Sun*. Arizona: Southwest Parks and Monuments Association.

Smith, Robert L. 1982. *Venomous Animals of Arizona*. Arizona: The Arizona Board of Regents.

INDEX

Page numbers in *italics* refer to figures and photographs in the text; entries in **BOLDFACE** type indicate plate numbers.

THE PETERSON SERIES®

PETERSON FIELD GUIDES®

BIRDS

ADVANCED BIRDING (39) North America 53376-7
BIRDS OF BRITAIN AND EUROPE (8) 66922-7
BIRDS OF TEXAS (13) Texas and adjacent states 92138-4
BIRDS OF THE WEST INDIES (18) 67669-X
EASTERN BIRDS (1) Eastern and central North America
 91176-1
EASTERN BIRDS' NESTS (21) U.S. east of Mississippi River 48366-2
 HAWKS (35) North America 44112-9
  WESTERN BIRDS (2) North America west of 100th meridian
   and north of Mexico 91173-7
   WESTERN BIRDS' NESTS (25) U.S. west of Mississippi
    River 47863-4
    MEXICAN BIRDS (20) Mexico, Guatemala, Belize, El
     Salvador 48354-9
    WARBLERS (49) North America 78321-6

FISH

PACIFIC COAST FISHES (28) Gulf of Alaska to Baja California 33188-9
ATLANTIC COAST FISHES (32) North American Atlantic coast 39198-9
FRESHWATER FISHES (42) North America north of Mexico 91091-9

INSECTS

INSECTS (19) North America north of Mexico
 91170-2
BEETLES (29) North America 91089-7
EASTERN BUTTERFLIES (4) Eastern and central North
 America 90453-6
WESTERN BUTTERFLIES (33) U.S. and Canada west of
 100th meridian, part of northern Mexico 41654-X
EASTERN MOTHS North America east of 100th meridian 36100-1

MAMMALS

MAMMALS (5) North America north of Mexico 91098-6
ANIMAL TRACKS (9) North America 91094-3

ECOLOGY

EASTERN FORESTS (37) Eastern North America 9289-5
CALIFORNIA AND PACIFIC NORTHWEST FORESTS (50) 92896-6
ROCKY MOUNTAIN AND SOUTHWEST FORESTS (51) 92897-4
VENOMOUS ANIMALS AND POISONOUS PLANTS (46) North America north of
 Mexico 35292-4

PETERSON FIELD GUIDES® continued

PLANTS

EDIBLE WILD PLANTS (23) Eastern and central North America 31870-X
EASTERN TREES (11) North America east of 100th meridian 90455-2
FERNS (10) Northeastern and central North America, British Isles and
  Western Europe 19431-8
MEDICINAL PLANTS (40) Eastern and central North America 92066-3
MUSHROOMS (34) North America 91090-0
PACIFIC STATES WILDFLOWERS (22) Washington, Oregon, California, and
  adjacent areas 91095-1
ROCKY MOUNTAIN WILDFLOWERS (14) Northern Arizona and New Mexico to
  British Columbia 18324-3
TREES AND SHRUBS (11A) Northeastern and north-central U.S. and south-
  eastern and south-central Canada 35370-X
WESTERN TREES (44) Western U.S. and Canada 90454-4
**WILDFLOWERS OF NORTHEASTERN AND NORTH-
  CENTRAL NORTH AMERICA** (17) 91172-9
SOUTHWEST AND TEXAS WILDFLOWERS (31) 36640-2

EARTH AND SKY

GEOLOGY (48) Eastern North America 66326-1
ROCKS AND MINERALS (7) North America 91096-X
STARS AND PLANETS (15) 91099-4
ATMOSPHERE (26) 33033-5

REPTILES AND AMPHIBIANS

EASTERN REPTILES AND AMPHIBIANS (12) Eastern and
  central North America 90452-8
WESTERN REPTILES AND AMPHIBIANS (16) Western North America, including
  Baja California 38253-X

SEASHORE

SHELLS OF THE ATLANTIC (3) Atlantic and Gulf coasts
  and the West Indies 69779-4
PACIFIC COAST SHELLS (6) North American Pacific coast, including Hawaii
  and the Gulf of California 18322-7
ATLANTIC SEASHORE (24) Bay of Fundy to Cape Hatteras 31828-9
CORAL REEFS (27) Caribbean and Florida 46939-2
SOUTHEAST AND CARIBBEAN SEASHORES (36) Cape Hatteras to the Gulf Coast,
  Florida, and the Caribbean 46811-6

PETERSON FIRST GUIDES®

PETERSON FIELD GUIDE COLORING BOOKS

PETERSON NATURAL HISTORY COMPANIONS

AUDIO AND VIDEO

EASTERN BIRDING BY EAR
cassettes 50087-7
CD 71258-0

WESTERN BIRDING BY EAR
cassettes 52811-9
CD 71257-2

EASTERN BIRD SONGS, Revised
cassettes 53150-0
CD 50257-8

WESTERN BIRD SONGS, Revised
cassettes 51746-X
CD 51745-1

BACKYARD BIRDSONG
cassettes 58416-7
CD 71256-4

MORE BIRDING BY EAR
cassettes 71260-2
CD 71259-9

WATCHING BIRDS
Beta 34418-2
VHS 34417-4

PETERSON'S MULTIMEDIA GUIDES: NORTH AMERICAN BIRDS
(CD-ROM for Windows) 73056-2

PETERSON FLASHGUIDES™

ATLANTIC COASTAL BIRDS 79286-X
PACIFIC COASTAL BIRDS 79287-8
EASTERN TRAILSIDE BIRDS 79288-6
WESTERN TRAILSIDE BIRDS 79289-4
HAWKS 79291-6
BACKYARD BIRDS 79290-8
TREES 82998-4
MUSHROOMS 82999-2
ANIMAL TRACKS 82997-6
BUTTERFLIES 82996-8
ROADSIDE WILDFLOWERS 82995-X
BIRDS OF THE MIDWEST 86733-9
WATERFOWL 86734-7
FRESHWATER FISHES 86713-4

WORLD WIDE WEB: http://www.petersononline.com

PETERSON FIELD GUIDES can be purchased at your local
bookstore or by calling our toll-free number, (800) 225-3362.

When referring to title by corresponding ISBN number,
preface with 0-395.